William V. (William Vicars) Lawrance

The story of Judeth

a tale of Bethany, with poems of home, heart, and hearth

William V. (William Vicars) Lawrance

The story of Judeth
a tale of Bethany, with poems of home, heart, and hearth

ISBN/EAN: 9783744736985

Printed in Europe, USA, Canada, Australia, Japan

Cover: Foto ©Thomas Meinert / pixelio.de

More available books at **www.hansebooks.com**

THE STORY OF JUDETH

A TALE OF BETHANY

WITH POEMS OF HOME, HEART, AND HEARTH

BY

WILLIAM V. LAWRANCE

Not what we see or what we dream
Should be alone the poet's theme;
For eyes deceive and dreams but cheat,
And give the bitter for the sweet:
The heart, if right, is better guide
To lead us than all else beside.

CAMBRIDGE
Printed at the Riverside Press
1889

To

MY BELOVED WIFE,

FOR TWENTY-FIVE YEARS MY COMPANION,

AND TO OUR ONLY CHILD,

HERBERT W. LAWRANCE,

THIS OFFERING IS DEDICATED:

TO THE MOTHER, AS A TESTIMONIAL OF HER WORTH;

TO THE SON, AS AN INJUNCTION TO HONOR

HER WHO HAS MADE THIS BOOK

A POSSIBILITY.

THE AUTHOR.

PREFACE.

In presenting this volume to the public, the Author feels that he has but imperfectly accomplished that which he sought to do, and that the work is but a dim shadow of the ideal which he would reach. Whatever faults there are, and there are many and serious ones, are in the infirmity of the writer, and not in the subject. It may seem presumption, and he is conscious of the justness of the charge against him, to attempt a work so far beyond his ability to do it the justice it merits. But in its reception by the public he hopes, that, while the work itself may not reach the standard he has sought to attain, yet the subject may receive that fair and candid consideration which it merits; and that, looking beyond the Author and his work, the higher ideal may be reached by the reader. Should this be achieved, he is content to be considered but as the guide leading the way to the beautiful gardens of Hesperides, although not being permitted to enter.

Before the simple and fragmentary story of the death and resurrection of Lazarus, given in the Gospels, we have stood wondering why a thing so momentous in its bearing and effect, not only in the life and future of the dead brought to life, but to the world of mankind, should be so lightly passed over, and left in utter silence. Far be it from us to seek to supply aught to this story, either in continuation or in supposition, well knowing that such attempt would well merit the bitterest rebuke that could be administered to our temerity. As it is given we leave it, adding nothing, nor detracting aught from it.

The method and purpose of the story of Judeth is seem-

ingly so plain and simple that it appears to the writer un-
necessary to even allude to its design. If this is not the
case, then the whole is a dismal failure, and any explanation
that might be made or elucidation given would not save it
from absolute and merited condemnation, and an immediate
banishment to that limbo of purposeless writings, the rag-
man's cart.

What is writ is writ, and it now goes to that inexorable
judge, the public, to receive approval or condemnation.
We may await its decree as the criminal the decision of the
court of last resort, who, though sustained by a conscious
knowledge of his innocence, knows that only the slender
thread of attenuated hope hangs on the word of fallible
man, and if that fail he is lost: yet, like that condemned
man, we may be pardoned if we should with him feel that,
if justice be awarded us, the decree will not be against

THE AUTHOR.

CONTENTS.

viii   *CONTENTS.*

THE STORY OF JUDETH

CANTO FIRST.

MORNING ON OLIVET.

I.

JUDETH.

AND this the daylight, this the balmy air
We call the source of life! How sweet, how fair,
Are all created things of Nature! See,
Where soars yon bird the ether light and free!
It seems a mote floating afar and high,
In this magnificently dreamy sky.
I would not know it were a bird, but guess —
If guessing were my mood, not seriousness —
It were a knotted skein of gossamer
Floating from thread intangible, afar,
Yet anchored to the earth, save that now faint
And throbbing through the air, more like a plaint
From heart care-sore than note of joy, his song
Floats downward to my ear.

II.

LAZARUS.

      Judeth, how strong
That picture there presents of eager soul
Striving to reach its destiny. The goal,
Which first invitingly in reach appears,
Sweeps farther outward, farther yet, as nears
The hoped-for rest; and yet with tireless wings
It soars and soars, and soaring ever sings
Its joyful song of hope unquenched.

JUDETH.

          The Soul!
I would not pain you with my doubt, nor roll
The darkling shadow of my life athwart
The golden sunshine of your hope, with swart,
Uncertain night, which settles close upon
The grave, when in it all of life is gone,
Yet such is my belief. The light gone out,
The house is cold and dark!

LAZARUS.

      What! Then you doubt?

JUDETH.

Nay, I do more than doubt; for I stand not
Uncertain of my faith, nor have forgot
The teaching of my youth, that man is clay,
The grave his home, and dust, when laid away,
Is all there is of him. My friend, in me,
Of straitest sect, behold a Sadducee.

III.

LAZARUS.

Nay, you but jest! In you and me, 't is true,
Flows the rich blood of Israel's ardent Jew —
In fact, so intermingled in our veins
That little else in them save that remains!
From it the warmth, the fire — hot passion — love,
Lurk hidden in our hearts in test to prove
We can be true in hate, in love, in pride,
True to our faith, the chief of all beside;
Our fathers' faith, religion, empire, name, —
Ours, blood-inherited, Altars and Fame!

JUDETH.

Religion! Well, yes; by that name as well
As any, if our meaning we may tell;
Mine is too plain. The god I serve this life,
And close the book at that. The vexing strife
Of Souls seeking their homes in fleshless dress
Is not a pleasant thought. If God will bless,

Let it be here and now with bounteous hand;
I want no sweeter and no fairer land!
Why should we seek a better?   You and I
Clasp hands and walk beneath this sunny sky,
With flowers beneath our feet songs in our ears
And hearts, while beautiful the earth appears,
In all the varied hues of Nature's dress
Clothes her fair form and sits in loveliness!
Is this not Heaven?   Ah! well I know for me
No brighter day dawns through Eternity.
What, then, would you ask more?

IV.

LAZARUS.
                              These fleeting years
Are sweet, fair Judeth, but too full of tears:
While Joy's few days are not enough for me.
My life, a Soul eternal born and free,
In dull obscurity but faintly glows, —
Just catches on this earth the quick'ning throes
Of being born to launch at last in song,
As yon sweet bird the brighter fields among,
Eternity's first day in opening dawn
Before me spread.

JUDETH.
                    I know that you are drawn,
Through the blind hoodwink of a blinder faith,
To a belief no witness, even, hath.
For who, of all the dead, returning bears
Remotest proof of Soul-life?   Where, too, fares
The risen dead whose sojourn sure would be
Sometime on earth through its eternity?
You dream, kind friend!   This clay you call the mould
Is all, and all must die when it is cold.
How cometh joy or pain to that which hath
Nor nerves nor vital parts?   How can God's wrath,
Or his great love, touch that which this weak hand
Can brush away, I cannot understand!
God's love and his great mercy speak through Death,
To us this consolation, Life is breath.

V.

LAZARUS.

If I could do such sacrilege to God
To even dare to think you but a clod,
Yet to yourself, the choicest earthly bloom,
I dare not do injustice.   In the Tomb,
The withered, dead, decaying sweetness lies
Forever hid from tear-o'erburdened eyes;
Can this be lost forever?   But one mould
In all the world can your fair likeness hold!
God works not all in vain, and no blind Chance
Here stumbles on divine resemblance:
Ah! no: immortal hands immortal made
Such beauty so that it should never fade!

JUDETH.

You lose yourself in compliments to me.
The grossest forms immortal, too, must be,
Else God would be but partial and not just.

VI.

LAZARUS.

And there you fail again: of fairest dust
The beautiful its fadeless beauty keeps —
More lovely grows as heavenward on it sweeps,
Refined, refining through the dateless years.
In grosser flesh the struggling soul appears
Cramped, all awry, — deformity's deformed:
From the coarse chrysalis the sun has warmed,
Comes struggling forth from its close-crowded home
The worm which has a butterfly become.
See! how it writhes to burst its prison cell —
Shakes from its wings its flight-impeding shell,
Pants at each breath in life's ecstatic pain,
Thrills with its pleasure until death again
Seems seizing on its vital powers, while wing
And body in the throes are shuddering.
But this is life, not death; and fold on fold
The cramped and crumpled wings are soon unrolled,
And, stretching wide their growing length, they gleam

In all the beauty of an artist's dream!
A few soft breathings of the buoyant air,
To try their strength and for its flight prepare;
Then, spurning its dull cell with proud disdain,
Soars skyward through the bright, unknown domain,
In flight forever leaving far behind
The prison-house where it lay dwarfed and blind.
So the freed soul from gross, imprisoning clay,
Clothed in God's beauty, deathless soars away.

VII.

JUDETH.

Your picture is most beautiful! If true,
I would be glad. The moth described by you
I, too, have seen; and when I saw it soar —
For I have watched them from my garden bower —
So beautifully painted, through the sky,
I oft have thought if I, too, thus could fly
To search a life of sunshine and of gold,
And leave forever here this sad and old
Abode — But how I prate! such cannot be,
Except for you and moths; 't is not for me.

LAZARUS.

Already stirs that soul within your breast
In its fierce longings for a sweeter rest:
Content not here, it gazes with an eye
Which, as from book, reads in the bending sky
Some mystery of which it hath a part,
And, reading thus, appeals to hope and heart.

JUDETH.

What moves you, brother, now in speech so grave
To talk of old things newly clad? I crave
You now unbend that face with brow austere,
And, with such words as is my wont to hear
From lips till now of levity the vent,
Speak in sweet phrase and simple.

LAZARUS.
                    Sister, pent

In this proud heart Ambition had its rule,
As you well know, and learning in such school
But feeds the thirst for more, and thus consume
The forces as the fruit absorbs the bloom
Until the sweetness and the freshness born
Of gentle blood were withered ere the morn
Of manhood touched the day, as you may know,
Who oft have watched and chid my dark'ning brow,
And I grew cynic.

VIII.

JUDETH.

And that was what best pleased
Me as I thought of you as brother.   How I teased
You just to let me call you so, for I
Have none, nor sister! you might one supply,
And Mary will the other.   Life is lone
To go through it still having neither one.
You are my brother, are n't you?   Do not frown,
As you have always done, and face me down.
Ashamed, somehow I feel, when in your eye
I read your strange, mysterious reply.
Are you ashamed to call me sister?

LAZARUS.

No,
But we our theme forget.

JUDETH.

Oh, no; true, though,
I did ask why you had so changed of late,
But I did scarcely mean it, I so hate
Philosophy, and those much harder names
Of things unknowable.   My pride but shames
My ignorance, and it, in truth made plain,
Shows but a heart as shallow as 't is vain.

IX.

LAZARUS.

Fair Judeth, — sister, if that please you best, —
The passions which stir in the human breast

Are deep, unsearchable ; but at the spring
We drink of truth, where never withering
Are flowers that bloom eternal on its course,
Full of the life that bubbles from its source.
He who drinks there thirsts not.   Soul cleaves to Soul ;
Like born of like, inseparable and whole
Becomes, as fruit from mingled juices grown,
The stock engrafted bearing fruit alone.
And feeding on such fruits the grosser part,
The mortal draws from the immortal heart
Its own eternal Immortality.

JUDETH.

Your speech to you is plain, no doubt ; to me
It is most vague and mystical.   Whence brought
This fine Philosophy which darkens thought ?

LAZARUS.

Philosophy is truth and truth is light :
They fail to see who lack discerning sight ;
The light shines but within, the outward eye
But night alone and darkness can descry ;
You need the inner light, where through the soul
The rays of truth their floods dilating roll.

JUDETH.

The Soul !   What mean you ?   I, as truth, deny
All source of vision save the mortal eye.
True, to the mind some truths come vague and dim,
Like wavering lights on the horizon's rim
When morn is breaking.

LAZARUS.

Why these lights you see ?

JUDETH.

Why ?   Sure the answer is most simple, " He
Who runs may read."   That faint and quivering ray
Is the fore-promise of the coming day :
Behind it speeds the swift and fiery Sun,
And Night, uncovered, blushes hot and dun.

X.

LAZARUS.

Because the sun is there, you see the light:
Without its rays all is eternal night.
Is not this true?   The twilight of the mind
Is but the gleam of the great soul behind.
That soul eternal, through the prison bars
Sheds the soft lustre of the risen stars.

JUDETH.

I said Philosophy and I were twain:
Its whys and wherefores are to me but vain
And empty vaporings.   I only know
That, as to me things seem, they must be so.
Philosophy, if I read right, should make all plain,
Else Wisdom, save for few, to man is vain:
Beyond that line lies dark and waste a land,
If I see not, how can I understand?
There lies the darkness, and, outstretched, my hand
Pierces its desert shadow, yet I feel
No touch upon me.   Ghostly somethings steal
Still nearer to me, until from the night
Drops down the curtain o'er unquickened sight;
And so the light shut close within me lies
A portion of the darkness, and my eyes,
As if they never saw, to me are blind,
Save to bright pictures glowing in the mind.

LAZARUS.

Those pictures glow not, save from light within:
The veil obscuring lies so sere and thin,
The shadow's fall across our waking eyes
Reveals the starlight in the Soul's clear skies.
The stars are there; it needs but keener power
To trace their glowing at the noontide hour:
So we, when life's day merges into gloom
Where fall the shadows round the hastening tomb,
With eyes earth-dimmed look forth with quickened sight;
"Lo!   It is morning, let there now be light!"

XI.

JUDETH.

My friend, — my brother, — tell me whence this change?
This wondrous wisdom, old and yet so strange,
Your heart has filled and schooled your lips to teach
With words prophetic and impassioned speech?
Has, in your absence, chanced it to your lot
To visit him, — you know, I name him not, —
Who by the Jordan's steep and rocky strand,
And thence throughout its valley's sweeter land,
Like prophet clad, Elias come again,
Cries doleful warnings unto all the plain?

LAZARUS.

John Baptist?   Nay, him I have not yet seen,
But travelled much the land where he has been;
And wonderful the tales one of him hears!
Wherever now this godly man appears
Great multitudes the desert places fill,
And follow him who leads them as he will,
With eager lips hang on his slightest word,
By fear or faith to deep conviction stirred.
God's Word he preaches from the Prophet's page,
And with its truths their waiting minds engage;
Their sins denouncing, scorns their pleasures dear,
Their pride, self-love, race, creed, in terms severe:
God's withering curse, a siroc's burning storm,
Is heaped on them who serve him but in form;
While Love and Pity ever wait upon
Those who to him in faith and trust have gone.
So great his fame, to him the Pharisee,
And with him came also the Sadducee,
To learn what mighty power was his to draw
The people to him; and to learn the law,
If such there be, by which he holds them thrall
To his strange teaching warring with them all.
Not that they hope to find in him aught good
For them to share, or for the multitude;
But that his words against him they may use,
Or turn his holy warnings to abuse,
Then mock, revile, denounce him as a fraud

They will expose though all the world applaud!
And seeing these, their lives and hearts he reads,
Weighs all through worth and judges each by creeds.
With scorn ineffable, such as the soul
Intensely pure must feel upon it roll,
The battle on, nor thought of compromise,
Thus to the vain, self-righteous throng he cries:
" Ye viper's brood, of earth the vilest scum,
Who warneth you to flee the wrath to come?
You must repent; the axe lies at the root
Of every tree that beareth not good fruit.
Unto the Lord shall be the soul's desire;
The barren tree is cast into the fire.
You Abraham for father boast!   If need,
God unto him of stones shall raise up seed.
Your ways are dark, your steps take hold on Hell;
Already burn with fires unquenchable
Your shrivelled souls! repent while yet you may;
For you the night of Death shall have no day:
God's mercies cease when hearts will not receive;
Rejected pardon hopes not for reprieve."

XII.

This much I tell, yet not the half I heard,
And telling this perhaps somewhat have erred.
The spirit of the truth proclaimed pervades
The very air: before his teaching fades
All opposition, and both high and low,
As penitents, for his baptizing bow.
His word is mighty; and throughout that land
Come flocking multitudes on every hand,
As if the wondrous teaching of the word
The deepest depths of human feeling stirred;
And whispering lips, awe-touched and white with fear,
Are asking, "Will Messiah soon appear?"
What meaneth it I know not, nor can well
Divine its purport; only thus I tell
The story as I heard.

JUDETH.
    Your words have strange

And subtle power e'en over me. The range
Of this unlettered dweller in the hills,
Whose magic eloquence so moves and thrills
The hearts of men, hath in it mystery
That I would fain unveil. Not that in me
Alone, dare I now hope, lies hid the power
That may be equal to such task or hour ;
My weakness left alone must ever fail ;
God gave Sisera to the hand of Jael :
When Truth and Error to the death contend,
How meagre oft the means are to the end !
But in the right the weak are ever strong,
While might's high citadel is sapped by Wrong.
So runs the tale from synagogue oft read,
How Jonah, when from duty he had fled,
Escaped the seas, at last to Ninus came,
Where he was sent God's vengeance to proclaim, —
Nor messenger such message ever bore, —
" Yet forty days, and Ninus is no more ! "
And yet they heed that warning strange, and hear
In it the voice of judgment speaking clear :
God's pardoning favor they in faith implore,
And Vengeance stalks regretful from the shore.
I oft have wondered how, in form uncouth
And maniac's cry, that people found the truth :
Why should the wise, the great, the powerful flee
Out from their sinful lives for such as he ?

XIII.

LAZARUS.

Because behind and in his footsteps trod
The Messenger of an avenging God.
No swifter fled proud Ahab's trembling steeds
Where fast before the girded Prophet speeds,
Than turned the heathen from his path accursed,
Before the cloud destroying on him burst.

JUDETH.

So I believe of these ; but can it be
That God in spirit speaks through such as he ?
Is our estate to topple to its fall,
And mighty things confounded be by small ?

LAZARUS.

God ever was and always is the same:
The sword which smites, and smites not in his name,
Turns back the edge on him who wields, and dire
The vengeance of his wrath's enkindled fire.
So mercy shown, if not evoked through prayer,
To him who shows hath blessing lean and spare.
Now from that Book you also have heard read·
That in the olden time the Prophet said, —
The whole I may not give in word and phrase,
But this their meaning and the truth conveys, —
" Receive you him who cometh now to bless,
The Voice that crieth in the wilderness ;
Ye who the coming of the Lord Christ wait
A highway build and make his pathway straight."
He now is come ; the people hear and heed,
And haste to him, forgetting caste and creed :
He is the " VOICE ! "   The Nations hear the cry,
And to his lifted standard soon will fly :
The heavens proclaim the wonders of his word,
In this the dayspring of the coming Lord.

XIV.

JUDETH.

You strangely move me ! and I now must see
This Sage and sacred Herald: if it be
Not now too much of you, my friend, to ask,
In burdening you with this a further task,
That you, as escort and also as guide,
Lead us to where the Jordan's broadening tide
Flows to that sad and death-distilling Sea
With its sweet waters from the Galilee,
Myself there to behold this mighty Seer,
And from his lips his wondrous message hear ;
While in his eyes I gaze, and gazing read
If truth or falsehood father his strange creed.

LAZARUS.

Your wish is but my duty, so prepare
At once the journey.   I will have the care
Of tents and meats, since now as locusts swarm
The multitudes o'er all the land.

JUDETH.
                    No harm
Will come to us from them?

LAZARUS.
                    Nay, as the sheep
Which graze upon yon hillside's rocky steep
They are as kind and harmless.

JUDETH.
                    Then away!
I am impatient for the coming day,
And the dusk shadows of the night will hate,
Since through their laggard course I needs must wait.
Martha and Mary, too, our way must share;
To them our purpose haste we to declare:
Delay no longer, since more swift my feet
Than yours to haste to joy, and far more fleet.
A time we part; and should we meet no more
I will await you at the morning hour,
Impatient of the bird's first matin call
From out the fig-trees by the garden wall.

LAZARUS.
Before the bird I shall awake you: come!
The day grows hot, so let us hasten home.

XV.

Now, while our friends the journey shall prepare,
Which we, as guests unbidden, too shall share,
We stop a moment and the time avail,
While lag the actors in our waiting tale,
To sketch in some bold strokes the scenes around, —
Map out the plan, a time survey the ground
Where soon the actors of a mighty Past
Shall move and speak, as ever changing fast
Scene upon scene, recurring act and deed:
These, shifting oft, each other oft succeed;
And in them bearing fruits the world alone
Shall reap in harvests as the years roll on.
A thousand years thrice told have come and gone,

Before the lifting of this day's faint dawn,
And through those years have voices far away
Proclaimed to man the coming of this day.
God's messengers, priest, prophet, sage, and seer,
Whose feet have trod these sacred valleys here,
Then, looking down the vistas lighted by
The beams eternal from the throne on high,
Have read the portent while the ages roll,
As letters written on a flaming scroll,
Far in the future, and proclaimed to man
The wondrous story of God's waiting plan.

XVI.

That time to-day; the land is Palestine;
Province, Judea, rich in figs and wine.
Hard by to Bethany on Olivet
The day has opened, and in shadows yet
The sparkling dews of morn in beauty cling
To pendant grasses, while the gay birds sing
Their morning songs perched in the olive-trees,
That, centuries gone, have wooed the fresh'ning breeze,
Just as to-day they woo and whisper there
In low, soft murmurings, to the morning fair.
Their tale, though soft, is as the earth is, old ;
Nor new the one they have this morning told,
While hither strayed the two we now have seen,
From the close city to the fresher green
Of field and grove : the why we need not tell,
Since youth is youth, in every age as well :
And its one story, if but rightly told,
Though new to-day, to-morrow has grown old!

XVII.

The maid is fair, is young and very fair!
Her eyes their night with lambent torches share :
Dusk cheeks that have the touch of shadow thrown
Across the milky skin, to blushes blown
In crimson tinge that on the surface lies,
Nor stains the blooming flower of health it dyes.
Like rippling shadows falling on the light,

Flow down her locks as sable as the night,
Save that across the shortened crests there gleams
The golden tinge where daylight softly streams,
Such as we see when twilight's ruddy glow
Touches the sea where darkling ripples flow,
Morn's promise shining on the topmost crest,
While Night and Shadow swallow all the rest !
Her lips apart, so red they seem to bleed,
Like cleft pomegranate o'er its gleaming seed,
Show teeth that stand, two gates in pearly row
Ajar, while speech and fragrant breath pass through !
Her dress — Oh, had I power from words to weave
The hues in flower, the grace and folds conceive, —
Throw out the lines, show, clinging as a kiss,
The folds that drape her bosom in a bliss
That makes them animate, yet fall away,
And the white, heaving bosom half display,
As in dim shadow touching but the light,
Two peaks of snow half veiled in dusky night !
Thence flowing down the girdled waist caressed
By golden cincture clasping silken vest,
In flood of color like Niagara's flow,
When o'er its sheen the sunlight casts its bow,
Falls round her form, and, thus emblazoned, gleam
In lights entrancing as a glowing dream,
As bare arms fall like flashes of soft white
With clasped hands hidden in its folds from sight.

XVIII.

And such is Judeth, save a hundred fold
Her charms outrival all that can be told :
We give but outlines, these but half expressed,
Then let imagination paint the rest.
Her years, these need we tell ? In northern lands
The fairest flower in blossom slow expands :
'Neath tropic suns, in garden and in bower
Both rose and maiden hasten into flower ;
No lingering dalliance in the smiles of Spring,
No coy delays that chilling north-winds bring.
Her sun to Eros speeds his gentle reign
With flowers to please, and hearts to soothe his pain.

To us a child, there she the woman grown,
In the full freshness of her beauty blown ;
The mind maturing with the body's growth,
Perfection's rare ideal lives in both.

XIX.

Companion of the hour, whose earnest speech
Has less of love and more of truth to teach,
Few words describe ; as few his story tell:
Let these suffice the telling, ill or well.
His name already is familiar grown ;
His native home, Bethany's peaceful town.
Whatever needs be told the story through,
His life in picture boldly brings to view:
A wondrous life ! so little known, and yet
That little still the world cannot forget!
A word describes him : as the arrow straight,
With face as gentle as its look sedate ;
Not large in stature, lithe in form and limb,
With eye whose lustre death alone can dim ;
Blue as the sky, and liquid as 't is blue,
Clear as the light, nor clearer than 't is true.
His golden hair falls o'er his polished brow
Like dash of sunshine crowning clouds of snow ;
His yellow beard both short and curling grew,
With cheek and lip still faintly blushing through.
And such is Lazarus, as we see him here,
Such, faintly pictured as he should appear.

XX.

By wealth not burdened nor made vain by fame,
His means were ample and revered his name.
Long lines of ancestors to him secure
A blood as noble as its source is pure :
Through these untarnished, on its currents run
From sire unspotted to reproachless son.
His kinsmen, too, sprung from this vigorous vine,
Through many branches spread the honored line.
Nor far remote, of kindred blood was she,
The fact sufficing, they ignore degree, —

Judeth, of tribe and house as his the same,
But not in line direct, nor yet in name.
Her father's station honored in the land
With riches that both smiles and place command,
A ruler in the synagogue was he,
In faith, if not in sect, a Sadducee.
She, at the home of Lazarus a guest
Of his fair sisters, lingers now to rest,
Whither from pent up city she has flown
To this sweet home scarce second to her own.
And finds she there home, life, and love so sweet,
From cares oppressive such a blest retreat,
That long she lingers, and, as day by day
The moments pass, they sweeten still her stay ;
Their hearts her home, their home a heaven to her,
Where Love rules all and each is worshipper.

XXI.

Adown the Mount of Olives in retreat,
They hasten now, nor stay their eager feet :
We watch them yet a moment on their way,
Bright in their hopes as is the glowing day,
Forgetful of the moment and the scene,
Sweet in its hills and valleys fair between,
That crowd the vision with their lights and shades,
Where gleams the sunlight or the shadow fades :
These, through their mem'ries and their past sublime,
Invite a moment of our grudging time,
To paint with feeble hand, in words that fail,
This land befitting its own marvellous tale !

XXII.

O Land, made sacred by the feet of him
Who bore the Cross down through yon valley dim,
In the far distance, where we still may see
That sad, sweet mount of suffering, Calvary !
O Land of Promise ! wondrous in the fruit
Of nectarine sweetness grown from bitter root !
The shadowy legends breathing still of thee
In those old mystic books of prophecy,

Paint not thy landscapes nor thy bitter Sea!
Thy mounts of promise and thy plains of palm,
Thy groves of almonds and thy vales of balm,
With frankincense and myrrh each story told,
As incense rise from out each page unrolled,
Until thy name prefigures to the thought
Something of all as we recall each spot!
Oh, for the tongue and pen once tipped with fire,
Of him who swept with master hand the lyre,
In those dim days when here with unshod feet
ISAIAH wandered through thy valleys sweet,
With heart of song and lips of burning praise
That give fresh glory to his name and days!
Or that could teach my stammering lips to sing
In the sweet numbers of the Shepherd-king!
Then could I touch the strings with master hand,
And, with a song that has a theme as grand,
Sing of this land, its glory and its fame,
Forgetting, as I sing, its abject shame!

XXIII.

Upon Mount Olivet at morning stand,
Beneath you, clothed in light, the Holy Land;
There paint in fancy that most lovely scene,
As then to gazing eye it must have been,
Imagination weaving in the flowers
In blooming valleys and in fragrant bowers;
In groves of palm as fringed with almond-trees,
In gardens giving sweets to every breeze;
The olive's dark'ning green on every hill,
The figs and dates that half the gardens fill;
With stately cedars, fair as those upon
The rocky heights of distant Lebanon,
Set in the gorges, with their fragrant shade
Refresh with verdure every opening glade.
Along the winding Kidron's fitful stream,
Where yet the Past with thousand memories teem:
Fair groves of trees like emerald islands sat
In the sweet valley of Jehoshaphat,
Made glad the weary souls who strayed among,
As sorrowing hearts made glad by wine and song:

Hard by this stream forgotten ne'er to be,
Lies the fair garden of Gethsemane.
Then sweeping out where the still Kidron glides,
The eye beholds upon the green hillsides
The white-walled villas gleaming on the day
Like pictures hung beside the winding way:
While thickly lie both hamlet small and town,
Embowered in trees from whence the odors blown
Make glad the hills, through valleys float along,
While every breeze grows vocal with sweet song.

XXIV.

Beyond the valley, on the rising hills,
Bursts on the view a sight that starts and thrills
With joy, such as the exile's heart alone
Can feel; and which in hope long fed upon,
When journeying from some far and distant home,
At first in sight of the dear shrine has come,
Beholds the glittering dome and blazing spires
That catch the gleam of morn's enkindling fires,
Where sits in queenly beauty, crowning them,
The white-walled city of Jerusalem!
Now with his sight, if we, too, could but feel
The fervor born of his unselfish zeal,
How would the heart with deepening passion swell,
The tongue inspired the wondrous story tell
Of the great glory of these mighty men,
Never to dawn upon this land again!
Yes! as that pilgrim, we in faith behold
The templed city with its shrine of gold,
As bursting into view in morning's glow,
Upon the hills it sits, with towers of snow,
Tribute of love and kingly virtues rare
As Pharsælus and Mariamne are:
Tributes to God and to his love divine
Where smokes his Altar in its sacred shrine,
With spire and dome resplendent in the light
Where tower and temple greet admiring sight,
All dim and distant from the haze burst through
In promised beauty of a nearer view,
But give faint pictures to the sight revealed,

Where Fancy paints what distance has concealed.
Give her free wings, and bare and desert sand
Glows at her touch into a fairy land:
Out of a mirage intangible and clear,
The bastioned towers and portalled walls appear.
Spire, minaret, and many a glittering shrine
Leap into air and on the vision shine,
And all that makes a city vast and grand
Stand forth in perfect form on every hand:
While grove and tree, lake, fountain, river, rill,
Environed landscapes with their beauty fill,
With spreading lawns, sweet meadows, twining bowers,
Ambrosial fruits, and ever fragrant flowers,
Soft-murmuring winds, low rippling of light waves,
And scent of flowers with rustling of green leaves,
Make perfect the delusion. Such the dream
Of those who thirst beside some fancied stream,
And pine for home, sweet fields, and restful smiles,
Where the fierce desert with no dream beguiles.

XXV.

We shall not enter in since now our way
Leads northward when shall lift the coming day:
Another time we too may tread the courts
Of its great Temple, view its famed resorts;
Then will we paint, if so it please our theme,
Its marvellous beauties that about us gleam:
But now we follow with the multitude,
To seek the Jordan's swift and swelling flood,
And him whose marvellous words have startled kings
With the strange tidings to the world he brings,
Presaging One who soon shall rear his throne
Where ruined empires shall have toppled down:
Of him will lessons learn, as by him told
In words as rugged as their truth is bold!

XXVI.

Nor we alone the winding valley thread
By ways that danger ever fills with dread,
Since our fair friend, with Lazarus as guide,

Martha and Mary; and with these, beside
Their servants and the train a generous care
Provides for need while they may sojourn there;
Companions all as we together go
Through the rough valley down to Jericho.
How fare we on there is no need to tell,
Since to them all the journey ended well;
The petty trials in such rugged ways,
The cares that vex, the danger that delays,
Are incidents that, at the hearth or board,
Food for the hour and gossip may afford;
But in the grander march life's journey through,
Fail to attract or fade upon the view.
Our story leads to graver days and themes,
Where action lives, nor man, the actor, dreams!
Thither we speed as one on flying train
Flashes afar through mountain-pass, o'er plain,
Down valleys sweet as fairyland, on steeps
So high the train along them seeming creeps;
By lakes whose waters quiver with white sails,
Through meadows whose fresh verdure never fails;
By cities gathering in their homes and marts,
A million eager feet and throbbing hearts;
O'er rivers whose deep arteries pulsing flow
With the vast wealth which feeds the plain below:
And yet, although the waking eye still sees,
The hastening traveller heeds none of these.
Beyond them all the goal of promise lies,
To this his thought on wing still swifter flies;
Whate'er it may be, yet this one thing sought,
The central figure of revolving thought,
All else absorbing: thus by reason's laws
The widening space to narrow limit draws;
By that strange magic of the mind's swift power
In one bold step we stride from shore to shore,
Until by thought concentrate we efface
In the mind's vision all external space.
So speeds our wanderer hastening from the sea,
The rocks behind him and the billows free,
Yet stretching out lie weary leagues of land
"Twixt him and home kept by a loving hand;
The miles but measure out the lagging hours,

As their perfume the presence tells of flowers ;
A continent, with all its scenes sublime,
Becomes to him a moving point of time
To mark the space where fails the ocean's foam,
And the sweet shimmer of his rising home :
And, closed the measure of a continent,
He dreams beside his hearth in sweet content !
So we this journey make, forgetting space,
As we rush forward in its morning chase,
Our thoughts fixed on the goal to which we tend,
Press the swift course until we reach the end.

XXVII.

A moment we might stop in brief delay,
As one who would an unknown sea survey,
To show his voyageurs, ere they trust the wave,
The ports of refuge and the rocks they brave ;
What chart he trusts, what kind his bark and sail,
Wherein he hopes success, and where may fail ;
How he discovery made of what he knows ;
How much is proof, how much they must suppose ;
So they, contented, trust their chosen guide,
And, having faith, to him leave all beside ;
Nor grow the dangers less, the seas less wide !
That might be well where all have equal rule,
The pleasant folly of communist's school ;
But who successful sails in unknown seas
Gives not his thoughts e'en to the whispering breeze,
But in his breast he hides both chart and plan,
Nor makes a confidant of any man ;
Knowing that, if successful, ample praise
Shall well repay for all unseen delays,
And that full time enough there is for all
Their curses, if misfortune should befall.
And thus shall we go on the journey through,
With secret chart the devious way pursue,
Buoyed by the hope that when we anchor cast,
Some cheers may welcome us from shore at last.

CANTO SECOND.

AT THE JORDAN.

I.

JUDETH.

How beautiful the morning! and how sweet
The breath from the calm waters! At the feet
Of the low hills lie the still waves, and glass
The heads of the near mountains. As they pass,
I see reflected in its mirrored breast
Cloud-shadows. On Mount Nebo's topmost crest
The glowing Dawn has fixed her torch of day,
And the pierced shadows swiftly flee away!
Come hither, Mary!

MARY.

          Did you call? In awe
I heard your rhapsody as I, too, saw
Through the drawn curtains peep the coming Dawn;
So I with haste my outer robe threw on
To join you here. How sweet the morning lies
Half-waking in the valley! Drowsy eyes
But catch the glow, else in soft sleep lose all
The day in losing this. I straight would call
To join us here Lazarus and Martha.

II.

JUDETH.

              List!
Now gently stealing through the dusky mist
On the hushed breath of morn I hear a song
Like liquid flow of waters float along,
From where yon tents lie darkly on the beach;
Its rising notes in trembling whispers reach
The eager ear just as from out the gloom
The gray tents into sight now slowly come,
As lift the mists above them. Hark! another,

And still another singer joins. Your brother,
And Martha too, if she is risen, call
And let us to the tents now hasten.   All
The valley now grows vocal with the song,
And loud and full the chorus sweeps along,
Like some swift stream chafing in barriers pent,
Finding in crevice small a meagre vent,
Runs first a silver thread scarce seen, then gray
With sand and earth, as wears the mole away :
Then gathering force, as widens still the breach,
The growing floods the deep foundations reach,
Then fiercer struggling in its hateful thrall,
Its stooping shoulders set against the wall ;
A sturdy Sampson, laughing thus to bear
The puny battlements of stormy war
On his broad back, hurls down the wall, and wide
The waste of waters flows on every side ;
While hollow echoes gathering through the plain,
The softened thunders murmur back again :
So sweeps the flood of music all before,
And echoing whispers run from shore to shore.
And have you called them?

III.

MARY.

> Ay, and they are here.

LAZARUS.

What charming sound is this strikes on my ear?
Ah, Judeth ! pardon, pray, my thoughtless mood,
The morning salutation due.

JUDETH.

> I should
Not e'en have noticed it, had not your speech
Called back my wandering mind.

LAZARUS.

> I pray you teach
To me the mystery of forgetfulness.

JUDETH.

I will.

Ah! here comes sister Martha, prudent still ;
She thinks of the damp shadows and raw air,
And brings our cloaks with her.   Hail, Martha! fair
And glowing as the morning.

IV.

MARTHA.

Still my care,

My sweet heart's sister, must be yet of thee ;
If thou wouldst more than this still hope to be,
Throw this about you ; Mary, this for you ;
Without my care what would you children do ?

LAZARUS.

Love you the same ; I know we could no more ;
For Love, in loving you, himself grows poor !
Judeth, you have not answered me.

JUDETH.

I will.

The answer is around you. Plain and hill,
Hark, how they echo with those wondrous strains!
Do you not hear the singing?   Yonder plains
Are vocal with the grandest melody
That ever swept its strains o'er land or sea.
Hark, how from yonder tents now sweetly rise
The incense wrought of songs of Paradise ! —
Not yours but mine, — the Paradise I know
Where joy fills life unto its overflow.
Can we not go to them ?

MARTHA.

You must have care,

There 's fever lurking in this murky air ;
Mayhap unguarded in those tents there be
Contagion rife or bloated leprosy.
Ah, listen to their songs !   One scarce believes
The heart which sings so sweetly ever grieves !
And this being so, that loathsome, venomed stain

Taints not this life, nor poisons healthful vein
With mortal malady. The song, so sweet
That Echo fain would linger to repeat,
Grows sweeter as the morning from the peaks
Falls glancing down the hills in golden streaks,
And rosy Day comes dancing on the sea,
And floods the land from Shur to Galilee.
Let us go thither.

JUDETH.

Good, my sister fair;
Let us now boldly to those tents repair.

V.

LAZARUS.

How beautiful the scenes around us! Night
Lay thick and sodden on the aching sight
When we, uncertain, down the winding steep
Approached our tents. We could do nought but creep
To our inviting couches kindly spread,
To slumber there upon a dreamless bed.

JUDETH.

Dreamless? Such dreams I never had as came
About my couch last night!

MARY.

Hush! do not name
Them ere we breakfast, else some evil thought
Corrupt, and of it something bad be wrought.

JUDETH.

Not of my dreams; for they were all of you
And yours, too marvellous e'er to come true:
And now I see —

LAZARUS.

Stay! let the telling go,
And look upon this scene! No dream is now
Sealing to earthly scenes our startled eyes,
Yet never dream so beautiful! Here lies
The waveless sea, golden in coming light
Where flash the morning rays. The mountain's height

Flames as on fire ; the skies, a grayish blue,
Melt into shadow to the west, and through
The valley breathes the flower-sweet laden wind,
Filling the white sails of the boats that bind
The Jordan's shores. The woods with odorous balm
Invite to its soft shades ; the groves of palm,
Green-tinted, wave aloft their feathery plumes ;
Along the way the oleander blooms,
Pomegranates ripen, and the olive's bough
With burdened wealth of dusky fruit droops low.
Amid this glowing beauty, wrought by One
By whose right hand all things done are well done,
Lie gleaming in the softened morning light,
Amid the green, a field of varied white,
Where tented wait on one man's coming feet
The pilgrims of all lands. Their song so sweet
Its notes have drawn us with no will to stay,
In captive bonds that lead our feet astray.
Shall we go further ?

MARY.

Oh, do ! And why wait
Our feet midway the road ? Now broad and straight
The way lies smooth before us : dull the ear
The songs they now are singing cannot hear.

JUDETH.

Yes, nearer still let us approach the throng :
Hark ! from the grove beside the way, the song
Rings out, and with a note so sweet and clear,
Each word, if we but listen, we may hear —
Stay ! let us catch the song.

VI.

LAZARUS.

I never heard
Those words before. How richly strain and word
Melt into each, so soulful yet so calm !
And yet that sung is neither song nor psalm.

MARY.

Be still and listen ! Now I catch the theme ;

A heart's hope woven with Judea's dream.
MESSIAH's coming, King of kings to reign,
Is the deep burden of the tender strain.

VII.

THE HYMN.

Hear, Adonai! perfect in thy grace,
    Our song in prayer;
Thy day of promise to thy chosen race
    This day declare.
Send Him, the Prince of Peace, the Conqueror,
    To us who wait;
Send with thy conquering hosts in holy war
    To his estate.

Bound long in chains, thy chosen seed remained
    As captives led;
The Holy City waste, thy house profaned,
    Thy prophets fled:
Yet thou didst hear and answer in the past
    Thy children's prayer:
Thy prophets have foretold our day at last,
    That day declare!

We watch the morning breaking through the chains
    Of dusky night:
Behold, the sun is risen! o'er the plains
    Sweeps in the light.
Come quickly, O Deliverer! in thy power,
    Thy people wait:
We run to bring thee, gracious Prince, this hour,
    To thy estate.

The messenger proclaims the day at hand
    Deliverance brings,
With wondrous grace, unto thy chosen land,
    Great King of kings.
Rise, rise, and sing! the day is sweet, the air
    A wondrous song
Of joy breathes to our hearts.   O soul, prepare:
    It won't be long!

We see him on the mountain in the light
    That golden falls;
We hear him in the winds that soothe the night
    With Zephyrs' calls.
He comes, he comes! His feet are on the hills
    Like purple Dawn!
His glorious presence all the morning fills,
    And doubt is gone.

VIII.

JUDETH.

How strange that song, if song it may be called,
That hath both prayer and praise in it! Appalled
Before that spirit breathing in those hearts
Our masters well might stand: the fears and starts
A tyrant feels, finds in them ample food,
With subjects hopeful and in such a mood.
This I can understand, for in my home
Lurk all fierce hatreds for the tyrant Rome.
I have imbibed them, — fed on them perforce,
Child though I am and woman. This of course;
But there is something more than this that makes
Me thrill with feeling undefined, that wakes
Within my heart a strange, new sense of power
Born of their hope that resteth on this hour,
As if the day itself were harbinger
Of hope fulfilled, which scarce the hours defer.
What think you, sister Martha?

MARTHA.

                I? No thought
Have I. On me so wonderful hath wrought
The feeling of this hour, that now I stand
In awe expecting — I know not what!

IX.

MARY.

                  And
I feel — I ought not say it, yet must speak —
I from my fast so long am growing weak.

MARTHA.

Why, what a speech !   And yet 't is ever so :
Before the appetite the grandest soul must bow
Or famish utterly ; and she, poor child,
Guiltless of such, with hunger now is wild.

MARY.

Why, Martha !   Sayest thy sister hath no soul?
Well, maybe not : a body hath she whole
And healthy ; and hunger sings a song
With tongue more clamorous than yonder throng, —
And it hath charmed me, too.

JUDETH.

                                        And since you speak
Of things so earthly, I with spirit meek
Confess the selfsame needs.

MARTHA.

                                        Then let us haste ;
The butler waits, and waiting viands waste
When long prepared, while the rich flavors fail ;
And such not eaten in their time grow stale.
Our brother Lazarus, where is he ?

JUDETH.

                                        See !
He wanders on as if unconsciously
Some power was drawing him within the charmed
And magic circle of its sway.   Disarmed
Of fear, it seems, he passes onward still,
A willing follower of some hidden will, —

MARTHA.

And, dreaming in forgetfulness, he leaves
Us here alone, the prey to fear and — thieves.
How stupid in him !   I will call him back.

X.

MARY.

Nay, Martha, let him go : a plain, smooth track

Lies now the way behind us, and the sun
Has swept the shadows from the plain. No one
Dare interrupt us on the way — and then
I am so hungry!

JUDETH.

I will join him : when
It suits his mood we will return.

MARY.

Your taste
I 'm sure I do not covet. On such waste
I do not care to feed, while dainty fish,
The tender lamb, lush dates and figs, — the wish
Outdone in them, — pomegranates ripe and red,
With generous grapes, I now prefer instead.
But then you have your choice.

MARTHA.

So far before
Is he, you cannot join in safety ; more,
The danger still will follow you along
In the low rabble of that gathering throng,
Then you will faint from hunger.

JUDETH.

Martha, dear,
Go to your tent, and of me have no fear;
Nor wait for us, we will return full soon :
The morning speeds apace, and brings the sultry noon.

XI.

MARY.

Then let us haste. I famish in the thought;
The thirst burns fiercest while the spring is sought.
When you grow tired of your airy feast,
Return to us ; the crumbs will wait, at least.

JUDETH.

Thank you, I will remember. Lazarus !
Wait, ho! my Lazarus ! He never thus
Has been so deaf when I have called him. Hear !

'T is Judeth calls.   He heeds not, and I fear
The looks of those who gather by the way.
And yet he said the sheep which yonder stray
Upon the hillsides more were to be feared
Than these swart men with shaggy locks and beard.
I will go forward.   Adonai, hear
Thy child !   Protecting, answer now her prayer.

XII.

They to their tents return, while Judeth still
Speeds on, her fear contending with her will,
Yet gaining as she goes upon the pace
Of Lazarus, whom all around delays.
Her courage rises as she, drawing near,
Finds in his presence solace for her fear.
Let us with them, and view the graphic scene,
In other lands than this could not have been.

XIII.

The scene is grand, if that be grand which awes
And in the beauty of its wildness draws
The soul entranced, with features not severe,
But in its rugged outlines soft and clear ;
A harmony in all swells through the whole,
And with its silent music floods the soul !
Near by the Jordan with its winding stream
Brings down its floods from where the blue waves gleam
On fair Tiberias' broad but placid sea,
And pours it babbling in its purity
Down the fair valley, lengthening on the view
Here in the plain, there cleaving valleys through,
Until its flood, first limpid as a beam
Ethereal, runs a pale and milky stream
Into the Dead, salt Sea, whose thirsty shores
Drink the cool tide which down its parched throat pours ;
But, like the Grave which swallows all the earth,
No living stream from its dark flood springs forth !

XIV.

The Sea ! What can we sing of sky and flood ?
Though most familiar, yet least understood :
The face of each a loved and cherished friend
Whose smiles in blessing ever on us bend ;
Whose light the joy, whose shadow still the cheer,
To hearts that love, and, trusting, do not fear.
Each has its clouds : reflected in the one
The face the other shows when looked upon ;
As cloud the brows of some ill-mated pair
With dark'ning frowns which they together wear.
When storms impend, the skies with thunders groan,
The troubled seas repeat in hollow moan ;
The tempests burst, the ragged whirlwinds sweep
The surging bosom of the boiling deep ;
While cloud to billow stoops, and wave to cloud
Lifts high its foaming crest, as hoarse and loud
The surges beat upon the sounding shore,
And drown the babel of the thunder's roar.
And yet the Sea is kind, the Sky is sweet ;
With thousand smiles they each the other greet ;
While changing oft to each their varying mien,
In every phase new beauty still is seen,
As when sea smiles to sky and sky to sea
In the full glow of morn's sweet witchery,
As we, the favored of that greeting, stand
On the green bosom of the glowing land,
To catch the radiance of the golden hour,
And feel the mystic presence of that power
Which speaks from out the bosom of the flood
Of beatific splendor, " It is good."
He made both sea and land, and spread the arch
Above them in Creation's wondrous march ;
He wrote his promise in the rainbow's form,
And as a garland with it crowned the storm,
Not as the victor, but as subject still
To the stern mandates of his ruling will :
So with his chains he bound the liquid sea
Which as to man flows fetterless and free,
Yet at the whisper of his slightest breath
The tempest's fury sinks to sighs of death !

As on the Galilee his gentle word
Of " Peace ! be still ! " the raging tempest heard,
And the hoarse waves, in murmurs low and sweet,
Crawled to the shore and kissed his naked feet !

XV.

But we forget ; and as we linger here
The voice of Judeth reaches Lazarus' ear,
And, turning quickly at the pleasing sound,
He stops, beholds inquiring faces round
That gaze on him in wonder born of fear,
Wrought in with hope and awe.   Again and near
Her voice he hears, and then upon his view
Appears the form of Judeth struggling through
The closing throng which press her round, and stay
Her further progress in the narrow way ;
Quick turn his feet, and soon his sturdy arm
The crowd holds back to save the maid from harm.

XVI.

" 'T is he ! " he hears in passing.   " No, 't is not ! "
Is answered back in Hebrew !   " Is forgot
The reading of the Word ? ' A prince ' it said."
" True, such indeed the reading ; he instead
Is neither prince nor princely born."   Behind,
In his mad haste the struggling girl to find,
He left dispute and disputants, and ran,
If such the pace which crowds from man to man,
Until at last he gained fair Judeth's side ;
She, scarcely seen, was struggling in the tide —
A rushing stream of human life — which poured
Its flood around him in a motley horde,
Drawn from all sides by cries, such as the word
Of him just spoken, now on all sides heard,
As others catch it up and send it on,
Wrong from the first, increasing still has gone,
Until the whispered guess a fact assumes
And this to them the truth its self becomes.
And thus in faith the tented city heard
With bated breath the hope-confirming word,

That he the promised had indeed now come,
For whom hearts open stood to give him room,
In joy awaiting to confirm the plan
When Truth exulting cries, " Behold the Man ! "

XVII.

" Oh, save me, Lazarus ! " was Judeth's cry,
With panting breath, when she beheld him nigh ;
" The horde would trample me !   Are these the sheep
You boasted of ? Yon sea now purpling deep
Would swallow me with not more greedy maw
Were I to trust it without bark.   Pray draw
Me from this vortex of contending life."
Then one approaching said, " Art thou not wife
To him ? " pointing to Lazarus.   " Nay, nay !
But what is that to you ? I need not say
I am a woman, since thou hast thine eyes ;
Should I be trodden if ye do despise ? "
Rebuked by words so bold, he backward pressed,
Apace, and forced with him all of the rest.
The action seen, and backward motion felt,
Like snow at touch of flame they crumbling melt
Around and from the two, and leave them there
A widening circle in the tented square.

XVIII.

As some strange beast by daring hunter caught
Which is for show to rustic village brought,
With muzzled snout and claws securely trimmed,
Still fierce of front, for battle strongly limbed ;
Unknown his nature while displayed his power,
His paws may grapple and his fangs devour ;
With restless pace he runs his shortened round
About the stake to which securely bound ;
Soon all the village hastening forth appears,
From gray-haired patriarch to the least in years ;
These crowd the circle which the monster's chain
Makes safe while yet its bonds his rage restrain ;
And there they watch in prudent distance safe,
Fly when he growls and when at rest they chafe ;

Crowd closer in when at the stake he lies,
And when he lifts his head retreat with cries, —
So closely gather at the circling line,
Whose human walls our captive friends confine,
This motley throng, uncertain if they dare
Approach these beings, both their fear and care,
Lest from them leap, omnipotent in power,
A sword to smite, or flame that will devour ;
Such as old Egypt's pride smote down, and laid
In dust her first-born by destroying blade ;
Or as the fire which went out from the Lord
And Nahab and Abihu both devoured.
Nor was the fear alone to those without,
Our friends within were filled with dread and doubt ;
While the strong heart of Lazarus misgave
Him, yet his look was passionless but grave ;
For Judeth, weak and cowering by his side,
Aroused his pity, manhood, and his pride.
Whate'er, were he encompassed thus alone,
In rashness or in zeal he might have done,
With her beside him, it deserved his care
To temporize ; when that should fail, then dare
The bravest deeds, else better wrongs endure
So that the end her safety may secure.

XIX.

She, trusting him, her woman's subtile skill,
She plied to read their temper and their will,
Since they the best are armed to meet the foe
Who both their strength and purpose fully know.
Let us with them the puzzling scene, too, scan,
And read as books their faces, man by man.
Around the circle, reading face by face,
No passion can we in one visage trace ;
A curious study here ! A Raphael's hand
Might faintly trace on canvas and command
Some truth in action, passive there, to tell
No living pen could hope to do so well ;
And yet for him there is a point his skill,
If he but touch, his touch would mar it still,
Because it is not in the grasp of men

To paint with brush, delineate with pen,
That wondrous power, beyond the grasp of art,
Which through each single mind moves separate heart,
And writes its message there, to speak through eyes
From which the wingéd thought to bear it flies,
E'en as the subtile fluid on the wire
Flashes our thoughts abroad in written fire,
While he whose hand may give the message wing
Can never touch the fount from which they spring!

XX.

Here Jews we see, Samaria's servile type,
For intrigue ready and for treason ripe ;
Yet, servile still, his bearded face declares
Whate'er his fortune little hope he shares ;
While from his eye the changing, fitful gleam
Shows he, in action even, still must dream!
Beside him, dark as night the burning eye,
Which shows fierce fires enkindled deeper lie,
Stands the swart Arab, child of desert lands,
Drawn hither from his barren, trackless sands,
Among the crowded tents finds ample field
Where his shrewd arts their golden harvests yield,
And hopes, in ev'ry crowd as this one made,
Some chance to ply for gain his crafty trade.
The Ethiop next, whose ebon face betrays
The focussed burning of the tropic rays,
Unlike his sun, whose blistering vapors burn
To living flame and blackened coal in turn,
His ardent heart with tender love aglow,
An odorous garden where all choice flowers grow ;
He, loving man because of man, but sees
In all things flowers to strew the paths of peace.
The Priest, the Levite, — chosen of the Lord
To guard his kingdom with a flaming sword
Drawn for the Law, — still with their greedy eyes
Seek place and power, and all things else despise ;
Their gain God's gain, and as they teach they mouse
Until their zeal has eaten up his house, —
These, too, are here to seek if from the hour
They may not add new lustre to their power.

XXI.

Then comes the Greek, we know him by his face,
A careworn dreamer of a glorious race;
The name is all: a mystic memory lies
Pale in the shadow of his soulless eyes;
Platonic now the fires, if not the love,
Which feeling hearts unutterably move;
Gone now forever all that was his own
In glory, while his fame to shadow grown.
Next him the Roman soldier, iron-browed,
With breast as heartless as his soul is proud;
Who, in things present, past, and yet to come,
Seeks still to add all glories unto Rome,
Whose darkling splendor now is toppling down
Since civic wreaths are turned to Cæsar's crown.
Here Sadducee and Pharisee in smiles,
Each thinking of himself, himself beguiles
With the fond dream that God in special care
Waits with bowed ear alone to hear his prayer!
The blind might feel upon his smiling face
His sanctified and self-asserting grace,
While in his heart lies hatred black and deep,
In couchant rest, but never known to sleep:
The tiger leashed, defiant, or at bay,
Than he is not more eager for its prey!

XXII.

Filled in with these and such as these, between,
Are hundreds more with varying aspects seen,
And on each face is writ with constant change,
In characters distinct as they are strange,
A wondrous sign — a portent — one may read,
And, though he understand not, still should heed;
For in it hope and faith in truth divine
Glowed in each feature, gleamed in every line,
Until the speaking countenance there shone,
Angelic, save it lacked the aureole crown.
These were of those who, hearing truth, believe,
Their faith from John, as children now receive;
And seeing Lazarus, with hungering souls

Their faith in him their eager hope extols.
They rush to him, believing now they see
In him a humble son of Bethany,
Their Lord and King, and ready are to greet
Emanuel, and worship at his feet:
So great their zeal for their expectant Lord,
So large the place they would to him accord;
Yet, when at last he cometh to his own,
His crown is thorns, a cross his earthly throne!
And these, who crowd in their expectant zeal,
Will let the world from them his kingdom steal,
Their Prince will crucify, then sit them down
And dream for ages of a vanished crown!

XXIII.

Judeth and Lazarus, when first they saw
The narrowing circle around them draw,
Were filled with fear lest violence towards them
Had raised a flood they had not power to stem.
But watching there the faces as they gleamed
In the bright sunshine which about them streamed,
They read them, and upon their pages saw,
Though much of passion, more of doubt and awe;
But nothing they should fear, save that a brand
Might yet be thrown by some mischievous hand
Among these masses, now so cold and tame,
And change the whole to a devouring flame
Whose withering breath, which once against them blown,
Would blast like bolt from hand Eternal thrown!

XXIV.

Judeth perplexed to Lazarus speaking turns:
" What mean they, Lazarus?   My eye discerns
No sign of anger in their watchful eyes,
But more of wonder, — questioning surprise,
As if we were to them of race so strange,
They knew not if to fear or worship."

LAZARUS.

Change

But just one thought in one o'erruling mind
And then this crowd, now peaceful, mad and blind
Will rage about us like that peaceful sea
When storms sweep o'er the plains of Galilee;
So we must hold our peace.

JUDFTH.

                    I understand :
But yet 't is hard to wait, — one's self-command
At such an hour in such a state as this.

LAZARUS.

One word missaid, one little step amiss,
And scarce a Legion of that Roman brood   .
Can save us.   Soon we would be fire and food
For this devouring horde ; so patience, all
In God's good time ends in the best.

JUDETH.

                    Then call
We on Him !   ADONAI hear !   Thy hand
Stretch forth and save us of thy chosen land !
Thou art our strength ; on thee must we rely
In our great need, then pass us now not by !

LAZARUS.

Judeth, your prayer so sweet to me, to him
A holy incense !   And my faith, though dim
And clouded, takes fast hold on it to rise
With it and upward cleave the cloudless skies,
And lay it at his feet.

XXV.

JUDETH.

                    'T is all I have.
A woman prays in danger, man is brave ;
And yet both lean upon the arm of God !

LAZARUS.

Yes, both ; and to escape his chastening rod.
But hark !   What sound is that ?   It swiftly nears
Where we are standing ; and to my quick ears

It seems a rising song.   Ah, see! a wave
Runs o'er this throng, and there is power to save
Us by this new diversion.   Now the ring,
Like mountain snows at breath of coming spring,
Melts at the touch of this new power, and flows
Around and from us.   Now, if these were foes,
They would o'erwhelm or bear us with the tide.
Since we are free, why longer here abide?
Let's to our tents, and, when well rested, tell
What here to us so wonderfully befell.

JUDETH.

They will believe us trifling.   How strange
All seems!   How wonderfully swift the change!
A moment past, we were hemmed in — a prayer —
The danger flees and leaves us free as air!
These are indeed strange people.

LAZARUS.

                          And yet kind.
But let us haste and leave these tents behind.
Ah, here they come again, a surging throng,
But now with laughing faces!   Praise and song
Following —   What is this which greets my sight,
That, were I now alone, my soul would fright
With a chill horror?   Is it man or beast, —
I cannot tell which one it favors least, —
Or hermit clad in skins?   Or can it be
John Baptist?   Yes, it·is, it must be he!
It is most wonderful that in such guise
The people hearken to him: wherein lies
His power to wield and sway them as he will,
To raise the tempest or the storm to still?
What fails to please too often we despise,
And virtue weigh alone with purblind eyes.
The leathern girdle and the cloak of hair
Oft make us scorn the sage enforced to wear;
The knotted staff, the stay of brawny hands
Our jeering laughter and contempt commands;
While matted beard and locks of tangled gray
Are food for scoffers loitering by the way:
And yet, beneath all these, unconscious lie

The wondrous attributes of Deity!
Not John the Baptist, nor the Prophets even,
Have the sole gifts, though much to them is given;
But man, the living image in the clod,
A temple is for the indwelling God!
But why should I stand talking, and delay
Our course, while he is coming on this way?
Let us go forth to meet them.

JUDETH.

       I'm content,
Since towards our tents our footsteps will be bent.

XXVI.

They hasten on; and, strange it may appear,
Unnoticed by the throng they now draw near,
Which scarce a moment past had held them thrall,
Hemmed in and pent within that human wall,
The centre drawn of all their staring eyes
Which now see not, or seeing but despise;
Since they must see the passion which inflamed
Their folly then, is that which now has tamed.
But there is one, the centre of them all,
With bearded face and stature straight and tall,
Locks long and flowing, eyes of dusky night,
Coarse-robed in camel's hair of dingy white,
With leather girt, and staff a riven bough.
He sees and steadfast looks upon them now
With eyes, to them, a strangely moving power,
Which, as they gaze, the very thought devour;
And yet so kindly in their gentle glow,
They seem with tears just ready to o'erflow.
Before him mute and motionless they stand
With feet that seem fast-rooted to the sand,
And eyes downcast, they wait his passing by,
And, waiting thus, they feel him drawing nigh,
Until his touch the shrinking Lazarus thrills,
With ecstasy his quivering being fills
To hush of thought, as sweetly he doth say,
" Blessed art thou to live in this blest day,
To have the love of the Eternal Son
Thy heritage;" and saying this, passed on.

XXVII.

With him the crowd which followed after goes,
Nor heed they, further than a glance allows,
Surprised, it may be, if they saw and heard
The touch he gave and the low-spoken word.
And so absorbed in him, who in his train
Leads them still further out along the plain,
Our friends they leave forsaken in the way,
Their senses to regain as best they may,
Not as Lot's wife, but like her fixed by awe
At the strange being they both heard and saw!
A moment thus, then Judeth, speaking first,
Said softly, " Lazarus, I pray you burst
This spell which is upon you! That strange man
Hath power phenomenal : there may be plan
And method in his craft, yet his kind eye
And gentle speech the thought of it deny."

LAZARUS.

My Judeth, were you speaking ? Your words seem
The ghostly whisperings of a troubled dream !
Did not some hand — I thought I felt a touch —
Upon my arm with pressure overmuch
Stay me a time?

JUDETH.

Yes, gently as a child.

LAZARUS.

And then I heard a voice speak low and mild,
Strange words to me, remembering ev'ry one,
Are without meaning ; that from me has flown.

XXVIII.

JUDETH.

The words I heard — and they were sweet as wine
From Eschol's vintage pressed, and yours, not mine,
The blessing — and the lips which thus bestowed
Spake as the oracle inspired of God.

LAZARUS.

John Baptist?   Ah, I know and feel 't is he !
None other hath such power.   And he to me
The blessing gave ?   Ah, now I understand
The words of promise and the loving hand !
Where has he gone, that we may follow him,
To learn the fulness of this joy, but dim
Portrayed in his prophetic speech ?

JUDETH.

The day
Grows on apace; we should no longer stay ;
Your sisters grow impatient.

LAZARUS.

True, and we
Must now return to them : but first to see
Whither the Prophet goes.   Yes, there they go
Down where the Jordan in its peaceful flow
Winds through the narrow plain.   And see ! adown
The roads which lead from each surrounding town
The gathering people fill. and plain beyond ;
While close about the Seer, wondering or fond,
They follow him where'er he leadeth.   Haste
We to our tents, and there a little taste
Of broken meats, which you now sorely need,
Then, with our sisters, after we will speed.

XXIX.

JUDETH.

My wants can wait, nor is it meet we heed
These temporal things, when mightier await
To feed the hungry mind.   Yet growing late
The hour, and I am flesh and blood, — gross flesh
That ev'ry day must be supplied afresh ;
And mortal, too, and that in every part,
And loving this mortality —   Why start ?
You know my creed ; it teaches this one truth,
As to mankind, there can be but one youth ;
That ended, then to age we stooping go,
In sorrow wrapped, like sackcloth worn in woe,

To greet the grave, and then — you answer, " Blest."
Yes, in its dreamless, everlasting rest!
I moralist — philosopher — have grown?
Thus far the truth of the grave charge I own,
And have grown wise to this extent, I find
The foolish ones leave happiness behind,
To chase a shadow for its emptiness —
For us to go unfed would scarce be less.

XXX.

While thus, she talking, towards the waiting tent
Their hastening steps along the way were bent,
He, answering not, but kindly on her smiled,
Pleased with her speech as prattle of a child:
For little else he heard, save the sweet flow
Of words unmeaning, in their cadence low,
Since through his mind, repeated often, ran
Those mystic words from that mysterious man;
Their hidden meaning, struggling to make plain,
Flashed through his mind and then grew dark again.
Like some fair landscape to the gazing eye,
Hung darkly curtained by a sable sky,
On which the lightning's fitful flashes burn
As failing lamps, now bright now dim in turn,
But nought revealing of the lovely scene,
Save mingled hues and misty depths between,
With never flower, or vale, or spreading tree,
Distinct or clear in night's obscurity,
So flashed his thought through mind's beclouded night,
While truth grew darkened in the feeble light.

XXXI.

Debating this with his own thought, while she,
Unanswered, drops into a reverie,
In silence thus the tents approaching, they
With loitering steps pursue their silent way,
Until midway the anxious sisters meet
Them in return, and haste their tardy feet
With urgent protest, question, and rebuke,
If not in word, still in both voice and look,

For their delay, of which the soaring sun
Tells off in hours to midday almost run.
Now they on either side have grasped an arm,
And thus returning hear their tale. Alarm,
Then wonder, fills their throbbing hearts to hear
The story as 't is told. So they draw near
The restful tents, the story done, with eyes
Cast down, and faces on which sits surprise
Mute in each troubled look. A time before
Their waiting tents that stand with open door
They pause, uncertain of their further course,
It may be, else from habit's silent force,
And then they enter, each with glances turned
Toward the near Jordan, with a look that yearned
For the fair stream, and him whose magic power
Was the great wonder of the passing hour.
Rest we a time with them; the way is long,
And he who follows to the end must needs be strong.

CANTO THIRD.

ECCE HOMO!

I.

WHY are we born so weak ? Why is the hand
So short that would lay hold on Truth ? The grand
Eternal thoughts of the All-knowing mind
Leave us in darkness : human eyes grow blind
Before his truth, which is the living light,
And with it still before, we grope in night.
Why are our ears so deaf they cannot hear
The wondrous message told for ev'ry ear ?
Two thousand years the world has heard it told,
Yet it is ever new while growing old.
New empires from the dust of old have sprung,
Their histories known and read in ev'ry tongue :
These in their fall give place to kingdoms new,
And these their course of empire still pursue.
Each race, each nation, passing o'er the stage,

Is known and read in its succeeding age.
Their peoples born, live, labor, hope, believe,
Give as they have, and where they lack receive ;
Their creeds, their gods, their rites of mystic faith,
Move ever on a plain and beaten path
The world can follow, reading, as it runs,
The deepest lessons of its mighty ones.
But God's bold writing on the staring wall
Has mysteries the gaping world appall.

II.

Six thousand years man stands beneath the sky,
And reads its ever-broad'ning mystery ;
And scarce a page it takes the whole to tell
Of his large wisdom learned thus none too well !
One pen-stroke from His hand, the lettered heaven
In written fires its history has given !
His fingers touch the mysteries of Time,
The scroll unrolls a history sublime !
At his command the shrouding curtains fall,
. And sun and stars are hid alike from all.
Yet man in his great wisdom, with a nod,
Denies these truths and cries, "There is no God ! "
Then gasps for his spent breath just snatched away,
His mighty wisdom turned to noisome clay.
And yet the world moves on without his hand
To wheel the stars, their courses to command.
A little dust dropped on the poising scale
To turn the balance here cannot prevail:
The hand which weighs the circling worlds heeds not
Such atom falling on neglected spot,
When counting in its worlds its million spheres,
As here and there a planet disappears,
Or, blazing through a thousand centuries, runs
The wasting conflagrations of his suns.
And yet how wonderful Salvation's theme !
Exceeding wild Imagination's dream,
That he, this God, will mortal man still own,
Stoop tenderly, and from his reigning throne
Lift up this creature from a world of night,
To reign with him and shine in endless light !

Not this alone the mystery of his plan
By which is brought salvation unto man :
This God eternal sends his Son to bear
Our sin and shame, and all our griefs to share —
E'en die for us ; yet those who saw him die,
Both God who sent him and his Son deny !
Why hangs suspended still the avenging bolt
To smite a world grown daring in revolt ?
Is Mercy endless in its saving grace
To spare eternally the human race ?
Bought at such price, his patient love denies
To Justice even, its own sacrifice ;
Denies that God whose mercies yet endure,
Through which alone we rebels are secure !

III.

Such thoughts awake when startling visions rise
From out the Past and glow before our eyes,
Where, from these scenes, as from illumined page,
We read the story of this wondrous age,
And reading stand before its truth declared,
To solve the mystery why one soul is spared.
So, as we strive, the wonder deeper grows
When mysteries solved but greater still disclose :
Behind them, Law dishonored, threat'ning stands,
The lash and sword in its avenging hands ;
And back of Law stands weeping Innocence,
With covered face but waiting to go hence :
While Love and Mercy at their altars wait,
With outstretched hands, imploring 'gainst her fate ;
While fragrant incense sweetens all the air
With the rich odors of their generous prayer ;
While over these the trembling heavens nod
Beneath the tread of the oncoming God,
Who, veiled in clouds, hides his mysterious face,
Whose smile can save, whose frown destroy a race.
On that dread march Jehovah Jireh made
Along Judea's hills in Christ portrayed,
Before his Messenger revealed we stand,
And lo ! now Christ himself is near at hand !

IV.

JUDETH.

Look! how they gather close about him. Fair
Is he, save that the sun has bronzed : his hair,
The tawny lion's mane, sun-scorched and long,
But silken-soft as a young maiden's. Tongue
Inspired his eye cannot describe. Clearer
Than midday sky, the zenith stooping nearer
Unto the earth, and of its blue a part !
It has the fire of suns that flame and dart
Both life and death in their alternate beams ;
And yet within its depths lie sweetest dreams
Of love and peace.

MARY.

If so, I fail to see
In him aught you describe, save, it may be,
The shaggy mane and beard. His bristling brows,
Bent in two frowning curves like bended bows,
Obscure the azure blue in murky night,
From which shoot flashes of a baleful light
That chills my blood.

LAZARUS.

You judge through your desire,
And see in him what you would most admire :
Your heart, romantic in its view of life,
Of saint would make a robber ; peace to strife
Would turn, then revel in the discord !

V.

MARY.

Nay !
You wrong me, brother, thus in what you say.
For I would fain believe him Prophet sent
To call the world to God, have man repent,
And peace unbroken reign on earth alway,
Than think him robber schooled from youth to slay
His fellow-kind. But him I can but read
As thus he stands before me. Faith and creed
To better vision fail to ope my eyes,
To see in him what I may not despise !

MARTHA.

Why, Mary ! Judge not, since not e'en a word
Have you from him in all his teachings heard !
The pomegranate forbidding first appears
In russet clad, nor outward promise bears
Of the rich stores within.   Cleft to the heart,
The sweets are seen as fall the halves apart.
So, from the dusty rock of Horeb's plain,
Gushed the pent waters from their hidden vein :
Elisha, clad in skins of beasts, still bore
God's truth within his heart ; so sacred power
May dwell to-day with yonder man.

JUDETH.

                                   Behold !
They gather closer still to hear him ! Bold
Are now his looks, and, hark ! his strengthening speech
Sweeps ringing out unto the farthest reach
Of this vast multitude, as, full and clear,
Drop his calm words into the dullest ear,
Hushing them all to silence.

LAZARUS.

                              Hark ye all !
Nor let us lose one of his words that fall :
The little distance gives us vantage-ground,
Where echo fails to reach in its rebound.

VI.

" Ho, ev'ry one ! " he cries in trumpet tones,
That in the distance die in quavering moans,
" Come to the waters, come ye all and drink,
Where flows the fountain to its crimsoned brink ;
Come ye who have no money, come and buy
Both wine and milk, and all your wants supply.
Why spend your gold for that which is not bread
When from his bounty ye may all be fed ?
Eat but the good and ye shall prosper then ;
The soul delight in fatness, blest of men
And God.   Incline thine ear, come unto me,
And then your soul shall live, and I with thee

A covenant will make, even the sure
Mercies of David, and they shall endure.
Behold my witness now to you I bring,
Commander, Leader, Saviour, ay, and King!
A nation thou shalt call thou dost not know,
And nations that to thee have long been foe,
Because thy God and Israel's Holy One
Hath glorified thee, unto thee shall run.
Seek ye the Lord while yet he may be near
And call upon him while he still may hear;
Forsake your evil ways, ye wicked, turn,
Unrighteous man, while yet the lamp doth burn;
For God invites, his mercy still endures,
His pardon purifies, his blessing cures.
My thoughts are not your thoughts, nor are your ways
My ways, saith God.   The heavens that yonder blaze
High over all, from earth are not less far
Than are my thoughts from yours; and yet there are
Such blessings in my word, which, like the rain
And snow that fall, returning not again
To heaven but watereth all the earth, until
Its flowers and fruits the teeming valleys fill
And man is fed; so it shall not return
Unto me void, but ye shall know and learn
That what I will it doeth, and at my hand
Shall prosper whereunto I may command.
Ye shall go out in joy, and thus be led
In paths of peace; the mountains shall be glad,
The hills break forth before you into song,
The trees clap hands, and earth the notes prolong.
Where springs the thorn the fir-tree shall abound,
Instead of briars the myrtle cheer the ground,
And ye shall know by these it is a sign
Ye shall not be cut off by hand divine."
Thus spake your Prophet as the voice of God
From his high throne, whence shines his grace abroad,
Proclaiming forth his mercies and his love
Unto your fathers, which you now may prove.
Repent, O Israel, while yet the day
Is yours, and for your coming Lord make way;
Prepare his road and make his pathway straight,
For now the hour doth for his coming wait.

Turn from your sins, O Israel! now turn;
Cannot your eyes signs of the times discern?
The heathen world your King and Saviour waits,
Impatient still at your unopened gates.
Lift up your gates and let the song begin,
" Behold, the King of Glory shall come in."
The valleys shall be filled ; mountain and hill
Brought low, the crooked ways made straight, and still
The roughened ways made smooth ; and then all flesh
Shall see Salvation's stream pour forth afresh.
Now is the day of your salvation, now
The hour when forth its living streams shall flow !
Behold the signs and portents which declare
The Lord to save his arm has now made bare.
The earth is sick from sin, the hills are faint,
The valleys in their groanings make complaint ;
Hoar Lebanon with cedars crowned bows low,
While Hermon stoops his ancient brows of snow;
The Jordan bears his burden of the wrong,
And flowing down chants mournfully his song.
The thirsting plains with hot lips faintly cry,
Because the brooks and rills have all run dry ;
While yon salt sea with its baked lips complains
Of desolation blasting all the plains.
Your cities cry aloud with woful call
From street deserted and from broken wall;
Profaned your Temple from its altar cries,
And clouds the air from useless sacrifice ;
While Gentile feet pollute the sacred courts,
And to its holy shrine the vile resorts.
God's house and altar by the heathen won
Have left your lands and cities all undone ;
And yet you boast of glory ! Proudly scorn
The Gentile hand by which your power is shorn!
Live in your name, which now is long since dead,
To leave you slaves and sycophants instead.
Of God deserted, vengeance on your path
Pursues you with the besom of his wrath.

VII.

Who are these come to me ?   From sable face
Which marks the sun-scorched Ethiopic race ;
In tawny skin and darkly piercing eye
The Bedouin of the Desert I descry ;
The sallow visage of the Greek I see,
The Roman mantle flowing loose and free :
Ay, ev'ry region, mountain, hill, and plain
Has sent its band to swell the gathering train.
What come you out to see ? is it a reed
Here shaken by the wind ?   Oh, hear and heed !
I am a man, my message is to men :
Repent, repent I say to you again.
But who are these who laugh me now to scorn ?
'T were better far that ye had ne'er been born,
Ye viper's brood with brows of hateful gloom,
Who warneth you to flee the wrath to come ?
Fruits meet for your repentance henceforth bring,
Nor boast descent from patriarch or king :
E'en of these stones, in these degenerate days,
Children to Abra'm God hath power to raise.
What boots it if your father Abraham be ?
The axe lies at the root of ev'ry tree,
And ev'ry tree, though robed in bursting bloom,
In promised fruit breathing a rich perfume,
That barren grows or faileth our desire,
To earth is hewn and cast into the fire.
Not ye, the people, nay, not ye alone :
The evil reacheth even to the throne ;
The king, the court, and those in places high
Our God insulteth and his laws defy.
Pollution sits in purple, and the fair,
The robes incestuous of the bridal wear ;
Red-handed Murder from each gateway frowns,
Unblushing revel midnight orgies crowns ;
Day mocks the night's debauch with lust and wine,
And lights the torch again at sun's decline.
From thousand altars flame your base desires,
While in the Temple pale God's altar-fires ;
For desolate is Zion, lone and sad
She sits now weeping and in sackcloth clad !

Return to her and comfort; hasten, bring
Your gifts unto her altars. Lo ! her king
In triumph now is coming to his own :
No more shall Zion desolate be and lone.

ONE OF THE PEOPLE.
What shall we do ?

JOHN BAPTIST.
Who hath two coats must one
Bestow on him who, now in need, hath none ;
And he who yet also hath store of meat
Must to his hungry neighbor give to eat.

A PUBLICAN.
My master, what, I pray thee, shall we do?

JOHN BAPTIST
Exact no more than what is just to you.

A ROMAN SOLDIER.
And what of us?

JOHN BAPTIST.
Do violence to none :
Speak no one false ; small wage is lightly won.

VIII.

I read your hearts, O People !   In your thought
There lingers much of wonder, more of doubt,
If I be the Messiah long foretold
Whom now your anxious eyes long to behold.
With water I baptize, but there is One
Whose coming now in faith I look upon,
My follower, the latchet of whose shoes
I am not worthy e'en to stoop and loose,
To whose dread name no mortal dare aspire,
He with the Holy Ghost baptizes and with fire :
Whose fan is in his hand, his threshing-floor
To purge, his wheat he will in garner store ;
The chaff, when purged the wheat by winnowing well,
He then will burn with fires unquenchable.

IX.

Haste, for his coming all your hearts prepare;
The world's salvation I in truth declare;
The promised day the Prophet long foretold
Is now at hand; through ages hoar and old
The sages saw this day, the day of days,
When from the seed of David God should raise
Emanuel up, THE CHRIST, the Blessed One,
To save his heritage through Sin undone!
Rise, shine, O Truth! and touch the smoking hills,
Until the earth beneath thy footsteps thrills,
And every knee shall bow, each tongue confess
The Lord is God, and his own righteousness.
Awake, O Israel! Ye nations, hear!
The Lord is God! He draweth very near!
Purge out your sins, for hath he not declared
He who repents he also shall be spared?
Although your sins be scarlet they shall be
Like wool, when cleansed, from spot and stain set free;
And though they are like crimson in their glow,
At his pure touch they shall be white as snow!

THE PEOPLE.

What shall we do?

JOHN BAPTIST.

Repent and be baptized.

VOICES.

We do repent, of that you are apprised,
And here await the cleansing flood.

JOHN BAPTIST.

Step down
Into the stream, to God allegiance own,
And I will follow.

X.

MARY.

Let us stem this throng —
Hark! Once again I hear that morning song
Come up from out the waters pure and sweet,

In woman's silvery tones. It is not meet
That she should breast the chilling tide with men,
And buffet with the waters. Hark! Again
From out the stream a hundred voices more
Catch up the song, and, borne along the shore,
It swells in mighty chorus, while the air
Is burdened with its slowly chanted prayer.

JUDETH.

Here now is vantage-ground, here let us stay.
Why should the throng at our approach give way,
And shrink from us in doubt and some amaze?
You, Lazarus, are the centre of their gaze!

LAZARUS.

I cannot answer you, but only know
The fact alone that, as you say, 'tis so;
And, better still, that when at morn they press'd
So close about us we were sore distress'd,
Since now it gives to us this vantage-ground,
Which else in this vast throng we had not found.

MARTHA.

Look well about you: in this motley horde
The noisome seeds of pestilence is stored.

MARY.

If so, from yonder washing we may deem
Pollution festers in the Jordan's stream,
And all its banks are sodden.

MARTHA.

Mary, still
Your words are wayward as your stubborn will.
All holy things are trivial in your eyes:
Have care, else you the truth of God despise.

LAZARUS.

Peace! Let us see and listen. This is strange!
As far around me as my eyes can range
Sweep out the plains about the purpling sea,
Ingirt with mountains that around them be;

And yet along each far and winding way,
Drawn near to sight by this most perfect day,
The throngs still come! In groups and then alone
The people from the uplands hasten down ;
While from the valleys upward winding still,
Through leafy grove and over barren hill,
They haste to hear this man whose wondrous power
Recalls Elijah from his cave once more :
While at our feet, in masses circling wide,
The Jordan's banks are packed on either side ;
And in the stream, behold, how still they throng,
And fill the air with shout and triumph song !
While he, whose fiery speech inflamed their souls,
With the chill waters now their burning cools,
Yet feeds the flames which warm the heart within,
Purged through the waters of its quenching sin,
And hallelujahs from the waves arise
In joyful shouts and cleave the bending skies.
They come and go, a flux and reflux stream,
And gather where the parting waters gleam ;
As his strong arm with plunging motion bends,
The shivering form beneath the flood descends ;
Like some coarse shepherd in the budding spring,
Who doth his flock to some clear brooklet bring,
To wash their shaggy coats before he shears,
Equipped among his pent-up flock appears :
The patriarch of his flock he roughly leads
Along the stream, nor his loud bleating heeds,
But, plunging in the stream, with roughened hand
Scrubs his long coat, then drives him out to land ;
The teeming ewes his careful fingers press
With tenderness that seems a half caress,
While his strong arms the old and feeble bear,
For age and weakness merit all his care.
So he to each his duty here fulfils ;
Somewhat of his own feeling, too, instils
Into these hearts, who by their faith alone
Believe in what his earnest hands have done.

XI.

MARY.

They are now almost done.

LAZARUS.

Goes down into the water.

Yes, now the last

MARTHA.

Ah ! how fast
He hath baptized them ! I can understand
Nought of his meaning, — where he gets command
For this strange sacrament; not in our law,
If I can read it right.

MARY.

Yet we may draw
By inference implied command.

JUDETH.

How so ?
I do not catch your meaning.

MARY.

Well, you know
That purity is one of our great laws.
No people ever had a greater cause
For washing than have these baptized to-day :
We all have gained to that extent.

JUDETH.

·I pray
You mercy, sister Mary, since your wit
Truth and occasion both to-day has hit.
But he is coming from the waters.   Grand,
Indeed, majestic is his mien.   Command
Sits in his eye, and yet so gently there,
Until aroused of it none seems aware.
How glows his face !   Encircling his white brow
A clinging light is shedding a faint glow,
As falls the sunlight over him.   Indeed !
Are not my words deserving of your heed
That you should gaze, forgetful of us here,
Out o'er the landscape?

XII.

LAZARUS.
See ! Now drawing near,
Who cometh yonder ?

JUDETH.
It is but a man
As other men, save that —

LAZARUS.
Save what ?

JUDETH.
Began
I that to tell, had not you rudely broke
The thread of forming thought just as I spoke.

LAZARUS.
Your pardon, then, I crave for my rude speech:
Impatience in such school is hard to teach ·
To be polite, and so itself restrain.
But now I pray that you would look again,
And tell me what of him who comes apace.

JUDETH.
I am and have been looking. In his face,
As he draws nearer, is that wondrous light
Which shines through sorrow, making sadness bright !
With measured pace he comes, and looks downcast
From sorrows yet to come or griefs long past :
No trace of fear, no line of evil there, —
An Angel's face in innocence !

XIII.

LAZARUS.
And fair
And sweet as woman's when her love and truth
Have made her perfect in her hope and youth.

JUDETH.
You said the last, not I. No woman born,

Hath half the beauty in her freshest morn,
As he who cometh yonder. Ah! How fair
The tender face, how rich the golden hair,
Now glowing in the sunlight with a blaze
Like molten gold aglow, a double sheen
Encircling and above the head is seen!
Majestic are his strides; yet, where they pass,
His feet are tender of the yielding grass
As if he feared to give it pain. But see!
A fluttering dove, which from a hawk doth flee,
Finds shelter in his bosom! while its foe
With angry cry hastes to the groves below.
How tenderly he wraps it in the folds
Of his white robe, and to his bosom holds
The frightened thing! Ah, me! How sweet such rest
When love is pillowed on affection's breast!

XIV.

MARY.

Doth that come from the heart, you needs must sigh
In speaking of it?

JUDETH.

Please excuse reply,
At hour like this, to such a question.

MARY.

True,
The hour is early, — is it late for you?

JUDETH.

I do not understand, save that at best
Of me or the occasion you make jest.
For me I care not, but a something swells
My heart with tenderness, and to me tells
That of this day, some way, there shall arise
The crowning work of all Earth's mysteries.
But we forget, while speaking: as he nears,
More beautiful his countenance appears;
And, as he looks upon the people, rise,
Floods of compassion clouding his sweet eyes;
Whilst Love absorbent in their light appears,

And Pity melts their liquid light to tears.
How strangely hath he all my thought possessed,
My reason captured, occupied my breast!
With not a word, thought, touch, or glance of eye,
Have I been noticed as he passeth by.
Who can he be that hath such power to move
At sight of him, enchain our will and love,
Wring from our lips confessions that might shame
Our cheeks to blushes, if we made the same
Unasked to dearest friend; and yet his will
A captive leads me, though reluctant still!

XV.

And yet, it seems, his glance in passing by
Would smite with terror, — at his touch we die:
Yet from his lips a word, and dried our tears,
Death glows in life, and banished all our fears.
But see! the crowd is parting ere he gains
The outmost circle of the nearer plains,
As if his touch instinctively it felt
At which the densely crowded masses melt,
And leave for him a broad, unbroken track,
A kingly way, from which the lines fall back,
Down to the river brink : there stands revealed
John Baptist, whom the crowd before concealed.
He catches sight of him whose hast'ning feet
Are rushing on the Prophet-seer to greet,
When, lo! transfixed with wonder and delight,
He stands as one heart-ravished by the sight.
And, hark! he speaks, as with his outstretched hand
He points to him in gesture of command.

XVI.

JOHN BAPTIST.

Hear, O ye people! Blessed over all
This day exceeding others ; now extol
The loving-kindness God to you hath shown,
Since Christ the Lord now cometh to his own.
Behold the Lamb of God which takes away
The sin of the whole world : again I say,

As I have said of him whom you now see,
That there is one who cometh after me,
Preferred before me, and in all before,
The one who was, and is, and is to come : adore
Him, since he is the Christ, not I. I knew
Him not, but knew, as I proclaimed to you,
To Israel he should be made appear,
And I, therefore, baptized with water. Hear,
And all ye people to my words give heed,
This is the Christ; he is the Lord indeed.

JESUS OF NAZARETH.

Beloved, I salute thee, and the rite
Baptismal at thy hands I now invite.

JOHN BAPTIST.

Nay; I have need to be baptized of thee,
Unworthy all, and comest thou to me ?

JESUS OF NAZARETH.

Nay, suffer it to be so as I will,
For thus all righteousness we shall fulfil.

JOHN BAPTIST.

Not as I will, O God, but as thou wilt,
Since to offend in me would now be guilt :
The blessing in the deed makes glad this day,
As I through thee shall wash all sin away.

XVII.

And as he ceased they to the water turn ;
The waiting crowd, of mystery more to learn,
Strain ev'ry power of eye, set ev'ry ear,
Of that which may be both to see and hear.
And thus in breathless pause, with lips apart
And hands pressed close to still the leaping heart,
They wait expectant, wondering, as they stand,
What new succeeding myst'ry is at hand.
Nor is it man alone which feels the power,
The solemn voicings of the passing hour ;
All Nature seems instinctive now to thrill

With the deep silence, and herself stand still :
The falcon, speeding for its fleeing prey,
Hangs poised in air and powerless, while, midway,
Between its foe and the far sheltering grove,
Rests on the wing the swiftly fleeing dove,
Both fixed in air like painted things of life
Bent to the action in the eager strife.
The ruffled sea has hushed its voice once more,
And its spent waves now creep along the shore ;
The Jordan hushes, too, its rippling song,
And rolls unbroken its swift stream along,
As conscious once again of godly will
As when at Prophet's touch its floods stood still.
The winds lie hushed, no tremor of a breeze
Stirs the green foliage of the silent trees ;
And Earth her thousand voices stills to rest,
And in the robes of silence wraps her breast :
The Heavens also are hushed, nor living thing
Gives voice to song nor strident note to wing ;
So deep its arch, bent in cerulean blue,
It stooping seems unto the eager view,
As if in listening it bent to hear
The voice of him whose breath wings ev'ry sphere,
While he who sits the circle of the Heaven
His stooping ear unto the hour has given.
Nor of that throng so hushed, are any there
More eager than our friends.   The very air,
Though hushed as death, seems boisterous to their ears ;
A trembling mist a shadow dark appears,
And were unwitting whisper breathed, its sound
As rapier keen with discords now would wound.

XVIII.

Judeth, whose eager eye's unvarying gaze
Clings breathlessly to Christ's angelic face,
Moves not, but rigid as a statue stands,
With quivering lips and tightly clasping hands ;
Her heaving bosom, constant in its sighs,
Pays equal tribute with her longing eyes :
Why, were she asked, all answer must forego,
Save the one refuge in " I do not know,"

With Mary, less of interest, little zeal
Is hers in this occasion now to feel.
Yet over her there came at last a spell
Which hushed her lips, but why, she could not tell;
While Martha's rigid form, like chiselled stone,
Showed nought of life save that she breathed alone,
And the fixed coldness of her features seemed
As if she saw while yet asleep she dreamed!
But Lazarus was a study as he stood,
With features changing with each varying mood,
The eye perplexed, the mind still left in doubt,
Of nothing sure, he was so tossed about.

XIX.

As to the Jordan's brink they slowly pass,
The stream lies waveless as a sea of glass,
Save where their feet, dipt in the sleeping tide,
Spread out the circling wavelets far and wide,
As deeper still they thread the trackless strand
With footsteps touching scarce the snowy sand.
The silent waters, motionless before,
Run swiftly out from the receding shore;
With liquid arms reach, longing to embrace
His sinking form, and fly to kiss his face
With crystal lips, then break into a song
Which zephyrs, catching, o'er the hills prolong;
While golden showers of soft, ethereal light
In halo veil him from the blinded sight,
And sit upon the waters in repose,
As o'er his face the trembling ripples close.
As lifts his head a golden arch is thrown
Above his brow and girts his head a crown,
While matchless beauty on his features glows
In radiant splendor, softening to repose!

XX.

In awe the people gaze upon that face,
More beautiful than aught of mortal race,
With lips apart, whose voiceless praise confess
The matchless beauty of his loveliness.

How long they thus had gazed in silence none
Might tell, had not the hotly glowing sun
His glory veiled in clouds of purple light,
Whose matchless splendor quenched the feeble sight,
Yet filled the heavens with glory such as none
With mortal sight might hope to look upon.
Then parting at the zenith, crystal sea,
Eternal Courts, Elysian Fields, the Tree
Of Life, in glory flash upon the view,
As Paradise from opening gates bursts through :
Whence, flying forth from out the hand of Love,
Came hovering down in form a milk-white dove,
With glowing radiance trembling o'er its wings,
Which through the skies a bright effulgence flings
In benisons for all the Earth, with light
To pierce the darkness of its utter night.
A moment thus the hovering form is seen,
With outstretched wings above the Nazarene :
Then on his head, amid the glowing crown,
The bird divine with folded wings sinks down
While from the cloud-girt gates of Paradise
The voice of God is speaking from the skies :
" This is my Son beloved ; I am in him
Well pleased." It ceased ; a shadow soft and dim
Veiled all the heavens, and visible there sat
Blanched terror on each face ; and seeing that
The people were in fear, John Baptist said,
" Beloved children, be ye not afraid :
Him whom you see I knew not until he,
Who to baptize with water first sent me,
Said, Whom thou seest my spirit brood upon,
The same is he, the True and Holy One ;
With Holy Ghost shall he baptize anew,
And ye with fire shall prove if you be true.
Behold the Lamb of God ! Repent, believe ;
The Strong Deliverer in your hearts receive :
My work is finished I was sent to do,
And I have run my journey almost through :
A highway now for Israel is laid,
Press on the conquest and be not afraid."

XXI.

His words are ended, and with outstretched hands
The Christ among the silent people stands :
His benediction, breathed upon the air,
Soothes with the solace of an answered prayer.
They feel the blessing of the spoken word,
Though but a murmur by the nearest heard ;
Then at its close the silent people wend
Their different ways, while friend communes with friend
Of all the day's strange scenes, but most of him,
Of whom their guesses are but vague and dim,
Compared with what the weakest might have known,
Had but their zeal pursued the Truth alone.

XXII.

That night, as in their tents in slumber lay
The eyes that watched through the exciting day,
No murmur rises on the silent air
To warn the Night if aught there liveth there.
Though strong the passions which those souls have swayed,
How soon the tumult of the storm is laid !
To-day they tremble with consuming fears,
To-morrow melt in agony of tears ;
To-night, forgetful of the day just past,
They sleep as if the night would ever last :
To-morrow's twilight throws no trembling beams
Athwart the roseate archway of their dreams.

XXIII.

But not unwatched, a time at least, are they
Who thus in silent slumber dreaming lay :
If they may sleep, yet there are sleepless eyes
Which, watching, wait beneath Judean skies,
But not for them, if of them thought, perchance,
Links still their being with rememberance :
So small the weight of our existence bears
Upon the little hour of life it shares !
Two are the watchers who before their tents,
Perchance, talk o'er the busy day's events,

While watching, furtive, on the plains below,
The tents which lie a misty field of snow,
While silence, creeping from the hills around,
At last has wrapped them in its hush profound.
We know the watchers, and will now draw near
Some fragment of their whispered speech to hear.

XXIV.

JUDETH.

How still the night! Methinks I almost feel
The silence from yon slumbering valley steal,
To seize upon my senses, and surprise
In slumber my but half-resisting eyes.

LAZARUS.

You must be weary from this busy day:
No longer wait, but go you in, I pray.
For me there is no sleep while crowding cares
Oppress, and busy thought my pillow shares,
As in review my past life now appears
To show how few and short my coming years!
No time for sleep is left, should I pursue
The work of life my hands shall find to do.
But hasten and go in.

JUDETH.

Why should I go?
When to your load of care I add mine, too,
It far outweighs dull sleep — and then — and then —

LAZARUS.

Speak, Judeth, if you will : those words again,
" And then," are haunting me to-night.

JUDETH.

If you,
What, then, of me? If I the mystery knew
Of this day's teaching, if I understood
But half the secret of my heart's strange mood, —
But all is dark to me.

LAZARUS.

Ah, Judeth ! still
That same old struggle with a stubborn will
Leaves you in doubt and blindness.   Just receive
The truth as I do, and in faith believe,
And then the light will break.

XXV.

JUDETH.

Of you all things
I gladly would receive, and on your wings
Of Hope would cleave ethereal space to find
Your Paradise, and leave all time behind ;
But still I cannot, — and there yet seems light
To-day a slender ray revealed to sight.

LAZARUS.

Judeth, you know I love you : would I teach
You falsely, feeling thus ?

JUDETH.

Nay, each to each
We should be crystal-pure, and nothing hide
That in it good or evil may betide.
I grant your love, for ever since a child
I saw it in your eyes, and when you smiled
I felt its kindling glow, and trusted you.

LAZARUS.

Since you were but a child ?   Yes, that is true,
And I now well remember it ; but then —

JUDETH.

Ah ! you have caught " but then."   I thought you men
Straightforward went and always to the mark.
Like me, are you now groping in the dark,
Uncertain of your way ?

LAZARUS.

Uncertain ? No,
The way is plain wherein I wish to go,
But dare I venture ?

XXVI.

JUDETH.

You oft to me have said
He is unworthy who holds back through dread,
His way being plain.   Your maxim taught to me
I now give back as fitting well your plea.

LAZARUS.

My plea? I have not made it yet; what need,
Since you confess it all?

JUDETH.

Confess?   Indeed,
I have confessed nought but of truth to you.

LAZARUS.

It may be that you mentally withdrew
What spoken words implied.

JUDETH.

Your words distress
Me, and I feel their unjust pain, nor less
Because in you I have put all my faith,
And followed where you pointed out the path.
You, who have always been so frank and plain,
Who never spoke if speaking added pain,
Be now yourself once more and speak your heart,
Nor let mere words us longer keep apart,
If one but frankly spoken makes all clear.

LAZARUS.

Then I will speak with no more doubt or fear,
As I have warrant from your lips to speak :
To hide the truth why should I longer seek ? —
Judeth, I love you !

JUDETH.

There is nothing new
In that, of which you should make such ado
In telling, as you know full well my own
Free heart to you in trust has long since flown.

XXVII.

LAZARUS.

Your heart to me?

JUDETH.

Why, yes; why not, I pray?

LAZARUS.

O Judeth! this to me thrice happy day
You make by this confession!

JUDETH.

Confession?
I do not understand — some wrong impression —
Some strange mistake — some — I — you — please ex-
plain —
But no — yes — how the thoughts whirl through my brain!
I have not heard aright.

LAZARUS.

Yes, I but said,
" I love you, Judeth; " and you answered —
You know your answer; words so dear and sweet
Would lose their flavor should my lips repeat.

JUDETH.

I did not mean — I did not understand —
This is a mean advantage by you planned —
Pray, let us now go in, the night is hot —
Nay, I mean chill, and we are heeding not —

MARTHA.

Judeth, Lazarus! The murk and chilly air
Will sicken. For the journey pray prepare
With bounteous rest, for with the risen day
We should be far upon our homeward way.
I now have slept, it seems, the midnight through,
And would be sleeping still had not of you
Some slumbering thought disturbed. I, waking, heard
Your converse low, and here and there a word,
And thought it better you forego the night.

XXVIII.

LAZARUS.

Most careful Martha! from your slumbers light
It pains me much to think it mine the blame
That you awoke. It was in truth my aim —
(And interest, too) I say that under tone —
That you, a time at least, had slumbered on.

MARTHA.

Nay, do not so regret my broken rest,
Since it was in your interest and was best.
Come, Judeth, enter in ; brother, good night!

LAZARUS.

Good night, my sister! Judeth, with you light
And hope — the best of life — hath gone within,
And where she sleeps there cometh near no sin.
The very Earth grows sweeter where she lies,
The flowers more lovely watched by her fond eyes :
If I but win the jewel of her love,
Her better self will in my bettering prove.
I yet would linger here to think of her
As some lone, wandering pilgrim worshipper,
Who, after weary months of lengthening leagues,
Slow travelled o'er, enduring their fatigues,
Kneels at the shrine which was his eager quest,
With streaming eyes and fiercely heaving breast,
And pours his prayers incessant at the shrine
Of God adored that grace may on him shine,
Then waits the light to fall, and sweetly roll
The burdening sins away from his sad soul :
So I, to-night, before the shrine of Love
Have poured my prayer, his wayward heart to move,
And linger still, uncertain of the hour
When he shall answer with assuring power.
But I must rest : the night fast speeds away,
Soon morning comes to clothe the sky in gray ;
To deepen into purple, as sweet song
Swells into chorus as it floods along,
Until the glowing Earth in rhythmic light
Shall blaze an anthem on the ravished sight!
Good night, fair stars ! I love you better now,
Since your pale light has kissed her vestal brow.

CANTO FOURTH.

IN THE WILDERNESS.

I.

WITH morning's light, full half the booths or more
Which, as a tented city, lined the shore
Where stretched the plain along the Jordan's strand,
Fold their white wings along the gleaming sand,
And, with the lengthening hours of growing day,
Join the slow caravan along the way
Returning to the homes from whence they came ;
Drawn hither by the Prophet's matchless fame,
Now well assured his task is well-nigh done,
And in the Christ's a greater work begun.
First in the van our whilom friends we see
With faces turned again towards Bethany ;
Yet in their hearts the fires of truth still burn,
And light the rugged way of their return, —
Not with the peace which lulls them to repose,
But one forgetful of our lesser woes.
As they pass by, scarce can we now forego
With them the homeward journey to pursue ;
So fair the day, so bright each kindly smile,
That lure us on and with their charms beguile :
But now our way leads otherwhere, and we
To choose, except through duty, are not free.

II.

Farewell, sweet plain ! our sojourn here is o'er,
Adieu, bright waters and delightful shore!
The scenes you witnessed consecrate your name,
And crown your memory with immortal fame.
Here would we linger, ravished by each scene,
Of vale enraptured, charmed by valleys green ;
Forgetful still of life and time, would dream
Our life away beside the Jordan's stream,
Or float resistless to its silent grave

Within the Dead Sea's still and lifeless wave.
Here would we drink of fountains whose sweet tide
In soothing music through the valleys glide,
Eat of its fruits its spreading groves supply
Whose leaves ne'er fade and blossoms never die;
Charmed by the songs its blushing maidens sing,
Until e'en life would madly from us fling!
But we must turn our steps, reluctant still,
And follow duty with subjective will,
Where leads before that bowed but stately form,
With stooping face as buffeting the storm,
Into the wilderness of doleful night,
Into the mountain's steep and craggy height,
Whither the Lord, led by the Spirit, goes,
Not to escape, but there to meet his foes:
And, in the weakness of the fainting flesh,
Be tempted of the Devil; who, afresh
As erst, in Paradise, our mother won,
His wiles would try upon God's only Son.

III.

On, on he goes, out from the pressing throng
From sight of face and sound of human tongue,
Within a wilderness so wild, into
A solitude so vast, to inner view
Was God himself concealed, the light shut out,
The spirit visible withdrawn, while doubt
The darkened shadows of its night unrolled,
And lay upon the earth a horror cold.
The weakness of the man, the frail, faint flesh,
Was on him now and wrung his soul afresh.
Now for the first the hand of God is hid
That erst the darkened way to him forbid,
And as the shadows drop in pall of night
Across his soul's horizon's clouded light,
Leaving a darkness gathering deeper still,
To pierce his heart with shafts that pain and chill,
He learns the bitter lesson of the fate
That follows the divine in man's estate, —
That he as man, not God, alone must stand,
Without the Father's stay and guiding hand;

That he must feel the sorrows of the flesh,
As man, with wounds that ever bleed afresh
At touch of pain, in deepest solitude
Must sit far separate in lonely wood,
No angel whispers soothing his sad hours,
No heavenly voice to stay his failing powers,
No smile divine his drooping heart to cheer
With the fond thought that God himself is near!

IV.

The Spirit that hath led him on thus far
Now leaveth him the uncrowned Avatar,
The Prince of Heaven of majesty now shorn,
And clothed in human robes in weakness worn.
The Angels that had ever thronged his way
With the bright glory of eternal day,
At God's command fled far beyond the bound
Of mortal sight, and there hung hovering round,
Without the veil along the bending skies
With quivering hearts and sleep-untrammelled eyes,
Watching their dear beloved they long to cheer
With whispers wafted to his earth-dull'd ear.
Dread silence reigns and hushed all earthly sound,
In solitude days speed in lengthened round,
And Night drops down his sable curtains gemmed
That veil his dusky brow star-diademed;
Where flashing worlds a million myriads roll
From zenith outward to each separate pole,
While fleecy clouds in folds of snowy white
Like ermine bind the sable robes of Night.
He knew those worlds, their orbits and their spheres,
Their course and time through unrecorded years:
He knew their source of light and what each bore,
How peopled and by whom, — their mystic lore;
For was he not before them and all Time,
And tuned Creation to its rhythmic chime?
The moon, the wrinkled, vitreous moon, a world
With fires long quenched when into space was hurled,
Companion was, and he conversed with her
Then face to face, as friend, not worshipper.
Well did he love all creatures of the hand

Creative, if 't were flower or system grand.
His shortened vision circumscribed by clay
Shut out the worlds that far beyond these lay,
Yet these he saw in memory shining clear,
As, speeding on, swung out each separate sphere ;
As sightless eyes remembered scenes behold
When they long years in rayless night have rolled,
Across the darkness of the vision's night
Sweep out in grand and never-failing light.

V.

The Sun he saw in all his glory rise,
And record days as points across the skies ;
He knew the limit of his farthest beams,
As woodmen know the source of hidden streams ;
Where other suns caught up his paling light
He knew, and the far bounds of utter night.
All Nature's vast profound a mystery
To man unsolved, then, now, and still to be,
To Christ revealed her hidden truths and laid
Them bare to him, from sun to smallest blade
Which parts the earth, a dainty point of green
And far too small unwitting to be seen.
With all communed the Master in this hour,
With heart of tender love. Each bursting flower
Unsealed its fragrant cup of sweet perfume
The kissing zephyrs ravished from the bloom,
And in his locks, wet with the nightly dews,
Mingled their thousand sweets of wealth profuse,
And, naught disturbing his unpillowed rest.
Upon his brow their soft, wet kisses press'd,
In tender love as soft as starlight's fall
On velvet sward, and soothing sweet withal.
Through all the day the birds their carols hold,
And sing a thousand songs that ne'er grow old,
In ev'ry note of which breathes love sublime
In praise of Him whom not to praise were crime ;
And as they sing from bough to bough they fly,
Wild in each quivering heart's sweet ecstasy.

VI.

And then, when darkness deepens on the day,
From hidden lairs come forth the beasts of prey;
Their white fangs gnashing with impotent power,
And threaten death, but only dust devour.
Although no chains restrain, no cage confines,
Their ravings drop to low, submissive whines,
As to his feet they cringing creep subdued,
No lamb less guilty of the shepherd's blood.
Surely the Lord is great when thus obeyed,
Obeisance by the powers of Earth is made
To him in all the princely homage due
From hearts of subjects loyal in love and true:
Yet all this makes his weakness felt the more,
By homage paid when he is shorn of power.

VII.

Is he not man? and man of woman born?
In weakness he a more than Samson shorn!
The Deity within, no less, was still
The Deity who heard the rhythmic thrill
When first in far Creation's tuneful days
The Morning Stars together sang his praise!
Still godly knowledge lives undimmed and clear,
Without a cloud to darken wisdom here;
All is in all complete; the Past is spread
Across the vision and unfolding. read
The pages of creation.   Infinite,
The mind immortal veiled in mortal sight.
This hid the Father's face as veil dropped down
Between him and the high, eternal throne,
Like that which shut the Mercy Seat from sight,
And in the Temple veiled Shekinah's awful light.

VIII.

The desolate, wild waste, with horrors strown,
A Paradise, were not God's smile withdrawn!
Thoughts, memories, — all Infinite could bring
From Time o'er past. sped by on dusky wing:

The plans evolved by Deity, vague forms
Unshaped, Creation's new chaotic storms
Upon the utmost verge of finite bounds,
Had drawn his heart unwearied in their rounds
And hushed all human cries for light, the while,
Had not the Father still withheld his smile.
He is alone, but not as mortals are,
Whom from their fellows Fate has thrust afar,
But yet with God above, whose ready ear
Their faintest prayer, a listener, stoops to hear,
And, hearing, flies on wings of urgent love
His prayers to answer and his fears remove.
Not as the prisoner who lacks for bread :
Though man may fail he trusts to God o'erhead
With faith, though man be deaf to all his cries,
His faintest whispers pierce the bending skies.
Not thus with Christ, to human weakness born,
His stay on God in this dark hour is shorn ;
Alone he bears temptations such as hurled
Man down to Hell, and lost through him a world!
Yet such the burden to redeem he bears,
And in this hour supreme no mortal shares
With him the peril! Should he faint or fall,
Lost, lost eternally! And with him all
Hope flies the sinking world ; but should he win,
The world is saved and man redeemed from sin!

IX.

When he for forty days and nights had led
His fast unbroken, tasting not of bread,
He was an hungered, and the fainting pain
A palsy seized his limbs, benumbed his brain.
His memory, which in solitude had cheered,
Like drifting bark when lost the hand which steered,
Fled here and there upon chaotic seas,
Through mists obscure, the sport of every breeze.
The mind, enfeebled through its failing force,
Ranged every field nor held to reason's course ;
Its failing powers launched wild the vaporing thought,
Amid strange visions saw all things distraught :
Of all uncertain, save alone that he
The Saviour of the world was yet to be.

X.

Again with friends he gathers at the board
With tempting meats in generous bounty stored,
And there divides unto the waiting guest
The bread to them which he in breaking blest ;
And yet, though frugal each divided share,
To him the meat a rich and princely fare.
Again the trees which crown each fruitful hill
Their ripened fruits invite to pluck who will ;
The vineyards round the terraced hillsides crown
With purple grapes, and stretching lower down
The figs and dates, while on the plain below
The later harvests for the reapers grow.
There, too, brown hands distended udders drain,
Else from the comb the amber honey strain ;
And all the land the hungry soul invites
To revel now unchecked in its delights.

XI.

Now Satan comes : the wily Tempter knows
The power and weakness of his human foes ;
That appetite is man's eternal bane,
And through desire his weakened soul is slain.
The mortal weakness of the Eternal one,
The man in him, through this may be undone.
And so to Christ he said, — his course well planned, —
" If thou be Christ, the Son of God, command
That of these stones there be made bread." What force,
What bitter irony of speech ! Of course
Divinity is here denied, with doubt
And with contempt his name is hedged about.
The task is easy, — pleasing, too, applied,
And satisfies his hunger and his pride :
The act which feeds will Satan, too, confound,
And unbelief will slay or sorely wound ;
Dissolve its bulwarks like a fleeting dream,
And prove him God incarnate and supreme !
Yet, Esau-like, he thus would barter all
The hope of man that stayed him since the fall,
His own fair heritage of God bestowed,

The Sonship and the throne he shared with God;
The love of angels, hymns of votive praise,
Eternal shores, ethereal worlds that blaze
In endless light, where Hope and Mercy reign,
Never to soar into those realms again,
But with man lost whom he had come to save,
And make of earth a universal grave !
For such a prize the wily Tempter played,
While Heaven stooped low and Earth beheld **dismayed.**
Was e'er before poised in such equal scale
Such destinies and yet the weak prevail ?
Ah ! had it been some weak and starving child,
Wayworn and weary and with hunger wild,
How quick his pitying lips in love had said,
" To feed my lamb, ye barren stones be bread ! "
Then at his touch their flinty hearts had grown
Yeasty and sweet as turned to bread the stone !
While Heaven to him rich blessings would accord,
And Earth aloud shout praises to her Lord.
He is an hungered, perishing for bread,
That Earth through him to fulness may be fed !

XII.

Now answers he, and with a visage stern,
That Satan well the lesson grave may learn,
And says, " It written is, ' Man shall not live
By bread alone,' whatever he receive,
' But by the word from out the mouth of God.' "
So answered he whose fame soon spread abroad,
When he, in answer to that power divine,
At Cana's feast turned water into wine,
And fed beside Tiberias' swelling flood
With loaves and fishes a vast multitude.
Some of his faith, some of his loyal love,
Still lives on earth, is left to man to prove
By cross and chain, by dungeon dark and lone ;
By martyred saints to hungry wild beasts thrown ;
By burning stake whose winding-sheets of fire
Torment the souls that in the flames expire ;
By prison walls whose black and reeking stones
Were long attuned to suffering martyrs' groans ;

By those who dare for him, whate'er the claim,
To meet contempt in poverty and shame,
Because, like Christ, for right they dared to stand,
And suffer for the truth with courage grand.

XIII.

Of further speech there was small need, and this
The Tempter felt, his wiles now gone amiss ;
Yet, thinking still advantage to regain,
Tries the resources of his crafty brain,
For well he knows that human strength is all,
Love purified, between him and his fall :
By that he still must stand, since from his sight
Is hid the face of God and Heaven's delight !
So, from the wilderness and silent gloom,
Unto the Holy City's templed dome,
E'en to its topmost pinnacle's vast height,
Where at his feet the city lies in sight,
Diminished, silent, voiceless, there and lone,
No sound returning from its streets of stone,
No life ev'n seen, except where lingering stray
Dwarfed forms diminishing along the way,
The Devil taketh him ; and then he saith,
To try his virtue and to prove his faith,
" If thou be Christ, the Son of God, make known
This day the truth, thyself from here cast down :
For it is writ, — commission full and large, —
' Concerning thee, he gives his Angels charge,
And in their hands they shall thee safely bear,
(See how the Word has hedged thee round with care !)
Lest thou at any time shalt dash thy foot
Against a stone.' "

XIV.

                    Again the doubt — dispute —
And mocking of God's power.   Why not attempt
And by God's promise prove himself exempt ?
Would not the hand of God or Cherubim
Uphold ? and thus confound the enemy
Of God and man ?   Why not the venture try ?
Thus man had reasoned, reasoning thus had tried

The God of heaven, and reason, thus defied,
Had fallen as falls the fool of wisdom vain,
Else saved, like Peter sinking in the main, ·
By piteous hand. But where the Angel throng ?
Where the Eternal Father ? Darkness long
Has hid both Cherubim and Seraphim,
Angels and powers of Heaven. Far, faint and dim,
Lie the Eternal Courts in shadows veiled,
To pierce whose heights his human sight has failed.
And yet alone upon that dizzy height
He holds with Satan now the desperate fight,
And with the Word against the Word destroys
The specious reasoning the Fiend employs :
" So it is writ again," the Christ replies,
" ' Thou shalt not tempt the Lord thy God.' "   Surprise
Confounds him in the answer meetly made
From lips which after that the tempest stayed ;
The Word a witness, too, against the Word,
The truth of God against the Fiend preferred,
Who wrested truth to lies, that they might turn
False witnesses. From mouths of babes men learn,
And age wise maxims oft receives from youth,
Where sages seek in vain to find the truth.

XV.

Now once again, the Saviour still to try,
Upon a mountain vast, exceeding high,
The Devil taketh him, that he may show
Him all the kingdoms of the earth below,
And saith, " All these will I give unto thee
If thou wilt now fall down and worship me."
Unwitting act ! Among those kingdoms vast
Arose the Future, Present, and the Past :
Yet blinded by ambition still his eye
Which once had looked unveiled on Deity ;
He thinks the things which had himself undone
May win from God his own beloved Son,
When he had failed ingloriously and fled
To Hell, where he o'er horrors reigns instead,
Believing still Ambition, once his bane,
May lure from Heaven a mighty prince again.

XVI.

And he had nought to give, this Jesus knew,
And scorned the empty boast and boaster, too,
Who spoke him fair and witting in his wile
The falsehood which might weaker faith beguile.
So from the Fiend he turns with scorn profound,
To view the grandeur of the scenes around,
Where, stretching backward, Time his circles run,
From the sweet morning's now returning sun
To where the shaping hand the worlds begun,
And earth, in darkling night a shapeless clod,
First felt the breath and living touch of God ;
And, springing forth from out its nether night,
Leaped blazing into God's eternal light,
Until the day it parched to ashes lies
A blackened ball from which all being dies.
He in the garden Adam sees and Eve,
Who for their sins in constant tears still grieve ;
And at her side the wily serpent sees
Whose arts first blind then win the heart they please,
As she doth pluck the tempting fruit and eat
With death to her and in it God's defeat :
So he believes, as he with mocking cries
Down to the Pit with horrid laughter flies,
And life throughout all shuddering nature dies !
While from the Garden, lashed by scourging rod,
They fly before the frowning face of God.

XVII.

He sees and weeps, because of man's lost state,
Hot tears that fall from eyes compassionate
Because of Sin through all the circling years
That fills the earth with misery and tears.
No pomp of power, no circumstance of state,
Or deeds heroic, triumphs of the great,
Can turn his gaze a moment from the tide
Where Sin's red streams the earth with blood have dyed !
What other eyes with mortal sight had seen,
If such with him upon that mount had been,
What other tongues had praised as noble themes,

Great deeds wrought out through man's ambitious dreams,
Grand empires built and wrought from human bones,
To draw fresh splendor from their people's groans,
Whose conquering heroes great are called in praise,
As bleeding hands high altars to them raise :
Hoar dynasties, long ruled by feeble kings
O'erthrown, forget these puppet-painted things,
As they in frantic haste now place the crown
On stranger brows again to drag them down !
All these he saw, and, seeing, saw the sin
Far back in Eden, — he who led him in,
When man's young heart, the temple then of love,
Pour'd forth itself in praise to God above
From crystal depths within which had not been
Aught but the face of God reflected seen ;
Now, all polluted, from this fount is pour'd
The bitter waters of this sin abhorred.

XVIII.

From Cain's rude bludgeon madly cast aside,
Red with the blood of fallen Abel dyed,
He saw strange weapons shaped with cunning skill,
With which man learned the art and use to kill,
When war gave license, or when might made right,
Fierce Rapine raged and Murder stalked by night.
The purple stream from bleeding Abel flowed,
A winding river growing deep and broad,
He sees with swift and constant current run,
Polluting earth and festering in the sun,
Beneath the feet of armies, where the slain,
Like reaper's sheaves, lay thick on battle plain.
To purge the earth and cleanse it from this blood
He saw roll in the world-destroying flood ;
Which drown'd all life, save but one lingering spark
Which toss'd uncertain in the lonely Ark,
That on the bosom of the waters sat,
At anchor safe upon Mount Ararat.
He saw the smoke rise black on Sodom's plain,
Its cities burned, their flying people slain,
Until of all along the salt sea's shore
Remained alone the little town of Zoar !

In Egypt next he saw a nation rise
Whose God and race its rulers soon despise,
Oppressed their lands, their burdens grievous grown,
Until as one the suffering people moan.
The voice of God he hears through Moses speak ;
He sees the chains that bind the pestilence break ;
And from that land, beneath the gloom of night,
To freedom speed a nation in its flight,
Then, swift pursuing, Pharaoh's mighty host
Engulfed beneath the meeting seas is lost !
Still on their march the fiery pillar set
By night, the cloud by day hath led them yet :
He hears the notes of Miriam's tuneful tongue
As she the triumph of Jehovah sung,
When in the waters of the rushing sea
Sank Egypt's king and Israel was free !
Then Sinai rears its awful head where God
On them his wondrous covenant bestowed,
To Moses in the smoking mountain given,
With lightnings girt and by the earthquake riven.
Scarce forty days communing there he stays,
Yet far from God inconstant Israel strays ;
E'en while he talks with God, below behold
That wayward people in rebellion bold,
A golden Calf, old Egypt's god, has cast,
And all to Apis bow the knee as in the past !

XIX.

Swift speed   the vision's changing scenes full fraught,
In ev'ry one a lesson grandly taught :
The Brazen Serpent here the Cross foreshows ;
In Horeb's Rock his smitten side there flows ;
The Manna falling in the wilderness,
The Bread of Life he gives the world to bless.
As Jordan's waves before their feet divide
To lead them safely on to Canaan' side,
So lead his footsteps through the purple flood,
Through Love's highway up to the courts of God.
Through this in faith had passed the hoary seers,
The priests and prophets of forgotten years ;
Through this must pass the saints in years to come,

With those who watch and wait in outer gloom,
To see the Star, Hope's harbinger to them,
Which shall arise and shine o'er Bethlehem.

XX.

Across the Jordan, on Judea's plain,
Jerusalem, in glory crowned again,
Arose in triumph, with her templed shrine
Refulgent in Shekinah's flame divine.
King David leads the princely line with lyre,
Whose tuneful strains shall ev'ry age inspire;
Her prophets next procession grand prolong,
Whose words proclaim the truth with trumpet tongue;
Then come her priests, who, years long gone, have stood
By altars sprinkled with atoning blood,
Grim in their service, yet with hearts that knew
No other faith, and, knowing this, were true.
Then spread before Judea's sacred land,
With holy memories strown on ev'ry hand,
Her verdant valleys and her fertile hills,
Where Hermon yet his honeyed dews distils;
Her empire, set by ever-widening bounds,
The jewelled boast, Judea's sacred grounds,
The Past declared, and in its lesson shows
How from the dust this godly nation rose.
Thence swept his vision down the future years,
O'er broken altars, worshippers in tears;
Her Temple razed, its glory in the dust;
The kingdom rent, a prey to faction's lust;
Barbaric hordes the people's hearts, instead
Of Eshcol's grapes, beneath their feet now tread.
One sign alone, a dim and shadowy form,
That lifts above and still withstands the storm,
As beacon gleaming through tempestuous night,
With fitful flame and still uncertain light,
Yet, broad'ning out its ever-bright'ning rays,
Shot swiftly down the course of coming days,
Until its brightness far outshone the sun,
And filled with light all lands it beamed upon.

XXI.

Then War grew hushed, or muffled his hoarse roar,
As this great light fills each succeeding shore ;
The brow of Hate grew smooth as on it burned
The beams of love, and frowns to smiles are turned,
As songs of joy are breathed from lips whose sighs
But answered tears which flowed from weeping eyes.
The desert waste, where late the wild beast's den,
Has now become the peaceful homes of men ;
The wilderness, the haunt of cruel foes,
Is sweet with song and " blossoms as a rose ; "
While mountains shout a glad and joyous song,
The hills its strains in echoing notes prolong ;
The rivers from the plains run to the sea,
And as they flow shout back the melody ;
The lakes and rills in liquid chorus break,
And with the murmuring brooks glad music make ;
The seas toss high their hands in glad acclaim,
And raise their anthems to its bright'ning flame ;
The oceans swell the chorus till it rolls
To tropic seas and echoes round the poles.
This wond'rous light, which sets all nations free,
Shines from the Cross that lifts on Calvary !
The song he hears with joyous notes arise,
Until the anthem fills both earth and skies,
At Bethlehem's low manger first began,
With " Peace on earth, in heaven good-will to man."
Then from the Cross, with mingling sighs and tears,
The swelling anthem greets the doubting ears,
And deep'ning still on resurrection morn,
Along the skies on angel voices borne,
It sweeps the heavens, a flood of joyful fire,
In one grand chorus from the heavenly choir.
Earth catches up the strain, and backward flings
The echoing song until all Nature sings
The praise of him who wrought Salvation's plan
Of " Peace on earth, in heaven good-will to man."
It was enough, and he could gaze no more ;
In sight of this, temptation lost its power :
A ruined world must be redeemed ; the seers,
Who walked by faith in him through all their years,

Must now be justified, the Law fulfilled, —
How, was not his to ask : the Father willed,
And his to do and suffer to the end,
While to that task mortality must bend.

XXII.

All this revealed, he then to Satan turns ;
His face aglow with indignation burns ;
Like gleaming steel his kindling eyes aflame
The pride presumptuous of the Tempter tame ;
His silence dreadful, and his withering look
More dreadful still than words in their rebuke.
That craven heart his boastful speech belies,
Since Satan's fear his power to give denies ;
His shrunken presence withers to a span
Before his awful judge, the God in man !
But if mere silence thus upon him wrought,
Far more the power when speech with scorn is fraught,
As now the Word which he believing owns,
With proof condemning his confusion crowns.
So, when the Christ, contemptuous of his power,
Feels in his soul the triumph of the hour,
With nought in action to his plea deferred,
Says, with contempt and scorn in ev'ry word,
" Get thee behind me, Satan ! "   Backwards reels
The Fiend as if each word a blow he feels,
While consternation fills his darkened soul
And clouds of Hell before his vision roll.
Yet, not enough this fierce rebuke to give,
The words that falsehood slay bid truth to live :
So, swift and sure, a keen two-edged sword,
He, cleft asunder, falls before the Word.
" Is it not written, too, false teacher, tell,
In Heaven known and in the Pit as well,
That ' thou the Lord thy God shalt worship, him
And only him, shalt serve ? ' "   Vague, shad'wy, dim,
Like smoke ascending or a lowering cloud,
The murky mists the lofty mountain shroud,
And in their gloom and through their deep'ning night
Satan, the Prince of Darkness, takes his flight !
As through the air resound his whistling wings,
Across the skies a golden twilight springs ;

Earth, hid from sight a moment, reappears
In all the glory of its natal years ;
No blight of sin, which darkened late its plains,
Upon her smiling face revealed remains.
From hills and mountains towering grandly there,
Shines forth the face of Nature sweet and fair;
The seas and rivers, brooks and rills, all fling
Glad hands to plains and mountains, while they sing
A song once sung on earth, but lost the strain
When Adam fell, which now bursts forth again.

XXIII.

And, catching up the song from plains below,
The heavens themselves in answer vocal grow.
At first a whispering echo faintly runs
From regions far beyond the farthest suns,
And, sweet as voices in the waving grass
When through the meadows sighing zephyrs pass, —
Aye, soft as night-winds as above they sing,
Across the pinions of swift-cleaving wing !
The heavens are filled unto the farthest sphere
With the glad chorus swiftly drawing near.
While mingling with the strain, one undefined,
Like sounds increasing of a rushing wind,
And through the mists ethereal brightness gleams,
The mountain glows in its dissolving beams,
The opening heavens reveal the coming throngs
With glad hosannas and triumphant songs.
Angels, Archangels, radiant Cherubim,
Led on by blazing hosts of Seraphim,
Princes of heaven, Powers in burning light,
Fill the whole skies with glory in their flight,
And Hell's dark shadows from their presence fly,
While Heaven's celestial glory fills the sky !

XXIV.

White-winged, white-robed, ethereal beings fill
The mountain top ; ambrosial dews distil
Sweet showers of incense through the glittering trees,
And load with balm the heaven-descending breeze.

Within the light which sits upon the crown
Of the broad mountain, swiftly floating down,
A grand pavilion, crystalline and pure
As heaven's far ether where no mists obscure,
Shuts in the mountain by its azure round,
And earth within is consecrated ground,
A heavenly court with heavenly ministers,
Their king enthroned amid his worshippers.
The mountain-paths now golden streets become,
The humblest flowers have changed to heavenly bloom;
Gnarled, stunted trees upon its distant sides,
Where Winter long a cheerless waste abides,
To pillared archways stretch their knotted boughs,
And gleam with jewelled leaves in golden rows.
The rocks which crowd this waste and bleak domain,
And make more desolate its arid plain,
To jewelled thrones at magic touch now turn,
On which the heavenly Princes sit and burn!
The caverned fastness, where some savage beast
In far seclusion held his bloody feast
From mangled kid or lamb from shepherd torn,
Which from the plain he up the heights had borne,
Beneath creative touch of unseen hand
Aloft and wide its narrow bounds expand:
The crystal points which crusted the dull stone,
And through the darkness with dim lustre shone,
Hang from the lofty archways white as snow,
And flood with light the broad expanse below.
Where reeking dews that drenched the broken walls,
Through which a trickling stream inconstant crawls,
Spreading upon them, moist, unseemly seen,
Broad, festering splotches of an oozy green,
Ambrosial showers of sweetly perfumed dew
Around the walls a misty dampness threw,
To feed and freshen where the mosses sprung,
Gardens of flowers in terraced niches hung,
Between whose banks in widening crystal played
The stream that shimmered in their darkling shade.
The lichens, clinging to the damp, gray stone,
To shady groves and blooming arbors grown,
With broad walks winding where the insect's tread
Its painful course had worn a narrow thread:

While flattened stones where ceaseless drippings fell,
So worn they scarcely now their nature tell,
Broad tables spread of pure and snowy white
That gleam and glisten in the prismic light,
And in bright radiance glow and flash between
The arbored gardens and the groves of green :
While on them spread by hands of angels placed
A feast such as no mortal e'er may taste ;
Ambrosial sweets, fair fruits from gardens where
The Tree of Life its fruits immortal bear,
And sparkling globlets, each as crystal clear,
The dripping nectar flowing with sweet cheer
Fresh from the stream which flows beneath the Throne,
The Fount of Life to the Evangel shown.
Such heavenly feast by angel cohorts spread,
Small need was there that stones should be made bread !
A princely kingdom his, beside it shown,
The world of Satan man would scorn to own !

XXV.

The need did not require so regal feast,
Where earthly lips the rich provision taste,
When forty days of fasting left scarce power
To stay a rage that could e'en stones devour !
Those who have felt such hunger well might deem
That this to him appeared a tempting dream
From mind distempered by the failing tide
Of vital force the vapid thought launched wide,
And through the misty mazes of such thought
The gleaming lights fantastic visions wrought,
While, straying on the confines of life's shore,
He tastes of feasts for mortals spread no more !
Not so the Christ ; the heavenly manna spread,
To him indeed became the living bread ;
The crystal flood, by angel hands bestowed,
To him a living stream of water flowed :
While he partakes, renewing leap the fires
Through his shrunk veins, and smiling Hope inspires
To rise on wings and cleave the azure dome,
And soar triumphant to his heavenly home,
Were man redeemed and sped the work of grace,

And earth no more to be his dwelling-place.
Nor his alone to banquet on gross things,
For while he feasts the wide pavilion rings
With song of praises, chants ethereal sung,
To sound of harp attuned to angel tongue :
A mighty chorus swelling on the air
Fills the whole mountain echoing everywhere
With lengthened notes whose joyful sounds proclaim
A thousand tributes to Messiah's name !

XXVI.

If human thought might shape angelic song,
If human notes its echoes might prolong,
If finite mind could know the infinite,
And pen of mortal theme immortal write,
Then such the song, from mountain height to sea,
Swept through the vale of sleeping Galilee.

Glory ! shout glory, the conflict is over ;
    The victor, we crown him Immanuel, God ;
Glory, shout glory !   He earth will recover;
    Oh, shout the glad tidings to worlds far abroad.

Alone in the conflict, the weak and the human,
    For man he with Satan the fierce battle sped :
The victory is won by the seed of the woman,
    And low in the dust lies the Serpent's bruised head.

All glory to God, the Adored, the All-giver !
    And glory to Christ ! and again and again
Sing glory to Christ, to the Lamb, and forever !
    With peace upon earth and good-will to all men !

XXVII.

Worn Nature fails, and when the feast is done
The heavenly songs through dreamy currents run,
Soft wooing Sleep, which whispers sweet of rest,
His yellow locks has to her bosom pressed,
And with her breath, as soft as zephyr blown,
Has kissed his white and waxen eyelids down ;

His parted lips her shadowy fingers close,
While Silence folds him in her sweet repose !
Now sinks the anthem to low-whispered notes,
Through heavy air a soothing incense floats ;
The shining hosts glide softly through the groves,
And lightest zephyr scarce the grasses moves,
All sound grows hushed ; the rustle of white wings
The faintest echo on the night-wind flings,
While heavenly watchers holy vigils keep
And guard in love the wearied Master's sleep.

XXVIII.

The night speeds by ; where yet the curtains drawn
The morn's pale lips have kissed the purple Dawn ;
The angel watchers, guarding still his rest,
So long and weary from his cares opprest,
Through the fringed borders of the trees again
See the dim twilight glimmering o'er the plain.
Softly white arms now glide beneath his head,
Gently they lift him from his downy bed ;
Broad pinions stretch beneath him, and once more,
Cleaving the crystal ether, far they soar
Out towards the valley and the distant sea
Where sleeps in shadow murmuring Galilee.

XXIX.

Now is the Word in truth to be fulfilled,
Not as the Prince of Darkness falsely willed,
But as God wills by his divine decree :
" He gives his angels charge concerning thee,
That in their hands they bear thee up." How grand
The prophecy and its fulfilment planned !
For in their arms they now their Saviour bear
With sturdy strength and yet the tend'rest care,
Until they lay him down in leafy shade
Where angel hands his waiting couch have made.
So softly borne, so tenderly transposed,
Not e'en his trembling eyelids once unclosed,
As he slept on throughout the downward flight,
On broad wings cradled on the breast of Night,

No dreams disturbing with a fitful start
The even pulsing of his tranquil heart.
The danger o'er, the shadowy mountains pass'd,
Safe in his humble couch he rests at last,
While heavy sighs angelic bosoms swell
As on their Lord they look a hushed farewell,
And, mounting high, they cleave the ambient air;
Just kissed by Dawn, they leave him slumbering there,
Until the Morn awakes with roseate beams
From the rich banquet of his heavenly dreams.

CANTO FIFTH.

THE MARRIAGE-FEAST AT CANA.

I.

AWAKE the song and touch the harp's sweet strings:
The soul rejoicing in its gladness sings
The new-old song since Adam in his bower
First sang the rapture of the nuptial hour.
Six thousand years! And these in centuries told,
And when begun the world was growing old;
Yet Love, the same and measured not by years,
No more than grief is counted by its tears,
Ruled human hearts, and in its roseate reign
Robbed e'en mortality itself of pain.
How can we sing of it in other lines
Than human thought through human heart divines?
Such best interpret: what we feel they teach,
As common passion hath a common speech.
There is but one green spot, one Paradise,
That hath enchantment to the wistful eyes
Of young and old, if they but live aright,
Save it be Love's deluded anchorite.
That spot is where two hearts together brought
Live on through life with but one common thought.
Love's Paradise they call it! Those without
For it have other name to mock, no doubt.
Not all who think they enter in that gate

Find Love within its borders roseate!
Love comes not in, is coy; and oft, when sought,
Asleep within some wayside bower is caught.
Seek Love out first, cajole and make him sure,
Then in your heart his presence will endure:
Mistakes mar all, be sure you have the elf;
His clever tricks sometimes deceive himself.
Count nothing gained until yourself you know,
That stranger self is still your mortal foe.
Be just to all; give ev'ry man his due;
His honeyed sweets may poison be to you.
These maxims writ, we now our tale pursue.

II.

Scarce had returned the caravan once more
To Bethany from Jordan's winding shore,
When invitation came with urgent haste,
In parchment writ, with many protests graced,
That on the marriage of a lifetime friend,
At Cana they should all straightway attend.
Well pleased were Mary, Judeth, and — well, now,
With Martha we can scarcely tell you how
She took the news.   She smiled, — she always smiled
When others did: in heart she was a child,
Pleased with the joys of others, while their cares
She all the burden on her shoulders bears.
At first when they were talking she began,
As was her wont, for them to fix and plan;
Then there arose a long and fierce array
Of obstacles across her further way!
With folded hands she next sat down and sighed,
And then in her own quiet way she cried
Herself to smiles again.   Meantime, deterred
By neither obstacle of time or word,
Judeth and Mary straightway set about
To make the journey; not a fear or doubt
Of its accomplishment in every part
One pulse-beat quicker stirred in either heart.
This was their motto, — may all such prevail! —
Do first your best, then if you fail, why fail.
A sturdy second Lazarus gave each plan,

A thing unusual found, they say, in man :
No matter ; still he had some interest shown,
At least in this one wedding not his own.
Strange freak in man ! In woman, grown or child,
Another's marriage always sets her wild !
This truth declare, which all the past but proves
Small wonder, then, to swift completion moves
Each small detail, until complete and done.
The journey thus auspiciously begun
Wore to its end : to please it may not fail
To give a portion somewhat in detail.

III.

The road they took when leaving Bethany
Along the valley of the Kidron lay,
Hard by Mount Zion, where the Jebusite
King David's hosts long held in stubborn fight.
Then turning up the valley where the road
Had worn its rocky way both deep and broad,
Beneath the city's high o'erhanging walls
Their little caravan in seeming crawls
As northward still its further course it bends,
Until beyond the city's walls it wends
In devious course, but not as one now sees
Where Art makes rugged paths broad ways of ease !
What Labor loses thus is Beauty's gain,
And Pleasure wins sweet recompense from Pain !
We may not tell — small profit if we should —
Of scenes unfolding on the way pursued,
But let our friends, as is the wont of those
Of kindred faith and feeling, joys and woes,
Who journey on together, tell the tale
Of the sweet valley or the lonely vale
As we pass by, as each remembrance brings
To mind and view the unforgotten things
Once wrought in them, and give to scene and place
A fame that Time itself cannot efface !

IV.

Jerusalem receding from the view,
Upon their vision opens strangely new
And pleasing scenes whose mem'ries dimly rise
And tinge with hues romantic to their eyes
That which, if all familiar or unknown,
Had dull to them and all insipid grown.
The skies are bright, the morning fresh and fair,
The breath of spices sweetens all the air;
The gardens on the hillsides, rich with bloom,
With beauty charm and solace with perfume;
While groves of dates, gardens of figs and vines,
Give promise of rare fruits and generous wines
To those whose toil and care their treasures yield,
Who prune the bough and till the fruitful field.
These they pass by with ever-watchful eyes;
In ev'ry changing scene feel new surprise,
From myriad charms and draughts inspiring drawn
From the sweet fount of purple-flowing Dawn,
Which Day renews with streams from crystal seas,
That round them flow with ev'ry fresh'ning breeze,
And cheers them as strong wine, while mirthful glee
Through early day holds constant revelry.
Yet of the hour the sweetness is the bloom,
And its retreating tide leaves nought but foam.

V.

The noon repast shared at some cheering spring,
When done, themselves upon the grass they fling
Beneath the welcome shade of tree or tent,
For rest and sleep, an hour most sweetly spent,
Where dreamy thought invites the god of rest,
A welcome guest to ev'ry weary breast.
Yet at such hour and in such place not all
Upon the drowsy god of sleep will call:
Perhaps another and a softer voice
Some of our friends to hear have now made choice;
A voice who hear with it are charmed withal,
And haste to answer its seductive call.
Howbeit, Lazarus and Judeth find

That sleep comes only to a peaceful mind.
How true it is that, be it smiles or tears,
The beams of hope, the shadowy gloom of fears,
The song of joy, the trembling note of pain,
The flatterer's kiss, the glance of cold disdain,
The slanderer's tongue, the voices that approve,
The hiss of hate, the honeyed words of love,
Each hath the power to shake the tranquil breast,
And rob the heavy eye of light and rest!

VI.

Long they communed apart from those who slept;
The lengthening shadows eastward slowly crept;
An hour goes by, and dips the sun's decline,
And yet he fails to give the forward sign!
The careless servants, careful of their sleep,
Half-waking to the shifting shadows creep;
The mules and donkeys, to the tether fast,
Are restless grown, now finished their repast,
Uneasy, stamp with hard and unshod feet
The burning sands with ever-constant beat,
Impatient from the flies their lives have curst,
And the sharp pangs of quick-returning thirst.
Now Martha, wakeful since the hour o'erspent,
Grown weary waiting, calls from out her tent,
With voice uncertain, " Judeth, Mary, come!
The heat is spent, nor are we far from home :
We must press forward, else we will be late
Arrived at Cana."

MARY.

Where is Judeth ?   Fate,
Or else I know not what, calls her away
With Lazarus, and even on to-day
She finds no time for sleep!

MARTHA.

What do you mean ?
Is she not here?

MARY.

The last of her was seen
By my poor eyes grown dull and dim for sleep —

Nor stealthier than she doth softly creep
The hunting tiger stealing on his prey —
As she with silent foot passed where I lay.

MARTHA.

You do not mean to say she has not slept?

MARY.

Of that I am not sure, — that is, except
One's ears have credit equal to one's eyes.
I did not see but heard her low replies
To Lazarus' questioning.

MARTHA.

Mary! Ah, well;
Of what we hear we cannot always tell,
Nor what we see.   Sometimes we find our eyes
Deceive, else ignorance assumed is wise.

MARY.

Or else ourselves we fondly would deceive,
And fail to see what we would not believe.

MARTHA.

That may be truth — it is — but who can tell?
False seeming imitates the true so well
We know not what is truth.

MARY.

I think I do.

MARTHA.

What is it, then?

MARY.

A thing not wholly new
In this old world ; and eyes as dull as mine
Somewhat of it are able to divine,
In this, that Lazarus and Judeth find
That double thoughts suit well a single mind.

MARTHA.

You speak in riddles ; therefore please explain.

MARY.

If you insist, I make my meaning plain,
And I had thought it glaring.   I will say,
Of Judeth and Lazarus speaking, they
Think each but of the other : double thought,
And but one mind in them, too, is it not ?

MARTHA.

There, that will do ; I think I understand,
So let us to the business now in hand,
For Lazarus calls —   Well, Judeth ?

VII.

JUDETH.

Hasten, all !
We have o'erslept ourselves.

MARY.

We ?

JUDETH.

Hear the call ?
The guard is mounting, and the hastening men
Will soon be ready for the road again :
Yes, here is Lazarus awaiting.

MARY.

Why,
The day sinks swiftly in the western sky,
And, judging from the far-declining sun,
There were two hours of rest instead of one.
Why not awake us sooner ?

LAZARUS.

Love forbade,
When burning heat is tempered by cool shade,
That I disturb your slumber.

MARY.

It is well

To blame Love with it, and your hot cheeks tell
The truth of your frank words.

LAZARUS.

You riddles love,
Else mock my kind confession.   We must move
If we would save the day.

MARY.

That is not lost:
It goes to God ; he reckons, in the cost
Of life to us hours we do not improve.
Which loses most, hours lost to sleep or love ?

MARTHA.

Mary, make haste!   In idle speech is found
The seas in which Time's sweetest years lie drowned.

MARY.

That may be true and is, for in them there
I see you plunge what time you have to spare.

VIII.

With this they mount, while laughter light and gay
Speeds them with cheer along the open way :
Nor does their talk a moment further flag,
Nor tardy feet along the journey lag,
Since their long rest ; while from the distant seas
Is felt the touch of the refreshing breeze,
Which kissed the mountains with its breath of balm
Blown through the groves of olive and of palm, —
Through fields of spices, gardens rich in flowers
Most fragrant now from their infrequent showers, —
Filled ev'ry sense with ecstasy, and strung
The harp of song in ev'ry soul ; each tongue,
Like golden chords of the Æolian lyre
Which tremble into tune when winds inspire,
Burst into song with strains as sweet and rare
As the rich odors wafted on the air.

IX.

What scenes are these we now are passing through!
What memories wake as they arise to view!
A nation's history from its earliest day
These sacred spots to gazing eyes portray:
Here have the feet of Abraham once trod
From Haran guided by the hand of God;
Here Jacob strayed with neither chart nor path,
A fugitive from Esau's righteous wrath:
And Lot here tented ere he chose for gain
His home among the Cities of the Plain.
With sandalled feet old prophets journeyed here;
And here unshod have wandered saint and seer:
The hosts of war have trampled down this way,
Red-handed Carnage hastened here to slay.
A thousand memories press upon the mind,
Shapes of the Past, in shadow dim defined,
Crowd thick the way, and fill the very air
With hosts departed, still in presence there!

X.

Of these they speak. What grandly solemn themes!
Who reads their story, reading only, dreams
Distorted things which vanish with the light;
But when the scenes burst in upon the sight,
And eyes beheld where these their sojourn made, —
For scenes remain although remembrance fade,
The ways they trod, the camp and altar shown, —
Then is the vision to the real grown,
Tradition turns her shadowy face, and, lo!
The living truth stands forth in light aglow.

XI.

The day is sped, the westward-sinking Sun
Across the circling heavens his course has run;
Behind the rising peaks in misty blue
He dips his fiery disc, then slides from view;
Yet, as he lingers, on these haunts of old
A benediction pours in showers of gold, —

A faint reflection of the blessing shed
From God's own hand on patriarchal head :
For, just before, the golden sunlight falls
On Bethel's white and far-reflecting walls,
Where Jacob saw the heavenly brightness gleam
A way to heaven which opened in a dream.
As from the rising ground our friends behold
The scene of that sweet story oft retold,
They cry with glad surprise, not at the scene,
Though lovely in fair fields and orchards green,
But that their eyes delighted gaze upon
The sacred source from whence their hope is drawn,
The spot where God revealed that Jacob's seed
Should be his chosen people, great indeed
In power and fame ; and from them, too, should spring
The hope of Israel, her conqueror-king.
Not all assured is Judeth of the scene,
So questions she of days that once have been.

XII.

JUDETH.

What place is this so charming in its view ?
The history old, the sight to me is new :
Somewhat the story of our land I know,
Its scenes of note, altars and shrines also ;
My father, learned in all his country's lore,
Hath taught me much in lessons oft conned o'er ;
And yet how little, in my too few years,
On Memory's page from out the Past appears !

MARY.

Upon that virgin page would you record
The buried deeds in misty records stored,
While living facts and truths unto us cry
That of neglect we should not let them die ?

JUDETH.

No, both I would secure, since from the dead
The living come.

MARTHA.

Behold, where lies ahead

A fair, sweet camping-ground! Our tents, when spread,
While we await the meal prepared for us,
We will survey the scenes, while Lazarus —
For he is versed in all our country's lore —
Will tell to us the wondrous history o'er
Of this dear spot, a shrine to all our race,
To us, I hope, a night's sweet resting-place,
Whose dreams shall be the hopes of waking eyes
By which we mount in triumph to the skies!

JUDETH.

It is most lovely now, as evening's glow
Burns softly on the city's walls of snow:
The hills beneath the mountains' falling shade,
That swiftly darken as the bright rays fade,
Give beauty to the scene, and sweetly stir
Within the soul of beauty's worshipper:
Nor wonder I that Israel alone,
With weary head here pillowed on a stone,
Filled with the vision of the day's decline,
Should dream of Heaven and messengers divine;
For surely to his sad and heavy eyes
This well might seem the gates of Paradise!
To which in dreams one bright'ning glance was given,
Along the golden way that led to Heaven.
But we are at the camp; the tents now spread,
The weary beasts are waiting to be fed;
While mind itself, by grosser wants subdued
In my weak flesh, cries out for rest and food.

XIII.

If it were meet, and there were time and space,
To paint the camp, portray the camping-place,
A picture fair and fine it would be, drawn
By pen or brush at sunset or at dawn,
Two points of time that bind with golden bands
The radiant world and its dim shadow-lands!
Where lights obscure a softened darkness throws
Across the arch where radiant sunshine glows,
And tingeing with its shadow earth and sky
A thousand hues, and each of varied dye.

This we forego, as pressing now our need
That with our friends we on our journey speed,
Since short the time to loiter or delay,
As speeds apace the coming wedding-day.
Yet, promise made by Martha, if forgot
By her full soon, by Judeth it was not,
That Lazarus should tell the tales of old
Of this fair land. To this she sought to hold
Him to the pledge, not by but for him made :
Nor was he vexed in this to be betrayed ;
Yet, punishment on Martha to impose
For her officious zeal, he sagely chose,
By leaving her and Mary, — supper done, —
To tell the tale to Judeth all alone !

XIV.

The night was beautiful, and softly lay
Its silvery robes where burned the golden day ;
The moon reclining on the mountain's crest
Poured floods of light from out the dreamy west,
Until the valley, narrowing to defiles,
Like sleeping maiden radiant in her smiles,
Grew still more beautiful, as filmy mist,
A silver veil, dropped o'er the brow it kissed,
From eastern slopes that watch above the tide
Where distant Jordan's milky waters glide.
The tents are pitched within a grove of palm,
Whose feathery leaves, now listless in the calm,
With inky stains the shimmering white sands dye
Where ghostly shadows in black mantles lie.
The mountain's crest, a slowly rising cloud,
The moon draws closer in its misty shroud ;
While voices of the night, so sweetly sad
They thrill with pain the hearts that might be glad,
Grew hushed and still, while over all there broods
The sweetest, saddest of Night's solitudes.
On such a night, amid such scenes, they stray ;
No shadowy lights across their faces play ;
They are too happy for their hearts to feel
The shade of sadness with its kisses steal
Across the brow or linger in the eye,

A misty vapor from a flood too nigh.
They talk, and as they talk is proudly told
The wondrous story of the days of old.
She questioning, to her in answer made
With fitting speech, and colors bright portrayed,
He tells the story for each hero meet ;
Though charming, we will not his tale repeat,
Lest what might please his listener would pall
On those who read, or, reading, might know all.

XV.

He told how Jacob forth to Haran fled,
While Esau's hate pursued his steps with dread,
With zeal that wrong upon his proud heart burned
When he of Isaac's stolen blessing learned.
A wanderer here before the face of man,
A mark upon him and his brother's ban,
At night he lay upon this sacred ground,
With sky o'erhead and savage wilds around :
He slept the weary sleep of toil and care,
Forgetting then that God himself was there,
Until the heavens open in a dream,
And floods of light divine around him stream,
While angels on a golden ladder bear,
From clouds descending, blessing to him there.
In after years returning here again,
An altar reared to witness his domain :
So, too, when from the bondage Egypt wrought
The promised land the sons of Jacob sought,
The tribe of Joseph, favorite son and dear,
Pitched their brown tents and made their dwelling here ;
While farther on, where Shechem greets the view,
The bones of Joseph now are resting, too.
And then he told with quickly dark'ning brow,
For wrong keeps long the coals of Hate aglow,
How Salem's prince the standard of revolt
At Shechem raised, with battle's fierce assault
Led on his hosts against the feeble son
Of Israel's mighty ruler, Solomon.
To fix his empire and his sway secure,
In selfish greed, and heart through lust impure,

At Bethel here and in the coasts of Dan
The worship of the golden calf began;
With priests and sacrifice from altars high
Whose shameful rites insult a gracious sky,
Until Josiah, coming to the throne,
Their altars razed and shameless groves cut down,
But left the sacred bones of prophets old,
Whose mausoleums still their ashes hold.

XVI.

Here he the story most abruptly closed,
For all but they in silent night reposed,
While he another tale to her began
As old as Adam and begun with man.
Shall we, too, listen? or with night now fold
Our robes about us and our dull ears hold,
While Zephyrs whisper to the opening flowers,
And kiss to blushes all the fragrant bowers?
Who says us nay?   Youth with its burning ear
Hangs on our lips the tale we tell to hear;
While blushing maidens with averted face
Creep closer still, — with rosy arms embrace
Each other, whispering with fragrant breath
The words conjectural our lovers saith:
Young men, half-conscious, seeming not to care,
With wise contempt and cold, indifferent air,
Turn half-averted faces, yet with eye
And ear well poised to catch the faint reply.
And married dames, remembering still the hour
When lovers' words for them had magic power,
Though now with wisdom bought at later day
Their better meaning and their truth might weigh,
Still stoop their heads to catch the whispered word,
As new to them as if they ne'er had heard.
Then all the old, no matter, man or maid,
Wife, mother, aunt, together are arrayed,
And, as the thoughts of other years inspire,
Each seems anew to catch the youthful fire,
And eager crowd to hear Love's tale again,
Once told to each — and told to some in vain!
The world gives sanction, so we, too, draw near,

With quickened heart and ever-ready ear,
To hear the wond'rous tale that is so strange :
The voice grows husky and its accents change
While he is speaking, bending low his head
To her, she lifting questioning face instead.

XVII.

JUDETH.

There is a tale, — I may not know it right,
If you so please, tell it to me to-night, —
How Jacob, wandering, came upon a well,
And what to him from that event befell.
I oft have heard, but do not understand —
Is not this Jacob's well so near at hand ?

LAZARUS.

No ; that one was in Haran.   Laban's sheep
It was his daughter Rachel's task to keep :
Here Jacob came, aweary of the way,
Drawn by the flocks athirst which waiting lay
About the well, for still the sun was high,
When Rachel with her father's flock drew nigh.
They with the flocks, he, questioning of the maid,
To him her father's name and race betrayed ;
And so he learned this maiden young and fair
Was she he sought, his uncle Laban's heir.
Straightway, when they to him the story told,
He from the well the stony cover rolled,
With his own hands, as strong as they were true,
For Rachel's flock the cooling water drew.
She, sore surprised, a stranger thus to find
With noble heart shown thus in act so kind, —
For with the herdsmen she was wont to strive
For place among them they refused to give —
Inquired his name, and if from journey long ;
He, answering in his father's native tongue,
Said he her kinsman was, and then declared
How largely she of his affections shared,
And he had hither come with her to wed.
She blushing hears, and hangs her queenly head,
While he, in love if ardent, no adept,

Kissed her, "and lifted up his voice and wept."
So runs the tale.

JUDETH.

Why did he weep, I pray?

LAZARUS.

Of that in truth I may not surely say,
Save he had lived so long and had not known
What pleasure was.

JUDETH.

And yet so quickly flown!
For those who give and take, not seldom miss
The joy ethereal lingering from a kiss.

LAZARUS.

You speak as one who judges, having tried.

JUDETH.

With you, at least, that charge can be denied,
Save as a sister's given.

LAZARUS.

Ah! who knows
But what that was the source of Jacob's woes?

JUDETH.

You leave untold this all-absorbing tale.

LAZARUS.

No matter, it to me is old and stale:
A man to win a wife his service hires, —
The sentiment, perhaps, the world admires, —
But when at last, his time of service done,
Another takes, and an uncomely one,
By fraud deceived, o'erreached, and played upon,
Contempt deserves as one unworthy shown
Of woman's love, and careless of his own.

XVIII.

JUDETH.

I know the story now: of Rachel's love
It were unjust her faithful heart to prove.

What was her loss, you men with force maintain,
Proved in the end to be for Jacob's gain
In two wives for the one, and Rachel, too!

LAZARUS.

Well, let that pass; it nothing has to do
With us or ours.

JUDETH.

Why not? If in their place
We put to test the virtue of our race?

LAZARUS.

Between us two it hath no lot nor part,
Since heart doth service here to loyal heart:
What it commands — desires — we freely give,
Since in its peace and love we hope to live.
For mine I speak, at least, and hope from thee
The same response in answer back to me.

JUDETH.

How can I tell? Another Rachel I,
And for a Leah you yet may pass me by.

XIX.

LAZARUS.

My Judeth, this is truth, thus more than true
The faith it is of Jew bestowed on Jew;
And yet you doubt what all my actions teach
With greater force than lies in human speech;
Will you not answer me to-night?

JUDETH.

Why haste?
The ripened fruit grows sweeter to slow taste.
The poisoned fig, if sparing we partake,
Thus sickens, and we shun.

LAZARUS.

Yet for Love's sake
You should believe and trust me.

JUDETH.

                  I should not
For Love's sake trust.

MARTHA (*coming forward*).

             This is a lovely spot!
Here I could dwell forever — Judeth! you?
And Lazarus is watching with you, too!
Ah! I had all forgotten he should tell
The story of this spot remembered well
By him. Ah-h-h-! You have grown chill, I fear,
And we had best go in again, my dear.
Good night, kind brother; at the break of day
It would be well to hasten on our way.

LAZARUS.

Yes, it is well that I her words should heed;
For if our journey makes no better speed
Toward Cana than I make toward love, why, then,
We all shall miss the wedding! Once again
Has my sheer arrow from the mark flown wide;
Still I in hope the better day abide.

XX.

Again they start, just at the dawn of day,
But we will linger not upon the way,
Though ev'ry foot we traverse to us brings
Swift mem'ries, hastening on their eager wings
To bear us messages from years long fled,
The voiceless stories of the sleeping dead.
Yet, as we pass, nor camp nor resting-place
Shall we more heed as hast'ning pen shall trace
Some outlines bold, some scenes long known to fame,
Where mem'ry clings or lingers still a name,
That yet to man as beacon-lights shall be
On rocky cliffs that tower in Time's broad sea.

XXI.

There Shechem stood, and near it Jacob's well,
Nor spot more famed in all of Israel;

Mount Gerizim, the Mount of Blessing named,
Opposing Ebal, Mount of Cursing famed,
Where on each height a choir of readers stood,
From this the Evil read, from that the Good,
While Israel beheld in awe the scene,
Whose waiting hosts the valley fill between.
Beyond these westward, toward the midland sea,
Samaria, famed for its delivery ;
Beyond it Dothan, where Elisha's prayer
Revealed the hosts of God encamping there ;
Then through the winding pass declining down
Behold the lovely plain of Esdraelon,
Where flows the Kishon through the winding plain,
Hard by whose stream the priests of Baal were slain.
Gilboa's heights upon the east appear ;
Despairing Saul, self-murdered, perished here,
Mad from defeat, which, following fast, befell
Just as foretold by risen Samuel,
Whose troubled spirit burst imprisoning clay
And at a breath blew all his hope away.
Then, as we journey on, Mount Tabor's height
Cheers with its woods of green the gazing sight,
Famed for its beauty and its charming views
When Spring the Autumn's purpling dress renews,
And Winter, touching but its highest crest,
Far Lebanon in icy robes has dress'd,
While yet his slopes, in dark and living green
With cedar crowned the circling year, are seen.
Still at his feet, along the Galilee,
The sleeping cities on its shores we see ;
And to the westward Esdraelon's vale,
Where Sisera fell by the hand of Jael,
Where Barak's hosts from Tabor poured their flood,
And flowed the Kishon red with Syrian blood,
E'en while the vales and smiling hills along
Reëchoed Barak and Debora's song !

XXII.

Still pressing on, and by a winding path
We pass beyond the town of Nazareth,
Then famous grown for its base turpitude,

Now world-renowned for its great gift of good!
Three days from Bethel, closing with the night,
And Cana cheers the long-expectant sight;
As sinks the sun adown the glowing west,
We slowly wind along the rising crest
Where sits the city, nestling like a dove,
Crowned where it clings by steeper heights above.

XXIII.

Why tell of greetings when we all well know
What springs of joy from such occasions flow?
Ben Ammi's house that night was glad with mirth,
And from its chambers as a flood streams forth
Glad strains of music, bridal-chant and song,
That on the evening breezes float along;
While gathering in came many a smiling guest
In festal garb and for the wedding dress'd,
And filled the house, which, as a garden blown,
Flamed in rich hues of flowers profusely strown.
Ben Ammi's daughter, with her maidens fair
As Hebron's lilies, for the rites prepare.
Shall we describe her? Why employ the time,
Or waste the value of a worthless rhyme,
When all the world the picture erst has seen,
Since ev'ry bride for once is Beauty's queen!
But we may not a word, at least, forego,
To paint the scene with flowers and smiles aglow;
Bold strokes we give, yet, while they may be few,
They are to nature and to beauty true.

XXIV.

Candace, daughter to Ben Ammi, born
Of gentle blood, would any home adorn;
Not born to wealth, yet frugal means supply
A generous store, but luxuries deny:
So that the costly robe with threads of gold,
And flashing gems to charm all who behold;
The golden cincture, coruscating bands
To clasp her limbs, and rings to deck her hands;
The golden crown upon her locks that flow,

A rippling sea of dusky waves below;
With silver veil, in threads so finely spun
It casts no shadow in the noonday sun, —
All these denied, yet in her simple dress
Of spotless white could any queen lack less
Than she, who thus by grandeur may be scorned,
Her jewelled self adorning unadorned!
What more can there be said to add in praise
Than this bold picture in itself displays?
Can eyes that glow like stars at dusk of night?
Can floods of hair in inky waves in flight?
Can brow that gleams a spotless crest of snow
Beneath which blooming roses gladsome blow?
Can neck as graceful as a swan's at rest, —
A column rising from a billowy breast?
Can lips as red as pomegranate cut through,
And teeth like seeds of pearl that greet the view?
Can form as graceful as the feathery palm,
When gently swaying in the light wind's calm?
Can smile as sweet as heaven's painted morn
The farther beauty of the bride adorn?
Then these are hers, and, though divinely sweet,
The picture drawn in all is incomplete.

XXV.

The sun is setting; on the western sky
The golden billows of the evening lie,
Reflecting shadows from the upward rays
That fill the glowing plain with misty haze
Softer than sunlight, yet with added power
That gives a golden glory to the hour:
And well it may! for ne'er before came down
Such glory here so grand a head to crown!
For, yonder passing up the winding height,
Full in the radiance of the lurid light,
Is one whom we when on the Jordan's shore
With heavenly glory saw enshrined before, —
Is one whom we, when Satan from him fled,
Saw on the mount with heavenly manna fed!
The Christ draws near! and heaven and nature glow,
While golden sunlight crowns his princely brow!

With him his foll'wers speed the upward way,
And mount the topmost height at close of day :
Ben Ammi's door swings open as they come,
And through it Evening's glory floods the room,
Nor ever was an earthly bridal blest
With brighter glory and such wedding guest !

XXVI.

Before they came, Judeth and Mary, drawn
From the fair bride, had to the house-top gone,
With other fair and comely maidens, bent,
As they, to witness ev'ry hoped event.
They talked as only maidens can and do ;
Grew rapturous o'er the fair dissolving view :
With hands upraised, and eyes with pleasure bright,
Gave voice in chorus to the heart's delight
A moment, then forgetting, it would seem,
That life was real in this golden dream,
Yet frail as fair, the shadow speeding fast
Across the golden sunburst ere it passed.
While yet remembering this the fairest thing,
The wedding-song is dying while they sing :
That note, it matters not how glad the strain,
Or for whom sung, no lips repeat again !
We might give voice to what they thought and said,
If something new and charming, but instead,
Whoever hears at such a time such speech
Needs here no lesson in their arts to teach.

XXVII.

The scenes around, the beauty of the spot,
Were soon by all who viewed alike forgot,
Save Judeth, who had drawn somewhat apart,
For sober thought with contemplative heart,
Her eyes fixed on the steep and winding way,
Whose chalky path, a silvery ribbon, lay
Far down the hills, where glowed as burnished gold
Reflected sunlight o'er the rocky hold ;
While Memory, gathering up the slackened thread,
Winds back the clue to other hours instead,

And through their misty veil, as light through trees,
Remembered faces of the past she sees ;
And, shining brightest of the loved and fair
Of all the faces she has gathered there,
She sees the one, since at the Jordan's tide,
Which in her heart has reigned there deified !
A start — a cry ! — now follows her fixed gaze ;
Her cheeks grow white, her eyes in fervor blaze ;
With rigid hand as that which points the road
At crossways set, she in the sunlight stood,
Which touches head and hand with generous glow
While lies in shadow all the form below,
Pointing adown the way where upward wend
Belated guest and home-returning friend.

XXVIII.

Her cry, her action — for no word she spoke —
Upon the ears of her companions broke,
Who, rushing where she stood in wild surprise,
With eager question and dilating eyes,
Gaze where she points, but fail with her to see
That which might rouse e'en their curiosity.
" What dost thou see ? " is questioned now by one.

JUDETH.

The Christ, whom John the Baptist calls God's Son.

HULDAH.

John Baptist ! What dost thou of that one know ?
He cometh not now hither ? If so, show
Him unto us.

JUDETH.

Nay ! him I did not name,
Save to declare his saying. To him came,
When we were at the Jordan, —

HULDAH.

What ! Were you
Of those who went his wondrous deeds to view ?

JUDETH.

Yes: we like others went, and it was strange
To see the multitudes! Each mountain range,
The valleys, hills, the desert wastes, the plains,
Gave up their hosts entire, till scarce remains,
Or did when we came back, throughout our land,
One who had failed to visit Jordan's strand.
While we were there — and short indeed our stay —
There came to him a stranger from this way,
To be baptized. This John to him denied,
Himself unworthy ; yet into the tide
He led him down, and in the milky stream
Immersed he him. As they came forth a gleam
As bright as the swift lightning filled the air,
And blazed along the heavens everywhere ;
And while expectant we the thunder wait
From out the skies now glowing roseate,
There downward sped a milk-white, hovering dove,
And sat upon his head : then high above
The bending arch a voice like thunder near,
Yet soft as whispering Zephyrs to the ear,
Spake, saying, " This is my beloved Son,
In whom I am well pleased, hear ev'ry one ! "
Behold! That man baptized with Heaven's acclaim,
Now hither comes! I know him as the same.

XXIX.

MARY.

Where? Which one, Judeth? Ah! I now can see
His shining face, and it indeed is he !

HULDAH.

Which one, I pray, — for many crowd the path, —
Is he you say this wondrous glory hath ?

JUDETH.

He with the golden locks which downward stream,
Around whose head the parting splendors gleam,
In robe of white fringed deep with band of blue
Full bordered round, to mark his lineage true.

HULDAH.

The dress does not distinguish : such is worn
By others on the way.

MARY.

He at the turn,
Where juts the chalky cliff out to the path, —
The one alone the golden ringlets hath.

HULDAH.

Not he ! I know him well, if he the one !
He is of Nazareth, and Joseph's son,
A lowly carpenter ; and even now
His mother waiteth on the guests below,
A kinswoman acknowledged of our host.

JUDETH.

I may have made mistake, or, at the most,
Some semblance, marked, distinctive, may deceive.
Call Lazarus, Mary : I cannot believe
My eyes misguide me, yet your statements shake
My faith in them somewhat.

HULDAH.

Sometimes we make,
When it would seem impossible, mistake,
When but to err is folly.   So with me.
This man our fathers knew from infancy,
And we since we have known our mothers, so
It now were doubting sight him not to know.

JUDETH.

I cannot doubt your words, nor yet my eyes ;
As he draws near, still greater my surprise :
For I have other witness I am right,
Since now my heart is seconding my sight,
And leaps with heavy throes and fluttering beat
At the near footfalls of his coming feet.

HULDAH.

I am surprised — I cannot understand —
Here, Lazarus is waiting your command :
Ask him of those approaching.

XXX.

LAZARUS.

I await,
My Judeth, your command.

JUDETH.

Then look and state
Whom those are who approach.

LAZARUS.

A company
Advancing up the winding way I see,
But they seem strangers ev'ry one — But stay!
The foremost of the first who come this way
Hath look familiar! Where hath been
By me that form and face so lately seen?
Where hath it been? Am I in thought so blind
That sight itself should now outrun my mind?
As they approach, a nearer vision throws
The light upon them that will soon disclose
Both form and feature, and — a glancing beam
Which doth through some cleft rock or crevice stream
Falls fair upon his face — What! Judeth, see!
The Christ, the Christ! I know him now! 't is he!
I know that face, the fairest ever seen —

HULDAH.

'T is strange, yes, wondrous strange! since he has been
To us familiar all these years, that now
You should be so mistaken! Hair and brow,
Dress, carriage, all are those of Joseph's son,
For such is he that you now look upon:
And then you know the proverb old that saith,
"No good thing cometh out of Nazareth."

JUDETH.

I only know what I before have seen,
And feel what I have felt. That brow and mien
Majestic now to sight and kingly are;
They for themselves the better truth declare;
And if his hands their menial task have done,

For labor he a nobler name hath won
Than kings can win : they consecrate all toil,
And princely honor of its jewels spoil,
And give to labor now the sovereign's crown.
He cometh in ; let us in haste go down !

LAZARUS.

Brave heart and true, my Judeth : in the day
That trieth us these words shall be my stay.

HULDAH.

This way ! The marriage now begins, and late
We all shall be if we here further wait.

XXXI.

The wedding-feast proceeds : Architriclin
Hath ordered still more wine should be brought in.
Dismayed, the servants to Ben Ammi go
With message that the wine is running low,
And fast is failing now their scanty store,
Nor in the town can there be purchased more !
Straightway Ben Ammi to his butler calls,
The thought of shame his honest heart appalls :
What can be done ? His close and grudging greed
Outweighed his honor, saving of his need ;
His guests, departing from his ruined feast,
Would speak of him but slightingly at least.
His kinswoman, Mary of Nazareth,
Hearing reproaches, to Ben Ammi saith,
" Peace, brother ! and reproach him not ; your good
To him is dearer than his richest blood.
Your needs he saw and strove to save in vain,
Yet what you count as loss shall be your gain.
There shall be wine enough and yet to spare.
Return within, nor doubting wait it there."

XXXII.

MARY OF NAZARETH.

They have no wine, my son.

THE CHRIST.

                    Woman, with thee
What have I now to do ? Dost thou not see
Mine hour has not yet come ?

MARY OF NAZARETH.

                    Thy day and hour
Are here.

THE CHRIST.

        Not mine. It is my Father's power
That worketh in me. If he now declare
The day at hand, I will the wine prepare.

MARY OF NAZARETH.

Demetrius, — Philip, — here ! Now hearken you :
Whatever he commandeth see you do.

THE CHRIST.

Bring here some firkins, all the house contains.

DEMETRIUS.

We have but six, yet they are large : on rains
We here depend for water.

THE CHRIST.

                 Take and fill
These level to the brim with water.

DEMETRIUS.

                    Will
These six suffice ? Our water is all spent,
But more may still be brought.

THE CHRIST.

                 I am content.
Now draw from these, nor of their contents spare,
And to Architriclin the flagons bear.

XXXIII.

They tap the draught, when, lo ! a ruddy flow
Pours its rich flood with foaming beads aglow,
And at the touch that marks the hand divine

The crystal stream flows reddening into wine!
The goblets filled, with pleasure and surprise
The guests behold with long-admiring eyes:
They taste; the flavor pleasing still the more,
Potations large and liberal they pour;
The vintage they discuss, the brand and vine;
Some to this vineyard, some to that, incline.
Though versed in wines through use and years of care,
All fail at last its vintage to declare;
Not dreaming that the wine their want supplies
Is pure, ambrosial nectar from the skies!
The wine of life, which cheers when looked upon,
Fresh from cerulean fountains sparkling drawn.

XXXIV.

Architriclin, the ruler of the feast,
Surprised and pleased at its rich, fragrant taste,
When first to him the wondrous draught was brought,
Nor dreaming it had been from water wrought,
Called forth the bridegroom and to him he saith
(His eyes denying his dissembled wrath):
"What mean you, sir, by this deception shown?
Your fault at once to guests deceived now own!
In all my life, and I am full of years,
I ne'er have seen what at this board appears;
And here to-night, of all these favored guests,
Not one but what at your offence protests."
"What have I done?" the astonished bridegroom cries,
His anger checked by his profound surprise.
"What have you done?" the ruler answering back, —
From rising laughter force his fierce words lack, —
"What have you not, would better you inquire!"
His words have now regained their wonted fire:
"No other man, as you have done, would dare." —
"I pray you," cried the bridegroom, "further spare
Your words and me! If I a wrong have done,
For my offence I will in full atone."
"Atone!" the ruler cried. "That cannot be;
Your crime is one 'gainst Time, not these, or me!"
"'Gainst Time? I am content, for well I know
That Time will soften and some mercy show,

Nor hold me thrall forever. Pray declare
To me and these around, — it is but fair, —
My grave offence."   Architriclin then said :
" Now every man his good wine first. instead
Of bad, sets forth when he begins his feast,
So that when men have drunk their fill, at least
So it is thought, they lose perception fine,
And thus deceives in giving them bad wine.
But you reject this rule kept in the past,
And keep your best wine even to the last ! "
Around the board the merry laughter ran,
Anew their cheer the wedding guests began :
What heart was there could feel the touch of woe,
What soul a sense of fleeting sorrow know,
When God's Eternal Son himself was there,
To bless with wine and in the feast to share !

XXXV.

A time they feast unconscious of the power
That wrought its generous blessing on the hour ;
So great the deed and startling, that the mind
Had doubted sight and thought the eyes grown blind,
Had not the witness each the other brought,
Convincing answer gave each doubting thought ;
While from the vessels they with water filled,
The ruby wine its fragrant flood distilled.
Slow were they yet the startling truth to tell,
For, since they doubted, others may as well.
At last low whispers of the wonder wrought
Are by the ears of one then others caught ;
Then, gathering force, the startling story grew
And moved, then thrilled the wond'ring household through.
A hundred tongues the hasty story tell,
And hold each list'ner by its wondrous spell :
The wine is tasted o'er and o'er again,
Nor is there lip but tries the test in vain ;
The vintage perfect, fruit and spirit fine,
Despite the process, still it must be wine !

XXXVI.

Who wrought the miracle? the question heard,
The answer given greater tumult stirred:
They taste again; some to the jar repair,
The servants question, test the vintage there.
The proof complete, the source and method sure,
Against deceit and witchcraft made secure,
Amazement deepens, and the more they try
The truth to solve, greater the mystery.
"It cannot be!" one puzzled guest exclaims
When his companion deed and doer names:
"Why, have we not lived neighbors all his life?
And there his mother, honest Joseph's wife?
Scarce is he known beyond his father's gate,
And not for wisdom in his humble state:
True, there was rumor once, that in dispute,
Before his wisdom priest and sage stood mute,
But that was years ago. How oft is found
That prattling babes our wisest will astound!"
"While you speak true, yet here is still the wine,
And these the witnesses: we must confine
Our speech to facts. We knowing him but shows
How little man of his own neighbor knows.
If he hath wrought this wonder-waking deed,
Of which of further proof there is scant need,
His be the praise, the glory, the renown, —
The Prophet's mantle and Emanuel's crown."

XXXVII.

Astonished at the zeal and fervid power
Of his companion, quiet till this hour,
The first stood mute, while gath'ring round them press'd,
With eager haste, full many a wedding guest;
And many tongues speak from the heart's desire,
And many bosoms heave with kindling fire.
Peter and John and Andrew then disclose
What each about his humble Master knows:
Strange stories, whispered, run from ear to ear,
While lip to lip still spreads the tales they hear.
Now Lazarus, the centre of a crowd,

With earnest speech and voice unduly loud,
Relates the story we before have told,
With fervid zeal and manner firm and bold,
Of Jordan's scene baptismal, and the flood
Of glory blinding all the multitude.
When all are done, a hush as deep as death,
Save the long sigh and gently sobbing breath,
Steals through the hall, and every wedding guest
Stands wonder-bound before the truth confessed;
Each eye pursuing with its silent gaze
The wondrous beauty of that saddened face
Of whom the prophet said, as true as brief,
"The man of sorrows and acquaint with grief!"
Whose meek eyes bending to the earthen floor
Refuse the homage when they would adore:
But, all the while they gaze upon him there,
His lips are quivering with a whispered prayer.
Delightful scene! and yet a scene most sad,
Where eyes must weep while yet the heart is glad!

XXXVIII.

Among the women, as the tale is told,
Well may we doubt what e'en the eyes behold;
As Mary, Martha, Judeth, all relate
The wondrous story of the Paraclete,
At Jordan's flood, when John the Christ proclaimed,
And him, their guest, the great Messiah named.
Amazed they hear; and as the glowing scene
Their fervid words portray as it had been,
Sobs, tears, and cries break in upon their speech,
As heart by heart the words convincing reach,
Until at last a shout of gladness rings
Out on the night, a voice in triumph sings,
And startles Judeth as she hears the strain
Remembered, as on Jordan sung.   Again
Their voices, clearing from the sound of tears,
Catch up the chorus that the burden bears,
And on that night once more are heard the notes
Whose echo yet adown the ages floats,
Still sweeping out o'er land and over sea,
The world's great anthem in its jubilee!

XXXIX.

Why further tell the story of this night,
That sweetens sorrow with a brief delight?
The tale is one too old, yet ever new,
That we should further in its scenes pursue.
The guests, some tarry for the morning dawn,
And some e'en with the midnight hour have gone:
Thus we, departing, out of life must go,
Some out to light and joy and some to woe.
Our friends, though ling'ring for a little day,
Soon turn their footsteps to the homeward way:
Their route obscure we leave them to pursue,
Though fair the scenes, now unrecorded through,
Though converse sweet, and scenes of beauty rare,
Beguile the way and charm away all care,
Until the safe return brings them again,
From Galilee through Jordan's charming plain,
To Bethany, where they once more may meet
The welcomes warm which will their coming greet;
There, for a time, we draw the misty veil,
And leave to silence the unwritten tale.

CANTO SIXTH.

WITHIN THE SHADOW.

I.

JUDETH.

ONCE more upon the mount, and for the last:
Can it be true that two long years have passed,
And growing in the third, since on that morn
We last stood here together!

LAZARUS.

     Now in scorn
The sun shines on us, and the morning light
Has more of shadow in it than the night,
Because my heart is darkened. What a change
One short hour makes, and everything seems strange!

How lightly beat my heart when on the path
We started here this morning ! Martha saith, —
It is a wisdom of her prudent heart, —
" When smiles the morn, at eve our joys depart ! "
Such is the truth with me.

JUDETH.

Who could foretell
This killing blow before it crushing fell ?
To think ! through all these years approving smile
Should in our bright'ning pathway still beguile,
Until it led to where the narrow track
Forbid the hope that we might still turn back,
And then the stern and life-dissolving word
Cuts 'twixt us two like a dividing sword,
And Love lies bleeding where we fall apart !

LAZARUS.

Thy servant surely hath a gentle heart ;
With such a message brought, he would allow
That we should stay a half hour longer now.

JUDETH.

He has, and gentle as a woman's.   Haste
We now our talk, we have no time to waste ;
For when, at yonder darkly frowning stone
Where he awaits, I leave you there alone,
Who then can set a meeting ?

LAZARUS.

What said he, —
What the message sent ?

JUDETH.
Here, read and see.

II.

LAZARUS (*reading*).

" Judeth, my daughter, blessed in thy name,
I hear strange rumors that our faith doth shame :
They are that thy sweet friends (God pity lend

That curse so dark should light upon a friend !)
Have joined a sect they call the Nazarenes:
I know not well just what that title means,
But they are followers of one who came
From out that city bearing evil fame.
Withdraw yourself from them, and straightway come
In most convenient speed with Haddan home.
Let partings, too, be short: the breach now made
Is final. See in love I am obeyed.
Your father,
      " Rahab,
          " Ruler at the Gate."

This is to us the very gall of fate,
And leaves us helpless, save the hand of Time
May soften as it sows his locks with rime.

JUDETH.

Yet we will hope: my promise, made at last,
I will with equal zeal and truth hold fast;
For, while it lingered as you pressed me on
Long after that to you my heart had gone,
I came reluctant, not for lack of love,
But that your heart I would still further prove:
So shall it stand firm-rooted as this rock,
Nor yield, as this may, to the earthquake's shock.
Bestowed, 't is yours, I cannot call it back ;
Though friends forsake and foes apply the rack,
My love is gone: if yours to me as true,
Then we for love will fight the battle through ;
And should Hope fail, why then let us be brave ;
They cannot rob us of a common grave !

III.

LAZARUS.

How bravely said, my Judeth! This repays
A thousand-fold the long, unhappy days
I hung 'twixt hope and fear upon each word
I from your lips, in doubt, expectant heard,
Until last eve your answer came, and brought
The joy I had so long and madly sought.

And in that hour I drank as sweet a draught
As e'er by lip from spring immortal quaffed;
Sweeter and richer in its cheer divine
To me than Cana's consecrated wine!
And now a hand as dear to me as can
The hand of man be to his fellow-man,
At one rude stroke strikes down the cup, and, lo!
From shattered fragments bitter waters flow!
And yet your words make sweet the poisoned flood,
As sins grow white through the atoning blood.
Your love makes sacrifice for me and mine;
Its answering fires around Hope's altar shine:
As you to me I to my pledge stand fast
While life shall warm, and mind and reason last;
And yet my heart as yours is not so brave,
Since I to meet you look beyond the grave!

JUDETH.

The grave? Beyond the grave? I had not thought,
As now I think, of that long-hallowed spot:
A place so welcome, peaceful, silent, where
We lose in rest all sense of pain and care;
A place where hearts desponding there may come
As some sick child unto its waiting home:
A place where age and want — the journey done —
With youth and wealth at last may be at one!
No matter there how fierce the adverse wind,
No broken tile in sheltering roof can find.
Beyond its portals never ranged my sight,
Since where I looked lay one eternal night!

IV.

LAZARUS.

Hath not the new faith taught, some glimmer thrown,
To light the darkness settled on your own?

JUDETH.

The grave! What is it? Is eternal sleep
The only recompense for those who weep?
He saith not so, the Master, whom I love,
And whom my ev'ry thought and word approve.

If I accept him and his faith in part,
I am but false in a divided heart ;
And yet I have been taught a creed that scouts
Eternal life, and laughs at him who doubts.
But now the warming truth of hope I feel,
As its sweet whispers to my dull ears steal,
Through love awake, which sees that nought is left
To it when we are here of life bereft,
Since stern decree no promise gives that life
Shall deck me ever with the crown of wife,
While cold and clammy the embrace and breath
Of bridegroom given at the hand of Death !

LAZARUS.

You freeze my veins at the detested thought !
The very picture hath within it wrought
A horror I would fly.   You make the tomb
An endless torture of eternal gloom ;
I, with my faith, flash hope upon the night,
And all its chambers are a flood of light !
Come, look within ; the curtains lift, and gaze
Into eternal realms of golden days.

V.

JUDETH.

I will attempt, my Lazarus, and pray
That to this light my Master lead the way ;
Since for his sake, his truth, I now must be
Forever separate from him and thee.
But now my hour is up.   O golden days !
Grown misty in my tears' unbidden haze,
Back to your light will look, as soon my race,
In exile dreaming of this hallowed place,
Shall gaze upon the Holy City there,
Of all the earth the place to them most fair.
And as to me this hour, so shall their home
Unto my wand'ring people soon become.
The foe is at our gates, the citadel
To heathen hands long since in weakness fell :
The march of hostile feet upon my ear
In thund'rous tread along the hills I hear ;

His camp-fires gleam from mountain-top and plain,
Presaging rapine and its horrid reign.
From this I turn to bid you all adieu,
Ye charming scenes that brighten on my view:
Though I from you may pine in hateful thrall,
Your pictures bright hang thick on Memory's wall;
No hand can mar you, and no bolt can slide
In prison-door and all your freshness hide.
Your sweetest charm is still my joy to tell,
And, since I take you with me, will not say farewell!

VI.

My Lazarus, I would it were as true,
And that I might not say farewell to you:
But this is not our lot.   Is hope, too, vain?
How does it answer, " Shall we meet again ? "
I cannot see beyond the rayless gloom
That lies this side and falls beyond the tomb.
But there is still one thing I know : my heart,
Bleeding, you take with you when we shall part ;
For you it lies in love forever slain,
I cannot call it back to life again !
Will you be patient with me in this hour?
The storm is spent when lightly falls the shower;
But when the drouth has parched the fertile plain
The clouds but mock us with the breath of rain,
And, though the Earth cries out in mortal pain,
The Heavens their mists its thirsty lips refuse,
And the hot air withholds the generous dews.
So are my cries to deaf, unfeeling ears,
And my hot heart denies mine eyes their tears!

LAZARUS.

Be patient with you!   Adonai teach
Me patience strong as I am weak in speech:
It falters, fails, and dies at every word!
O that my love were now a flaming sword,
That it might hew all opposition down,
As conquerors cleave their way to earthly crown !
Your heart my kingdom, in it there to reign
I would risk all.

VII.

JUDETH.

I said my heart lies slain
By Love, and now is prostrate at your feet,
You reign in it and over it complete.
No hand can wrest it from you, and no power
Can change or turn it from you evermore.
But I must haste! How swift the time has flown,
And Haddan now has long impatient grown.
If I could on this mount forever dwell
With you apart, — might never say farewell, —
How gladly would I linger till the gray
From these dusk locks had chased the night away!
Were we to part but soon to meet again,
I might defer the sharp and bitter pain;
But now! what matters it if go or stay,
If to your bosom prest, or on the way
To Love's long exile, nevermore again
Back to your arms escaping from the chain!
My smiles are bitterer to you than tears,
Your smile to me a mockery appears!
Oh! let us part! How can I linger on
When hope forever from my heart has gone?
And yet, and yet I turn again and turn;
I feel your bleeding heart still for me yearn,
And reaching out blind hands afresh I cry
That I may still within your bosom lie!

VIII.

LAZARUS.

I cannot speak! Let all of my past years
This bitter guerdon of my many tears,
Let all my heart, let all my nature, prove
The wondrous fervor of my voiceless love,
Which, choked by grief, in trembling silence stands,
And reaches out to you imploring hands!
I cannot say farewell! I pray you go
With feet so silent that I may not know
Of their departure; then that quivering kiss
While these lips breathe they nevermore shall miss:

A sacred seal, it rests there with a vow
Which from all lips forever parts mine now!
O life of my best life! from thee is drawn
Its glory, as the day its hues from Dawn!
Do not depart just yet! Reach back your hand
And clasp my fingers, 't is my last command:
Why still withhold? What! and is she now gone
Without a further word? Up! follow on!
We must some plan for meeting now devise,
Some way to write to baffle cunning eyes.
I had not thought my foolish speech she heard,
Or she would ready take me at my word!
The way lies clear along the dusty road,
Where floats in gray their dust-departing cloud,
And I, too late, pursue upon the track
Of feet which at my call will not turn back.
And yet what matters it, now she is gone,
Since in this way no more could we live on!
A bitter draught were better drunk in haste;
While we delay we linger o'er the taste.

IX.

Within a mansion near the western gate, —
No palace wrought for lord of high estate,
But generous in its comfort and design,
Nor scant its fittings nor unseemly fine, —
We enter now by invitation kind
A friend familiar once again to find.
Now, as we pass beyond the entrance-door,
With hasty glance let us this home explore.
Beyond a court, where all the household care
With fowls and beasts the spacious courtyard share;
From this, divided by a narrow wall
Which shut the garden from the sight of all,
Was seen a bower, for such was it in size,
A feast entrancing to admiring eyes:
There, in the centre of a leafy shade,
A cooling fountain in the sunlight played;
Around it, glowing in their tropic bloom,
A wealth of flowers in color and perfume.
The aloe here and balm now scent the air;

The bay and box-tree deck the borders there;
While myrtle twines its branches vivid green,
With oleanders flashing bright between.
The rose of Sharon and the lily fair
The inner circle of the fountain share;
While flowers of Rimmon and its russet fruit
The garden's beauty and its wealth dispute.

X.

From these we pass, and turning to the stair
To mount to upper chambers we prepare:
The marble steps, a short and winding flight,
Gleam as the snow in their unspotted white;
A sacrilege to household deities
It seems to set unholy foot on these.
But we ascend, the upper porch invade;
A terraced hall shut in by balustrade,
Whose sheltering eaves and awnings many-hued
Shut out the sun, or give his light subdued.
From this the chambers of the household lead,
Through archways curtained just to suit their need;
Dim niches wid'ning in the dusky light,
Great doors with panels carved and gilding bright,
Well-stanchioned walls and tessellated floors,
The strength and beauty of the home secures.
We tarry not, but hasten to the door
Which stands ajar invitingly before,
From which low voices heard in broken speech
In fitful murmurs scarce the list'ner reach.
We pass within just as a gentle wind
Blows wide the door but carelessly confined;
Our presence mingling with diffusive air
The breeze they think alone has entered there.

XI.

Here curtained windows draped in varied hue
The light subdued, as, softly sifting through,
Floods all the room, and makes the outer day
In contrast seem a cold and cheerless gray.
Rich rugs from Smyrna; purples, too, from Tyre;

Damascus lends its hues of gold and fire ;
Elam's famed woods and Gilead's fragrant fir,
Lebanon's cedars, ebony from Ur,
Inwrought with flowers and carved in rich design,
In mirrored polish in the soft light shine :
A wilderness of beauty, yet a bower
That hath no songster and a single flower !

XII.

We heard soft voices as we entered, now
We gaze upon the speakers.   One fair brow,
Though bent so low the face is scarcely shown,
To us, though sadly altered, still is known.
A silken robe of pattern rich and rare,
Shows still her taste in what best suits to wear ;
The jewelled throat, the thin and bloodless hand,
The tender heart of pity now command ;
While faded face and dark and dreamy eye
Show sorrow passing that will not pass by,
And tears unshed that at the surface lie.
The languid motion of the drooping form,
Which bends as if upon it beat the storm
Which long has swept, is sweeping still, that breast
With waves whose tossings nevermore find rest ;
Shows now a wreck, such as the stormy sea
In painted boat, which rode the waters free
In calm and sun, by storm at last despoiled,
Drives fast ashore upon the breakers wild.
And this fair Judeth ! We can ne'er forget
Her lovely face last seen on Olivet :
How could we dream a thing so wondrous strange
That days so few could make so great a change !

XIII.

But hush ! again she speaks.   We had not seen
Him whom to her companion there had been,
Until addressed, nor shall our story now
Wait but a word, and this we must allow.
He was a man, a Jew, and full of years,
As from his snowy beard and hair appears :

His brow is broad, low, wrinkled, knit, and stern ;
Receding sharply, bald his crown.   You learn
Much from the shape of head, the masters teach,
But more from eye, from gesture, mode of speech.
Both have we here, with form not slightly bent,
As if on earth his mind was most intent ;
His shrunken limbs were clothed in silken gown,
And in its folds his hands lay shrunk and brown :
Such is the man in look and in attire,
And such old Rahab, Judeth's doting sire.
Now what the world in truth may of him say,
Which meets and grapples with him ev'ry day,
One thing, no matter how he shows his heart,
His love is natural, and in it no art !
And should he kill her she must needs but know
The hand that loved in love but dealt the blow !
How this can be, when from effect to cause
We trace this truth through Nature in her laws,
Our reason gives no answer ; all we see
And know is that they are, not why they be.
To him she speaks, and speaking lifts her face
Pathetic in its sweet and simple grace.

XIV.

JUDETH.

I have still but one answer, one alone ;
When that is made, my plea and speech are done.
If there can naught abate, can nothing move
You in the name of pity and of love,
Then let us cease ; you, me to make forget,
And I with you to plead for mercy yet.
I die each day a death that in the night
Moves but a short space on with morning's light ;
And yet as surely as the shadows run
Around the dial with the wheeling sun,
So sure the sands of life are running fast,
And each grain dropping hastens to the last.
I cannot check their course : if you will place
Upon my silken vest your sidelong face,
And there await with close and listening ear,
The dripping of my heart's blood you will hear,

For through this wound its richest flood is shed,
Which now runs low in thin and purple thread.
If you had rather see that stream run dry
In this slow death, as day by day I die,
Then be it so; if rather I should live,
Recall your curse and Lazarus forgive.

RAHAB

That Nazarene! The tomb would be more kind
Than bonds of troth which you to him should bind.
Because I love you thus, I would you save;
His arms are far more cruel than the grave!

XV.

JUDETH.

They are so now, or to my heart appear,
Since to my arms the grave lies very near,
And in it is, to this o'erburdened breast,
The promised sweetness of untroubled rest,
While far beyond its darkened portals glows
A Heaven where no cruel hands oppose.

RAHAB.

Judeth, my daughter, cease this foolish speech!
My curse upon the hearts such folly teach!
High time indeed was it that I recall
You from the folly of such maddening thrall!
To think the last of all my generous line,
Whose tenets still our crowning glory shine,
Should all forget, — my teaching, too, forego,
And follow leaders in a creed so low
Its birthplace reeks infectious with a name
That honest lips refuse to speak for shame!
Nay! nay! A thousand times I still must say,
And to your latest breath will answer, Nay!

XVI.

JUDETH.

That ends my plea; but for that Teacher's sake
Their best defence my stammering lips shall make,

Nor you, though cruel, dare not me deny:
You taught me truth and know they cannot lie!
What I have seen the pledge of truth my word,
Nor here relate what I from others heard.
At Cana's feast I saw his power divine
Change crystal water into ruby wine:
At Jordan's stream I saw from clouds above
Shekinah's fire, descending like a dove,
Rest on his head and burn, a kindling flame,
And all around irradiant became!
And at Capernaum of Galilee,
That city nestling by its inland sea,
Where we in sojourn passed delightful time
In listening to the Master's words sublime,
In one short day three miracles he wrought
On souls despairing that his mercy sought.
Of these three, two occurred before my eyes,
And filled the gaping throng with mute surprise.
The first a woman, haggard, pale, and lean,
From abscess dying, and by law unclean;
She pressed upon the throng where he passed by,
With eager haste, hope burning in her eye,
And touched the 'broidered blue of his short stole,
And in an instant was made pure and whole!
Two blind I saw, beyond physician's might,
Both at his touch receive anew their sight.
Man's skill, his magic spells, deceptive art,
In work like this might do the whole or part,
But one thing which he wrought upon that day
No man dare answer for it in that way.
Jairus, ruler such as thou art, there
A daughter had most comely, young, and fair;
Seized by a mortal sickness skill defies,
Before the Master could be called she dies.
I saw her in the throes of mortal pain.
If she died not, Death ne'er shall kill again;
And yet (this I saw not) when Jesus spoke,
From out that death as from a sleep she woke!
But this I saw, — her living, sound and well,
Without a trace of sickness left to tell
Of wasting fever and the days of pain
When at his touch she was restored again.

XVII.

RAHAB.

There, that will do, my daughter! This long strain
Has weakened vitals and distorted brain
Until your vision changes desert sands
Of Fancy's realms into enchanted lands.
Oh! what have I now done, what fatal deed?
The voice of those who warned I would not heed
Until too late. I fear the fatal draught
Of this stark madness has been surely quaffed.

JUDETH.

My father, what you hear you still refuse,
And of my fancied madness make excuse;
For, save for this, my tale you must believe:
Too well you know my lips would not deceive.
Like that proud city where these works were wrought
Who saw, confessed, and then received him not,
So you reject the truth, my word deny,
And through the lack of reason make me lie.
How weak the pretext! Nought such plea avails,
And to convince yourself it wholly fails:
So nothing more have I to answer now,
Since to me reason you will not allow.

RAHAB.

Peace, child! In love and sorrow I command:
Its loss, if lost, is charged not to my hand.

JUDETH.

Father, will you yet hear and grant one prayer?
It is the last I make to you.

RAHAB.

To spare
You pain, and if in sparing I can please,
Ask, — nay, command : I grant you such as these.

XVIII.

JUDETH.

Nay, it will turn my pain to pleasure : this
It is, and nothing I can see amiss
In granting it.   Our cousin Martha you
Most surely know is wrought of caution : true
She is what you now call a Nazarene, —
And say by it you know not what you mean, —
No matter : what I want is this, no more ;
Now, I was wrested almost from her door,
And left scant time to say a brief farewell, —
No word of explanation.   I would tell
Her something of the cause.   Six moons or so,
And not a word since then between us, who
Scarce any week, in all these years gone by,
Sent not a letter and received reply.
This is the prayer by love to love preferred :
To her I now would write, if but a word, —
A simple greeting love from me must claim, —
And underneath it simply write my name.

RAHAB.

Request most simple ! nor will I confine
Your letter to one simple written line :
Write all you wish, save that you nothing say
Of this new — something, call it what you may ;
Nor write to Lazarus, nor of him speak.
I trust your truth ; command you will not break :
There, child, just see how easy 't is to please !

JUDETH.

Yes, father, in such little things as these :
But then I am content.   The day is warm,
And I must sleep ere I this task perform —
You are not gone ?   If you anon can spare,
Send Haddan hither.   Kiss me ; softly, there !
I now would woo coy Sleep, whose heavy wings
To these sad eyes no soothing solace brings !
I will be true in his firm faith in me,
But oh how hard, how hard the task will be !
If I can sleep one little, shortened hour,
It then may be that hope will cheer once more.

XIX.

The evening shadows from Mount Olivet
Fall over Bethany ere sun is set;
Now through their deep'ning shades that trail along
There came, with night's ever-returning throng,
A messenger to Martha's open door,
And in his hand a written missive bore:
'T was Haddan; and in low obeisance bent
He gave to her the letter Judeth sent;
And as he gave would then have turned away
To journey back, had she not bade him stay.

MARTHA.

Stay, Haddan! haste not from us to depart,
For weary somewhat journeying thou art:
A cup of wine, some figs, I pray, partake,
For your kind care in this, for Judeth's sake;
Pray go you in; a servant to the stall
Will lead your beast and there await your call.

HADDAN.

I may not tarry: Rahab gave command
That when I gave this letter in your hand
I should return straightway.

MARTHA.

            A breath at least
From dust and heat is due to man and beast.

HADDAN.

Well, as you will: I am content to do
In this affair what seemeth best to you.

MARTHA.

Stay! just a word: how doth our Judeth seem?

HADDAN.

Like one asleep and walking in a dream!
She answers all we ask; talks some, and yet
Her eyes remain for hours with sad gaze set
On nothing, while her face is white and thin,
Her robes so loose that two could get within.

MARTHA.

What of an answer back?

HADDAN.

Just at the gate
She touched my sleeve, and said for me to wait
And bring what answer you saw fit to give.

MARTHA.

You will await its writing?

HADDAN.
Yes.

XX.

MARTHA.

Long live
You and your children! Pray you walk within;
Your wine awaits : to write I must begin.
Here, Mary! Lazarus! hasten! Haddan brings
Love's own sweet message on his snowy wings.
'T is Judeth sends it, but to me : yet all
May catch some fragrance as its sweet dews fall.

MARY.

A letter? And from Judeth? Who hath brought?
'T is passing strange that she of us has thought!

LAZARUS.

Hush, Mary! I but now believed that you
Had learned humility both deep and true.

MARY.

I have at his dear feet bowed low, but yet
The old rebellious heart makes me forget.

LAZARUS.

Enough! Let us now hear the letter read.
That is her hand, but weak and faint, instead
Of her strong characters.

MARTHA (*reading*).

" My dear beloved,
The love of God, or pity else, has moved
My father, that he gives me leave to write.
Until this hour, since on that hateful night
I entered here from you just snatched away,
No word would he allow nor letter. Nay!
Beyond these walls my feet have never gone,
And all the faces I have looked upon
Were father's, Haddan's, and my maid's. No word
Beyond what they would bring me have I heard, —
No syllable of you nor of the Cause.
But writing of this further I must pause :
He has forbidden it. But I may tell
How I do love you all so true and well ;
How ev'ry day, how every separate hour,
Your love, your kindness, do my thoughts devour.
And in the silence of my chamber here,
I can but think that you are very near !
And when the wind sighs in its sweetest moans,
The sounds half-syllable your very tones.
And where the lamplight darkly wavering falls,
I see your shadowy faces on the walls !

XXI.

" You are so near to me, at morn I miss
From off my lips your nightly honeyed kiss ;
And yet I 've felt it there to me so plain
That I reached out my hands to you in vain, —
You were a shadowy vision ! Oft I see
Beside the blue-tinged billows of the Galilee
The Master — There ! that line blot with a tear ;
It came before I thought, from memories dear.
I have grown thin since last you saw me ; this
Because I am kept in : my walks I miss,
And the long climbs up on Mount Olivet —
Its radiant glory, how can I forget !
And its fair scenes and — I must hush my heart
And let those days in silence now depart !
Oh, how I love them, Martha ! them and you !
You must not think your Judeth's heart untrue ;

It is so true it has grown sick without
You : if of that you could have smallest doubt,
The thought would shame you, could you now but see
The fading shadow that responds for me.
I passed my mirror — accidental now —
And saw reflected there both form and brow,
And thought it was some ghostly stranger guest,
Who by mischance was in my garments dressed,
And would have spoken it as such instead ;
But at my smile the strange delusion fled,
And left a mask in place still standing there,
That had my eyes, my teeth, and dusky hair !
If you could touch me with your hand, — could kiss
My lips, — I know your power would equal his
Who raised Jairus' daughter — there ! again
My thoughts reflect that written on the brain.
But I must cease, though scarce begun to write,
And bid you all a long and fond good-night !
Send by the hand of Haddan message back,
And let your letter nought of interest lack ;
Since, strangely as it seems, my father did
Not message back from you to me forbid, —
Nor from another, if such choose to send, —
And if, beside you, yet I have a friend.
At least from you I shall expect reply :
But I must cease this letter now.   Good-by !
Since Haddan doth me patiently await,
And I would meet him with this at the gate.
Thy sister, Judeth, kisses this to thee ! ''

XXII.

LAZARUS.

And not a word in it to or of me !
I have a letter written long, — would send
It to her, if I thought 't would not offend :
Would Haddan carry it ?

BOTH.

And pray, why not ?
You heard his interdict.

LAZARUS

True! I forgot,
And I will haste, and, as you women do,
Will send it all and add a postscript, too!
But we must write at once, for Haddan kind,
In his return should not be kept behind.

XXIII.

The letters done, and Haddan through his wine,
Just as the last hot rays of evening shine
On Nebo's crest beyond the silent sea,
He mounts and rides, with heart both light and free,
Back to the city, whose still-open gate
Will not upon his loitering footsteps wait.
All watch him start, and many greetings go
With him to her who waits for him below
In that fair home, in all its wealth possessed,
That hath no spot in which her heart finds rest.
He brings her Martha's letter: if he bore
Within his sash another letter more,
No eye has seen it; even his were blind
To aught like this, just as his heart was kind.
And more: he carried with him not unknown
The sorrows of that home which now had flown;
While in each heart a singing bird now sung
Its song of joy with notes from silvery tongue!

XXIV.

The lamps are lighted in old Rahab's home,
And hast'ning footsteps hither go and come:
The beasts and fowls inconstant clamor keep
As one by one they settle into sleep.
From out the garden, flashing still with bloom,
Floats through the house a faint but sweet perfume:
Rest settles down with shadows of the night,
And Care prepares to wing her silent flight.
Now Judeth, restless of the long delay
That follows on kind Haddan's lengthened stay, —
Forgetful that the hour's delay to meet
May make the hour of meeting doubly sweet, —

Glides from her room and through the trellised hall,
A shrinking ghost that hugs the shelt'ring wall,
Down the stone stair which to the garden led,
Nor Night more silent than her hast'ning tread:
There, as she passes by the inner wall,
Behind she hears a voice as softly call
As night-bird's cooing; turning, face to face,
Meets Haddan there within the shadowy place.
No word he utters, but her fingers clasp
Some object slipping from his ling'ring grasp:
" Go to your room," he whispers, " his command,
That he the answer bear in his own hand."

XXV.

Back through the dusk with eager feet she fled,
No echo whisp'ring of her coming tread:
With breath hard drawn she urged her eager flight,
While her loud heart-beats startle the still night.
Ent'ring within, the lamplight's softened glow
Shows a rich flush on upturned cheek and brow,
As she, with hard-clasped hands and thankful prayer,
Holds in them the dear message hidden there.
She has not read, indeed she does not know
If in it be the words of joy or woe:
Nor yet by word or look has she been told
If aught within the parchment pages hold.
She knows instinctive — that is woman's pow'r,
Her strength and refuge in the trying hour —
That Lazarus sends it; that her fingers clutch
What is to her made sacred by his touch.
She does not open — nay, she did not look
Upon it, while her fragile fingers shook
With eager haste from sound of coming feet,
As they the crumpled parchment now secrete
Within her bosom's snowy depths to lie
Secure from closest search and prying eye:
While ghastly pallor spreads from cheek to brow,
So richly flushed with blushes until now;
From head to foot she shivers with a chill,
As one grown sick from grave and sudden ill.

XXVI.

Her father enters at her low command,
But him to welcome she can hardly stand;
He sees her ashen face and trembling limbs,
Her eye unsteady, that dilating swims
In its deep socket, half engulfed in tears,
The two fold witness of her joys and fears.
Pained in her looks such weakness to behold,
His eager fears make him unseemly bold
To haste to her with quick, impetuous stride,
His fear o'ercoming now his haughty pride;
And to the winds his studied sternness flies
As with alarm, all else forgetting, cries,

RAHAB.

What ails thee, daughter? What of care or pain?
The body's weakness or the troubled brain?
If these oppress thy heart, their pangs endure,
And in this parchment find for them a cure.
Here is the answer, Martha — noble friend —
Doth to thy loving letter in love send:
It came unsealed, inviting me to read,
Of which, had I suspicion, was no need;
And so I thank her, — in your answer say
As much, — and send it back the coming day,
If it so please you.   Kiss me now good-night;
I leave you with your friend and dreams more bright.

JUDETH.

Thanks, dearest father! you have made me glad;
With such kind friends I should no more be sad.
So he approves her letter!   I will see
If his approval is approved by me.

XXVII.

JUDETH (*reading*).

"Bethany, Abib, second month and year:
Dear Judeth, — and to me you are most dear, —
At Haddan's hand — God give his soul sweet peace! —
Your kindly letter I received, and these

Most hurried lines, it please, Mary and I,
By his returning hand, send in reply.
Your saddened parting gave us all great pain,
But this your letter makes to us quite plain,
And the occasion; so that all the more
We love you, dearest, — better than before,
If that could be! We miss you from our home
And hearts, and hope and pray the day will come —
May God speed on its hours! — when once again
We make one household, you in it to reign.
We are all well to-day; but housewife cares
Somewhat upon my frugal patience wears,
Since Mary has grown zealous in the Cause,
And somewhat from me needed help withdraws.
I said we all were well: I spoke too fast;
My brother has for months appeared downcast, —
A kind of weakening in a general way,
But little ailing, save that for a day
Or two he hath grown feeble like and weak,
But nothing serious, as I may speak.
I ofttimes think of those times past when we
Went down to Jordan and the Galilee;
Do you remember, should I ask? and yet
How many learn such lessons to forget!
But, speaking of these times, I would recall
One thing that happened, — let it speak for all, —
When down in Galilee, you know, at Nain,
The Master raised the widow's son. Again
We saw and talked with him, and strange the tales
He tells of what he saw. My credence fails,
They are so wonderful! And they relate
That, of the blind man at the eastern gate
Who sat and begged, — blind from his infancy, —
You know him, and have passed him oft with me,
And gave an alms at every asking — well,
The case is wonderful of him they tell.
I did not see it, but the Pharisees
About its spreading fame are ill at ease.
That he was blind I know, and so do you,
And that he sees is known now to be true
Throughout the city. Now but one thing more, —
Of this I should have spoken just before.

The Master supped with us since you were here,
And Mary was content to leave the cheer
And household duties to my care, and seat
Herself — the careless child — at Jesus' feet!
I did protest — I know I may have been
Somewhat impatient; yet I did not mean
To be — that she should aid me with the cares
And vexing duties of the house affairs.
You know how trying oft that such things be,
When all the house is filled with company.
She looked so innocent — God bless her life! —
It seems a sin that she should taste of strife;
And then the Master, lifting up his head,
And smiling as he did so, gently said :
'O Martha, Martha, thou of many things
Dost trouble make; know that but one thing brings
Thee rest : as Mary has, choose that to-day,
The one good thing which naught can take away.'
O fie! There, Haddan calls; his figs and wine —
Light fare to guests, and they will lightly dine —
Are finished, and he would away, while I
Have just begun to write! Well, please reply
At your first day, if that day be to-morrow :
Each day's neglect is but an added sorrow.
Your friend in love,
                    "Martha."

XXVIII.

JUDETH.

                              She much imparts
Of news to me, and shows the loving hearts
Her home doth hold for me. Ah! what is this
My careless eye would now so nearly miss?
A postscript! Well, they say a woman's letter
Is not complete without it. All the better,
For in it are the sweets. No, 't is a line
With hurried pen, and hand both weak and fine,
From Mary, added in a hasty scrawl
So dim it scarcely can be read at all.
" Dear Judeth, on this closely written page
I find a vacant corner I engage

To write a line while Haddan waits. Be strong,
For it is better far, we suffer wrong
Than do it. Know my love and his are true:
We pray, we think, we live and work, for you ;
Your cause is ours : the Master bids you stand,
Nor fails the cause that resteth in his hand!
To further write ill with my mood accords,
And struggling thought drown in a sea of words.
Your sister,
      " Mary."
                Thanks, a hundred times!
Those words to me are as the sweet bells' chimes,
That tinkle at the High Priest's feet, with smell
Of incense offered breathing prayer as well !
O sweet heart-sisters, how your words do still
The tempest in this bosom, — softly fill
Its sighing chambers with a calm, sweet peace,
Like Galilee when its loud ravings cease !

XXIX.

But here lies on my heart still one more weight
That I must lift, for in it lies my fate.
Have I deceived ? Am I a recreant grown,
That e'en his love would blush to know and own ?
He is deceived : bear I a guilty part ?
Shall me my conscience judge or shall my heart ?
Both, and their judgment here I will abide ;
Whatever they decree Love shall decide.
O Love's sweet messenger! on thy wings
What new delights this speaking missive brings !
I clasp thee to my heart, and fondly cling
To thy sure promise, faith's best offering ;
And wait and pause, until the time complete,
Anticipation drinking ev'ry sweet.
There ! I will read, and, eyes, let loose your springs ;
Joy, plume for flight your highest-soaring wings ;
Cheeks wreathed in lilies, bloom in rose once more ;
And, lips, resume your smiles so bright before ;
While I now drink with heart of thirsting pain
From the sweet spring which Love has found again.
But stay, the door ! I would not curious eye

Upon my love's sweet message now would spy :
There, now all's safe. Ha! Does the polished steel
The joy which fills my heart, unconscious, feel ?
It gleams and burns, and o'er my form and face
Throws back in smiles its truth-repeating rays.
Well may you smile, my old familiar friend,
To know my tears and sadness have an end ;
For all these moons, since my return, when seen,
Bathed in a flood of tears my face has been.

XXX.

Sweet messenger ! Uncertain yet, I hold
Your snowy wings and kiss you fold by fold,
As if my lips that thus you fondly greet
Can taste within, the dainty, hidden sweet.
I now unfold ; the softly rustling leaf
Would cheat my ear with a sweet, vague belief
That from the breath he breathed upon each word
A whispering echo in each one is heard !
Now I can read — stay ! what is this ? The date
Is Chislu ! This is Abib : separate
So long ? And yet to me it doth appear
That ev'ry month hath been a dreary year !
And he hath written, waiting, hoping on,
To reach me with it all this time now gone !

(*Reads.*)

" Dear Judeth, how your cheering smile I miss !
And yet my lips glow with your parting kiss :
But just to think ! it has been o'er a week
Since I have seen you, or have heard you speak !
The sun hath lost its brightness, and the skies
Are dull and leaden to my hopeless eyes.
I could have borne this better, — could now bear
The heavy burden, did you not, too, share :
That is the load which deepens all my grief,
Since what I bear to you brings no relief.
I daily walk out to Mount Olivet,
But find there nothing for me but regret.
You know we thought the views were beautiful;
Now suddenly they have grown tame and dull.

Two scenes there are that I can look upon
And find no vestige of their beauty gone.
One is Jerusalem, for thou art there,
And thoughts of thee still keep it fresh and fair ;
The other Bethlehem, of nothing shorn,
Since Christ, our dearest friend, was in it born.
O Judeth ! such two hearts, if all else fail,
Could change to Paradise Gehenna's vale !

XXXI.

" I often sit where we last sat the morn
When you from me, I well may say, wert torn —
Why did you leave me so abruptly ? Why
Would not you hear my heart's despairing cry
When I ran after you in maddening chase,
In that as fruitless as 't was eager race ?
Did you believe I meant what I there said ?
My meaning was the opposite instead ;
I was not ready for the parting : nay,
For that Time's calendar has not a day !
But you must go I knew ; I would prepare
Some way — some hand that might this message bear ;
That was not done : we trust but Love and Chance
To cure this fault and still our cause advance.
And in that hope I write, and trust, and pray,
In constant faith in you, come now what may.
I will not now write more, for words avail
As Love is true, without it they but fail ;
But will await to see how these few speed :
If aught they lack, between the lines pray read.
I know you think me cool if I end thus,
Yet words are but Love's chains.
                              " Your Lazarus."
It is most brief, — so brief its shortness pains.
If it is true that " words are but Love's chains,"
Yet Love loves words if they in love are breathed :
They are the flowers in which his form lies wreathed —
But stay, another page ! Now chide not this,
Until we know if aught we do not miss.
Its date is Abib, caland week to-day —
My love, your kind forgiveness now I pray :
Impatient was I of your lines too few,
And judged before I read your letter through.

XXXII.

(Reads again.)

"May God be praised, my Judeth, he should send
To us in Haddan such a noble friend !
But stay ! I may be now too fast to write
To you this letter you did not invite ;
For not a word to me in all you wrote
Was sent, as I can all your letter quote,
I was so eager listening, and heard
From end to end and never missed a word.
I said as much to Martha, but her plea
Was your restraint : this seemed enough for me,
Since I remember well the pledge you gave
To meet me here or join me in the grave.
Since you have gone, how often have I thought
Of this, and light have of the Master sought ;
And he doth make it plain, — so very plain
That I can never fear or doubt again.
Oh that I could but see and talk with you !
Could give his words, so noble and so true
Their very force convinces.   Thus, he saith,
There is no second life except through death.
The seed that falls into the ground there dies,
But from that seed a second life shall rise.
How true !   We tried it in the garden here,
You must remember, from a ripened ear
Of corn ; and when you hunted for the grain
The empty husk was found where it had lain !
Where was the life ?   Was it or lost or fled ?
Not with the grain, for that we saw was dead.
Life never dies ; it changes its abode :
From seed to plant it goes, from man to God !
The Grave keeps nothing : dust in dust is lost ;
The life it never claims, whate'er its boast.
' If man dies, shall he live again ? ' cries Job.
' When that the worms destroy this outer robe,
This house of clay, yet in my flesh shall I
See God ! ' How can he if the soul shall die ?
No, no ! Not in the grave, but far beyond,
Cry out my hopes, with faith as sure as fond,
We two shall meet again when Death shall part,
And, living, join the loving hand and heart.

XXXIII.

" Believe this, Judeth, O my love, believe!
I know the truth your heart would now receive
If you could see the Master, — hear his speech,
The wondrous truths his simple lessons teach ;
Your doubt would now be gone, and you, with me,
The truth of what I say would plainly see.
Pray pardon me that I so use the time
To press upon you now this truth sublime,
That you might wish to use for other things
That I should say ; but, darling, somehow clings
The thought upon my thought, which you expressed,
That in the grave alone you could find rest.
I cannot shake it loose ; and more, to-day
Your words upon my heart their burden lay :
In them my soul grows sad, until I seem
Like one who, not asleep, walks in a dream.
I 've tried — now try — to write of something gay,
But this is ever rising in my way ;
And like a veil let down, intensely black,
Hides ev'ry smile, and keeps the sunshine back !
And then I feel so strangely ! Through my brain
Shoots, as I write, a fast recurring pain :
There falls a blackness on the quivering page,
And then — What? Haddan calls? It seems an age
Before I heard from you, and now to me
It seems there lies before, Eternity
Ere we shall meet to speak again, — two seas,
And this small point of time dividing these !
If this the end now here, O Judeth, live
The life of faith ! Thy heart, believing, give
Unto the Master ! — I must close — they call —
My love, my heart, my life, — you have them all !
And ever yours they are in truth, and thus
I write you from my heart.
                              "Your Lazarus."

XXXIV.

Ah, sad, sad heart ! This neither soothes nor cheers,
And my expectant smiles are drowned in tears !

Why should he write so sad ? why should he wring
My quivering heart until each separate string
Would snap with pain, had not his love the power
To soothe somewhat the agony of the hour !
Sure of his love — and yet not of it sure
If there the grave ! How can I this endure ?
Should he lie dead — O God ! what means this pain
That seizes now upon both heart and brain ?
I must not think it, yet there lies before
The shadow trailing through my open door.
This must not be ! I will such fate defy,
And with bright smiles bid all my fears go by.
Nay, I will laugh this sadness from my eyes,
And turn to song my heart's desponding sighs ;
Forget such sorrows while I court Hope's smile,
And write sweet words his sadness to beguile :
Words which, of love beyond physician's skill,
Has power to cure his heart's distempered ill.
Unto that task at once I will address
My powers to please in words that charm and bless :
Most confident am I at eve's return
From this a perfect cure in him to learn.
So, World, good-by ! Good-night to sighs and tears !
O Love, send words whose sweetness soothes and cheers,
And I will write them in my heart's red wine
And Love shall glow and run along each line,
Until the message, full of healing balm,
Shall fill his troubled heart with holy calm !
Good-night, sweet love ! I kiss your eyelids down,
And from Care's brow smooth out each knotted frown.

XXXV.

The sun hangs low along Judea's hills,
The twilight's fitful glow each valley fills,
As Haddan rides, despondent now and slow,
Along the Kidron's valley, all aglow
With golden beauty, as if now he bore
Some evil news to those who wait before.
He winds along the way, nor heeds how late
The hour as he goes through the city's gate.
More careless still, he winds along the streets,

Nor e'en salutes the wondering friends he meets,
Who stare in wonder as they fall behind,
Since he to all was courteous, frank, and kind.
At last through Rahab's waiting gate he rides,
Dismounting then along the court he glides
To reach old Rahab's room, when in the way
He meets with Judeth! Lion brought to bay
Looks not more fierce, altho' his frown belies
The humid softness of his gentle eyes.
" Why hedge my path, you bold and careless one,
When you perceive I would this meeting shun ? "
" Have you my letter? "   " No, I left it there."
" I mean his answer, then."   " None such I bear."
" What! none from him?   Did he not write me ? "   " No."
" O! Haddan why do you torment me so ?
If it were not — if I but dare — you see
You have, and so advantage take of me."
" Nay, Judeth! speak not so : you make my heart
Bleed doubly sore by this most unjust smart."
" Why, Haddan! what is wrong?   Is he — I know
There is sad news!   Pray tell me, Haddan !   O !
My father's God! what shall I, shall I do ?
Your very looks declare my worst fears true."
" Peace, Judeth, peace!   It is not near so bad
As you imagine — yet the news is sad.
Take this!   I would have spared you till I saw
Your father and his counsel asked.   But draw
What comfort there is in them from these lines,
For much warm light there is beyond them shines,
As sorrow seen through Love's dissolving tears
Distorts the vision magnified by fears."
She seized the packet — down the court-yard flew —
An instant more and she is lost from view,
As down the long and dimly lighted hall
She mingles with the shadows on the wall :
Faint, fluttering footsteps echo on the floor,
Their softened cadence dying toward her door.
Upon the night a sudden brightness gleams,
And through the door upon the darkness streams :
With sudden quenching of the flashing light,
Roll back again the heavy folds of night ;
A moment, then upon the breathless air

In wail is heard a broken heart's despair.
From Judeth's room the light flashed on the eye,
And echoes there her low and wailing cry.

XXXVI.

A wild commotion follows soon below:
Lights flash in hands that hurry to and fro,
To centre soon at Judeth's silent door,
Through which her cries had pierced so late before.
They wait — they listen! Rahab gently calls:
No answer on their waiting ears now falls;
Out through the night the quivering echo flies,
A lessening shade of sound until it dies;
And silence, startled by his voice, once more
Returns the watchful sentry at her door.
Her father, by this deathlike stillness stung
To agony, his hands in terror wrung,
Till Haddan, trembling, to his side draws near,
And, stooping, whispers something in his ear.
Old Rahab starts at the low-whispered word,
Stands waiting as if he imperfect heard,
Then lifts the latch: the light an instant blinds,
Until relief from shading hand he finds;
And, entering then, before their startled eyes
Upon the floor Judeth unconscious lies.
They lift her up; her stiffening fingers clasp
A written parchment crumpled in her grasp:
With trembling fingers this her father wrings
From hand which to it yet unconscious clings.
They gently lift her to a low divan,
And there, with chafing hands and cooling fan,
Sweet pungent spices, aromatic wines,
Revive her: then her father reads the lines
Writ on the crumpled parchment, short and dim,
E'en in that light scarce legible to him.
They read :
　　　　　" Dear Judeth,
　　　　　　　　　　Pray our thanks receive
For your kind letter ; nor too much, dear, grieve
At this short answer. Lazarus is ill,
Yet his disease does not at all times kill.

I cannot now write more; Haddan will tell
You all.
　　　　"Your sister in sad haste : Farewell!"
"O Lazarus!" now Judeth feebly cries,
"They hold him from me while he yonder dies!
Oh, give him back to me, or let me go
And in the grave with him there hide my woe!"

CANTO SEVENTH.

INTO THE NIGHT.

I.

WE look upon the face of one beloved
As something beautiful.　The heart is moved
By the soft cadence of the rippling thrill
Which quickens as we gaze, and leaps until
It seems the sturdy blows must break the bars
Of its pent bound which with its freedom wars.
We love the flowers so beautiful, which grow
In our fair gardens.　As we watch them blow,
Our hearts are glad because their smiles are sweet,
And make the earth more lovely for our feet.
We love our homes: of all the fair of earth,
No spot so fair as this!　Here Love hath birth,
Of Love's fair children born ; and here abide
The smiles of God and ev'ry grace beside.
The grave hath none of these.　Its ev'ry grace
Death steals; of beauty robs the form and face,
And makes them all unsightly, so that love
Becomes a memory, lifting us above
The sodden earth where still our treasures lie :
Is it because man is not born to die?
Is it because the man immortal springs,
Like bird exultant, on Hope's buoyant wings,
To higher heights of life, that here below
We drink from springs which from such sources flow?

II.

When flowers fall and wither at our feet,
Doth Love mourn long because of their lost sweet?
We scatter them upon the grave, and yet
When strown the withered garlands we forget.
Why is this so?   Were these dead flowers the last,
Would we not to the withered buds hold fast?
The home is broken, one by one they go;
The hearths that know them, soon no more shall know;
Forsaken, desolate, with weeds o'ergrown,
Where moles but hide beneath the broken stone.
Why should this be?   A Paradise below
Will man on earth unwilling still forego?
At parting, turn not back regretful eyes
While from it mounting to the azure skies?

III.

Read we the lines, unwritten, from the page
Which here these truths in man our thoughts engage:
The rose may wither and its blossoms fall,
And soon its beauty shall be lost to all;
Yet in the flower a second blossom grows,
The hidden roots a second life disclose.
The rose that dies, in seeming, is not dead,
Although in withered bloom its leaves lie shed;
In it this promise man cannot deny:
Though leaves may wither, blossoms never die.
The home lies desolate, yet from its door
New homes as sweet have but gone out before:
Though walls may crumble, hearthstones may decay,
The home itself shall never pass away!
Behold a truth which hidden in this lies, —
The body perishes, man never dies:
For what is dearest and is loved the most,
Once made, though it may change, is never lost.
There is no death if man dies not.   Decreed,
The fruit bears in it self-producing seed:
And as we follow out these natural laws,
Behind it all still lies the great First Cause.
Why further seek?   It is enough to know

That flowers still bloom, reviving grasses grow :
How ?   Here we pause, and silently we stand,
For life we see, but not the guiding hand.
Because that power we fail at last to find,
Shall we deny the living power behind ?
God's truths man questions, says they cannot be,
The proof he gives is this, — he cannot see !
As well the blind might say there is no sun,
Through lack of sight to prove that there is one.
If breath should wait man's power to analyze,
How it gives life, with all the ifs and whys,
The world would die while waiting — and in vain —
And not one breath of sweeter air would gain.
If truths so simple he cannot disclose,
How can he hope God's wisdom to oppose ?
Thought follows thought, and in the train we see
Dissolving vistas of infinity,
Where life and death work out their perfect plan
To leave evolved the best of all in man.
We leave this question where we found it, dark :
Our arrows fly no nearer to the mark ;
Yet hoping, ere these pages are wrought through,
Some clearer light may burst upon the view,
And we may see more clearly and divine
That which we feel, yet cannot now define.

IV.

The coming morn is purpling Olivet,
But in one home the lamps are lighted yet
In Bethany's fair town, nor passing feet
Belated here are heard upon the street :
The silent hour in eastern towns is this,
The sweetest, which in other lands we miss.
And yet within that home no hour of rest
Has hushed in sleep and soothed the troubled breast;
And from its windows, watching for the dawn,
Where trembling hands the curtains have withdrawn,
Are eyes now wet with tears, whose eager gaze
A prayer is wafting in the glance they raise.
That face familiar and the home is known,
And both to us on yesternight were shown.

Let us go in with lightly muffled tread,
With feet now bare for sandalled ones instead,
And greet the watcher as she waits the light
With Hope's good-morning to her sad good-night!

V.

We pass the outer portal through the court,
And should we tarry here our stay is short,
Since darkness hides, or dimly here is shown,
All that a curious eye may gaze upon.
Along the lighted hall our steps we turn,
Ascend the outer stair where lamps still burn,
Until our feet have reached the chamber door
Where we the anxious watcher saw before.
We pause ; the house is hushed like halls of death,
Save that a whisper faint as zephyr's breath
Rustles the ghostly curtains in the light
Each moment deepening on the fading night.
We pass within : the light has now grown strong,
And on the floor the shadows lie along,
From lamp and window, while the glowing day
The lamplight robs of its illuming ray,
As lifted curtains let the crimson beams
Flow through the room in bright and gladsome streams,
Which, falling on the watcher's upturned brow,
Upon it sheds a golden glory now,
And in this crown of light, sweet in its grace,
A saint prefigured, shines forth Mary's face.

VI.

A moment yet upon the eastern skies
Is fixed the gaze of her far-reaching eyes ;
All else unheeded now has ceased to be
So eager is her soul's intensity :
And as she looks with ever steadfast sight,
Forward she leans as if to meet the light,
Then, springing up with almost joyous cry,
She greets the sun's first rays along the sky
With hands hard clasped, and lips which tremble there
In a hot outburst of soul-thankful prayer.
Why turns she to the light, — why to the sun,

And not the Temple, as the Jew had done?
She is a Jew, and yet at this calm hour
She turns unto the newly rising power,
The Sun of Righteousness, whose coming brings
Health to the sick and " healing on his wings."

VII.

As ends her prayer, in low and gentle hum
Hushed voices from the room adjoining come :
She hears the sound, and, softly passing through,
A scene not all unpleasing meets her view.
Upon a bed in snowy whiteness dressed,
A suffering form in fever's hot unrest
Lies tossing there, but now the throbbing brain
A time sweet respite has from maddening pain.
And this is Lazarus ! Stooping o'er him there
The gentle Martha, soothing with her care
And words of comfort, answering, if she can,
Those questions woman answers best for man.
When in the battle — in the wearing siege —
Where kings have rule and man to them is liege,
Where sturdy hand gives hard and telling stroke,
Where servitude bears unrequiting yoke,
Where homes are wrought from Nature's rugged soil,
And raging seas invite to desperate spoil ;
There man by man stands fast to aid and stay,
Guide in the road, and cheer along the way :
But when disease the strong has prostrate bound,
When grinning Death looks in through gaping wound,
No hand like woman's then to give relief,
No voice like hers to soothe our pain and grief !

VIII.

Hark ! she is speaking, yet can scarce be heard
The half-articulate, dissolving word.

MARTHA.

Peace ! We a messenger without delay
Will send, and soon he will be on the way :
Mary will write the letter, and I know
Friend Rahab will her earnest prayer allow.

MARY.

Whatever, sister, he doth now desire,
It matters not, of me if he require
Life-service, or if life itself demand ;
I freely give all with a willing hand.

MARTHA.

No such stern task : for Judeth he would send.
In us he hath both sister, nurse, and friend,
But something more than these this hour he needs.

MARY.

And when the messenger for Judeth speeds,
Why send not one unto the Master, too?

MARTHA.

Aye, both ! I had forgotten.

LAZARUS.

What say you ?
My ears have grown so dull since this fierce pain
Hath burned and seared my ever-aching brain
That every sound is far, is very far,
And whispers on my quickened senses jar
Almost like smiting thunder.   You will send
The messenger ?

MARTHA.

Yes, brother, to that end
Mary will write and start him on his way.

LAZARUS.

Did she not send a letter yesterday ?
Of this there is some memory undefined
Now fleeting in the chaos of my mind.
How is this ?

MARTHA.

Yea, she sent to you a letter,
Which I will read to you when you get better.

LAZARUS.

Nay, read it now, I pray you ; it will be
Almost as if she now should talk to me.

Pray read it, sister, else I cannot wait
Her coming unto me.

MARTHA.

It is not late —
It scarce is risen morning, and indeed
The sun is lingering on the hills — but I will read:
" Dear Lazarus " —

LAZARUS.

Did she write that ? Is 't so ?
And writ in her own hand ?

MARTHA.

Here, I will show,
And you can see the writing.

LAZARUS.

Dear, sweet hand
That writ my name so sweetly ! — It is grand
To stand here thus this morning with the skies
A well of blue — but deeper are your eyes.
O Judeth, you do little know how rich —
How rich —

IX.

MARTHA.

O God ! his eyes begin to twitch,
And the wild light glares fiercely forth again,
As Fever's dusky wings o'ercloud his brain !
I feel its angry surges in his breath
As if its tempest now drove on to death.
Haste, Mary, haste the messenger to bring
The Lord beloved on Love's returning wing !
The fever now renews its fatal fires ;
When they burn out, then life itself expires.
Judeth will have full time if still delay
The feet that hasten o'er the nearer way :
While now the feet that speed to Him must fly
Across the miles which yet between us lie :
So grave the need, so pressing is the care,
For life grows faint, and Death waits not to spare.

X.

Speed the swift messengers! and there is need
That wings be added to their hastening speed.
For there is one still swifter in his flight
Who surely comes to meet the shades of night,
Which gather now in desolating gloom
About the borders of the opening tomb.
No skilled physician with his utmost care
Can stay the chilling currents rising there ;
No tender hand its patient ministry
Can backward turn a fate that is to be.
The voice of Love but calls to death-dulled ears ;
The failing heart is moved no more by tears ;
Sad faces which with scalding floods now burn
With hopeless eyes to dark'ning windows turn,
Where fall the shadows o'er their hope and day,
As night comes creeping through their curtains gray.
How sweet is night when with it comes repose !
But oh how dark when burdened by our woes !
Judeth comes not ! Why still this long delay ?
The morn was early, short indeed the way :
And hearts that love find wings when Love in pain
Cries out to them — nor will he cry in vain.
At last the messenger returns alone,
His message in his troubled face is shown :
The prayer refused, no other word is sent,
So breaking hearts must be with this content.
How much of bitterness unknown we bear
In silent, scornful interdict of prayer !

XI.

Speed the swift messenger, and bid him ride
Through lowly vale up rugged mountain-side,
For Death draws near — the Saviour still afar —
To let him in, life's gates now swing ajar.
The day is past ; the gloom, a double cloud,
Falls in the sombre pall of night and shroud ;
Yet he who in the morn rode forth, again
At the lone gate draws not returning rein,
Although the watchers, weary at their quest,

Cease not to listen, nor, discouraged, rest.
Why comes he not, or messenger at least?
Fear with his lingering absence has increased,
Since danger lurks in the broad light of day,
And stalks forth boldly in the open way.
Unconscious, Lazarus since the morning's dawn
Has tossed in fever as the day wore on,
And as the night turns to the ebbing tide
His life flows backward to the shadowy side
Of the great shoreless, ever-widening sea
Whose billows bound the wide Eternity.

XII.

Still lags the messenger: can he not find
That friend so ever constant, ever kind?
Have now his feet, in their long, tireless round,
Wandered afar to Israel's utmost bound?
If he but knew, on wings of love would fly
That soul of pity moved by sympathy.
Time could not stay nor distance force apart
The suffering friend from Christ's most loving heart!
Life lingers still as wears the night away,
Yet paling burns its torch at coming day;
Then for a moment it anew revives,
As life with death in their last conflict strives.

XIII.

The morning deepens into broader dawn,
The shadows fleeing from the light are gone,
And at the window once again is there
That watcher kneeling in a wrestling prayer
For life to him who yonder lies in pain,
Until the Lord Christ shall return again.
Hark! in the silence of the lonely street
Are echoes heard of slowly coming feet;
They draw still nearer! What the message borne
To those within? Shall they rejoice or mourn?
"The Master comes not!" Such the message brought:
Now are these stricken hearts with grief distraught;
Since hope through him has fled and Death appears,

And with their Lord's neglect now mocks their tears.
Their grief before this hour, though deep, had been
A sympathy to sorrow next akin,
Such as we feel when loved ones wracked with pain
In anguish cry, but soon are well again.
For them Death hath no fears, for well they know
That Christ the monster could with touch subdue ;
And when he comes, this best of earthly friends.
A word from him and all their sorrow ends.
So beat our hearts in careless hope possessed,
While scarce a troubled thought disturbs the breast,
As we beside some loved one sit content,
Nor see the threatening bow remorseless bent
To wing the poisoned shaft in deadly flight
The heart of our beloved with death to smite,
Until the veil, by hand revealing, drawn
Shows bow unbent — the hurtling arrow flown —
Still quivering in that breast before our eyes,
And our sweet friend, thus stricken, gasping dies,
While horror freezes with its deadly chill
Our heart, which in its agony stands still !

XIV.

So falls the blow on them.   At first their grief
In Christ had hoped of sure and swift relief :
No doubt obscured the blue of faith's fair sky,
Nor could they dream that Lazarus would die !
And so they watched with just enough of fear
To start in eyes of love a doubting tear, —
Not that he would not come, but, coming late,
Would leave too long the scale in hand of fate.
As still delayed his needed presence there,
Their hearts grew sorrowful in anxious prayer :
Then hope would spring anew in doubting breast,
And for a time would hush their fears to rest :
And so they hoped, doubted, believed, and prayed,
While yet the messenger through weary hours delayed,
And, when he came with his dread answer, still
Saw not the shadow of the coming ill,
Until it came in night so black and dread
They saw not Death until all hope was fled,
And he sat visible beside their dead !

XV.

The pent-up brook, which from its rocky source
Through mountain gorges holds its headlong course,
And brawling frets the banks its floods restrain,
Leaps from its rocky hold, and through the plain
Flows murmuring on, now singing as it flows,
Glad in its freedom which no rocks oppose,
Beneath blue skies, which smiling back its smiles
On troubled past which now no more beguiles :
No storms disturbing, on its gleaming sands
It rests contented as its breadth expands,
Within green banks beneath wide-spreading trees
Whose shadows cool while through them sings the breeze,
And bright flowers gleam along the mossy side
Whose stooping blossoms kiss its blushing tide,
Nor clouds affrighting with their angry frown,
Nor in its bosom drenching floods pour down.
And so it smiles and flows, and smiling sings
Its song made up of all these gladsome things ;
When, lo ! with skies as bright and earth as fair
As ever sun and summer painted there,
When with no note of warning, not a word
Of threatened danger's distant coming heard
From storm unseen, which o'er the mountains breaks,
Whose thunder, echoless, their caverns shakes,
Down through the gorge from whence the stream has fled,
With deepening thunder o'er its rocky bed,
Rushes an avalanche, whose watery wall,
A towering flood, engulfs and swallows all
Until the steep is reached ; then one wild spring
And the hoarse waters madly downward fling
Their seething torrents, and the gentle stream,
Which lay so sweetly in its summer dream,
Its flowery meads, its grassy banks and groves,
Its scenes of beauty which it courts and loves,
Its pride, its boast, its blessings broad and free,
All sunken lie in this devouring sea !
So lie man's hopes, his joys, his all o'erthrown
In the fierce floods of grief which bear him down !
Since. like the stream, he holds his destined course,
And like that stream life's storms rise at its source.

XVI.

At first the blow in silence they receive,
Benumbed and stricken far too deep to grieve;
So fierce it falls, the darkened senses reel
Beneath the shock, so great they cease to feel.
As when the spear the throbbing vitals gains,
The quivering shaft within the wound remains,
The steely blade which deals the deadly blow
Stops in its course the ruddy current's flow,
Until some kindly hand unkindly draws
The barbed death, and yet its hindering cause,
Then spouts the blood in torrents through the wound,
And the red life is poured along the ground, —
Thus sank this shaft so deep within their hearts,
The blow benumbing deadens all its smarts,
Until some hand to soothe their tearless pain
Withdraws the barbs the bitter floods restrain,
Then drowning eyes grow blind in floods of grief,
Which, wept away, bring solace and relief:
And after tears, with moanings low and faint,
Each thus bewails her loss in sad complaint.

XVII.

MARTHA.

O Lazarus, my Lazarus, how still
You lie!   And never, ah! never more will
Those white lips speak to me!   I clasp thy form
And kiss thy parted lips now coldly warm,
But passing through them there is now no breath,
Save the cold, icy chill which comes with death!
I kiss thy closing eyes and eyelids down!
Thy fair warm hair the death-damps softly drown:
I kiss those hands, so ready to bestow
Those gifts upon me I no more shall know!
Poor, faded hands!   Like flowers upon thy cheek,
They now are waxen grown, death-palsied, weak!
No pressure in them!   No responsive thrill,
As on thy breast they lie so white and still!

XVIII.

MARY.

My sad heart's love, my brother ! Can it be
That he who lies so still is dead to me ?
How joyous was thy heart, how bright thy smile,
My grief to lighten and my care beguile !
Thou wert my very life ! and in thee lived
This drooping heart which at thy touch revived.
Thou wert my sun ! and now, thy light withdrawn,
My soul in darkness careless journeys on :
Thou wert my tongue and thou my song it sings !
Thy fingers touched my heart's melodious strings,
And all my being quivered with the strain,
So sweet its tender ecstasy was pain !
And thou art gone ! A shadow of thee lies
Before my face to mock my yearning eyes.
Yes, thou art gone ! Thy spirit, wandering far,
Hath shot its glimmering light to farthest star,
And in the bosom of Eternal Truth
Renews the bloom of its unfading youth !
I should not weep ! but yet, but yet my heart
Thy saddened going out hath torn apart,
And it lies bleeding in the dust undone,
Since sorrow has before my joy begun !

XIX.

MARTHA.

I cannot give thee up ! Once more a child
As thou wert when upon me young life smiled
In peace and innocence, when mother died
And left thee, fair-haired prattler at my side,
And I but able then by this white hand
To lead thee out along the chalky sand
Where Kidron's stream a dusty channel lay :
There we for hours would with its pebbles play ;
Else, underneath the stately olives, we
Strayed in the Garden of Gethsemane,
And sang our songs as only children sing
When life is young and care is free of wing.
My youth is lost in thee, and as it dies,
Along thy open grave it withered lies !

XX.

MARY.

Thou art not dead ! I feel thy pulsing heart
Against mine throb, returning life impart;
Thy temples answer to the warming glow,
As the chill blood resumes its quick'ning flow !
And — oh the folly of my love's desire,
That from dead ashes kindles living fire ! —
Those heart-throbs are my own ! my burning breath
But warms with fitful glow the brow of death !
O God ! why art thou hidden from my eyes ?
Why are thine ears grown deaf to pleading cries ?
Why didst thou smite this unoffending clay,
And snatch from it the living breath away ?
My father's God, now hear me, I implore !
The Master send, that he may life restore ;
For he hath power, if he but speak the word
That in her sleep Capernaum's daughter heard !

XXI.

MARTHA.

Why shouldst thou die ?   Are now the Master's ears
Deaf to our cries, his eyes grown blind to tears ?
On other works was he then so intent
He would not heed the message to him sent ?
So thou hast died when he had power to save !
Forgotten now, thou goest to thy grave,
Forever hidden from our loving gaze,
To be bemoaned through all our coming days !
O Christ beloved ! what have we done to thee
That in this hour we should forsaken be ?

MARY.

Hush, sister ! calm the sorrows of thy breast;
He knew, and, knowing, did for us the best;
We may not judge, while yet our eyes are blind,
Him, when we know his heart is wondrous kind !
His ways are not our ways, yet seemeth hard
Our prayer should fail to win his slight regard.
But let us learn the lesson herein taught,

Though bitter, and with hard conditions fraught,
That Lazarus must die, and now prepare
The last sad rites which now demand our care.

XXII.

MARTHA.

O gentle heart! your words my thoughts engage,
For wisdom grave and counsel wise and sage :
My love for him, the dead, my judgment blinds ;
In bitter words my grief expression finds,
For it is hard to say, " Thy will be done,"
When in our hearts we pray still for our own !
Nor is it meet we with our lips express
That which in truth our hearts dare not confess.
Good by, sweet brother ! Rest thee in thy sleep :
May he thou lov'st thy soul in his peace keep !
Since 't is his will ; nor is it mine to say,
No matter what I wish, unto him nay !
I kiss thy lips, thy cheeks, thy brow, adieu !
A long, a last farewell !

MARY.

And so I, too,
Now kiss thy lips, thy cheeks, thy brow, thine eyes ;
Each kiss now warm on thy cold features lies,
As my hot heart upon thy pulseless breast
Throbs agonized to be with thee at rest.
Farewell ! O loved and lost ! I cannot tell
The agony of this last, long farewell !

XXIII.

And so they part, and leave the dead beloved
For the last rites by creed and faith approved ;
Of mourners hired, the solemn funeral song ;
Their doleful wails that discord still prolong ;
And with their friends who come indeed to mourn
With them the bitter loss so hardly borne,
Now sit apart, and each condoling guest
Speaks words of comfort as it seemeth best.
But oh how harsh such words to mourners' ears,

Though they be softened by the hush of tears!
Instead of melting, they the heart may steel,
Awake some conscious pain it would not feel,
Or, feeling, witness in the soothing thrill
That love in tender message whispers still.
And, as they sit, there enters at the gate
A messenger whose haste no form will wait,
Scarce the frank bidding friend to friend may show
Who would in love attend the house of woe.
We know the face; 't is Haddan's, and surprise
Looks out from paling cheek and startled eyes:
The meaning of the scene, well understood,
Chills his warm heart with his receding blood,
So sudden wrought, to him so unforeseen
Has the swift ending of his sickness been:
For he from Judeth now a message bears
Winged with her love and ever-constant prayers
That health returning soon, a blessed guest,
Companion dwell with Love in Lazarus' breast:
With lines too long, though filled with love's lush sweet,
For us now scarce to mention, not repeat:
While in his hand for Martha he has brought
The written whispers of her tenderest thought.
O sad love-message! Saddest ever writ
When Love's dead eyes are ever closed to it:
How many breaking hearts such words would save,
Received too late, but hasten to the grave!

XXIV.

They bid him enter to the darkened room
Whose softened light has naught in it of gloom,
Save the sad hearts whose chambers have no light
Since the closed curtains shut within the night.
In quiet greeting Martha takes his hand:
Thus they, a moment sorr'wing, silent stand;
Then meet their eyes; hers fall, weighed down with tears,
Which in their flood the calm before it bears;
While in his eyes the gathering mists appear
Which tell of heavy clouds of weeping near.
The storm blows past; the clouds of gathering rain
Hide in the depths of bright'ning eyes again,

And he essays some words of greeting now
With quivering voice and swiftly clouding brow.

HADDAN.

I had not dreamed such ending, and so soon!
A life so sweet! nor morn had kissed the noon
Of its sweet midday hour.

MARTHA.

Alas! nor I:
I had not dreamed that one so fair could die:
But then the sweetest flowers of all die first.

HADDAN.

Not all the sweetest, else the earth accurst
Would thorns and brambles bear, nor set a rose
Where now the bitter fruit of Sodom grows.
This is most sudden; and no warning word
Was even at the home of Rahab heard,
Save but your message, most imperfect told,
That brought his answer back so seeming cold.

XXV.

MARTHA.

There was a letter sent to Judeth.

HADDAN.

True!
But in the hasty reading of it through
The graver truth to Rahab was not seen,
Since he, in reading, read the lines between,
And thought it some device, to him made plain,
In which you sought advantage grave to gain.
Not till this morn the note withheld he gave
To Judeth.   Pardon now I come to crave
From her and bring her answer.

MARTHA.

Thanks to you:
We knew her heart was loving, kind, and true,
And that such cold reply was not from her.

HADDAN.

Nay, she at heart a bitter sufferer
Could never wound the heart that it must needs
Her own should suffer, if through her it bleeds:
And then she is herself now feeble grown
With grief and care, and wholly broken down.

MARTHA.

Now while I read her letter, generous friend,
The servants will your several wants attend;
And I will call you to me, by and by,
For some instructions following my reply.
O sad, sweet heart! how little did you know
The bitter darkness of your coming woe,
When your white fingers eager, throbbing, penned
The words within to your now mourning friend!
How can I read the sadly sweet refrain
Which runs along the trembling cords of pain!
And look, in thought, within your tender eyes,
Beneath whose lids the rising fountain lies
So near the brink, my loving hand, I know,
With tenderest touch, must cause the floods to flow!

XXVI.

(Reads the letter.)

"My dearest sister :
How can you excuse
The bitter coldness that would dare refuse
What in your letter asked? My father, kind
As he would be to me, with fear is blind,
And sees in all things, where the new Faith grows,
Some threat'ning evil he must needs oppose.
It is not you nor Lazarus that fires
His hot heart's passion. He, in fact, admires
Aye, loves you both; but creed he sets above
All things, except for me it be his love;
And that in its sharp selfishness so pure
That what might tarnish he will not endure.
I write this much excusing him, to say
Your letter was withheld; and this delay
Prevented answer back. I am so pained

To learn that Lazarus has nothing gained
Upon his fever; yet I hope your fears
Have made him worse than even he appears:
For I will tell you of my dream, and then
I know that it will cheer your heart again."
(Dear heart! you know not yet our grief's extremes,
Else you would seek not cure in fleeting dreams!)

XXVII.

"This morn had soared somewhat the risen sun,
And I my morning sleep had almost done, —
A sleep disturbed through all the early night
With horrors which the shrinking soul affright, —
When all at once it seemed, like speeding thought,
I to a mount of flame was upward caught,
Borne in the arms of one whose noiseless wing
Supports our flight while to his breast I cling.
I could not see the face, nor did I know
If it were born of heaven or earth below,
If it were angel bright, or spirit blest
That bore me panting on its quiet breast;
Until upon the Mount my feet were placed,
And then I saw 't was Lazarus' arms embraced!
The hills I saw around, and vales below,
Touched with a golden glory, burn and glow,
Like we beheld above the Jordan's stream,
When Christ baptized, the heavens' refulgent gleam.
The Kidron's valley and sweet Mamre's vale
Lay in the splendor, burning soft and pale,
While, to the sight, white-walled Jerusalem
Shone in the setting radiant as a gem!
Its glittering spires and holy, templed shrine
Gleamed with a splendor wrought by hand divine;
While bending arches pillared from on high,
A templed earth reflects against the sky!
In such a spot he set me down to rest,
My hot face pillowed on his tender breast,
And with cool lips he kissed my burning brow, —
So plain they were I feel his kisses now! —
And whispered in my ear, ' Rejoice! at last
The burden of our sorrows now is past.

No more shall cruel hands us part ; no more
Shall stoop the neck which once the burden bore !
Thou art now mine ! The courts of this sweet heaven
Behold ! for us a nuptial couch is given,
A heavenly choir our bridal song shall sing,
While heavenly hands ambrosial dews shall fling,
With flowers of Paradise, along our way,
Which ne'er grows rough no matter where we stray.
Hark ! hear you not the minstrel choir's sweet strain ?
And scent the dews that fall in odorous rain ?
Behold the bright and ever-changing showers
Where fall as snow the many-colored flow'rs ! '

XXVIII.

"And as he spoke, a breath about me stirred ;
In it my ears enchanting music heard ;
Upon my brow a mist of odorous dew
Its prismic shower of cooling incense threw,
While bud and blossom in the crimson rain
Fell soft as snow upon a sunlit plain.
Again he clasps me to his breast ; his breath
Is sweet as incense, as to me he saith,
'Here shall we dwell eternal in the light
Of this fair home, which never knoweth night.
Kiss me soft kisses. Even so, my own ! ' —
And as I turned to kiss, lo ! he was gone !
While through my open window golden day
Poured rich and warm, and on the carpet lay
So dazzling bright the ever-changing stream
That I could not believe it all a dream !
So, sister Martha, in this dream behold
The bright'ning future of our joys foretold ;
And soon, so very soon, I hope to see
My home restored in hearts its wont to be.
And Lazarus tell " — (Poor child ! she does not know !)
"This much my father, jealous, may allow —
That I have not forgotten : further need
I not to write, for he the rest can read.
But I have too much written, and now fails
My o'ertaxed strength : yet little it avails,
Save that my hope may feed it with such food

As this, which now, I pray, may do thee good.
Give Mary love ; and say to her, each line
She wrote found lodgment in this heart of mine.
Pray trust me, sister Martha, I would come
If I had liberty to leave my home.
An answer I expect ; though smiles are coy,
Earth glows to-day and fills my soul with joy !
Good-by, sweet hearts ! I wait your answer back ;
Until it come, my heart is on the rack.
Ever your loving
           " Judeth."

XXIX.

           How can I
Send back the one unchangeable reply ?
'T is cruel-kind to paint with hues aglow
And mask from sight Death's cold and clammy brow ;
Or hide in roses faces dead, but fair,
For hands to find when gathering garlands there !
How can I rudely break the silvery charm
That holds her heart, with truth's too dread alarm ?
I cannot, cannot ! Mary, warm of heart,
Adept in love's most tender, soothing art,
Write back my answer. Say that I embrace
And kiss to smiles again her tear-sad face ;
That in our bosoms warm we softly press
Her throbbing brow, and, as we press it, bless
Her with a love that ever will abide,
That with her dwells, — walks ever at her side ;
That she may lean upon the arm that binds,
Though she the one she seeks still absent finds ;
While, mingling tears with those her sad eyes shed,
We mourn together Lazarus now dead !

MARY.

Sweet sister, I could nothing better write :
I pray you, just those simple lines indite,
And close with invitation that she come
With Rahab, if it please, to our sad home.
Leave Haddan then to tell them all the rest.
Such things by mouth are better far expressed :

Let him depart : it deepens but a woe,
When it must fall, to long suspend the blow.

XXX.

Why linger more upon this saddening scene
To pluck at funeral wreaths which yet are green ?
The fading fragrance of the withered bloom
Breathes all too strongly of the open tomb !
Yet, at the coffin of a treasured friend,
We, lingering sadly, o'er his features bend
For one last look upon the sacred face,
One lingering kiss, one clinging, last embrace,
Then, as we go, at ev'ry footstep turn
Our glances back upon the gloomy urn
Where sleep the ashes in unbroken rest,
Blessed in repose as only such are blest,
Of our lost love, alive to us, though dead,
And ever present, yet forever fled !

XXXI.

The gathered friends have many words of praise ;
The warmest those who knew him all his days :
And such judge best ; and praise by them bestowed,
A sweet discharge of duty gravely owed,
And happy he, deserving, claims such meed,
Since words from such are eulogies indeed !
The city round the garb of woe takes on ;
And ev'ry house, it seems, has lost a son :
For fathers speak with half-averted face,
As if each hearth had now a vacant place ;
And mothers weep as if for children borne
That from their yearning bosoms had been torn :
While sons and daughters whisper of the dead
As if from each home-circle he had fled.

XXXII.

So gathering groups in home and open street,
As they with solemn faces sadly meet,
His death declared, inquire with flattering speech,

And eyes that glance in questioning, each to each,
Why he had died ? Why had the Healer stayed
When for his coming groaning hearts had prayed ?
When but a touch of his all-healing hand,
With potent power that doth e'en Death command,
Had healed him sick, or, all too late, that power
The fleeting life itself may still restore.
Disputes ran high : but he who all denied
Had still the better reason on his side,
Since all the graves their tenants still contain,
With never one restored to life again.
The sick were healed ! Why not ? Physician's skill
Rebuked disease and baffled gravest ill :
The lame man walked ; Bethesda's troubled pool
Whoever stepped within made clean and whole.
The dumb were made to speak ! The magic art,
Which charmed the devils forth, here did its part.
The blind received their sight ! this too had been,
And darkened eyes the light again had seen.
The dead are brought to life ! A tale is heard,
That such, too, have been raised when long interred.
So theme and answer pass from man to man :
Some silent keep, some answer as they can ;
But all the burden of their speech is why,
If Christ could save, he should let Lazarus die.
Nor was it strange this questioning the hour,
The ways mysterious of almighty power :
Infirm in purpose, despot in his will,
Man, judging God, disputes his judgment still.

XXXIII.

No further waiting, since has come the day
The funeral rites no longer can delay :
The Master's ears have now indeed grown deaf ;
His ready hand will offer no relief :
Hope flies each breast where lingering it had stayed,
And plans complete for burial are made.
Forth moves the train now slowly from the gate,
Where he went in and out in life so late,
With bounding heart, rejoicing in the pride
Of manhood that with Death himself had vied.

Afresh the tears from pent-up torrents flow,
And loud and shrill the gathering notes of woe ;
While pipe and psaltery lead the doleful train
With funeral notes which deepen mortal pain.
Without the city's close confining walls,
Where softened shade from feathery palm-trees falls,
The rocky tomb stands waiting for its prey,
With gaping mouth wide open to the day,
Its hungry maw now ready to devour
This blasted fruit that falleth in the flower!

XXXIV.

He rests within.   The stone fast seals the door
Which his still hands shall open nevermore :
The world without to him as nothing grown,
The world within encircled by this stone,
Dividing-wall between the two must stand ;
To break it down lies not in mortal hand.
From Abel's dust to Egypt's mummied kings,
No living flower from out their ashes springs :
" A thousand years are but as yesterday "
To those who in their cerements waste away, —
A thousand years, a moment's space in time
That marks Eternity in march sublime !
And yet its æons circling into space
Leave not a footstep in the vacant place,
If such could be that dust so long endure
Like floating motes within the ether pure ;
And through it all the dead sleep sweetly on,
As if their sleep had its first watch begun.

XXXV.

Yet when that voice which spoke to being life,
And stilled old Chaos from eternal strife,
Shall speak, the dead will rise, and from the tomb
Then shrouded kings in tattered shreds shall come,
While from their bones the clinging dust will fall,
And sweet, young flesh be clothed upon withal :
The beggar from his lazar-tomb shall rise,
His rags the woven robes of Paradise !

Nor will it call in power a greater skill
Than that which lies in a creating will,
To bid the atoms of the scattered dust
The grave has lost in its unfaithful trust
To fly to each, and to each other cleave,
Till form renewed the spark of life receive,
And perfect man walks forth before the throne,
He knowing, and to all creation known!
Nor need we wait the great, eternal day
To feel the quick'ning of consuming clay:
No law here bounds the all-creating power;
All time to God is his accepted hour;
For he made Time, and it has hoary grown
In the long service wholly still his own!
And he who is the Ancient of all Days
Himself has set his bounds to Time and Space.
Earth hears his voice; the circling worlds on high,
Touched by his finger, in their orbits fly:
He can create — destroy — renew again,
And nothing to his hand shall come in vain!
Now, should he cry against this hollow tomb,
" Ho! Lazarus, come forth! " he forth would come,
As sweet in youth, as fair in life to see,
As if no death forevermore could be!

CANTO EIGHTH.

THE SACRIFICE.

I.

JERUSALEM, the holy, favored, blest,
Of what grand hopes hast thou not been possessed!
Well might the Saviour say, when on his sight
Fell the dark shadow of thy coming night,
"Alas! alas for thee, Jerusalem,
That killed my prophets, and that stoneth them
Sent unto thee! how often would I bring,
As doth a hen her brood beneath her wing,
Thy people unto me, but ye would not!

Your homes are desolate, your fame forgot;
And now I say to you, no more shall ye,
In peace and glory crowned, my coming see,
Until my praise you shout in loud acclaim,
' All hail who cometh in Messiah's name ! ' "

II.

O fair, rich city !   God hath made his home
In thy grand Temple.   Ages yet to come
Will look with wonder on thy favored lot,
Thy golden blessings all too soon forgot :
That heavenly care which o'er thee stooping threw
The sacred mantle God around thee drew ;
Thy prophets calling from the unseen land
The power to smite, the wisdom to command,
And to the eyes of subject and of king
The door of mystery wide open fling,
That they may read, whoever choose to look,
The Future's pages as an open book ;
And wonder if of all our human-kind
There ever could be men so madly blind.
And further, reading from this wondrous page
The history of this once most glorious age,
Amazement seizes on the sense, oppressed
To see a land above all others blessed
With rich abundance, present and foretold,
So full that room there scarce was left to hold ;
That even darkened minds in sombre light
Could run and read, and running read aright,
The glowing page on which imprinted burned
The living letters read by lands unlearned, —
That they would Christ deny, their Prince refuse,
Spurn him with scorn ; revile, contemn, accuse ;
And — crowning madness ! — God himself defy,
Then Christ, their hope, betray and crucify !

III.

Now through its streets we wander where his feet
Have pressed their stones with kisses wondrous sweet,
And look upon this haven that might be,

No mortal eye again as then shall see.
We will not stop its story here to tell,
Sublimely told so oft, nor further dwell
Upon its scenes, save as the hour require,
Somewhat to note the things that shall transpire.
The streets are thronged with busy crowds that go
Along their narrow windings to and fro :
These thousands, hastening on their several ways,
As this impels and that their speed delays,
Bear in their bosoms severally and whole
The powers that all the world of man control,
Which, singly or united, when 't is hurled,
From centre to circumference shakes the world.
We may not follow each, we cannot all ;
Duty to such a task does not now call :
While human hearts with human-kind still share
A common lot, they have no common care.
And yet our eyes grow humid when we meet
A fellow-sufferer helpless in the street ;
His tale of sorrow we with sighs may hear,
In pity feel our hearts to him draw near,
And yet along the streets we wend our way,
If it be on to labor or to pray ;
His sorrow soon forgot, until it come
To dwell a guest within our sheltering home :
So we this hour forsake the crowd for one
Who still before us on his way has gone.

IV.

Rahab, just passing from his closing door,
As we approach, now leads the way before.
His eager steps and bearing plainly show
That something pressing strongly moves him now.
We now would enter, and for this had come
To visit him and his within his home ;
But since he goes, his steps we will pursue,
And learn his motive and its end in view.
The curious crowds, from ev'ry nation drawn,
Attract our gaze as still we hasten on.
Their dress each caste in varied color shows,
While form and feature race and clime disclose :

The Arab from his desert home, the Greek,
The Syrian from beyond Mount Hermon's peak,
The sable Afric, and the yellow son
Of Asia, land and race that day unknown,
Save here and there, like bird of plumage strange,
Storm-tossed or blindly led, seeks wider range ;
For in the line of commerce of all lands
Jerusalem a welcome gateway stands.
Still as we go, we note the scenes around,
While Rahab leads us on o'er unknown ground.
What means he now by this long, tortuous chase
Through streets obscure and strangely winding ways ?
Has he pursuit discovered, and would throw
From off his track his close pursuing foe ?
Or is he bent upon some deed of shame
That neither friend nor foe should know or name ?
Whate'er impels, untiring on his track
We follow, with no thought of turning back,
Although a thousand charms may here supply
Their pleasing stories for both mind and eye.

V.

He passes beggars who persistent wait
At ev'ry crossing, sit at ev'ry gate :
Blind, halt, and lame ; of ev'ry ill distressed ;
Alone, in groups, of ev'ry plea possessed ;
Whose piteous cries for alms in pleading tones
Should move to mercy even hearts of stones :
And yet old Rahab in his silken dress,
Who with his gold might each one cheer and bless,
But draws his skirts the closer, with a frown,
As on these pleading faces he looks down,
As one might look upon a whining cur,
Save that the dog would greater pity stir !
But Rahab now hath sterner work on hand
That doth his zeal and sympathy command ;
Some questions grave that burden with their weight,
And nearly touch his heart in church and state.
These well excuse his air abstract and grave,
And pardon of his better nature crave !
For who can think of God's own starving poor,

Whose hands outstretched appeal at your own door,
When honors wait and heads are bowing down,
That hands which bear may now bestow the crown !
Who would endure that hands which beg or toil
The festal garments by their touch should soil?
And mar the pleasures of the festal scene
By leprous faces that are thrust between?

VI.

But none of these upon his thought to-day
Doth 'gainst its burdening care abstractly weigh;
Since nobler deeds, if any such there be,
Make for old Rahab now excusing plea.
The Council calls, his earnest help to crave,
Upon a subject weighty, too, and grave,
Which touches close their honor, creed, and rites,
Their fame and place, and action swift invites,
Unto the end that these be saved, and God
Receive the honor thus in them bestowed.
The rumors come, and thicken as they come,
That Christ restoreth speech unto the dumb!
That lame men walk! the deaf are made to hear!
The blind receive their sight! and even near —
If he had looked — was one whom he had known, —
Nay, one who had from youth to manhood grown
Up in his sight, blind from his birth, whose sight
He touched, and turned his darkness into light!
If this were not enough, they further said,
He healed the sick, and even raised the dead!
All in the name of God; and worse and more,
He fed the hungry from miraculous store,
And preached the gospel to the dying poor!

VII.

No; these he could not see, as in his haste
The burdened streets full in their midst he paced,
To meet the Council, which would ways devise
By which the Christ they might alone surprise,
Still that kind voice, that hand of pity stay;
Because he heals, the tender healer slay;

He of all men who wrought the best among
The hopeless, homeless, helpless, friendless throng,
Who, for his mercies and his grace alone,
To hate implacable must now atone!
On to the Temple, where its spacious courts
Once sacred held as worship's sweet resorts,
Forgotten now, to commerce open thrown,
And the world's market for its traffic known!
Deserving well the censure it receives,
" Lo, you have made my House a den of thieves! "
Where are the singers who in chorus grand
Chanted those psalms now sung in ev'ry land,
The poet-king sang to his sacred lyre,
And kindled song into a quenchless fire?
Where are those bands whose golden horns proclaim
The majesty of Adonai's name?
Whose pleasing strains with harp and psaltery join
Their tribute praise to God through love divine?
Where are the priests who read from sacred scroll
The wondrous teachings which their race extol;
How blessings strown like sands along the shore
Which were to them a promise evermore
That he who led their fathers safely here
Would still uphold if they would serve and fear?
Where are the mighty men of valor?   Where
The daughters of old Zion brave and fair,
Whose beauteous faces hallowed all this scene,
And thronged their court in days that once have been,
The glory and the pride of Israel?
For in her daughters Judah did prevail:
Her mothers were her strength, and with the Lord
Found grace when man was beaten by the sword.
Where are the smoking altars, where the priests,
The holy vessels and the bleeding beasts,
The sacred offerings from the hand of love
Which brought down blessings from the throne above?
Gone! gone forever! and their glory fled;
While gather daily in their place instead
A motley throng, whose gentile feet profane,
With their unclean and soul-polluting stain,
These sacred pavements once sublimely trod
In ancient time by foot of Israel's God!

VIII.

Through these he passes, even to the door
Where stands the offering, now concealed no more ;
Nor sees he where the money-changers bring
Their tables for the market, where the ring
Of changing coins must pain the pious ear
Of those whose wont had been to worship here ;
As usurers, their traffic made with those
Who, in God's house, of market-wares dispose.
No thought hath he of those who, for a price,
Make profit in his courts for greed and vice ;
Or from the shambles sell the fatling slain,
And coin the altar's stolen blood for gain.
A braver work hath he ! He who hath scourged
These desecrators from his house, and purged
His altars of pollution, now must pay
In blood the loss sustained that market-day !

IX.

So now he mounts to Gazzith, by the wall,
The Council-chamber of the Temple hall,
Where secret conclave of the ruler Jews
Debate how best they may the Christ accuse.
He enters, and the last is he in place ;
And ere he sits he scans them face by face.
Not that he doubts or fears, but would inquire
The hopes and aims their several hearts inspire.
Full-robed, old Annas for the high-priest sat
In state ; his bead-like eyes, half hid in fat,
Malignant gleamed at some disturbing word,
Or grave report which he but just then heard :
From this distracted, when old Rahab came,
He turned and bowed, deferring, called his name :

X.

ANNAS.

Here is Rabboni Rahab, hear we him ;
But first to him the pith somewhat will limn
Of such reports as have been to us made

Of the pretended Christ, his course to aid.
Now, of his famous cures I need not speak,
Since they foundation have most frail and weak,
And like all tales that fill the country round,
When search is made, why, nothing can be found
But idle rumor, some old woman's tale,
Told for the hour when other stories fail.
You all have heard them : healing of the lame,
The sick, the blind, the dumb, — I need not name,
You will remember : yet, when he doth feed
The multitudes who perish of their need,
Stills the wild storms, and at our very gate —
Though we deny, it is beyond debate, —
Creates in eyeless cells most perfect eyes,
And then those rolling balls with sight supplies ;
Makes on the shapeless stump an arm to grow,
And through a withered limb the new life flow ;
All at a word, and in that awful name
Our lips dare not pronounce, — our cheeks with shame
Should burn, as we stand idly by and see
His brazen claims and gross profanity.
But more, friend Rahab : he makes claim to be
Equal with God — his Son — Vicegerent here !
This Temple will o'erthrow, and on it rear
A kingdom of his own. So to prepare
His foolish dupes in this belief to share,
Pretends — for it is all pretence, we know,
And all conspire with him in this to show
His godly powers — that he can raise the dead
(And they believe it) even, it is said,
And give as names, this witchcraft to maintain,
One widow's son who liveth now at Nain.
We have sent there, our messenger brings word
It was some falling sickness now averred
That aileth him. Again, they boasting tell
That for our friend Jairus, trusted well,
His daughter dying suddenly, 't is said
He, with a word, restored her from the dead ;
When we have proof direct, in truth supreme,
That what seemed death was but a palsying dream.
You see he preaches that the dead will rise,
And through these specious frauds the proof supplies !

XI.

RAHAB.

If this were all, I see no proof in this
That man to soul makes metamorphosis.
The gravest charge in it is being God, —
Or so he claims to be, — and has avowed
That he and God are one! The gravest charge,
I say, is that he should the Word enlarge,
When he his curse, with bitter emphasis,
Declares 'gainst those who read that Word amiss;
And yet by word and deed would poison mind
With teachings in that book you cannot find.

ANNAS.

What! Would you argue, and our cause abuse, —
Instead of Christ, his judges here accuse?

RAHAB.

Not judges, but their judgment, I impugn.

LEVI.

Let us, the judges, judgment here attune
To the occasion, nor be drawn aside
By that alone which counsel will divide.
Whatever else we each believe, one thing,
Methinks, will all our minds in concord bring,
And that the work in hand.

XII.

ZADOCK.

True, friend; but still
The slighting speech of Rahab soundeth ill
In answer to the kindly words and grave
Which Rabbi Annas, without question, gave
For his own guiding. And the best essay
To prove man hath no soul, we see to-day
In the occasion and the slighting speech,
Which proves in teacher what his faith would teach.

RAHAB.

What! Am I here insulted? It is time
That change should come when words are made a crime,
And covert jest is turned to earnest.

ANNAS.

Peace,
Now, brethren; let these words unseemly cease:
In our hot passion we too soon forget
The common cause in which we now are met;
Like dogs that guard the sheepfold in the night,
We leave the flocks to wolves while here we fight.

ZADOCK.

Yet to the sheep, the cause of strife thus borne,
Small matter if by dog or wolf he 's torn:
The wolf without hath honor, being bold;
The dog within, a thief who guards the fold.
In open war we honor daring deeds,
And praise the foe who for his country bleeds;
But treason hath no friends on either side,
In blood accursed his hands are doubly dyed.

LEVI.

With him within we fight the common foe;
When he plays false, will give returning blow.

RAHAB.

If you mean me, I am content to wait
And fight the common foe without the gate;
But as I fight will take good care to lend
A helping hand to generous foe or friend!
Your words to-day are idle winds o'erblown,
And with their sound rememberance is gone:
Let us bestow our counsel.

ANNAS.

Good! Well said!
A hot heart governed by a cooler head.
Rabboni Rahab, whatsoe'er your creed,
We in the common good are all agreed;
And we will gladly listen to your speech,

Well knowing what we hear will please and teach.
Be pleased to let us hear you.

XIII.

RAHAB.

Spoken fair :
My words shall be but few, yet they may bear
Food meet for all your earnest thought and care.
The Passover draws near; and he again
Will then return, if not with us remain :
He hath warm friends in Bethany, and there
He may, while lasts his sojourn here, repair.
There we might lay our plans, some plot devise
Through which he may be taken by surprise.
Now here the people will at least befriend,
And, if attacked, with open arms defend.
Those friends of whom I speak are of my blood,
And I have long against their cause withstood, —
In fact the brother, Lazarus, you knew,
A worthy man, and of your faith most true.
But him beguiled, this faith hath led astray,
And all I have disowned on from that day :
And yet I love them! Judeth for long years
Midway hath lived between our homes, — her tears
Are many since my interdict: to save
Them from a fate to them worse than the grave
Is now my hope in snatching up their stay ;
Then they may see the folly of their way.
This is my plan at large ; we have full time,
When that the roost is known, the bird to lime !
My means are ample and my ways are sure :
If this the plan, the prey we shall secure.

XIV.

ZIDONIAH.

A word, grave Annas, Rabbis, one and all ;
I have held peace, and rise but to recall
Some things we should consider ere we place
Our hands to acts that savor of disgrace
In eyes of men, and bring upon our cause

The certain vengeance of our outraged laws,
To us revealed by God.

ZADOCK.

Stay ! but one word ;
Have you, my brother, all these rumors heard ?

ZIDONIAH.

I have, and that is why I speak. I read —
And there is none more firm in faith and creed —
That when our king shall come, Messiah reign,
The days prophetic shall return again :
Then wondrous signs will fill the land, the air
Be thick with rumors : Earth and Heaven declare
The time appointed when the dumb shall sing
The praises of his name ; the lame shall fling
Aside his staff and leap for joy, the blind
Shall see, and deaf ears be unstopped. We find
These things to-day, — nay, of them we complain,
As work of evil hands in ways profane.
Should we not pause ? These truths dare we deny ?
In our own strength can we the hosts defy ?
Pray let us pause, and reason's course pursue,
And know if as a fact these things be true ;
And if found true, what is the better plan ?
Where lies our road ? Shall we serve God or man ?
If he be Christ, the madness of the hour
Is to resist and thus our hopes devour.
Wisdom and Truth through God the way prepare,
And victory lies for whom these ways declare.

XV.

ZADOCK.

You must be mad to seek his cause to crown,
Which, when you do, you drag our honors down !
Why now accept what we perforce believe ?
If not deceived, we others may deceive ;
Our hopes, our fortunes, lie along that way :
It would be madness to ourselves betray.
I grant you quote fair Scripture : those who do
These works can quote it just the same as you ;

And thus their wicked hearts their work prepare
To suit the Word, and by that Word ensnare.
Nay, good friend Zidoniah, he but smiles
His sweetest on us who the truth beguiles.
That traitor false to truth in truth but hides,
While lurking treason in his heart abides :
The honest man, bold in the truth, with blows
Smites to the dust relentless all his foes.
Will God, who Pharaoh's hosts o'erthrew, 'gainst Rome
With shepherds' staves and shouting rabble come?
Our King shall ride the whirlwind : in his hand
His sword as sceptre smites a fleeing land ;
Before it falls Rome's conquering eagles prone,
And he his footstool makes of her proud throne.

XVI.

ANNAS.

Well said, bold Zadock ! had we men like thee,
Our land oppressed already would be free ;
And when Messiah comes, no better hand,
Nor readier one, shall seize the conquering brand !
But for that time, if we would best prepare,
Destruction of the false demands our care ;
To that Rabboni Rahab points the way,
The means and method wait another day.
Discussion longer I would gladly hear
If further good from it there should appear ;
This is not plain to me, and so, to end
What, if pursued here farther, might offend,
Will close our meeting, hoping, praying still,
Whate'er we do, it be not fraught with ill,
And that we bear toward God and man good-will.

XVII.

So ends the conclave, and with speech profuse
Each to the other words of heat excuse :
To Zidoniah, and to Rahab most,
The others of their love or friendship boast ;
They well receive excuse and protest made,
While o'er each face, in faint and varying shade,

Grim hate, distrust, and deeper passions pass
As shadows darkly in a hidden glass,
And through these smiles unconscious now appear
The hidden images their false hearts bear.
And it is ever thus when pride and hate,
Together bound, be it in church or state,
The offspring of such union, more accursed
Than that of Sin and Death, of Hell the worst,
Feeds on them both, devouring, as they grow,
The panting breasts from which their life must flow,
Until this birth an incubus becomes,
And at the last its hideous self consumes.

XVIII.

Let us return to Rahab's home once more,
To meet and enter with him at the door:
The smile has fled which on his lips we saw,
They, trembling at the corners, downward draw;
And yet, although his eyebrows darken down,
His forehead wears no shadow of a frown.
Some friend in want, perhaps, he chanced to meet,
Some saddening rumor heard along the street,
Something oppressive to him, — something grave
That he must meet, and, meeting, sternly brave;
But how, disturbs him more than does. the cause.
From this some trouble, it is plain, he draws,
But light indeed, if he could surely know
What the result of the returning blow.
So, thought-absorbed, he at the threshold stands,
His blue-fringed robe grasped tightly in his hands,
And thinks, — but in a self-consuming thought
That hath no present action in it fraught.
The chaos stirred within his whirling brain
Obscures all thought instead of making plain;
Yet fires intense conceal their lurid glow
By their dense vapors rising from below:
The fiercest storms stretch forth the blackest wing,
From dark occasion mighty actions spring!

XIX.

How long he stood, or would have stood, like stone,
An image into pulseless marble grown,
Uncertain, when the voice of Haddan wakes
With sad speech which upon him rudely breaks,
As he in low obeisance slowly bends,
And with a trembling hand to him extends
The parchment letter Martha by him sent.
A startled look on this old Rahab bent;
Drew back his hand, retreated then a pace,
Glanced at the letter, then at Haddan's face;
Essayed to question, yet his lips were dumb, —
Refused to ask for answer sure to come:
He stamps the stones, impatient of his fears,
Then bows his head, moved by his servant's tears,
For Haddan, troubled by his master's mood,
No longer can restrain the rising flood.
"Speak, Haddan!" cries old Rahab; "is it true,
This tale I hear? The truth must come from you."
"Alas, my master! you may well surmise
The truth convincing from these flowing eyes;
A grievous tale of death, and sadly told
In that poor body lying stark and cold.
The comely lad has no disturbing dreams
As from his sisters' eyes run sorrow's streams;
That parchment tells it all, to Judeth writ, —
Her soul to his in love undying knit" —
"Peace, Haddan! you forget, and should not seek
Occasion of forbidden things to speak.
Now go within, and see you hold your peace
Until I bid you speak: your weeping cease,
And bathe your eyes until each lingering trace
Of grief is washed from tell-tale eyes and face;
Then wait my call within the court below,
As I shall now to Judeth's chamber go."

XX.

To Judeth's chamber let us, too, repair,
A lovely bower and she the flower most fair!
We have not seen her since that sorrowing night

She lay so pale beneath the softened light
Which fell on her closed eyes when but a fear
Seized on her heart of coming sorrow near,
And smote her down, while Death's gates swung ajar
And showed his misty shores not dim nor far!
But from her letter we may judge aright
That hope revived, and, smiling through the night,
To her in dreams bore promise sweet of bliss
That mortals only know in worlds like this.
This day had been exceeding bright to her,
And at her shrine she knelt, Hope's worshipper;
And saw in the sweet mirage o'er her cast
The Eden of her joy and rest at last!
So goes the traveller in the desert lost,
Where hot sands drive by fierce siroccos tossed,
The sky, a flaming arch, pressed closely down
On scorching plains, waste, desolate, and brown,
The losing battle of the way he makes,
Reels tottering on till hope his breast forsakes,
Then falls at last exhausted, — panting lies,
The glare of death already in his eyes, —
Sees in this death-dream valleys fair and green,
With flowers and verdure glad'ning all the scene;
Broad lakes spread out with ever-wid'ning shores,
Adown whose steeps a sparkling river pours
Its cooling floods through groves of waving trees,
Which ceaseless murmur to caressing breeze.
Soft voices call, a thousand joys invite
The panting soul to share each sweet delight;
He hears their calls, his hot lips, baked and dry,
Bleed as he strives imperfect to reply;
His quivering limbs he strains in eager pain
The treacherous sands that mock to mount again;
There reeling stands, his heart in drunken glee
From sounds he hears and sights his dull eyes see:
Thus gazing on this scene of rest and bliss
That hath no eye to drink its sweets but his,
Entranced he stands, enraptured by the sight!
His soul in quivering transport of delight,
Unconscious of the death which round him lay,
For fear and suffering now have fled away:
With one glad cry he rushes down the steep
Into the valley of eternal sleep!

XXI.

Her dream, as charming, with its visions fraught,
Through all the morning in her fancy wrought
Sweet pictures, glowing in a world of flowers,
With singing birds in cool and fragrant bowers,
With softened sunlight slowly sifting through
The rustling leaves from skies intensely blue ;
While music sweet as Love's unwritten strains
Sends the hot current leaping through her veins,
And thrills her soul until the bonds of clay
In fervent flame, it seems, must melt away.
And dreaming thus, the pictures slow unroll
As in the reader's hand runs out the scroll,
New scenes portraying in their graphic dress,
And each made sweeter in its power to bless :
While ever at her side there wanders one
Whose praise to her is breathed in undertone
In pleasing streams that ever constant run
As shadows chasing the inconstant sun.
So plain each scene, so bright each image grew,
They pass before as clouds across the blue :
She hears the voices, sees the red lips move,
Feels the warm breath in the soft kiss of love
Hot on her cheek, which blushed a crimson glow,
The guilty blood suffusing throat and brow :
In ecstasy of love she softly cries,
And, washed in tears, still brighter gleam her eyes !
Too bright the picture now for her long gaze ;
Her heart is pained, as eyes by midday's blaze :
To hide the view while she the memory holds,
Her face she buries in the divan's folds,
And to its silken curtains whispers now
The sadd'ning words of her betrothal vow,
Until they lose all sound of sadness there,
And woven in the pictures seem most fair !

XXII.

Her ecstasy of joy in sleep is drowned,
And then by other visions still is crowned,
Brighter than day-dreams seen through Love's soft eyes,

And gay as wings on which an angel flies!
Yet what those dreams no mortal tongue can tell,
If in them sunlight glowed or shadow fell,
Save from the pictures on her brow we trace,
Which in its smiles outshines an angel's face!
And thus she lay through morning's golden hours,
Enchained by Sleep's still softly wooing powers,
All care forgotten in its shadow fled,
All tears of sorrow dry; while joy instead
Plants thick as poppies in celestial field
The flowers of Peace which milk of Lethe yield,
While heavenly smiles lie on her upturned face,
Kissed by the sunshine's softly pencilling rays.
Dream on, fair Judeth! Earth hath not such sweet
For thy sad lips, such paths for thy fair feet!
Her ways are thorny, bitter are her fruits;
The cup she gives her earthly kiss pollutes;
A crimson tide flows mingling in her streams,
Your purest joys you drink from them in dreams.
Drink long, drink deep, fair maiden! ere the flow
Shall mingle in Life's darker seas of woe.
Be glad in dreams! A cup is at thy lips,
And never smiles again who of it sips!

XXIII.

She woke, but how need we now stop to tell?
The story that awaits we know too well!
Her dark eyes glancing up in their surprise
Meet the fixed gaze of Rahab's eager eyes,
Whose very look a spell upon her cast,
And like the serpent's charm still holds her fast;
His piercing glance with fear benumbs and pains,
Chills the hot currents in her shrinking veins,
And palsies speech, until the course of thought
Itself is stayed and ev'rything forgot!
A moment thus in helpless fear she lies,
Then breaks the spell, and starting up, she cries,
" Where am I? What is this? You, father, here?"

RAHAB.

Hush, daughter! Calm this wild and needless fear!

Yes, I am here; what is there in that strange?
My absence you might note and mark the change,
Since from your mother's death your good my care,
Your joys to plan, from grief and trials spare:
And o'er your couch many and long the night
Have my lone eyes watched for the coming light,
While you slept on, as you were sleeping now.
Will you not still your father's care allow,
Whose love undimmed seeks in your comfort rest,
As in your blessings he is ever blessed?

XXIV.

JUDETH.

Nay, chide me not, dear father: that you came,
Should I object, would fill my heart with shame.
That was not it, but this: upon your face
My startled eyes the signs of sorrow trace;
For that dear face to me is like a book
On which the eye, accustomed long to look,
Learns ev'ry line and mark that meets the view,
And at a glance detects each tracing new;
So, as I look, about your mouth and brow
Some strange, new lines are plainly written now.

RAHAB.

You may be right: in truth, I feel you are.
Affairs of church and state have brought new care;
And I just now have from the Council come
To seek an hour's relief with you at home.

JUDETH.

I am so glad, my father, that you feel
That in this feeble hand is power to heal
The mind made sick with cares that needs must be
Borne by kind hearts to shelter such as me!
Sweet father, let me chafe your furrowed brow,
That looks so dark and haggard even now;
And let me sit once more upon your knee,
My throne of state you know it used to be,
And, with my arms your neck encircled round,
With kisses soothe your sore heart's bleeding wound.

You will not let me ? Then on the divan
Rest while I read to you, — or else we plan
Some new diversion when the fasts are done,
And days of our rejoicing have begun.

XXV.

RAHAB.

How like a child you prattle, Judeth !

JUDETH.

So
I am, and happy as the day ! My woe,
Which sat so heavily upon my heart,
Is fled, and darkened clouds now fall apart,
And from the rifts my sun is shining through.

RAHAB.

How so ? I thought your grief would not allow
The thought of sunshine, since I, cruel, drove
The riving bolt which tore you from your love.

JUDETH.

I thought the blow had killed, — and so it should,
But out of evil cometh still some good ;
And if we wait on sorrow to the end,
We ofttimes find in it a helping friend.

RAHAB.

How ? Hath this sorrow turned into a joy,
And findeth hope in what should hope destroy ?

JUDETH.

I thought you hard, my father, — that your hand
Should separate, and Lazarus be banned,
And I from them cut off. And it was hard,
When on my very thought was set a guard,
Forbidding it to breathe his name, and not
Because upon that name was stain or blot
Save one of our belief. This could not change
My wedded heart : this new belief, though strange,
Within my being hath so twined about,

To purge my heart you needs must pluck it out!
The longer here confined, the closer round
And deeper in my heart his love hath wound.
Not prison walls, nor courts where all is gay,
Can conquer love, nor pluck belief away.

XXVI.

RAHAB.

For your own good, you I have sought to save
From peril of mistake so great and grave :
If I have failed in this, the bitter pain,
Not in the deed, but that 't was done in vain.
I might have been content to own your love,
Could I from you this curs'd belief remove.

JUDETH.

Nay, that belief but strengthens love, and gives
It richer food on which it grows and thrives :
The two inborn, and cherished by the fire
That quickens faith and softens our desire,
Binds even closer heart to heart, and weaves
The meshes round my life, nor in it leaves
To me a choice.

RAHAB.

Then is it all in vain,
My love, my care, my teaching? Will the pain
Of your neglect be added to despite,
And my old heart bleed from this bitter slight?
You cling still to that banned, forbidden faith,
And Lazarus love through life unto his death?

JUDETH.

Father, I would not wound your guarding love,
And aught that child can do will do to prove
That you lie deep within my heart. My faith
Is not of me, nor is my love. He saith
That he is true who to his heart is true ;
A lesson old, and one I learned from you.
Would you now ask me falsely to deceive, —
Denying this, renounce what I believe?
Which is the better, — truth in life, though wrong,
Or falsehood lived in the angelic throng?

RAHAB.

I want you to be true ; and, since a child,
The light of truth has on your pathway smiled.
And I have taught you, — trusting to no one
The task ; and if 't were well or illy done,
It was the head, not heart, that in it erred.
I guarded ev'ry thought, weighed well each word,
As gems and gold are weighted in the scale,
To give you their true value.   Should this fail,
Now that my head, like Hermon crowned with snow,
Is blossoming to death, it bringeth woe
To my old heart that hath not hope nor cure.
I want my daughter as the snows are, pure
From all that can defile : for this I taught ;
For this, when from your trusted friends I sought
To snatch you, and by that I hoped to save
From what to me is darker than the grave.
Will you not give them up ?   Renounce, resign
Their love and faith you hold, for me and mine ?

XXVII.

JUDETH.

I know 't is true, my father.   Ev'ry line
That marked your life is reproduced in mine.
And I have lived in you as thought and guide,
And where you walked I, too, walked by your side.
I had no self from you distinct, apart :
The very beatings of my separate heart
Were timed to your desires.   Since I have known
The Master, thought and faith have separate grown ;
While in my love for Lazarus, there grew
A force that separated me from you ;
Not as a child, — that surely could not be, —
But as a woman, separate and free.
I would be all you ask as child, but here
The duty to myself is no less clear,
I cannot give them up.

RAHAB.

You cannot ? say
You will not, then 't is I will find a way
To wring them from you.

JUDETH.

O my father! stay
Thy wrath, and force me not by words unkind
To speak in haste, for wrath is always blind.

RAHAB.

Ah! wrath is blind, but blinder are the eyes
That will not see the course where duty lies,
Nor will be led therein.   Stay! have you heard
From Bethany to-day?

JUDETH.

No, not a word,
But wait in instant expectation now —
And time sufficient for it I allow —
An answer back to me: why do you ask?

RAHAB.

Sometimes the frankest faces wear a mask
To hide their hearts.   No matter; not a line
Of such I see in face so frank as thine,
Nor should I ask the question.   Tell me why,
Since this is so, you still my prayer deny?
Your love is hopeless: I will not consent
To such a union; nay, I will prevent
It, not to thwart your love, but you to save
From that to you far darker than the grave, —
The loss of caste and station.

JUDETH.

I care not
For these, save that you love them.   All forgot
By me are these vain things of life; my thought
Is full of those grand lessons taught
By the Messiah, and with these to guide,
And Lazarus walking ever by my side
In love made constant. I can all forget,
Save thee alone, without one poor regret.

RAHAB.

Still Lazarus and that faith!   You cling to these
As the vile leper to his dire disease.

JUDETH.

Why not? the one brings solace to my pain;.
The other heals, nor leaves a leprous stain!

RAHAB.

I talk, persuade, and even plead, to one
Whose duty is to do, not argue. Done
Are idle words; your answer I require.
Let it be yes or no!

JUDETH.

Nay, spare me, sire!
You know my heart, and as an open scroll
The truth now written there I would unroll
To farthest fold, were it still further writ:
What more in words can I now add to it?
Is there yet pleasure wrung from out my woe?

RAHAB.

Will you renounce them?   Give your answer.

JUDETH.

No.

RAHAB.

As you decide, my further task is light:
My door lies yonder, and beyond the night
Is waiting you.

JUDETH.

My father, as you will!
For now I go to him who waits me still:
No home have I to shelter me from harm;
No stay to lean upon except his arm.
The Master I will meet there, and his smile
My heart will of its bitterness beguile.
Oh, I could fly to meet them, if thy frown
As night upon my heart did not come down!

RAHAB.

You should make haste, before the outraged Law
Hath hanged him on a tree.

XXVIII.

JUDETH.

When last I saw,
The little children gathered at his feet,
While he to them the story did repeat
Of God's great love : should he be hanged for that?

RAHAB.

We well may guess the plot which he is at.
So robbers with the guileless children toy
While yet they plot their village to destroy.
But I no further argue.   You have said, —
And from this hour you are to me as dead ;
While that same arm you boast as your support,
You soon will find to reach you has grown short.

JUDETH.

What mean you, father?   Oh, what horrid fate
Is hidden in your words?

RAHAB.

Your lost estate
Is bitter without curses, nor could I
A bitterer from burning hate supply
Than in that paper hid.   Take it and read,
You that my old heart wrongs in lonely need
Of love like yours ; then tell me which is best, —
Dead Love's embrace or Rahab's sheltering breast?

JUDETH.

Oh, hard, my father, be it yet thy will!
If Love cannot embrace, it will not kill.
If Love be dead, then soon, ah, soon! will I,
Glad of escape, up to his bosom fly:
There, sheltering on his breast, not cold to me,
Forever in his arms my rest shall be!

XXIX.

Ah! what is this which trembles in my grasp,
And would escape from my uncertain clasp?

Frail as my life, yet on it, as a thread
Suspended, hangs that life. I look with dread
Upon its hidden mystery to see —
A letter! And from Martha unto me.
There should no terror in it lurk, no pain, —
Yet kinder hands than hers have ofttimes slain.
Now I will open and its hidden message read,
Tho' from each word my heart, sore wounded, bleed.
Be firm, poor fingers! Steady, in thy task!
When this complete, 't is all of ye I ask :
Hold fast the page, while my unsteady eyes
Read the sharp words from which my poor heart dies.
I cannot see! Has light forever fled ?
Stay! What is this I read ? " Lazarus is dead! "
Dead! Dead ? He said to me he would not die!
Nor is he dead! Behold! the opening sky
Reveals him with his arms outspread to me :
I come! I come! dear Lazarus, to thee!

XXX.

As some light bark, outspreading ev'ry sail
On seas becalmed, is caught by sudden gale,
Unsteady rides the fast increasing waves
A moment, as the battling winds it braves,
By sudden lurch upon its bow is thrown,
Then, shuddering, poises ere it plunges down ;
Its yards, like wildly pleading arms, on high
Implore the pity of a frowning sky ;
While wild and high the seas around it pour,
And in the flood it sinks to rise no more, —
So Judeth sinks beneath this sudden storm,
As death's cold billows sweep above her form,
Save that to her now streams the beacon light
Across the flood, the harbor safe in sight!

XXXI.

Above her now aghast old Rahab stands,
With quickly clasping and unclasping hands ;
His quivering lips are ashy in the light,
His parchment face a livid, brownish white :

So swift the work by cruel Love begun,
He scarce has spoken ere the deed is done!
He cannot think, — hath not the power of thought
To understand the woe his hand hath wrought.
A sudden faint, a spasm of swift pain,
Is all, and she will soon revive again:
Such thought at first he may have had, but now
The pallor deepens on her upturned brow;
No flush returning to the cheek — no breath
To lip, he inly cries, "is this thing Death?"

XXXII.

As the fierce tigress, eager, panting, springs
To seize her mangled cubs the hunter flings
Down her dark den, and with caressing tongue
Strives to revive again her murdered young:
So Rahab, when he saw his daughter lie,
Her white lips silent, with a startled cry
That in the tremor of its rising tone
Had all the anguish of a dying groan,
And arms uplifted, hands outstretched and wide,
He threw himself full length at Judeth's side.
There prone he plead with her, kissed and caressed,
Folded her lovely head against his breast.
Parting her locks, he laughed as through her hair
He kissed her forehead damp and deadly fair;
Then laid her down upon the low divan,
Chafing her clay-cold hands anew began,
Unconscious still that life itself had fled,
And that his eager hand caressed the dead!

XXXIII.

At last he starts from his delusive dream,
As truth's cold lights upon his vision gleam.
With eager foot he hastes across the floor,
And face to face meets Haddan at the door.
" Fly! Haddan, Fly! The leech in hot haste call;
Arouse the house, and send them one and all,
Some here, some there, relief and aid to give,
That from her death trance Judeth we revive!"

No second word he needs, for long in call
Has he awaited, pacing through the hall,
For this dread hour, assured that it would fall:
Nor had he idly waited; but instead,
Now ready at his hand around are spread
The waiting needs an hour like this requires,
Which, soon supplied, the anxious nurse inspires.

XXXIV.

The leech is brought, and willing hands apply
The arts reviving long and faithfully:
Old Rahab, aimless, hastens here and there,
Alternating from hope back to despair,
A hundred questions asking, without stay
For answer ere again he hastes away.
His look is pitiable, and his cry,
Ever the same, is " Do not let her die! "
Alas! appeal for her is now too late;
His own rash act has hastened on her fate,
Which had delayed if he his rage had stayed,
And smooth the way of grief by soft words made:
Aye! even death he might have turned aside
Had Love been stronger in his heart than Pride.
How vain is pride, how false to all our good:
Mad when 't is free, and bitter when subdued;
False when it serves, and fickle in its reign,
Forgetful of our pleasure and our pain!
Self is its all, and in it all complete
It drinks the draught if bitter or if sweet;
Place and its own, these gained, the rest
Beside is lighter than the buffoon's jest.
Yet he who dwells within its gilded halls,
Whose airy coldness hearts of love appalls,
Lives separate, alone, a desert in his breast,
Fear his companion, Solitude his rest!
Love hath no place within except to serve;
Friends are unknown, as such the name deserve;
Of kindred, power may win, blood hath no ties,
Save but the choice to honor or despise;
The poor it knows not, though their lineage springs
Untarnished from the richest blood of kings.

Pride ruled in Rahab's heart, and for its gain
Hath robbed him of his all in Judeth slain!

XXXV.

But all regrets are vain ; old Rahab's brow
Is darkened by a cureless sorrow now :
How much of self-accusing grief is wrought
In the fierce current of his bitter thought
No lip can tell, nor suffering heart compute,
Since those the tale might tell are hushed and mute.
The mourner's wail is heavy in the air,
With notes that breathe the echoes of despair ;
And as the tale of death goes sadly round,
The answering wail but shows of some new wound,
Still adding to their grief ; as Nature grieves
Departing beauty of the Autumn leaves,
Not for the leaves thus fallen, but because
Inexorable Death is constant in his laws,
And the first leaf bears in its early fall
The sad presaging of the fate of all !
So in the fate of Judeth, falling thus,
Is whispered now the death of Lazarus.
So come our griefs : a shadow on the light,
Then thick'ning darkness hiding half the sight,
And then the black and desolating night!

XXXVI.

We close this picture, dark'ning in its gloom
With the thick shadows of the closing tomb,
With Rahab solitary and alone
Shut up with grief.   A low and plaintive moan,
A shivering chill like wind at evening blown,
In low and whispering sighs through aspen leaves,
Shakes his bent form, and shows how deep he grieves.
Now one had thought, who saw him on that day,
Sweep with a word his fellow's scorn away,
Who in the hot and fast increasing strife
Showed but contempt for paltry things of life,
And in his tenets rested in the faith
That life was breath and lack of it was death,

That he would have no tears to shed for those
Who in the grave their weary heads repose.
Yet now he sits with head bent low, and eyes
Set hard on space to search Death's mysteries ;
But what he sees his lips refuse to tell,
And keep their secrets for a time right well.
Hours speed on hours ; the night in swift retreat
Hastes to the arms of dawn on dusky feet,
And yet he sits there : Rest and Sleep defied
Have fled, Despair still lingering at his side,
And whispering in his ear, " Be strong, be brave !
For all of life but endeth in the grave ! "
So, ever in the presence of our fate,
We with our pride and conscience hold debate :
And when the hand of death hath touched the brow,
We who have known declare we do not know.
At last arousing, first his stony gaze
Hath caught the glitter of a steely blaze,
Cold, cruel, deadly, in its gleam of hate,
Which marks a soul defying fear and fate.
This, melting slowly, as the morning's beam
Purples the east and falls on hill and stream,
To softer glow, which lights his eye instead,
While sad and sorrowful he shakes his head,
And mutters hoarsely through his snowy beard,
" Even my one sweet lamb he hath not spared !
Have I done right ?   Should I judge this new creed ?
I have not seen, but now I feel the need —
And Lazarus, too, lies dead !   Why is God's ear
Deaf to the cry of love and will not hear ?
Jairus' daughter felt the touch divine :
The hand that raised her up can now raise mine !
Oh that the Christ would come !   Not as I sought,
But that I, too, may know his mercies wrought."

CANTO NINTH.

WITHIN THE GATES.

I.

THOU All-Eternal Mystery! First Cause,
Creator, God; the Law unto all laws;
Before thy great creation now we stand,
With sightless eyes and flesh-enfeebled hand,
And stretch our arms, as blind men in the night,
To feel the path they cannot find by sight!
We cannot draw the veil behind which, hid,
Lie Mystery of mysteries. If we did,
For our presumption we would surely find
Our prying, earthly eyes of sight struck blind;
We, left in night to grope along life's road,
And, seeking that denied, lose that bestowed.
We do not ask to see, — nay! would we hide
Our face in terror from that portal wide,
And with our brows low in the dust await
The awful closing of the flaming gate
To thy Eternal Courts, if earthly eyes
Were ours, with which to gaze on Paradise.
Not Icarus' waxen wings and plumage ours,
Content we use the cautious father's powers.
No, not that sight, but let a golden cloud
With silver curtains our weak vision shroud:
Then take our eyes and consecrate their sight
To the swift burning of that fadeless light;
And give them powers unfailing to pursue
The swift, prismatic, ever-changing view:
Then take the heart, and give it power to feel
The grandeur which these opening scenes reveal,
And melt it with thy love until it flow
A liquid flood of feeling all aglow,
In which all hateful things on earth here found
Shall in it be forever sunk and drowned:
Take, then, the brain, and purge of all impure,
Give power to know and strength that may endure;

Write on its folds the words we may repeat,
Paint on its forms all pictures there complete ;
And then the hand with cunning strange endow
To weave the colors into fields that glow,
To paint the softened scenes, and touch with pen
The words of Truth until they glow again.
So wings our prayer, as to this task we turn,
And wait thy answer in the fires that burn,
Inspiring thought and opening to the sight
The cloudless Universe in glory bright,
Where thou, O God ! thy throne hast set to reign :
Without thou givest, all our work is vain !

II.

Shine, light Eternal ! in descending rays
Let all the heavens around in glory blaze !
Fill earth and sky until our feeble sight
May see ascending spirits wing their flight,
And watch their course through ether's deep profound,
Where stars are lost and worlds themselves are drown'd,
Until their glory paling in the light
Is hid within the blazing Infinite.
The dawn is breaking on the Soul's dim sight !
The shadows part — the clouds now flee away —
The zenith glows and Heaven's eternal day
Dawns through the mist of finite sight, and clear
The hills of Beulah through the rifts appear !
We stand transfixed before the sight revealed ;
See in what shadow earthly eyes are sealed, —
How small the space our little world contains,
And of the Universe its smallest grains !
What seemed but stars, each wheels a blazing sun,
And their appointed courses steadfast run ;
And in their train draw through the realms of space
Their wheeling satellites in endless chase.
To eyes that can behold each mighty world,
As through the heavens it flies a meteor hurled,
The faintest shapes that fill the infinite
Float large and dense upon the wondering sight :
As eyes to sight, so ears attuned to sound
Catch the faint echoes ever floating round ;

Thus sweetly tuned, upon the quickened ears
Swells the sweet music of the gliding spheres!

III.

We are of earth, but not upon the earth:
Floats far below the place which saw our birth,
While yet our eyes are fixed upon that sphere
Of many sorrows, yet to us still dear.
And, watching, there we see two beings rise,
With wings fresh-plumed to mount the shining skies:
Their bright robes, woven of the mists of light,
Now shine refulgent in their upward flight.
They spring exultant through the bending air,
Whose buoyant wings them heavenward floating bear,
Swift as the light from the Eternal Throne,
That at God's thought through all his realms has flown.
Two Souls they are, new-born to this estate,
Sprung from yon earth and grovelling there of late;
Now, free at last, through God's unbounded grace,
Fly forth exultant to his dwelling-place.

IV.

To us they are familiar: in the clay
We walked together in earth's lowly way.
Our paths, not yet divided, we pursue,
And keep our earthly friends still here in view.
There seems no haste: their twining arms are wound,
In Love's embrace, each other's neck around;
Her face is upward turned, his downward bends,
A smile to both a heavenly beauty lends;
And rising they converse, yet hushed their tones,
Silence their harshest word his whisper owns;
And yet so pure the air, so quick the ear,
We can the lightest sigh they utter hear,
For whispering echoes catch each trembling sound,
And breathe it deepened on the air around.

V.

How like those scenes we never may forget,
We have beheld on lowly Olivet,
Where they together walked with lingering feet
In those bright hours which were of earth so sweet,
Before the cloud which grief brought in its gloom,
And through its shadow showed an open tomb!
Long parted by the cruel hand of hate,
They mourned on earth their hard and hopeless fate ;
Sighed out their spirits in unbroken grief
That saw for them in death alone relief, —
But not as they now find. The wildest dream
Of their fond hearts gave not the faintest gleam
Of this first joy they feel as floating out,
With not one fear, no lingering, shadowy doubt
That savors of the earth, to cloud the brow,
Crowned in its first immortal sunshine now!
So, basking in its halo of delight,
On Love's soft pinions now they take their flight,
Not with the heavy wing the mortal flame
Bears the glad heart as soars the soul the same,
But one of ether woven, fledged anew
With the soft filaments of ethereal blue.
Their hopes and fears, their joys and sorrows known,
We, while on earth they journeyed still, have shown
So we, as now their whispered converse hear,
Will tell their story e'en to mortal ear.

VI.

JUDETH.

How light the soft air feels, as in my hair
Its fragrant breath is gently stirring there,
Sweet as your own when on fair Olivet
I breathed it when our lips in kisses met!
Your arms that now embrace me have more power
Than when they held me in that parting hour.
For then they were too weak my flight to stay,
While now they bear me upward and away
From earth and pain.

LAZARUS.

My love was strong to hold,
But fleshly arms are weak.   The spirit bold,
In fettered clay sinks ever further down
When it would rise : defeat, the mortal's crown,
And all his laurels, are but bleeding thorns
Which make the wreath that his own head adorns.

JUDETH.

Let us forget the earth, for it is sad,
And as above we soar let us be glad.

LAZARUS.

Nay ! let us not forget, that would be wrong :
The saddest notes are in the sweetest song ;
And then beneath us are some friends that we
Are hoping soon in this sweet life to see.
I did not you forget, but on the wing
Above those distant hills hung hovering,
Waiting and watching for you.

JUDETH.

Ah ! I know.
You came to me in dreams, and on my brow
I felt your loving kisses.

VII.

LAZARUS.

Yes, and more :
The night I died, your slumbering soul I bore
In my soft arms, plucked from your sleeping clay,
Up on my flight to Olivet.

JUDETH.

I lay,
They told me, long as in a trance.   I know
The hour you came : the heavens seemed all aglow
With light like this around us, and I felt
Myself uplifted, and my being melt
Into a flood of joy, and on the height
Of Olivet, when we had ceased our flight,
I felt my feet touch earth, and then your breath —

And in it seemed to me the chill of Death —
When on my lips your kiss of parting fell,
As through it breathed a sigh in soft farewell,
And you were gone!

LAZARUS.

No, no; not I, but you.
Like thought, you to your clay-cold body flew,
When earthly voices called, and left me there,
But not as you did once, in wild despair,
For I knew you would come again.

JUDETH.

All day
I felt so happy, though in death you lay,
Which I knew not, and wrote to Martha so,
A sad and mocking letter in her woe.

LAZARUS.

Fair Judeth, — and you are divinely fair,
But not more beautiful than when we there
Strayed on the Mount of Olives, — I would know
What think you now of Death, — if joy or woe
Lies buried in the grave?

JUDETH.

Woe still there lies,
But Joy is risen, and with us now flies
To God's Eternal Courts.

VIII.

LAZARUS.

The Master taught
Sweet lessons to us, and with love so fraught
That it was heaven then brought down to man,
And in his love this joy I feel began!

JUDETH.

Oh that I could behold him once again!
The brightness of his smile this hour makes plain,
Since it was brought from heaven.

LAZARUS.

Look below!
Where yonder star is radiant with the glow
Of light consuming.

JUDETH.

Pray, what star so bright,
That burns so fiercely on the brow of Night,
Is that we see? The whirling suns, so vast
They crowd divided space as they rush past,
Seem not more grand; their light a taper's spark,
Which seems to make the shadows still more dark
Compared to its increasing flame.

LAZARUS.

Our earth
Is that you see. The flames now leaping forth
Is but the glory of the Holy One,
That far outshines the brightness of the sun.

JUDETH.

Why, I see not the earth, but only see —
What is it? Not the hills of Galilee?
Is this thing possible? Lifts Tabor there
His green-browed summit: Hermon, faint but fair,
His snowy head reveals; and Jordan's stream
Pours down its floods in light. I see the gleam
Where lies the Dead Salt Sea, a burning glass,
Across whose waves no ruffling billows pass.
And who are they along the steepy shore
Where Jordan's waters now tumultuous pour,
That climb the heights which guard the narrow plain,
Returning towards Jerusalem again,
Still hid in shadow, save that fitful rays
Of this strange light upon its Temple plays?
Is that — can that be Christ, whose presence burns
And all the shadow into brightness turns?
Yes, it is he! And from his raiment streams
The wondrous light which from him upward gleams,
And shows Judea, blazing as on fire
From Nebo's crest to Carmel's rocky spire,
While all the earth beside, without this light,
Lies floating in impenetrable night!

IX.

LAZARUS.

Yes, that is he; and, following in his train,
Are his disciples from the Jordan's plain;
Their faces you can see, and call the names
Of those who walk within the lambent flames.
When on the earth, you may have seen the light,
Its small, thin ray intensely strong and bright,
Shoot through the blackness of a darkened room,
And flame a gilded halo on the gloom:
That ray, which through its wondrous course has run,
Was but a part of the consuming sun.
So is the glory of the Christ, concealed
To us on earth, through God from heaven revealed.

JUDETH.

O wondrous power! A glory all untold
To eyes where sin the clouds obscuring rolled:
How weak we are, immortal still in part,
Who sin pursue with eager, panting heart,
When, could the eye look upward and believe,
New sight through faith in God it would receive.

LAZARUS.

Your heart grows full when these dim glories rise.
Wait! hold your peace, and further mount the skies:
The day grows brighter as we hasten on;
Our wings, but faintly touched by rising Dawn,
Now speed our flight as conscious of the way,
Like birds that fly to meet the breaking day.
So let us soar, thus cleaving less'ning space,
Our flight a glorious and continued race;
As, clasping hands in silence for a time,
We rise to light, and drink its floods sublime!

X.

Shall we in silence, too, their flight pursue,
Nor paint the scenes that open to our view?
Still it were better Silence set his seal
On lips that falter where they should reveal;

Nor hand unequal to the task essay
To paint the colors of the rising day,
Than feeble drawn and weak the scenes portray.
Now here the task so far exceeds the power
Of mind, that lives on earth its little hour,
That shadows faint and dim in neutral hue
Confuse the mind with their distracting view;
Yet he who draws and he who reads, of earth,
Have all the weakness of a common birth.
He teaches best who stoops through shadows dim,
And lifts the darkened reason up to him;
While he who soars above his fellow-kind,
At best a lost, blind leader of the blind!

XI.

On sweep the pair! Eternity of years
In the great calendar around appears;
The whirling worlds their chosen circles run,
And follows each his own retreating sun.
Great fields of vapor cooling to the view
Roll their vast clouds around some planet new;
Vast wastes volcanic, arid, cold, and dead,
Show here a world from whence all life is fled.
Loud-bursting flames flash on the gathering gloom,
Whose raging fires a burning globe consume.
A flying comet, with its spreading train,
A conflagration whirls along the plain;
While scattered through the mazes of the sky
The living worlds in grand procession fly;
Their continents between broad, gleaming seas,
With plains and mountains, rivers, rocks, and trees,
Invite to rest in flowery vales that glow
In their soft sunlight, gilding all below.

XII.

Beyond all these, to where the circling dome
Touches the confines of th' celestial home,
They upward rise, in awe and silence bound,
Their souls absorbed in mystery profound.
But now they lift their awe-filled, wondering eyes

Up to the shining gates of Paradise,
Which flame above them as two burning suns,
Watched at the portals by God's holy ones.
Far in the vastness of the vast abyss,
That sweeps beyond the sight that looks on this,
Rise battlements, which gleam in crystal white
And burn like walls of fire from inward light.
These on the arch of Heaven unyielding stand,
As bastioned granite on the solid land ;
Above these walls, as sweeps the eye afar,
With not a cloud the vision clear to mar,
The hills of Paradise, like fields of snow,
In beauty and in light celestial glow.
Before the gates, a bright and shining way,
An outstretched crystal sea unbroken lay ;
And on this journeyed many pilgrims there
In shining robes, with faces bright and fair,
All toward the gates which shone as suns afar,
To light their pathway from the utmost star.

XIII.

Here poise these spirits in their upward flight,
Descending then upon the way alight ;
Fold their white raiment o'er each heaving breast,
And pause a moment as for breath and rest,
Then hand in hand go forward to the gate
Whose trembling valves just opening for them wait.
No question there, — no passport need they show,
The seal of their acceptance on each brow :
As they draw near, back slide the noiseless bolts,
And from its rest each golden barrier vaults ;
Wide swing the doors, and through the portal past
Their feet are safe in Paradise at last!
Before and after them a shining throng
Fill the broad streets and crowd the way along,
While thousands more within the portals stand,
Waiting for friends who journey to that land ;
To welcome them, and lead them to the home
Prepared and waiting until they should come,
Glad voices, mingling, join in loud acclaim
To greet their friends and calling each by name ;

While silvery laughter freights the fragrant air
From happy hearts as friends commingle there.
No saddened faces hidden griefs conceal,
Nor tears of anguish Sorrow's wounds reveal:
Hope fills each heart, and in each beaming eye
The fount of tears is now forever dry.
As come and go this never-ceasing throng,
The shining ways are filled with rapturous song!
Some rise and soar aloft to radiant heights,
Some to the lower hills confine their flights.
Angels and cherubim commingling join
With the bright hosts of spirits now divine:
While beings strange of unknown world and race,
Yet with the glory of the human face,
From many shores unknown to earth and man,
A ransomed race, or saved by other plan,
Else favored by that God who virtue guards,
And makes of heaven the crown of their rewards,
All gathering within the court await
Their friends, or welcome to that blest estate.

XIV.

Not all in waiting friends shall there receive,
Nor yet do they the absent ones now grieve;
Why, is not ours to say : we only know
That which we see, not why it should be so.
Around where Lazarus and Judeth stand
Are gathering now a bright and shining band:
Some, from the throng beholding them, proclaim
With shouts of joy the well-remembered name ;
Some from the fields of light, on hast'ning wing,
Fly to the gate, and with them others bring,
To welcome home at last, beloved and dear,
These friends of earth, arrived in safety here.
We may not name them ; once on earth well known,
But long from there, both name and memory flown :
So frail the tenure of our earthly fame,
So light and fleeting the most honored name !
Mayhap a father Lazarus greets with smiles, —
An infant sister, when on earth, beguiles :
A glorious being in perfection now,

With Martha's voice and Mary's face and brow!
He knows her, greets her, smiles his pleased delight,
And looks upon her as a glorious sight.
His father and his mother, radiant, too,
Their youth eternal charms his earnest view;
With wonder fills his soul to see such change,
More beautiful by far than it is strange.

XV.

To Judeth flies a spirit grand in height,
The charm of glory filling her rapt sight,
As in embrace, as fond as it was sweet,
His blooming lips her cheeks with kisses greet,
While gleam his eyes, nor brighter star e'er shone,
With Love's sweet glances, looking in her own.
And well she knows by whom she is caressed,
And that she trembles now on Jadath's breast,
Her only brother, playmate of her youth,
And now forgotten save in Heaven forsooth.
How flashes memory back from scene to scene,
And gathers up the threads that once have been, —
A moving picture full of light and shade,
Whose colors once she thought could never fade!
And yet from them no cunning can devise
The glorious being that now greets her eyes,
As her old mother, crippled, bent, and blind,
And to her couch on earth had been confined
Long, weary years, as long as she could mind,
Springs from the throng with joy of mother's love
Still in her heart, nor purer that above,
A heavenly being, fairer than the one
Whose bending neck her arms now hang upon.
A moment overcome by joy supreme,
She stands as one awak'ning from a dream,
Then clasps her fast, as if she feared escape
Into that once distorted but loved shape,
And looks into her eyes, whose glorious light
Now fills those chambers long condemned to night,
Such as she saw in those to blindness born
When Christ into their eyes awoke the morn.
Sweet smiles press out the wrinkled lines of pain,

So deep, it seemed she ne'er could smile again :
Each supple limb, now straight and lithe as reeds,
The twisted, shapeless thing of pain succeeds.
How glorious is the sight, how grand the power
That to the suffering mortal brings such hour,
In this a world of joy, and here to rest
Forever with the souls of mortals blest !
Yet this is but the portal ; here they meet
The souls beloved awaited long to greet :
Beyond — look up ! The home that is prepared
Befits the souls that have its glories shared !

XVI.

The greetings done, on swift but viewless wings
Each into air self-buoyant upward springs ;
Judeth between her brother floating there
And her sweet mother, smiling, young, and fair ;
While Lazarus, upon his father's arm,
Soars, clasping to his breast his sister's form.
No jealous fears, no lover's selfish mood,
Stirs the sweet current of his ichorous blood,
So broad is Love, so pure his passion here,
That all are drawn within the circle dear.
No narrowing limit here affection bounds,
No icy blasts that blow o'er earthly grounds ;
No fears to chill, no hates to fire the breast
With Passion's rage that blasts the soul possessed !
One broad, eternal love, with God the source,
Holds on unbroken in its even course,
Until the glowing heavens, with it aflame,
Good-will and Love their only law proclaim !

XVII.

Let us with these the onward flight pursue,
And what we may of Eden's glories view :
Hills of delight with heavenly verdure dressed
Thrill with their charms the now immortal breast,
As from the spreading plains they tow'ring rise,
Kissed by the glory of the sunless skies :
For here no sun, its feeble rays but lent

By the Creator of the firmament,
Pale in their struggle with absorbing Night,
Since God himself diffuseth now the light.
Great valleys stretch beyond the utmost sight,
While rivers clear as crystal through them flow
To seas that in the azure distance glow ;
While on their borders stand the trees which bear
Their fruit immortal, and whose blossoms fair
Fraught with such odors that for mortal breath
To breathe would in its ecstasy be death !
Along these fields the ransomed and the blest
With hosts of light and angels walk and rest.
Friends joy with friends ; eternity of years
But strengthens love and ev'ry tie endears ;
Angelic hosts fill out the circle grand,
And add delights to them on ev'ry hand.
No narrow vales are these with earthly bounds,
That man might traverse in his yearly rounds ;
But empires vast, illimitable, shown
With but one season and one tempering zone :
And yet, if judged by Earth's swift-circling year,
In daily rounds its changing fruits appear ;
While flowers celestial, blooming everywhere,
A thousand sweets from ev'ry garden bear.

XVIII.

O'er these we speed ; and swiftly flying train
With us compared but crawls along the plain.
Not e'en the meteor in its dizzy flight,
Which cleaves the skies a blazing train of light,
Flies with such speed as we ; and yet so vast
The regions passing and those to be passed,
That in the air we seem to poise aloft,
And catch the perfumes rising sweet and soft
From the same fields of flowers and fruits below,
That change not to the sight as on we go.
Although a thousand varied aspects cheer
The fields with bands celestial wandering here,
The hills with gentle swells of florid green
Add pleasing contrast to each changing scene ;
Yet they seem scarce to rise above the plains

Where rivers wind like shrunk and shrivelled veins :
But if beside these mole-hills of this land,
The Himalayas, measuring, we should stand,
Their wondrous height would shrink into a span,
And Kinchinganga scarce o'ertop a man :
If to these rivers, shrunk and sluggish there,
The streams of Earth in contrast we compare,
The Amazon a summer brook would seem,
And Mississippi's flood a trickling stream ;
While by each sleeping lake and spreading plain,
If we would measure continent and main,
Atlantic's boundless seas a shallow bay,
Pacific in some inlet hides away,
While continents in valleys such as these
Would all be lost within their flowery seas.

XIX.

All these are strange, and yet familiar seem,
Like forms and faces rising in a dream :
Something of life that we have lived is here ;
Something of memory, faint but ever dear,
Yet beautiful beyond the power of thought,
Which has in dreams of wildest fancy wrought.
The colors eye of flesh cannot conceive,
Nor of our light the faintest patterns weave :
The forms, the shapes, the richness of the flowers
That weave their festoons into gorgeous bowers ;
The birds of plumage — sweeter still of song —
Fill the bright trees where'er we speed along ;
And forms and shapes in dazzling hues and dyes
Startle the thought, the eager eye surprise.
We cannot wait here further to declare
More of these wonders ever strange and rare,
But must speed on to where, before our eyes,
Gleam far and fair the plains of Paradise ;
While, as we journey, question and reply
Reveal each scene and thought in passing by.

XX.

LAZARUS.
What lands are these, my father ?

FATHER.
These below ?
The Border Lands to which all worlds may go.
They seem but narrow and their bounds confined,
And yet exceed the grasp of mortal mind.
Here, circling round the Throne Eternal, lie
The lands which all the common wants supply, —
Not at the hands of toil which hardly wring
The Summer's harvest from reluctant Spring,
But ever blooming, ever ripening there,
Eternal fruitage without toil or care !

LAZARUS.
Why call them Border Lands ?

FATHER.
Because they bound
The Courts Eternal in their circuit round,
And all these worlds — these people blest — can share
In mutual use the bliss unfailing there.

LAZARUS.
All share them here ?   Then are there homes apart
Where friend may join with friend and heart greet heart ?

XXI.

FATHER.
Nay, more than that !   Behold ! I will you show
The glory of this land as on we go.
For now we pass the confines of the Blest,
The land of homes, Elysian's perfect rest :
Far as your eyes can reach stretch out these plains,
Where Spring eternal in its verdure reigns ;
Where Summer's fruits still ripen through the bloom
That Autumn's harvests sweeten with perfume.
Behold ! how varied is each shifting scene,
Where landscapes new and changing intervene !

Scarce do we note one feature in our flight
Before it fades and others greet the sight;
And yet great continents are here unfurl'd,
And each new scene is a succeeding world!

LAZARUS.

What mean you, father? Are these worlds unknown
To us whose hosts dwell here beside our own?
We passed such by as upward here we sped,
But through the air so rapidly they fled
I did not note their fields, save that I saw
Their vastness, which my heart then filled with awe.

FATHER.

And did you think our little mote afar, —
You long had lost it as a paling star,
Save that the Son of God, grand in his grace,
Has flown to it to save our fallen race,
And from the Throne Eternal on its night
The love of God falls with diffusive light,
Until there shines out through the closing gloom
That sacred spot where Christ doth make his home, —
Aye! did you think that for that world alone
Here in these Heavens, where God has set his throne,
And in this light Eternal, out of space,
Was built for earth-born man a dwelling-place?

LAZARUS.

How could I know? I had but faith in this,
That in the far beyond lay rest and bliss!

XXII.

FATHER.

True, man is but as dust; his feeble eyes
Claim they can search and read the bending skies,
And yet see not beyond the clouds that pass,
While dumb he stands before a blade of grass!
How can he know? how can he understand
The wonders of these worlds, their systems grand?
That in each star there rolls a blazing sun
Which with its little worlds their circuits run?
Yet this is truth; and as we sweep along,

I will point out the homes these plains among,
Where dwell the peoples of full many a star
Which you from Olivet have watched afar,
Not dreaming in the twinkling of its rays
Were souls that you might meet in other days.

LAZARUS.

You startle me by this strange truth declared !

FATHER.

I all your wonder once myself have shared :
But look !   A curious plain is that in view,
With rising hills the valleys piercing through,
Small lakes its seas, with waters thick as oil ;
Wide-spreading trees grown from an umber soil ;
Strange flowers, whose colors paint each teeming field,
Which odors rank as incense constant yield ;
And curious homes, most beautiful withal,
As palaces, whose people, dark and small,
Dwell joyful there, blest in the scenes which late
Had cheered their hearts when in their first estate.
Before you here a mimic world you see,
Earth's nearest star, the glittering Mercury ;
So called by us, and man, most wondrous wise,
Some day will filch this name, too, from the skies !
I name this one, but thick as shine their lights
Across the bosom of Earth's darkest nights
Lie spread these worlds exact in counterpart,
Each as original : the plastic art
Of God's creative hand renews in Heaven
The varying scenes that in each world is given.
Now we draw near our Earth's allotted place,
Small it now seems and circumscribed in space ;
But when you see its continents and seas,
And then compare the known of Earth with these,
A blush of shame should tinge immortal cheek
To know our kind, so boastful and so weak,
Who would the mysteries of God explore,
Yet scarce can bound his country's nearest shore !
While o'er its seas and lands in regions vast,
The night of ignorance so densely cast,
He cannot pierce, until the light from heaven,
Through truth in Christ, to him the power has given.

XXIII.

LAZARUS.

Has Heaven for man in mysteries no end,
And yet grow deeper as we upward tend?
And what new scenes are these we now draw near,
Which to my eyes most beautiful appear?
Not since we left the glowing Border Land
Has any seemed so beautiful and grand!
What! Are we stooping to a downward flight,
That all grows plainer to my nearing sight?
Why now descend?

FATHER.

This is our mother Earth.

LAZARUS.

This? This is not the land which gave us birth!
The peaks of Hermon I can nowhere see,
Nor the blue waters of the Galilee:
This cannot be our Earth!

FATHER.

Yes, ours; but not
That beautiful, that love-enchanting, spot
Which gave us birth.

LAZARUS.

Oceans I see most grand!
Dividing continents of teeming land,
That our Judea and all Palestine
Would hide in their abyss, yet hand of mine
Would cover up their highest mounts, if there
With yonder towering peaks we should compare.
What are these lands? They cannot be our Earth!
Or else not there those beings strange had birth;
For human eye ne'er saw in all our day
Such beings as in yonder valley stray.

FATHER.

I grant you true; nor has our slothful race
Spied out on Earth that people's dwelling-place;
And yet, as ants that in the desert thrive,
That lovely region is with them alive;

The time will come their night will break away,
And through its clouds shine forth Emanuel's day.

XXIV.

A cry of joy here breaks upon the ear
From the fair lips of Judeth, soaring near:
All turn to her their fond, inquiring eyes,
To read upon her face her glad surprise,
As she with shouts renewed calls out to them:

JUDETH.

Behold Judea and Jerusalem!
The plains of Jordan and its stream I see!
Old Nebo's front and sleeping Galilee;
And, drawing nearer and still nearer yet,
The heights beloved of dear old Olivet!
But oh how changed!   Their borders, far and wide,
Stretch on and on, and swell from ev'ry side.
The vale of Kidron, now a mighty plain
Through which its brook a river runs amain,
Now swift and constant in its onward flow
To the broad plains of towering Jericho.
Mount Hermon rises with his crest aglow
In golden light where gleamed its peaks of snow;
And Esdraelon to Carmel's rocky height
Lies sleeping there, a valley of delight;
While Kishon's stream from Tabor's grassy hills
Pours down his flood and half the valley fills.
Sweet Mamre's plain! once dear to Abraham,
Thy groves of oak and shades of feathery palm
Are yet as fresh as when he sojourned there;
While now in beauty far beyond compare,
Once known and named on earth " The Vale of Tears,"
Where Adam Abel mourned a hundred years.
Here Sharon, sleeping yet beside the sea,
More beautiful than brightest dream can be!
But where the towns?   From Dan to Bethlehem
There is no vestige now remains of them;
But, in their stead, what lofty domes arise
To kiss with golden spires the bending skies!
A land of palaces, which upward spring

From ev'ry hill in which man dwells a king,
Make beauteous cities set in fields of green,
With fresh'ning groves and gardens fair between!
Of all the cities of our hills and plains,
Alone in place Jerusalem remains;
Yet with no vestige of its earthly fame
Save uncrowned hills and its immortal name!
But crowding its white walls, which now no more
Guard it within as on the earthly shore,
Rise palaces for homes in beauty grand,
Along the spacious streets on ev'ry hand.
But what is that I see beyond it rise,
A flaming glory filling all the skies?
A city on a hill, whose farthest bound
Sweeps out of sight in distance dim, uncrowned!

MOTHER.

That is the City of our God, the grand
Jerusalem the Golden!

XXV.

JUDETH.

O fair land!
How dim my eyes, how frail my sight, to see
The ever-changing glories found in thee!
My powers now fail me! Sinking in my flight,
I fall to Earth pierced by this great delight,
Which cleaves my life as does the feathered dart
The soaring eagle's bold, exultant heart;
And I, like him, stung by its fainting pain,
Drive headlong down to meet the rising plain.

BROTHER.

Nay, sister, we will stay you! Our tried wing
Its strong support will to you succor bring;
Or, if the flight too long, a short delay
On yonder mount we will our journey stay.

JUDETH.

Pray let us, then, alight. Foot I would set
On thy fair brow once more, dear Olivet!
O Lazarus! your words come back again,

You spoke to cheer in that dark hour of pain,
When on the earthly mount we, weeping, strayed,
And, full of grief, our parting hour delayed!
Your words to me were dark and mystic then;
For I but saw with the dull eyes of men,
Earth-blind and doubting: but upon this ground
The light eternal of their truth is found!

XXVI.

LAZARUS.

And I rejoice that our immortal feet
Kiss its green sward, its flow'rs unfading greet;
And that its sunshine, bright'ning here again,
Hides the last shadows of forgotten pain.
O native hills, how glorious to my sight!
My heart leaps up, and thrills with new delight,
When I behold them stretching far and wide,
A heavenly rest, forever glorified.
Here through these valleys in the sunless day,
Life an eternal song, we now may stray,
Eat of the trees whose fruits immortal grow,
Drink from the fountains which unfailing flow,
Rest in the groves whose odors fill the breeze,
Lulled by the music of their singing trees,
While Memory's golden moments flood the soul
And all its shadows from its sunshine roll!

XXVII.

MOTHER OF LAZARUS.

Yes, here you may abide as suits your will;
That is your home, and this your native hill.
Where stand those palaces o'erwrought with flowers,
Whose honeyed sweets in coolness there embowers,
There stood old Bethany; and there our home
On Earth, from whence your tardy feet now come!
We, in these homes of sojourn, ofttimes meet,
And in the circle, now increasing, greet
The dear home-faces. There apart for you
A chamber set: would you now come and view
The heavenly mansion where we all may join

The broken circle in a home divine?
But think not that the home you now behold
Is wrought and fashioned as our home of old:
These heavenly mansions are for our delight,
For rest and joy in days that have no night:
Tongue cannot tell its beauty yet to be,
If you would learn, then with me come and see.

JUDETH'S MOTHER.

And thou, my child, in yonder city fair,
Once our Jerusalem, are mansions rare,
And there a home awaits us when we will,
And to it all of earth are gathering still:
With me, if thou wilt go a moment, come,
And as it shall be, see thy shining home!

XXVIII.

While these are gone, we here awhile await,
And further view the scenes in this estate,
Not to describe, that lies not in our power,
But just to note the wonders of the hour.
No desert land is this, nor treeless waste
The hills of ancient Canaan has displaced;
No beetling crags nor swift and rocky steeps,
No waste of sands that o'er its valleys sweeps:
But teeming fields with heavenly vintage grown,
That Migdol's slopes had joyed of old to own;
With valleys broad, a waste of fruit and bloom,
With groves inviting, rich in rare perfume:
While breath of spices freight the softened air,
And floods of music charm the list'ner there.
Nor hid the singers, who from hill to plain
Catch up and echo back the softened strain,
Like those so oft at feasts in ancient days,
Who toward the city crowd the flow'ry ways.
They may be maidens led by Miriam's hand
That sang the songs of her triumphant band;
Or Barak and Debora, who proclaim
Their people's triumph in Jehovah's name!
Upon the plain of Mamre, at the Oak,
Where God to Abraham in blessing spoke,

It may be now one of the throng we see,
Again he walks beneath his favorite tree!
So, at the Jordan, with the shining host
Elijah views the spot where he once cross'd;
John Baptist, gathering with the multitude,
Stands once again beside its widened flood;
While Lot reviews that land of evil fame,
Once swept to death by Heaven's devouring flame,
And plucks from trees since grown that sea beside,
Whose bitter waters stir beneath no tide:
Their fruit of myrrh and ashes grown below,
Here with their honeyed sweets celestial grow.
We may not speak of those who crowd the sight,
Sojourners in these valleys of delight,
Who come and go forever without tears
Or sighs to darken lives of endless years.
But turn to grander heights, whose way of gold,
Like that which Jacob saw in dreams of old,
Let down through fields in floods of crystal light,
Whose slow ascent reaches the lofty height
Where on the plains of the Eternal One
Stands Zion's City and the Great White Throne!

XXIX

A thousand glories of the god of day
Would scarce be equal to the feeblest ray
That pours from Zion in a flood so vast
That blazing worlds in it would shadows cast;
And yet so soft its radiance that the light
Touched with a grateful glow the gazing sight,
And thrilled it with a power the mortal feels
When softened color light's sharp glare conceals.
The dome of blue, the arch of earthly skies,
Is here replaced by vault of changing dyes;
A thousand hues successive shift and change,
These followed by a thousand still more strange,
And each so pleasing in the shade and hue
That with each change the eye is charmed anew;
While o'er fair Eden's fields and Paradise
The light shines out and fills the utmost skies.
The walls rise high and fair in purple stone

Of blazing amethyst to earth unknown,
So pure that through the range, from height to height,
The domes within rise tow'ring on the sight,
Which we as through a crystal now behold,
With spacious courts and pavements laid in gold.
Each gate, a single pearl, swings open wide,
And angels guard the way on either side,
Not to defend, but welcome as they come
The wayworn pilgrims to their rest and home!

XXX.

Our friends returned, with them we will ascend
The golden way and to the city wend,
And with them enter to the Courts of Day,
Across whose portals Night can never stray.
The watchman at the gate, celestial born,
Bright as Aurora at the coming morn,
In pleasing garments clad of heavenly dyes,
Angelic beams upon admiring eyes.
Obeisance low he makes as we draw near,
His smiles seraphic charm away all fear,
As he to enter bids us through the ports
Into the grandeur of the heavenly courts.
As we, approaching from the heavenly plains,
Were charmed and cheered by those melodious strains
Of music, such, if on the mortal ear
It fell, the soul would agonize to hear, —
So heavenly tuned the notes of pipe and string
To the rich voices that its anthems sing!
So now within these gates enraptured stand
These souls, transported by the numbers grand,
As singing breezes, vocal with each strain,
Through echoing courts repeat them o'er again.
At last her speech, which for the time was hushed,
To Judeth's lips with sudden impulse rushed,
And with a cry from soul entranced she flings
Her hands aloft, — her song triumphant sings,
As Miriam sung, from foes pursuing free,
When Pharaoh's hosts lay buried in the sea!

XXXI.

JUDETH'S SONG.

Praise Ye our God, for he is mighty ; praise ye him, for still
    his love endures,
And he has triumphed over our last enemy and victory
    secures !
Praise him ye Heavens that now are, and praise him Earth
    that soon shall pass away !
Praise him ye Moon and Stars of Night ; praise him, O
    Sun ; and glorify, O Day !

Ye shall be soon no more, but in your stead the heavens
    your likes shall here contain ;
For he who made you all shall keep you, for his hand it
    maketh nought in vain.
Praise him ye White-robed Throng, ye burning Hosts that
    in his courts eternal blaze !
And ye Angelic Choirs, ye Saints redeemed and Souls Im-
    mortal, sing his praise !

Praise him ye farthest Stars that roll in dim Oblivion's far
    and gloomy night,
That have for earthly eyes, which dim obscured by clay, no
    place or gleaming light !
Praise him Elysian Fields, fair Border Land, and Eden ever
    blest of all !
Your glory is his light divine ; your Day, his smiles which
    sweetly o'er you fall.

Praise him ye Mansions fair on yonder plains, ye Lakes and
    Rivers smiling there !
Praise him ye Hosts of highest Heaven, who with glad songs
    his glory shall declare !
Praise him Eternal City ; praise ye Walls and Gates and
    Streets of burning gold !
Praise him ye Courts of Glory, Palaces, and Thrones of
    Saints, which I behold !

Praise him Archangels towering now in light ; praise him
    ye Seraphim divine !
Praise him Cherubic hosts and Powers unnamed who in his
    glory burn and shine !

Praise him Eternal Years, which nevermore shall end and
    nevermore shall die !
Praise him ye saved of Earth and Time, — of Sun and Stars
    through all Eternity !

Praise him transcendent Arch which spans, in glory crowned,
    Jerusalem the Golden ;
Thy pillars, of the turquoise wrought flamboyant, by his
    right hand now is holden!
Praise him all Earth, all Heaven, all Time, all Worlds ; and
    praise him every living creature !
The glory of our Lord and King in majesty shines forth in
    every feature.

Praise him anew ye Choirs of Heaven whose strains ring out
    eternal with sweet praise :
Upon your melodies my soul entrancéd soars unto him, the
    Ancient of all Days !
Eternal, loving, tender, just, Almighty Father, God! to
    thee I sing
The song of one glad soul redeemed, that bows and wor-
    ships thee, its King !

Faint is my song in failing breath, but all of life and heart
    and faith inspires !
And I would die, if there was death, of joy which my whole
    being fires !
Accept, O Father, faltering praise that my poor lips, un-
    taught but loving, bring :
The one grand blessing now I crave is at thy feet to sit, and
    there forever sing !

XXXII.

At her first note of song the lambent skies
Grew yet more lovely in their brilliant dyes ;
And as her notes swelled out, the glowing light
Benignant fell, a glory soft and bright,
With halos such as we in day behold
Where streams the sunlight full on burnished gold,
Save that its beauty faintly here portrays
The wondrous glory of those heavenly rays.

The friends around, when she her song begun,
Themselves entranced, stood silent ev'ry one ;
While in the streets and courts the shining throng
Half-stayed to hear the soul's triumphant song :
For oft had they in these entrancing days
Heard souls redeemed burst forth in songs of praise,
As through these gates with welcome smiles they passed,
To know they were at rest and home at last !
But as these strains arose, and higher rung
The melody of her inspiring tongue,
When grander swelled the tribute of her song
In thought which challenged e'en the choral throng,
That by the Throne its tribute anthems sing
In praise forever to the heavenly King,
Then stayed they, breathless, by its power enchained,
Which in each strain new force and beauty gained.

XXXIII.

Soon through the glowing air the hosts of Heaven
Throng to the gate as flames a summer levin,
In flashing bands that poise in upper air
As if they hung enchained in transports there ;
With stooping heads, and faces all aglow,
Drink in the strains that greet them from below ;
While gathering courts and streets begin to crowd
With throngs whose hurrying feet speed from abroad,
And upward from the plains the golden stair
Is filled with hast'ning forms, divinely fair.
Still sweeter grows the song, still richer fall
The silvery numbers list'ning hearts enthral,
Until the rising flood of melody
Sweeps out as billows on a stormy sea,
Save that the waves that beat the sounding shore
In floods of liquid song their billows pour !
And as the echoes on the beaten coast
In the high cliffs and mountain crags are lost,
So, rising higher in its upward flight,
Sweeps on the song in ever-new delight,
Until the shining ranks that wait upon
The courts of God and dwell about his throne,
The choir whose songs eternity has known,

Catch the sweet notes, and hush the tuneful tongue
Upon whose strains the ear of God has hung ;
And Heaven grows silent as he stoops the ear
The song of the glad soul redeemed to hear :
With joy unbends the broad, Eternal brow,
And all the heavens in smiles benignant glow ;
So sweet to God the songs triumphant rise
Of souls redeemed who mount the shining skies!

XXXIV.

When from her lips the echoes died away,
And silence, new in Heaven, around her lay,
A moment life itself restrained its breath,
And kissed with ashen lips the cheek of Death ;
Then through the waveless air a mighty sound,
That shook the Throne itself, with swift rebound
Swelled up in cheers and shouts of glad acclaim,
And rapturous praise to the Eternal Name,
Whose love had wrought so grandly in the soul
Which with such praise his name could thus extoL
Then gathered there about this joyous band
Of all the angel hosts the great and grand ;
With them the saints who mortal were at birth,
And who long time had walked the lowly earth ;
For some were there a thousand years before,
Had trod like them the far Judean shore.
Here Moses shone ; Elijah, robed in white ;
Miriam and Aaron ; Israel's famed knight,
Brave Joshua ; King David, Seth, and Lot :
Old Abraham, fair as the morn ; and not
The least, nor yet the last, Isaiah stood,
With meek Elisha, in that multitude ;
And all their faces shone as never sun
With brightness far too grand to look upon.

XXXV.

And there was joy supreme ! In realms below,
The grandeur of its flights Earth cannot know.
Seraphic greetings cheer the quivering souls,
The smile of God across their vision rolls :

The saints exult; fair beings from afar,
Who claim for homes the farthest shining star,
Greet them with praise; and kisses soft as down
The smiles of the beloved delightful crown.
Then through the streets, aglow with blazing gems,
White-robed the throng, and crowned with diadems,
Lead on our band to Zion's crowning hill,
Where sits the Lord of Hosts, eternal still;
And from his throne of light directs the course
Of the far realms of the whole universe!

XXXVI.

How shall we tell the glories that arise
And fill with awe our wonder-wid'ning eyes!
How shall cold words the fervid lights convey
Of the bright vision's dazzling array?
Where mansions tow'r in their majestic heights,
Like terraced hills, succeeding flights on flights:
Each flight is wrought of its peculiar stone,
Of lustre such as Earth has never known;
Nor is one house, of all we passing meet,
Whatever court we view or on what street,
Like to its fellow built in form or kind,
Nor known of Earth, by mortal hand designed.
One laid in beryl ends in chrysolite;
The next of jacinth, emerald crowns its height;
From amethyst to chrysoprasus rise
The towering walls the next to greet our eyes;
While sardonyx to sapphires next succeed,
And sardius and jasper others lead!
In others chalcedony crowns the wall,
While diamonds give their light and glow to all,
As wrought between in ever-changing hue
A thousand shades of beauty charm the view.
So pure the stones, so limpid is the light,
What might obscure, reveals to outer sight;
And ev'ry mansion of those tow'ring homes
Clear as the day to gazing eye becomes.
And these, how beautiful! The charms of earth
Are pitiable and all of little worth
Compared with these; and language hath not name,

So poor it is, their glories to proclaim!
Nor can it tell the beauty and the grace
Of those who throng each shining dwelling-place.
If you would see or dream of what is shown,
As falls the light successive through each stone,
Where thousand softened hues prismatic fall
From ev'ry height and each succeeding wall,
And burn and blaze, a flame that is a joy
That, while it cheers, it never can destroy;
Within these courts and homes set laden trees
That shed their fruits with perfume on each breeze;
There gardens plant, in them a thousand bowers,
Where springing buds burst ever into flowers;
Set fountains, where their ever-changing streams
Cast up white mists through which the white light gleams;
And fill these gardens, groves, and bowers with song
That hath no like in earth or human tongue, —
Then gather there the children of some home
Who through the sorrows of our Earth have come,
And here united, an unbroken band,
Forever housed in this delightful land,
Robed in its hues celestial, with the light
Of God's Eternal Throne before the sight,
And this is Heaven! with Eden still below,
Where, as they will, their wand'ring feet may go!

XXXVII.

Still up the height! and yet so soft th' ascent,
The gliding foot scarce to the pavement bent;
So grandly beautiful each changing scene,
That left behind seems like it had not been!
And, as they journey, close at Lazarus' side
Elijah, Moses, and the Saints divide
His time in converse of the Earth below,
And its fair scenes they once had joyed to know.
So they conversed until of Christ they spoke,
Then forth in loud acclaim in song they broke,
And sang with voices sweet a heavenly psalm
Of thanks to God and glory to the Lamb;
While Judeth led with still a sweeter strain,
And sang in low, soft notes her song again.

Thus journeying with song and converse blent,
Up the bright way together on they went,
Until they pass the veil whose crystal hides
The Throne of God, and light from light divides:
When, lo! the Throne, and Him who sits thereon,
To sight immortal blinded, now is shown.

XXXVIII.

It is a glory tongue can never tell,
If tipped with fire, attuned however well,
That mystery mysterious power concealed,
Never to mortal sight to be revealed
Until the spirit mortal cease to know,
And flies forever from the world below.
Such God's decree, and our two friends now find
That in his presence they at last stand blind,
With groping hands, that in the glorious light
Reach out and touch the borders of the night!
Abashed, confounded at this sudden change,
To them as cruel as to others strange,
They cry aloud in agony of fear.
Then they who know, their cries of pleading hear;
And quick as thought an angel by them stands,
And folds in his their outstretched, trembling hands;
He soothes their fears with words as kind as sweet,
And leads them forth with slow and faltering feet
Back through that veil, as clear as filmy glass:
With throbbing eyes in darkness sealed they pass,
When, with a blaze of glory, bursts the light
With all the outspread scenes before the sight,
More beautiful to them, from night set free,
Than they had dreamed that aught of Heaven could be!
So sweet is sight to those who have been blind,
That, when again this gracious gift they find,
A thousand beauties do their eyes explore
In form familiar never seen before!

XXXIX.

A while in silence they about them gazed,
Drank in the beauty that around them blazed

Transfixed upon the heights, where glowing lay
The Plains of Glory stretching far away ;
And farther on beyond the outer walls,
Where, sheer in space unfathomed, downward falls
The plummet sight, their eager, quick'ning gaze
Catches the light of upward-streaming rays,
And in their beams they recognize the Earth,
And the fair spot on it which gave them birth !
" Look ! Look ! " cried Judeth, with a glad delight ;
" Our little world once more beams on my sight !
Oh, how I long to tread those hills again,
And snatch our loved ones from their life of pain ! "
Abashed at what she said, her hands she threw
Before her eyes and hid her face from view.
" Fear not, my sister ! " then the Angel said ;
" Full many spirits to those shores have fled,
To plead with those who linger on Time's strand,
And win their spirits to this heavenly land.
And more, my brother, — let not this dismay, —
To yonder Earth are calling you away
Fond voices, weak and hoarse with falling tears ;
While yonder, near that earthly tomb, appears
He whom the worlds obey, and at his call
Your clay reposing there shall break its thrall,
While your plumed spirit shall return again
And take once more its burdened life of pain."

XL.

" Shall I not, too, return ? " fair Judeth cried ;
" And with my burdened life walk by his side ?
To dwell forever here, of sorrow free,
With him enchained, would not be Heaven to me !
May I not go with him ? " " Stay, spirit, stay !
Angel of light ! Nay, drive me not away !
How can I dwell on Earth, and Heaven know
As I have known ! It would be Hell below !
Unsay those cruel words ; or, if for me
Is this hard fate of Heaven's divine decree,
Let her stay here until I shall return,
A light on Zion's Hill for me to burn ! "
" Nay ! I will go, sweet Lazarus, if leave

To me is granted." " Hush! do not so grieve,"
Said Raphael, the Angel : " I will show
You what is to be wrought on Earth below,
And of the glories for that land in store :
When you behold, you will refuse no more
To fly to it and of its burdens bear,
That you may here still brighter glories share ! "

XLI.

RAPHAEL.

Proud mortals! and you now may well be proud
Of the grand joys which were to you allowed!
Few other souls, not yet divorced from clay,
Here in these courts have trod the golden way :
And never eye still dimmed by mortal sight
Hath passed the veil and gazed upon the Height
Where the Eternal sits enshrined in light !
Had but your gaze endured the burning Throne,
That heavenly eyes in joy may look upon,
No more could Earth resume its feeble sway,
Nor you return again to mortal clay.
Your cries proclaimed that still the mortal part
Clung to your soul and clogged ethereal heart !

JUDETH.

Are not our souls yet pure ?

RAPHAEL.

          No ; earthly mould
Its taint upon the spirit still doth hold :
You must return to yonder Earth again,
To suffer on to your allotted pain,
But not as mortals blind and in the night,
Who walk by faith, for you shall walk by sight!

JUDETH.

Then be it so ! We would be wholly pure,
And not a taint of sin would I endure :
In sackcloth I would walk in thorny ways,
In pain and tears, through all my weary days,
To free my soul of Earth !

RAPHAEL.
Thou shalt be free,
And pure as light, so it is writ of thee,
Yet purged as if by fire.

JUDETH.
I care not how,
If it be thorns or gold that crowns my brow,
If I am worthy of the crown.

RAPHAEL.
No soul
Shall be more worthy, if thy faith extol
The name of him who shall thy leader be,
For he will ever guide and counsel thee.

XLII.

LAZARUS.
Why should we thus, the living of the dead,
Through all these scenes of glory here be led,
Then at the pinnacle of bliss destroy
The golden vision of our crowning joy,
And dash us, humbled, smarting with the pain,
Headlong from these crowned heights to Earth again?

RAPHAEL.
Why, is not mine to answer. All I know
Is that the Lord, the Saviour, there below
Hath need of you and sent you to the skies,
That to the blind of Earth you may be eyes.

LAZARUS.
But I had faith, believed and trusted him, —
And yet that faith was shadowy and dim, —
While now the glory of his truth outspread
Lies fair before me and all doubt is fled.

RAPHAEL.
To cheer your heart, and make your courage strong
In the fierce conflict you shall wage with wrong,
I am permitted to in part reveal

What yonder clouds in darkness now conceal, —
The coming years of struggle to the soul,
As centuries succeeding centuries roll
Through Time's abyss until the triumph come,
When Earth a Paradise in Heaven shall bloom.

XLIII.

Look where the Earth in darkened night is hung,
The palest of the lights those worlds among;
And now in night and darkness it would roll
With not a ray to gild from pole to pole,
Were not the Christ himself the saving light
To lift it from the deep abyss of Night.
How rich indeed that Earth when feet so fair
Would stoop to tread in pain its borders there!
Should mortal soul redeemed through his great love
Reluctant leave these shining courts above,
To dwell a time with creatures of his clay,
When he, the Lord, forsakes the shining way,
His throne and God, to tread these paths of pain,
And be at last by man despised and slain?

LAZARUS.
Be slain? I had not heard of that!

RAPHAEL.
'T is true
He had not taught this mission unto you;
But to your sight, though shadows thick oppose,
Somewhat that future I will now disclose.
Turn to the world once more! Behold the rays
Of springing flames which from its surface blaze:
Now, as they rise, their deep'ning beams expand,
And into sight float clouds, then Earth, then land!
And swelling out this widens by degrees,
Until the mountains rise and roll the seas;
Then from the shadows shines the hidden sun,
Until the trees spring forth and rivers run.
Yet over all, except in one bright spot,
A shadow lies, obscuring like a blot
The face of Nature, as do passing clouds,

Whose shadow half the smiling plain enshrouds.
Judea's hills are in its flames aglow,
And Hermon burns around his peaks of snow :
The Jordan's stream now in its light we see,
And day is breaking over Galilee !
Through Asia run now points of gleaming light,
And Europe, too, is waking from its night :
The bordering seas are bright'ning in its beams ;
Across their waters now it broadly streams ;
Until the islands, long to man unknown,
Come forth to light and continents are shown ;
And on the Earth, in all its circle round,
From pole to pole, no shadow more is found.
This is the light of Truth, which from the skies,
In Christ revealed, a dying world supplies !
And it shall spread until all Earth below,
As now Judea's hills, shall burn and glow :
Then, with the dayspring come, the Earth restored,
Shall shout the praises of a risen Lord !

XLIV.

LAZARUS.

The sight is wonderful ! Then Christ must die ? —
Shall he arise again ?

RAPHAEL.

Yes ! Through the sky,
As you fled up to Heaven, so he shall soar,
While Earth shall shout and all the saints adore !
But he shall come again, and Death shall yield
Himself a captive ; and the grave, unsealed,
No more shall claim its prey ; and Sin shall die,
Man, saved at last, ascend the opening sky !

LAZARUS.

I am content again to dwell below,
And all the bliss of Heaven a time forego,
If I can draw one soul from endless pain,
And for a struggling race redemption gain.

RAPHAEL.

I might for you the veil from Hell withdraw,

Where wail the lost, condemned by broken law,
But it would pain your soul, and of your joy
The sweet remembrance of its peace destroy.
Nor is there time.   Behold where yonder come
A company, and nearing now your tomb!
The Saviour comes to bid you now arise,
Recall your spirit from the smiling skies,
And you must haste on wings of speeding light
To cleave the air in swift-descending flight.

XLV.

LAZARUS.

He calls! I go.   Farewell, sweet Judeth!

JUDETH.

Stay!

Shall I not go?

RAPHAEL.

Yes, now; and haste away.

JUDETH.

Farewell, sweet spirit! Angel of the light!
Ah! now I gladly take my downward flight
To that fair clay I see in yonder home,
Decked in its weeds and waiting for the tomb:
Above its form my father, bending there,
Breathes out his soul in agony of prayer.
I come, sweet father, now I come!

RAPHAEL.

Farewell!

But we shall meet again.

LAZARUS.

In Heaven to dwell?

RAPHAEL.

Ah, yes! to dwell where yonder glowing light
Shall never more make blind your gazing sight.

XLVI.

As fall two stars from midnight's zenith down,
So swift they speed from the Eternal Throne,
And, like their flame dissolving in the blue,
They swiftly pass and soon are lost to view.
Yet in their track along the course they fled
A golden halo lingers where they sped,
Such as we see along the midnight play
In Boreal flame or lambent Milky Way.
Long time the Angel gazed in rapt delight
To see the grand, the soul-inspiring sight
Of two such souls descending from the skies,
Who had but sipped the sweets of Paradise,
Now hast'ning back to earthly miseries,
That they might save some mortal soul from sin,
Some earth-blind heart unto the light may win,
Forsaking glory, peace assured, and Heaven,
For which their souls in bitter paths had striven,
Well pleased that they the Master's will may do,
In lowly way the finished journey through.
" Earth is redeemed! " Raphael exultant cries ;
" Redeemed! " shout back the sweetly bending skies !
To Echo long he bent his listening ear,
As it went ringing on from sphere to sphere,
Until the farthest star caught up the word
And the Eternal Night its murmurings heard.
Then spake he once again, with bated breath :
" The reign is broken of the conqu'ror Death !
Men to the Cross for love of Christ aspire ;
And love of Christ will set all hearts on fire :
A thousand years will wait upon the day
The Crimson Flood shall wash all sin away."
He turned and vanished from our entranced sight,
Then on our mortal eyes sank down the night.

CANTO TENTH.

RESURGAM.

I.

In grief our hearts grow selfish, and our own
Afflicting pains that pierce we feel alone;
And we forget, as we tumultuous grieve,
That others bear still greater wounds and live!
Beside the dead we pour unnumbered tears,
And start in horror at a word that cheers;
Look on the smiling faces gathered round,
And make each smile a self-inflicted wound;
Asking ourselves why any heart is glad,
And think the world should weep when we are sad.
Our tongues refuse to sing, — we think it wrong
That other tongues should tremble into song:
We mourn the dead, who have escaped from pain,
With eager hands would snatch them back again;
Accuse the fate as cruel which relief
Has brought through death, because it brings us grief!
We count, too oft, the worth of friends by sighs,
And think none kindly but their weeping eyes;
E'en hate the sunshine, and where'er we go
Would drape the smiling skies in weeds of woe!
And yet, in after days, when we look back
Along this dark and desolated track,
We gather flowers of memory, planted there
By gentle hands which smoothed the path of care,
That grew where smiles their sunshine on them shed,
Where in the track of tears all flowers lay dead!

II.

So mourn our friends for Lazarus in his grave;
So, in their selfish love, his presence crave;
Forgetful of their faith both old and new,
Which offer rest and heaven, the journey through,

To all the faithful; and that make the tomb
The gate to Paradise, and not to gloom.
Their days are spent in waiting and in tears;
Their nights in wasting sorrow dark with fears;
While those who seek to comfort, ofttimes bring,
For balm of healing, sorrow's sharper sting.
Instead of hiding from the stricken heart,
They show the purple shaft and reeking dart;
At sight of which the sore wound leaps with pain,
And bleed afresh its pallid lips again.

III.

Accustomed forms about the mourners bring
Those comforters that cheer less than they sting;
Whose ostentatious grief to stricken hearts
Far more of form than feeling thus imparts,
To that which it seems best should private be,
And makes of mourning but a mockery.
It is not ours these sacred rites to tell,
Nor yet in words of censure on them dwell:
They are of the dead Past, so let them lie
In that Past buried as we pass them by.
If not such as survive, their forms still show
That we are kindred in the touch of woe;
And have respect unto the law of grief,
Since it is lasting and our joys are brief.

IV.

Now that which grieves his sisters far the most
Is the occasion by the Saviour lost,
While yet in life the panting Lazarus lay,
To snatch from Death his still reluctant prey,
And teach the world another lesson wrought
Through faith, and to their hearts with pleasure fraught.
They could not see in it the lesson taught,
That faith in God no bounds sets to his power,
But holds him equal to the darkest hour:
They could not see upon the shrouding pall
The hidden radiance of his blessing fall,
No more than we, who look upon the face

Of our dear dead, can on that marred page trace
The sign, invisible on features fair,
That shows beneath a hidden blessing there.
They saw as mortals see, with mortal eyes,
That which upon their bleeding hearts now lies,
While Faith's dim ray had cast its feeble light
Across the borders of doubt's darker night
But to the threshold of the open grave, —
There fixed the power to succor or to save,
Nor looked beyond to where the mortal lay
Dissolving at the touch of foul decay!
They had not learned the lesson of Christ's love,
Which they were yet to learn and he to prove,
That those who trust him in his love shall find
The hand that smites may still be wondrous kind!

V.

Four days of mourning have with slow hours fled
Since Lazarus within his tomb lay dead;
And each gray morning to that stricken home
Saw faithful Haddan, ever sorrowing, come,
And bring each day some message from his lord,
That if not cheer some comfort might afford;
Until the third day morning, when he bore
The broken vessel from his own sad door
In token that fair Judeth there lay dead,
And that with her the hope of Rahab fled,
While o'er her clay he bows in broken pride,
For in her death the heart of Rahab died!
The fourth day dawns, a morning sweet and bright;
While yet it trails the sables of the night,
Old Haddan bears a message, sad and brief
As are the whispers grief bestows on grief,
From Rahab to his mourning friends, but still
The few short words with strange emotions thrill.
Upon a parchment, traced in trembling lines,
A heart in grief unwritten grief divines,
Where lie the tears upon the blotted page,
Like leprous spots on yellow cheek of age.
The thought of Rahab weeping for his dead
Makes woman's deepest grief seem light instead:

The shaft must reach that proud heart's deepest springs,
That tears from eyes of such as Rahab wrings.

VI.

RAHAB'S LETTER.

" Friends in affliction sore and dark as this,
Your cousin Rahab greets you with a kiss,
And prays you, as you sorrow, so forgive
A weak old man who hath few years to live,
Since she he loved in death now darkly lies,
And in her death this old heart hourly dies!
Her faith was yours, now in that faith I come,
And through it look to hope beyond the tomb.
Oh for one touch that hand divine might give,
That I may see my Judeth rise and live!"
In these sad lines, so darkly writ and brief,
Is told the story of his hope and grief;
A strangely written, blind, and halting faith,
That gropes in darkness, from the gloom of death,
Out of the shadows where a glow of light
Falls as a mist along the breaking night, —
That would believe because a fierce desire
Drives the blind, grovelling soul first to aspire,
Then draws it from itself by that same power,
To feel a longing never felt before,
And try the wing uncertain, as some bird
Too soon by storm from nest protecting stirred;
Distrusting still its sense so vague expressed,
By hope inspired and then by fear distressed.
But Martha soon the way to light discerns,
To question Haddan now abruptly turns.

MARTHA.

How fares thy master, Haddan, pray thee tell?

HADDAN.

Save for his grief, I may say fairly well;
And yet his grief has so wrought on his soul
That, were it healed, he would indeed be whole;
But if not healed, a malady so grave
Is more than his old heart alone can brave.

MARTHA.

How doth he bear himself about her death?
Hath any change been wrought in Rahab's faith?

VII.

HADDAN.

I may not say that it hath wrought a change,
But then his speech to me seems sometimes strange.
On yester-night he called me to her side
And asked if I could see, since she had died,
A trace of death upon her face or brow.
Now I was startled, too, I must allow:
If it were fancy or the light, or hues
The ruddy flowers about the room diffuse,
I cannot tell, nor would I care to say,
But she as sweet as one asleep there lay;
I almost fancied that the eye, half hid,
Was opening then the softly quivering lid,
And for a moment stood with staring eyes,
Expectant that the sleeping maid would rise!
It was a pleasing fancy, but it fled
To leave the sad assurance she was dead.
But Rahab talked of her in curious strain,
And said he knew she would arise again;
That she but slept, and if the Christ would speak,
At his command the icy bonds would break.

MARTHA.

Why, Haddan, you surprise me!

HADDAN.

Not so sore
As he did me. I never heard before
Words of the Christ that were not spoke in hate.

MARTHA.

To see his change into a faith so great
Is wonderful! And then he really feels
That it is true the Christ restores and heals?

VIII.

HADDAN.

I so believe : for through near half the night
He held me in long converse, — did invite
Me to detail to him each separate feat,
And his strange cures ; and then the same repeat
With time and circumstance.   I won his smile,
And so was pleased I could of grief beguile :
Then of a sudden on my speech would break
His cheerful voice with " Judeth will awake ! "

MARTHA.

Is it of this life or the one to come
He spoke ?
HADDAN.
Of this ; and yet he wavered some
In his long-fixed belief that death ends all,
So strong is mind to fixed opinion thrall :
But with his old belief his hope now wars,
And what best pleased of late his heart abhors.

MARTHA.

His faith so new, and yet so strong, has shamed
My doubting heart, that still the Christ hath blamed
Because he did not come and save from death ;
While here is Rahab, who from childhood hath
Been taught there is no soul — that life is all
There is for man, the grave eternal thrall ;
While he the Christ contemned, denied his power ;
Has cut our friendships from the very hour
He learned we were his followers ; denied
Judeth our fellowship, and has decried
As foolish tales the story of his deeds :
And yet with that same Christ he intercedes,
In faith that he who hears and answers prayer
Will hear him as he cries, and, hearing, spare !
Oh that the Christ would come !

A SERVANT (*entering*).
The Christ draws near.

MARTHA.

Where comes my Master ?   Is he not now here ?
Then I will go to meet him : pray thee wait,
Kind Haddan, for me at the outer gate,
Nor speak to Mary anything of this,
Lest something in the story be amiss.

IX.

With hast'ning feet and throbbing heart she sped
Along the way which from the city led,
Where from the heights into the plain below
Winds the steep way that leads to Jericho.
And just without Bethany's farthest bound,
Where through the shady groves the roadway wound,
She met the Master at the generous shade
Near by the tomb where Lazarus was laid.
Nō tardy feet were hers along the way,
No doubting heart to hinder or delay :
Hope winged her steps, and joy her heart made light,
And in his smile the day once more grew bright.
Yet, as she met him, in regret she cried,
" Hadst thou been here, my brother had not died !
This well I know, and, whatsoe'er it be,
Ask thou of God and he will give it thee."
With sweet compassion for her grief and pain
He saith, " Thy brother shall arise again."
" I know he shall arise at the last day
When all the dead shall rise."   " To thee I say,"
Spake Jesus, conscious of her inward strife,
" I am the resurrection and the life :
He who in me believes, though he were dead
Yet shall he live again."   He further said :
" And whosoever lives, and thus believes
Through me, eternal life at once receives,
Nor waits he for the resurrection day.
Dost thou believe ? "   This Martha answered, " Yea,
Lord, I believe thou art the Christ, the son
Of God, and through thee liveth ev'ry one."
As a fond mother on a trusting child,
At Martha's faith the Saviour gently smiled,
Pleased at her words, and with the joy it gave
To his fond heart her further grief to save,

X.

As lingered his disciples by the way,
Cheered by the softness of the beaming day,
He saith to her, " Why tarry Mary's feet
That they come not her waiting Lord to meet?"
No further word she waits, no further needs,
But homeward now the trembling Martha speeds,
So eager in her thought the word to bring
To cheer her sister in her suffering.
It chanced that Haddan met her at the door,
Where he for her had kept his watch before,
And at his call her sister quickly came;
Surprised to see her eyes with joy aflame,
She said, reproving, "Martha, why so glad
When ev'ry heart about you now is sad?"
Then Martha whispered to her secretly,
" The Lord is come, and calleth now for thee!"
New light returning to her eyes grown dim,
" Where is my Lord, that I may go to him?"
She cries: " Haste! lead me! haply his great love
From my crushed heart its burden will remove."
" Then follow me!" cried Martha: " care for those
Who mourn with us disturbs not their repose."

XI.

With silent feet together now they go,
Then those within alarmed cry: " In her woe
She goeth to his grave and weepeth there;
In her great grief she needeth now our care."
They rise and follow, and a gathering crowd
Assembles fast and fills the dusty road;
Unconscious why they go, are blindly led
To where the Master waits for her, instead
Of to the tomb. Thus seeming to our eyes
The goal in sorrow's way before us lies,
And what seem ways of grief, if still pursued,
Lead in the end to unexpected good!

XII.

When Mary comes to where the Master waits,
The sight of him naught of her tears abates ;
But deeper sinks the rankling shaft of woe,
And drowns her eyes by the fresh torrent's flow.
With hastening steps at first, then falt'ring, slow,
She at his feet fell down and sadly cried,
" Hadst thou been here, my brother had not died."
Now when the Saviour heard their wailing woe,
Saw Mary's eyes like streaming fountains flow,
His soul was troubled, and he inly groaned,
Until the echoing skies above him moaned,
While shadows darkling o'er the sunshine crept,
And Earth grew hushed and still, for Jesus wept !
Man's woes poured out a fountain deep and wide,
And in its flood all human tears were dried !
" Where have you laid him ? " presently he said.
They answer, " Come and see," then gently led
Unto the tomb where Lazarus lay dead.
The Jews, astonished at the Master's grief
Which thus in open weeping found relief,
One to another said : " Behold his love :
It doth his very soul in sorrow move !
Could not this man, so loving, tender, kind,
Who at a touch doth open eyes born blind,
Whose tender hands the leprous death defy,
Could not he too forbid that Lazarus should die ? "

XIII.

Here at the grave a moment Jesus waits,
As if within his soul he still debates ;
Then, with a sigh that trembles to a groan,
He gently bids them roll away the stone.
" Stay ! " Martha cries. " Do not the covering raise ;
It is not best : he hath been dead four days."
Christ answering, saith, " Said I not unto thee,
Wouldst thou believe, God's glory wait and see ? "
Abashed and awed, she from the Lord retires,
But yet his speech her trembling heart inspires.
Along the flinty groove the smooth stone rolls ;

A nameless dread seizes the waiting souls.
In silence rapt a time the Saviour stands,
With upturned face and tightly clasping hands ;
His eager eyes search out the bending heaven,
As if to him a foretaste here is given
Of that dread hour when he shall come to die,
And in the tomb, as Lazarus, lifeless lie !
If so, does thought of waking stir his breast
With its first flutterings of his troubled rest ?
Now part his lips; his voice the silence breaks
In a low prayer which sleeping Echo wakes,
Like murmuring breezes in the whispering grass,
Or midnight voices when the night winds pass :
" Father, I thank thee now thou hast me heard,
As thou dost always hear ; give to my word
Thy power, because the people wait to see.
Teach them to know 't is thou that sendest me :
Show forth thy glory, Father, most divine,
And let its heavenly beams around me shine."

XIV.

Not as before, when at the Jordan's flood
He, glorified, at his baptism stood,
Fell burning flame from out the midday heaven,
While thunders roll and flashed the blazing levin.
But now a calm instead, like breathless night,
Hushed the warm air which glowed in soothing light,
Like fires that in the warming furnace glow,
When rising blasts increase the heat below,
Before the flames with white and angry glare
Leap out and burn e'en those charged with its care.
Expectant Nature holds its shuddering breath,
While hollow moanings fill the halls of Death,
As trembling stands the grizzly Terror by,
Shuddering at defeat he knows is nigh.
Above their heads the bending zenith burns
With glowing fire and flashing light in turns,
While from the silence softly on the ear
A sound like beating wings draws swiftly near.
All eyes are upward cast to catch the flight
Of some swift bird of prey in mazy height,

But in surprise they range the glowing air
With eager eyes and find still nothing there ;
And while they gaze, the God incarnate speaks,
" Lazarus, come forth ! "   A golden glory streaks
The azure vault and runs from east to west,
Gilding the sea and purpling mountain crest;
While o'er the Earth anew the morning springs,
As Hope leaps forth with life upon her wings.
Along the shores of Death its thunders peal,
The tomb it shakes and bursts its hoary seal,
And on the ear of sleeping Lazarus breaks,
Like trumpet's brazen note, — the dead awakes !
No spectre from his tomb before them stalks :
In grave-clothes bound, the living Lazarus walks !
Through haggard lips his struggling breath he draws,
While yet the reeking napkin binds his jaws.
So quick the chilled blood starts along its course,
The living flesh at first feels not its force ;
The staring eyes the day so quickly finds,
The light benumbs them and its brightness blinds :
So, with closed eyes and fettered foot's slow tread,
He walks a living man, but looks the dead !
But soon the surging flood which stirs the heart
Sends out its tides anew to ev'ry part ;
The tingling fingers feel the genial glow,
The stumbling feet are steadied by its flow ;
The pallid lips are tinged by health's red flush,
The ashen cheek glows with a mantling blush,
While from the wide and wildly staring eyes
Looks forth the soul in its unmixed surprise.
Yet speaks he not a word : while all are glad,
Of all their faces, his alone is sad ;
Still on his heart the light celestial lies,
While earthly shadows darken now his eyes !
Now speaks the Christ in accents hushed and low,
" Loose ye his hands and feet and let him go."

XV.

At first the soul expanded seemed confined
In its clay tenement, whose limits bind
The heaven-plumed spirit in its narrow bound,

And spurned impotent at the grovelling ground.
Here those swift wings, so late to cleave the skies,
Can now no more with their gross burden rise:
Mortality, the victor once again,
Over the stooping soul asserts its reign,
And unto Death it bows, a slave supine
In mortal flesh, this essence all divine.
Oh sad, sad scene! No prison-house so dread!
The grave to us gives liberty instead!

XVI.

The Master greets him with a brother's kiss,
In its return a time he seems remiss;
Abstraction seems to fill his sluggish brain,
Returning thought comes slowly back again;
For still before his heaven-enlightened eyes
The visions of celestial worlds arise.
How like to one who walketh in a dream
Where gladsome lights about his pathway gleam,
When life is dark and saddening in its cares,
And few the joys his heart o'erburdened shares:
Through flow'ry fields that in rare beauty glow
With Eden's glory in this world below,
And, walking, plucks the fruit and fragrant flowers
That load the garden and bedeck the bowers;
Else, softly lying in some leafy shade,
Drink in sweet music there entrancing played,
While eyes of beauty please with charming wiles,
And lips of pleasure cheer with glowing smiles;
White hands the amber nectar there bestow
With words that charm in music whispered low,
And Earth has fled with all its cheerless gloom,
Else in the dream a paradise become:
Then let harsh words break on his sleeping ear,
And for his dream reality appear
In faces harsh, seamed o'er with care and pain,
The narrow cabin with its fittings plain,
While skies without hang lowering on the day,
In whose dark shadows flees his dream away!
How rueful now he views the scenes around,
Scans his own hearth, surveys his sterile ground!

With anguish of a soul so born for joy,
He sees rude hands his ev'ry hope destroy ;
There silent stands with anguish in his face,
Until he feels his loving child's embrace,
As her soft arms steal shyly to their place,
Then love tumultuous fills his heaving breast,
And peace at her soft touch has brought him rest.
So Lazarus felt when he at first awoke,
And on his mortal vision dimly broke
The scene around, the Master standing by,
And all his friends in loving sympathy.
So for a time he bowed his gloomy head,
And to their kind caresses nothing said,
Until his sister Mary, bathed in tears,
With face made beautiful by smiles, appears,
And, rushing to him with delighted cries,
Close to his heaving bosom fondly lies ;
With arms clasped tight about his stooping neck,
Upon his ample breast her head thrown back,
Smiles in his face with eyes that in their night
Tell through their tears her heart's untold delight :
A picture she of Judeth in their flight,
When they from lessening earth soared upward, far
Beyond the light of farthest shining star.
If it were thought of her, we may not say,
That roused him, but the shadow fled away
Which veiled his face, and into light it broke,
And for the first he, smiling, to her spoke.

XVII.

" Dear sister Mary, pardon, if I seem
Cold and neglectful, for a wondrous dream
Has filled my soul, and from its charms I still
Its glories feel that all my being fill.
I cannot name its wonders ; words will fail ;
The colors of this Earth to nothing pale :
I must stand silent, while the lights that burn
Die out and I to sombre Earth return.
And you are beautiful ! yet not so fair
As Judeth is, — or was at parting there
Upon Mount Olivet.   I hastened here,

And now before you in my flesh appear:
Still you remind me of her when she lay
As you do now, when hence we soared away."
" I do not understand you ! " Mary cries,
Her dark face paling with distress'd surprise ;
" Your mind is wandering still, and visions keep
Their spell o'er you that held you in your sleep —
Stay ! 'T was not sleep, but death ! What visions come
To light the darkened chambers of the tomb ? "
" None to the tomb ; for I escaped from thence —
Where ? would you ask, and whither come ? and whence ?
I may not answer now, since Martha waits
And all my friends around." Mary debates,
Uncertain of her course, or how pursue
This subject further, fearing to renew
A theme which, followed by whatever path,
Would in the end lead up to Judeth's death.
Meantime her arms release their ardent hold,
While his the waiting Martha now enfold,
And loving tears her heart of grief beguile,
O'er which is thrown the rainbow of his smile.
Soon other friends with joyful greeting press, —
Kiss hands and face and tenderly caress,
Uncertain which their duty claims the more,
Their friend to greet, or Christ, their Lord, adore.

XVIII.

Meanwhile had Haddan, first in sore surprise
At what he sees revealed before his eyes,
Recovering from his awe, with hope inflamed,
That for a time the dread of Christ had tamed,
Approached the Master where he silent stood,
With head bowed down and in dejected mood,
And said : " Rabboni, hearken to my prayer !
Thou dost remember Judeth, once so fair,
Friend of these three, the ruler Rahab's child ?
Of her fair life Death hath our house despoiled.
My master saith if thou but will, she lives :
This day to me that bright assurance gives.
I pray thee come to him apace : his grief
In thee or death must find a quick relief."

The Christ to him at first makes no reply,
But Lazarus searches with inquiring eye
To know his thought, as Martha has made known,
Fair Judeth's death in tender pity shown.
Yet well he reads the secrets of his breast
That hath the heart of Lazarus oppressed.

XIX.

When Martha sees that Haddan pleads her cause,
To his support with eager haste she draws,
And, further aiding on the case she pleads,
Old Rahab's letter to the Master reads.
" Come hither, Lazarus ! to thee would speak :
Wouldst thou that I fair Judeth should awake ?
Thou know'st her secret soul, with her hast soar'd
To where the Father sits high and adored :
Shall I call back her shining spirit blest
In yon bright Paradise of endless rest ? "
To Lazarus Mary and then Martha turn,
His paling cheeks with fitful blushes burn ;
His eyes suffuse with quickly rising streams,
In dewy mists through which their brightness gleams ;
Contending hopes combat his rising fears,
While selfish love in his behalf appears.
If she returns, her smiles will cheer his days,
Make glad the paths of life through which he strays :
To him a source of joy will she become,
And light the chambers of his deepest gloom ;
Yet at what cost ! This Heaven to her denies,
And all his gain must be her sacrifice !
He knows how great the glory she foregoes
To journey with him through this vale of woes :
The bliss eternal now by her begun,
Secure in Heaven, again is to be won,
With sorrows constant thronging all her life,
Her soul a battle-field of ceaseless strife,
With dangers grave that she may be undone,
And lose the victory and her waiting crown.

XX.

'T is but a moment waits he to decide
The answer, which, when made, he must abide,
And then with low-voiced speech he simply says,
" My will, dear Master, as thou wilt, obeys."
" Why, dost thou not desire," here Martha cries,
" That Judeth from her sleep should now arise?
Why, art thou lost to love, and feeling too,
Forgetting that which is to duty due?
I fear me that the shadows of the tomb
Still hold thy senses clouded by their gloom."
" I see too clearly, Martha," he replies,
" Not shadow, but the light which blinds my eyes;
And this now makes me gravely hesitate
To call her back to Earth's unblest estate.
Yea, Master, as thou wilt! Be mine the pain,
To her the blessing and eternal gain."
" 'T is not to man the glory, but to God;
For this my feet the thorny ways have trod,
That I for man the crooked ways make straight;
In lowly fields my Father's bidding wait:
Shall mortal man do less, as he hath power,
To serve his own and glorify the hour?
I know thy heart, its pity and its love
For her who might dwell in the courts above;
But there is work for you and her, when done
Will glorify as day the rising sun.
Go tell thy master, Rahab, the Christ saith,
' It will be done according to his faith.' "

XXI.

As to the town their homeward steps they turn,
The thronging people of the wonder learn;
And, meeting Lazarus in grave-clothes clad,
His smiling friends around with faces glad,
With them the Christ and the disciples, too,
At once believe the wondrous story true.
To all the town he is familiar known;
In all the land around, there scarce is one
Who hath not seen him dead, or shortly heard,

From those who knew, the sad assuring word ;
And now as plainly do their eyes behold,
As witness of the truth so strangely told,
The dead alive and in his grave-clothes walk,
The voiceless lips in pleasing converse talk ;
While eyes, late closed in death, with reason's light
Look into theirs, remembrance in their sight.
The further rumor, that the Christ had wrought
This miracle, around him quickly brought
A wondering throng, whose curious eyes now sought
Him in the way ; and many is the gaze
Now fixed on him in wonder and amaze.
Some are his followers who long believed ;
Some from this hour alone the truth received ;
While all now praise, save those whom hate makes blind,
And they this hour no fault in him dare find.
This truth stands forth, they cannot now deny,
And for a time at least dare not defy ;
But harbor in their hearts a secret hate
That for its hour propitious needs must wait.

XXII.

At home arrived, no banquet ever spread
Was half so grand as here awaits the dead
Now made alive, for love and joy afford
The wine of life that crowns the festal board,
And they all sup together with the Lord !
A constant throng with smiling faces greet,
And rippling laughter rises where they meet.
The gardens ravished of their choicest fruits,
Here friend with friend for honor now disputes
In their bestowal, while the sweetest bowers
Give generous tribute in abundant flowers.
For Mary roses blush of radiant dyes,
Abundant lilies cheer grave Martha's eyes ;
While mingled flowers, still breathing sweet perfume,
With fragrant breath o'erflow each open room.
Gay garlands deck the walls around, instead
Of weeds of mourning gathered for the dead.
For Lazarus' brow the laurel wreath is twined,
White immortelles among the leaves combined ;

While purple myrtle Christ's fair head adorns,
Foreshadowing a bleeding crown of thorns!
And yet, among these hearts so light and glad,
The two who bring them joy alone are sad, —
The one because of bliss a time now lost,
Or, if regained, yet won at bitter cost;
The other, for ingratitude, which brings
To death and shame so many earthly kings,
And now is waiting for occasion given
To basely crucify the King of Heaven!
And it is thus, and evermore shall be,
To man here born to earthly destiny:
The one who lifts his fellows from the night
Of mortal gloom into the better light
Must pass through persecution's bitter tide,
And see himself by those he helps denied;
Scorned by the hearts that owe to him their joy,
While their mad hands his dearest hopes destroy,
Then cast him out, derided, scorned, contemned;
While they grow great on what their lips condemned!

XXIII.

Now while they joy who gather at this home,
Forgetting past nor think of days to come,
One guest from out the portal quickly glides,
And Haddan, mounting, to Jerusalem rides:
His message borne is one now full of cheer,
Yet burdened with a dim and distant fear;
Since from the joyful living has he sped
To greet the mourners watching by their dead.
At first his steps are light, as his who bears
Sweet words to comfort hearts oppressed with cares.
He feels from his own soul the burden rise
To wing his footsteps as he homeward flies;
While bearing in his hand the full reprieve
To those in sorrow's chains who hopeless grieve.
But, as he nears the city's towering walls,
From its wild flight his soaring spirit falls;
The joys that filled the hearts he left behind,
As strains of music faint along the wind,
Have lost their charms; while grief to which he goes

Renews again the shadow of its woes,
And faith, that rose with Lazarus from the tomb,
Sinks down again within its charnel gloom, —
Forgetting that the hand which raised has still
Its cunning left, nor languishes its skill.
How true his heart our hopes and fears declares;
In doubt each breast consuming torture shares!
We faith forego, in darkness still pursue
The shadow of our fears the journey through,
When right before, inviting to our eyes,
The Paradise of hope benignant lies;
So near its bounds, if we but stoop the ear,
The songs of its sweet singers we may hear.

XXIV.

While Haddan rides let us speed on before,
And reach the city ere his journey o'er;
And, by the prophet's new-awakened power,
Turn back the dial to the morning hour;
Then, entering Rahab's hall, with muffled tread
Pass to the silent chamber of the dead!
Not altered much the room since for the first
Its pleasing beauty on our senses burst,
Save that the sunshine through the windows wide,
Except in light subdued, is now denied,
And the bright presence of the soul it cheered
Is lost in ev'rything the spot endeared.
There broods a silence in the very air;
Nor sounds a footfall now in hall or stair:
Like spectres glide the servants on the sight,
And one expectant waits the fall of night;
So deep the shadows in their gloomy fall
That darkness weaves into a funeral pall.

XXV.

And yet the room which should the darkest be,
And shrouded thick beneath Death's canopy,
" Has most of cheer and sweetness in the air, —
The one green spot left blooming fresh and fair!
Is it because the sweetest flower lies there?

Is it because the touch of love has made
Its brightness such that it is slow to fade, —
Like white immortelles plucked, which sweeter grow
In the clear, waxen beauty of their snow?
With head in reverence lowly bending there,
We enter in, our feet unshod and bare,
And eyes whose tears stand ready now to start
At the sore touch of woe upon the heart.
What means this scene?   It is not one of death,
For life is rife in ev'ry fragrant breath:
The flowers long plucked have not a withered leaf;
The wreaths here twined as tokens sad of grief,
And fragrant spices, freshen in their bloom,
While bud and blossom yield a fresh perfume.
From scattered flowers to chaplet on her brow,
All, all are fresh as if but plucked just now!
While, sweetest of them all, before our eyes
In all her wondrous beauty Judeth lies!

XXVI.

Oh had we Raphael's art, Angelo's power,
And could we draw their colors from each flower
To twine in garlands, and on canvas paint
Each blossom, with its shading deep or faint;
To start the life upon the pictured scroll
Until it breathed a living force through all;
To weave among the flowers each tinted shade,
To catch their wrinkled brown where'er they fade,
And set the buds each on its separate stem,
In beds of green bright settings make for them,
So that the eye beholding, their fresh bloom
Would cheat the senses with unshed perfume, —
Then could we tell, in pictures fair to see,
The wondrous sweetness of their witchery:
Undreamed of, save in some fair paradise,
Whose charming bound beyond our vision lies,
Where death holds not, as here, high carnival,
And sorrow decks with flowers no funeral pall.
How bright such picture in its flowers and gold,
How sweet the story in its beauty told!

XXVII.

But we must tell in slow and halting speech
What art and brush can far more truly teach,
And leave to thought, where lacks the ready eye,
The shades and colors it must needs supply.
Had Death been bridegroom to this fair young bride,
More bounteous hand had not her couch supplied;
Love could not find in all the smiling land
Desire to crave and beauty to command
One thing now lacking not on her bestowed,
That lack of care in thing most trifling showed.
And yet, in all that beauty so profuse,
That lack of nothing even made excuse,
The dead of all was the most beautiful!
With rounded cheek, and lip still fresh and full,
And waxen lids with lashes dark as night,
Shut in the eye and veiled its darkened sight,
While fair above them, peerless in its snow,
Gleamed the white marble of her matchless brow.
Her hands with waxen fingers lightly rest
Unclasped and loosely on her quiet breast,
As if in careless moment she had thrown
Them thus in restless slumber lightly down.
We watch her eyes in fear lest she awake,
And by her glance the spell enchanting break;
Expectant wait the bloom upon her cheek,
Or see her pale lips part and hear her speak!
She is not dead! we say, and so believe
With Rahab, who may yet in anguish grieve;
But still with hope expectant constantly
Believes what he now feels he soon shall see.

XXVIII.

And he sits there with bowed head bending low
In trembling hands that clasp his wrinkled brow,
His white hair falling scant and loosely down
O'er their thin backs, now shrivelled, gaunt, and brown.
He does not weep as he sits silent there,
Although his lips move in a whispered prayer;
Absorbed with that within, his soul is lost

Beneath the sea of sorrow tempest-tossed;
Though now in calm the bitter waters rest,
Nor moves a ripple o'er his tranquil breast!
Is it his hope, or is it his despair,
That to his breast brings peace unbroken there?

XXIX.

It must be hope, for see! he lifts his eyes
To Judeth's face, and in them gleam surprise.
Expectant still he waits and watches on
Until the seconds are to moments grown;
These run to hours, and still his placid face
Is altered not, nor lifts his earnest gaze.
Now he approaches from his lowly seat;
A moment stands in silence at her feet,
And gazes on her form as Parsee priest,
For rising sun watches the reddening east,
And like him still in rapt devotion there
His thin lips tremble with a whispered prayer.
Next to her side he glides with silent tread,
And stoops a moment o'er her love-crowned head, —
Would kiss her brow, but, for some unseen cause,
When touch his lips her hair, he then withdraws,
And with a sigh of sorrowful regret
Kisses with eyes, — his lips denying yet!

XXX.

He would withdraw again to wait and muse,
But this his still unwilling feet refuse,
And lingering at her couch his fingers stray
From bud to flower, from flower to bending spray;
Here lift a leaf, there press another down,
Toy with the purple myrtle of her crown,
Smooth out a ringlet wandering on her brow, —
Touching with trembling hand her fingers now,
Which, as he lifts them. like a clinging vine
Whose waxen tendrils what they touch entwine,
With all the lightness of their slender grace
Cling to his hand, and, clinging, half embrace!
At this he starts, and there is in his look

A gleam of joy that o'er his aged face broke
Like set of sun across the winter snows,
And cheering light on sorrow's bleakness throws:
But when he turns and sees her death-sealed eyes,
The light of joy along his features dies,
As fades that sunset in the gloomy shroud
Where spread the wings of the oncoming cloud.
Then sweeps across his bosom's placid rest
The storm returning to his withered breast,
And for a moment there beside his dead
To grief's swift blast he bows his helpless head:
As traveller, lured upon his homeward way
By the fair promise of the closing day,
Yields to the storm which veils his guiding sun,
And into night drives him now helpless on !
" How long, O Lord ! " he moans, " shall this endure ?
For sin and grief on earth is there no cure ?
My faith in thee and in thy strength abides ;
And still its light through all this darkness guides :
My spirit for my guilt now inly moans,
My flesh in sackcloth for its crimes atones :
What is there more in me thy justice grieves ?
My soul repents and now in truth believes ;
Thou canst, if thou but will, this clay revive,
Speak but the word, and she again shall live ! "

XXXI.

As ceased his prayer, a moment in the room
The light grew shaded into misty gloom ;
The air, disturbed, shook lightly in their rest
The silken curtains which the windows dress'd ;
Then o'er the brow of Rahab swept its breath,
And trembled lightly on the lips of death :
Nor yet was open door nor window found
From which it came through all the house around.
As Rahab lifts his head, in golden streams
The light within the room a glory gleams ;
Nor yet uncurtained window doth invite
From skies without the midday's blazing light,
But in a flood it self-created pours,
A sea of light that hath no bounding shores !

From ev'ry side, above, around, below,
Streams the soft light in ever-bright'ning glow,
Like boreal beams upon the Arctic snow ;
Or light from midnight skies when comet's train
Enfolds the earth and fills the heavenly plain ;
Or such as blaze along the tropic seas
Cut by the ploughing keel or ruffling breeze.
Now on the stillness hushed as silence there
Comes with a trembling sound upon the air
A sigh, such as when breathes across the strings
Of unstrung lute the wind in whisperings,
And following it, in faintest monotone,
The sigh increases to a quivering moan.

XXXII.

With eager gasp and eye of anxious gaze
Old Rahab glances up to Judeth's face.
Still calm and pale in snowy whiteness gleams
That lovely brow within these mystic beams.
Her eyelids lie like white seals softly press'd ;
Upon her eyes their fringéd curtains rest,
A dark line traced upon the bloodless cheek ;
While yet her lips, half parted as to speak,
Are still and white, like petals of a rose
When first from waxen bud the leaves unclose ;
And shut within, and partly hid beneath,
Gleams the white pearl of her unrivalled teeth.
A deeper sigh convulses Rahab's breast,
In darker gloom his soul seems now oppress'd ;
The inward groanings of his spirit rise,
And intermittent mingle with his sighs ;
And as he watches now his Judeth dead,
He looks as one whose hope and faith have fled :
And surely his new faith and hope are strong,
To thus endure in patient waiting long !
How many tried and proved have soon forsworn
The faith in which they have been bred and born !
The test is not that we believe ; the sure,
Undoubted proof is that we still endure :
Remembering, where fails the mortal's power,
In man's distress is God's propitious hour.

And this is Rahab's faith and hope, — his stay;
And, set on these, he will not turn away.
He saith He will reward most surely send
To him whose faith endureth to the end:
What more can mortal ask, what more demand?
'T is but in want we need the helping hand:
If then our needs our faith's endurance try,
He who permits it succor will supply.

XXXIII.

A gracious promise Rahab sweetly feels,
And peace again within his bosom steals;
Then, with a sigh as soft as zephyr blown,
He softly says, "Thy will, O Lord, be done!"
As if the touch of the Archangel's wand,
Or trumpet blown that shall the dead command,
Had called the sleeping girl with power so great
The dead must feel in dust inanimate,
So through her death-sealed ears the whisper came,
To it responsive thrills her quivering frame;
The throbbing heart renews its work again,
The hot blood speeds to palsied limb and brain;
The icy dews melt from the clammy brow,
The pale cheeks flush with health's returning glow;
The trembling eyelids from their slumbers wake,
Her parted lips the seal of silence break,
And Judeth rises in the midst of flowers,
Like sleeping beauty in her summer bowers!
Nor trace of death upon her features lies,
No shadow resting in her sparkling eyes,
As she about her looks with wondering gaze,
Through the dim light now paled to twilight rays,
Which seems to her the dim and spectral gloom
And shadowy darkness of the chilling tomb.
Nor hath on earth the mortal eye e'er made
Such change from day to night's Plutonian shade:
Nor could endure the soul so great a fall,
Were not its powers to mortal bondage thrall.

XXXIV.

Robbed of its powers so late intensified,
To range the trackless heavens far and wide,
Her mortal sight obscured does not descry
At first Old Rahab where he kneels near by :
So lost in hope's abstraction to all near,
He the awak'ning sleeper does not hear.
The clearing mists soon lift before her sight,
And hidden things stand out against the light :
First are the flowers, — they startle while they please, —
And next her father's snowy head she sees.
A time she fails to recognize or know
The bowing form and head of crowning snow ;
So gazing round, now slowly from the gloom
She notes each separate object in the room ;
Strangely familiar and yet strange they seem,
Like home-wrought visions rising in a dream.
Since she has slept, fair hands have kindly wrought
Some sombre spell in this familiar spot ;
Enchantment here has with its magic wand
Touched here and there and changed on ev'ry hand,
And yet so slight to eye like hers alone
Throughout the room the changing touch is shown,
Save in the weeds of mourning : these declare
The hands that wrought in grief with tenderest care.
From these returning, with a touch of pain,
Her eyes rest on her father's form again ;
His brown and shrivelled hands his face still hide,
Sunk deep within the pillow at her side :
With gentle hand and soft and tender touch —
The lightest breeze his locks might stir as much —
She from the pillow with a soft caress
Smooths back one long and singly wandering tress
Which from his thin locks there dishevelled lay,
White as the pillow, in a frosty spray.
At this, with start and cry of glad surprise,
His head he lifts, gazes into her eyes, —
Clasps her white hand as from his knees he springs,
And, kissing with hot tears, he trembling clings
To its warm grasp, then clasps her to his heart,
As if he feared she would again depart,

Or else she is some vision of the brain,
That if escaped would melt to air again;
But reassured, she soft caresses giving,
That what he held was real, warm, and living,
Kisses her cheeks, her lips, her eyes, her throat,
And kissing breathes a low and cooing note,
Such as the mother's when to her warm breast
Her laughing child in fond embrace is pressed.
She, too, with kisses that his cold cheek burn,
With health's red lips repays his love in turn:
Each silent still, too glad in heart to speak,
Since words in hour like this are cold and weak.

XXXV.

This may seem strange in Rahab stern and old,
In life severe, in heart reserved and cold;
Such as we knew him when her love denied,
His hard heart turned away from pity's side:
But that was Rahab. Sadducee and Jew,
Who scorned the heart another creed held true,
And late had joined in the pursuing cry
Against the Christ he sought to crucify.
That Rahab is no more, but in his stead
This new one here, by faith and love now led,
Who hath the Christ within his heart received,
And through his mercy in his truth believed.
Such is his power, whose love divine controls
The hardest hearts and moves the darkest souls,
That at its touch, like Rahab here, they prove,
That love for Christ but deepens human love.
And Judeth, loving heart, as sweetly gives
In love's own coin the same as she receives,
Glad that her father is made glad, and she
Shall be restored to Love's sweet unity.
This reaches out to Lazarus the first,
Whose faith and love her father lately cursed;
Then Christ, then Mary and Martha, too:
In these she will her earthly joys renew,
Though with their love she may regret the skies,
While tasting here some sweets of Paradise.

XXXVI.

"Are you so glad, my father, I awoke?"
Thus first fair Judeth, smiling, to him spoke;
" I had my fears that, as you one time said,
You'd rather see me laid among the dead
Than keep the faith which you to me denied,
And in which faith I had most gladly died."
" My daughter," answered Rahab, "I have learned
That faith and love like yours cannot be spurned.
I now believe the Christ, though from this hour
I must forego all place of trust and power;
Yet what are these, if we their worth compare
With the calm peace and blessing we now share?
Thy love, my daughter, and thy smiles, are more
To me than all I ever dreamed before:
And when I add to these the Christ I gain,
All earthly power to me seems weak and vain."
" Dear father, I rejoice," fair Judeth cries;
" While yet your bold words cheer, they more surprise:
And yet I should not say so hard a thing,
The one whose love sustains through love to sting;
For you were ever tender, good, and kind,
Nor could I aught in you revengeful find;
The very hardness of your rule, like fate,
Nor place to bitterness it gave, nor hate."
" Thou sayest well," her father answering said:
" 'T was not by hate, but love, that I was led;
Whate'er the course that was by me pursued,
The way I sought led ever to your good,
Or so I deemed, and, looking to that end,
All other things to it were made to bend.

XXXVII.

" But tell me, daughter, what is there that lies
Beyond the vision of these earthly eyes?
Is death a sleep that comes without a dream,
Or is it what we all would have it seem?
What mysteries lie hid beneath its veil?
Is life but breath, and do our senses fail?"
" My father, to your questions answer made

Would rob our time, already much delayed,
For it is meet my maidens now be called :
Too long this robe my fettered limbs has thralled,
And I would rise, but, ere you go, would give
Some answer to your question.   Yes, we live
Beyond the grave, from whence our spirits rise
To find their rest above our bounding skies.
Our faith was false ; but mother, through her pain,
Walked in the light, nor was her suffering vain :
A glorious being now, she shines above,
Most beautiful to worship and to love ! "
" What ! didst thou see her, that long sufferer ? "
" Yes, and sweet converse had I there with her —
But of this I another time would speak " —
" Nay !   Tell me now, since you the mystery break ;
I would hear farther still " —   " Stay, Haddan comes !
I would with him converse, for sweetly blooms
My Rose of Sharon and my Lazarus lives ! "
" What power of sight to you this knowledge gives,
Since from our friends not one poor, halting word
Have we since yesternight from Bethany heard ? "
" How know I this ? " cried Judeth.   " With these eyes
I saw him at the Lord's command arise."
" You saw him ?   Do not mock at me, my child !
Too far already has your speech beguiled."
" To prove the truth that I have seen and heard,
I will relate each action and each word
That has transpired, and, when I tell it through,
Call Haddan in and prove me false or true.
First call my maids, I now must have their care ;
Death's bridal robes I would no longer wear."

XXXVIII.

We will not stay here longer to relate
The joy among the household, small and great, —
How nimble hands remove the mourning weeds,
How joy delirious moping grief succeeds ;
While for the doleful mourner's sad refrain
Gay laughter echoes through those halls again.
With Judeth waking as if from the grave,
Faint hearts come forth again, now strong and brave,

And songs succeed the low and lingering wail,
While roses bloom on cheeks with weeping pale.
From far and near the throngs rejoicing come,
And gratulations fill old Rahab's home :
Where flowed so late the sympathizing tears,
On ev'ry cheek a welcome smile appears.
The wonder spreads ; each tongue its part supplies,
With many tales now busy Rumor flies ;
A thousand lips repeat the marvel strange,
And on each tongue the stories grow and change :
Nor should we wonder, since of Christ the deeds
Each day succeeding still the last exceeds,
Which fill the land until all stand aghast,
And wonder what the next when heard the last.
But still more startling that which hast'ning wings
From Bethany of risen Lazarus brings.
His was a name with friends and circle wide,
His death and burial could not be denied ;
No more could man against the truth maintain
That he alive walked not the earth again,
And that the Christ, the truthful witness said,
By his command had raised him from the dead :
A living witness he of truth and power,
For Christ now filled the measure of the hour.

XXXIX.

As rumor spread, it coupled with his name,
Not hurtful in its speech, fair Judeth's fame :
They were old friends till Rahab had forbid,
Because his child in following Christ was led
By Lazarus and his sisters.   'T was opined
That this through love had preyed on Judeth's mind,
And she grew sick from this, or was confined
By Rahab's orders to her room, where she
Was there allowed but scanty liberty ;
That, while she was of freedom thus denied,
Young Lazarus fell sick, and seeming died,
Of love the victim ; and when this she heard
In deadly swoon she fell, it was averred,
Which was so like to death in ev'ry way
That all her friends, in sorrow and dismay,

Believed her dead save Rahab ; he held fast
The hope that she but slept, unto the last.
Now all who knew him knew as well that he
Was of the straitest sect a Sadducee,
Whose tenets held the dead will not arise,
And life beyond the grave to man denies.
Thus Lazarus' name with Judeth's was combined,
And in the rumors rife their deaths were joined :
So thus, in following back effect to cause,
Were each alike judged by the hidden laws
Traced to the hand of Him whose power alone
Has hurled grim Death down from his ancient throne.
Christ Lazarus raised up, and by his power
Was Judeth's life restored the selfsame hour.

XL.

The tale which Haddan brings in facts and words
With that which Judeth told in full accords,
And Rahab, had he heart to doubt, receives
His daughter's marvellous story and believes,
Although his former faith, his friends declare,
Is still unaltered by this strange affair.
Nor does he yet to them the truth disclose,
For friends are harder kept, he finds, than foes :
And so the tale goes out that by strange chance,
Now well assured, she lay but in a trance,
And, through his care and love, his child adored
Again to health and life was thus restored.

XLI.

But Haddan knew, with all who shared their grief,
That he had changed in heart and in belief ;
That, if his friends were in their hearts deceived,
Yet Rahab was not, but the truth believed :
None better knew than he that death was sure,
And Judeth was beyond all mortal cure.
The first of all his friends his faith to share
Was Lazarus and his two sisters fair :
For, ere the day had sped which brought the word
That Lazarus to life had been restored,   .

The selfsame day it was which Judeth broke
The seal of death and unto life awoke,
Went Haddan back with urgent message sent,
To which fair Judeth words persuasive lent,
That all with Haddan soon returning come
And add their blessing to his favored home ;
And with them bring, more secret in the way,
The Christ, to bless the pleasures of the day.
In this behest how speeds he, ill or well,
It is not meet we stop the tale to tell,
But leave imagination to portray,
In colors cheerful and in setting gay,
Such scene that must, beyond compare, be sweet,
When friends like these in happy union meet,
The storm behind them and the skies above,
A golden glory from the beams of love.
How true the mind can paint the eager haste
Of friends long parted love's sweet feast to taste !
A hundred mem'ries on each other crowd ;
A hundred pledges of affection vowed
Make up the current of such days as these,
Where all of life thus lived is lived to please.
Ah, sweet those hours, in all their varied round,
These life-long friends in such communion found !
With Martha's love, her sweet and tender care,
And Mary's smile to cheer and solace there ;
While Lazarus, still somewhat sad to leave
Those heavenly joys, can here no longer grieve,
Because his care would rob somewhat of zeal
These loving hearts the glowing rapture feel.
Nor was there face of all who gathered here
Than Judeth's sweeter, nor was heart more dear ;
With her bright face and ever-beaming smiles,
She of their sadness and their love beguiles,
Glad she escaped again to Earth below,
To plant sweet flowers in hearts where brambles grow !
Nor of them all was heart more full of joy
Than Rahab's, saved by what he would destroy,
For now he finds, when sat with him at meat
The Christ, a friend in whom is counsel sweet,
And learned grave truths there is not power to teach
In mortal tongue by weak and halting speech.

XLII.

More of these days, so few though sweet to all,
We cannot now back from the past recall,
But leave these lives in the sweet ecstasy
Of moments such as these and short to be,
Before the deep'ning shadow and the gloom
Shall fall upon another head and tomb,
To leave a night far darker than which fell
Upon these homes, — a night the shades of Hell
Stretch out o'er earth and sky their murky pall
When Earth's hoar pillars totter to their fall :
Yet with a morn whose rising brings a day
From which the light shall never pass away,
But in its grandeur deep'ning shall shine on
Until the footsteps where the Christ has gone,
Along Judea's plains and hills, shall burn
To light a world awaiting his return.

CANTO ELEVENTH.

THE EARTHLY TRIUMPH.

I.

JUDETH.

ONCE more we stand upon Mount Olivet,
With much to cheer us, little to regret,
Since first upon that morn we lingered here
And gazed upon these scenes now doubly dear ;
Since, woven in them, twine the brightest hours
Remembrance hangs in its delightful bowers.

LAZARUS.

Well may you speak of this enchanting scene,
Since it to me the very gate has been
That led by ways, to my o'er-eager sight,
Which sweetly wound through gardens of delight,
Where you beside me, ever faithful, strayed

Till of this Mount a Paradise was made.
As we here stand upon this apex crowned
Itself with light and beauty all around,
So tower our lives to this ecstatic height,
With heaven above and earth beneath us bright,
While the horizon's verge in clouds of dun
And shadows murk enfold the setting sun.
So fall the shadows now upon our day,
But all its brightness shall not pass away.

JUDETH.

Why speak so gloomily? and why this tone
In your strong voice that hath despairing moan?
Is earth less fair to us than it should be,
Had we not gazed upon eternity?
It should be brighter, since we know where lead
The ways we tread on earth, with feet that bleed
From thorns of care and wounds from stony hearts,
Which pierce and bruise the torn and broken parts;
Since they shall tread the golden streets, nor feel
No more the wounds their soothing touch shall heal.

LAZARUS.

Not for myself I fear, but more for you,
And those who are unto the Master true:
The day is coming, now is almost here,
That shall dismay the stoutest hearts with fear;
For he, the Christ, will then be snatched away,
And men of wrath our Lord and Master slay.

JUDETH.

This cannot be! for hath he not the power
To smite them blind, and triumph any hour?

LAZARUS.

True, he hath power, but not with man to war, —
The ways of violence he doth abhor:
His kingdom is of peace, his reign is love,
As seen on earth and as we saw above.

II.

JUDETH.

A glorious kingdom then ; where it shall stand
Shall bloom as Eden all the smiling land.
And is he not most tender ? at the feast,
When at the table he was honored guest,
Dear sister Mary, with her tender care,
Spoke of my sleep and sweet awak'ning there :
How sweetly smiled on her his eyes benign
A benediction we all felt divine,
And said that, since you lay there, was the tomb,
To him at least, robbed of its night and gloom !
What could he mean ?   His words could not imply
That he, like mortal man, was born to die ?

LAZARUS.

His words are plain, what ambiguity
Is there in this, the plainest speech, to thee ?

JUDETH.

He does not mean his death ?

LAZARUS.

                                What else but that ?
Would you his plainest meaning still combat ?

JUDETH.

Shall he who conquers death to death succumb ?
The very thought leaves me for answer dumb.

LAZARUS.

He yields to death that he this death may slay,
And in his blood wash all our sins away.
Then shall he rise, and, from the tomb set free,
The prince immortal of our hope shall be.

JUDETH.

Why, we arose from death, and yet his thrall
Doth hold us still !

LAZARUS.

                The Saviour dies for all.

He dies that we may live, so he doth teach;
And in his death there shall be life for each.

JUDETH.

If he should die, shall we then be immortal?

LAZARUS.

For us he opens but the gloomy portal
Where yawns the grave, that we may there pass through,
And thus through death begin our life anew,
Such as we have just tasted.

JUDETH.

This is strange!
And far beyond the short and narrow range
Of my poor thought; and, as I know not why
He should, do not believe that he shall die.

LAZARUS.

Still he so says, and what he says is truth,
Which we, if we believe, accept forsooth.

III.

JUDETH.

We must not let him die! The Pharisees
Against his life pronounce their hot decrees
Of hate and death, because of mercy shown;
And gnash on him, and seek to hunt him down.
And well you know that your own life they seek,
For in your life restored his teachings speak;
A living witness here you stand to-day,
And draw to him thus many more away.

LAZARUS.

These are but first beginnings, — but the shade
Which clips the light by rising storm-cloud made:
Not for myself I care, but for the cause,
When he is dead, which still the thunder draws.
The leader gone, like scattered sheep our band
Shall fly defeated, driven from the land:
And thou, my Judeth, whither shalt thou go
When this red flood shall darkly overflow?

JUDETH.

I ? Where thou goest, that shall be my place,
If here it be in honor, there disgrace :
I know no life but thine as shared with thee ;
Where thou shalt pitch thy tent, that shelters me.
If toil and sorrow to their tents invite,
There will I go and follow day and night;
If death with shadows covers thy bowed head,
I in that clammy couch shall make my bed,
That I may rise again, and soar with thee
Triumphant to yon far Eternity.

IV.

LAZARUS.

I ask not this of thee ; too well I feel
What yonder angel's words to me reveal, —
That he who wears the crown invites the sword,
And man through suff'ring gains his high reward.

JUDETH.

Wouldst thou forego the crown to shun the pain
When life eternal through it we shall gain ?
We know we were forbidden to the heights,
The Throne Eternal and its rapt delights,
Because we were not pure, were not assayed
In life's fierce crucible, and perfect made.
I would be pure.

LAZARUS.

      Nay, I do not deny :
This bitter cup, I would now pass it by
Thy tender lips, nor have thee drink its gall.

JUDETH.

And to be pure I would now drink it all,
And thirst for more.   But what is this I see
So strange and curious in its pageantry ?
What means this long procession, winding down
Along the way which leads to Bethany town ?
It is most strange we had not of it heard,
Or rumor in our ear some breezes stirred !

LAZARUS.

It all is new to me! Let us descend;
And as they through the Kidron's valley wend,
Beneath the shadow of yon olive tree,
Or the sweet coolness of Gethsemane,
We there may watch them pass.

JUDETH.

Down from this height
Is not so easy as our downward flight
When from the skies we as the lightning sped.

LAZARUS.

Nay, rather is it to us now instead
The type of what our way through life shall be
When we shall follow him of Galilee.
Watch well your steps, the stones will cut your feet:
He walketh best whose footsteps are not fleet,
O'er darkened roads with pitfalls spread and snares,
And standeth well whose way with Prudence shares.

JUDETH.

And he who lingers lest he suffer pain
Can never hope the roughened race to gain!
Bleed my poor feet upon the cruel stones,
If the won race for half the pain atones!

V.

Let us descend and watch the coming throng,
Who fill the radiant air with cheers and song:
And it is wonderful to look upon,
A marvel passing and a dream when gone!
Their hast'ning feet the roughened way pursue,
While lies before them, spread in ample view,
The western slopes that to the Kidron run,
And now are glowing in the morning sun,
Save where the shade from palms and olive-trees.
Lies dark and changing in the gentle breeze,
Or Mount Offence its short'ning shadow flings,
Dark'ning in shade the Garden of the Kings,
Beyond which Ophil, burning in the glow,

A flame throws back on Kidron just below.
Before, the winding roads on either side,
Like wavering threads, the fields between divide;
Some through the valleys to the Jordan's plain,
Some o'er the slopes divide and meet again,
All leading to the central road and great
Which threads the city at St. Stephen's Gate, —
So named to-day, the Sheep Gate called of old,
When wolves and sheep together held the fold, —
Which lies before us, and where brightly falls
The gleaming sunshine on the snowy walls:
While on Moriah's high and templed crest
The brighter glories of the morning rest,
Like benediction soft and sweetly given,
A kiss of fire in glory sent from Heaven,
While in the shimmering of the fallen rays
The golden gates below in glory blaze!
Such is the scene apart from man that charms
The eye beholding and the bosom warms;
With man now entering on the broad'ning stage,
These scenes, grown animate, the eye engage.

VI.

Now is the Passover: the tented fields
Lie white before us, and each canvas shields
From sun and dew some pilgrim come to lay
His offering on the altar, else to pray
With face towards the Temple as a shrine
Where dwelt in cloud the form of God divine;
His eyes enchanted with the glorious sight,
His hungry heart filled with a rapt delight!
While more and larger crowds, like vultures drawn
At scent of prey, fill valley, field, and town.
These hither pass and thither swiftly glide,
As runs the swaying crowd from side to side;
Untouched by passion, cold as ice to all,
They watch their harvest, garnering at the fall.
No bleeding feet attract their scornful eye,
No beggar's plea arrests as they pass by;
The leper's cry for answer gets a stone,
And curses harsh return the dying moan;

And in the coming throng with Christ they see
A plenteous harvest for cupidity.
As human harpies of the battle-field
While hot the conflict safely lie concealed,
The battle over, nurse and surgeon go
The wounds to bind, to soothe the groaning woe,
These, bent on plunder, careless of their tread,
Alike prey on the dying and the dead,
Glad of the wounds they scorn to heed or bind,
Because these silent lips to crime are kind:
So these to-day, for sordid, earthly gain,
Rake in the dirt, but pass the golden grain.

VII.

And others, too, there are whose lives have run
Along the shallow groove where first begun,
In line so straight, in path so narrow made,
A world too wide the edge of rapier blade;
Themselves so small the broadness of a hair
A great highway that all may journey there.
But then they live a life of broad expanse,
The world they know and gather at a glance;
No task fatiguing, since within their eye
All things material and perceptive lie.
Their faith is easy and their creed is slight, ·
Since, when they walk at all, it is by sight;
And if they worship — and they always do —
The God they follow ne'er is lost to view:
Religion is the best of life to them,
And all who serve not with them they condemn,
Because himself the narrow man prefers
To be the worshipped by the worshippers.
He, when he prays, thanks God alone that he
Is not as others, but a Pharisee;
And lost are man and prayer to God while rise
Like incense prayer from hearts such men despise.

VIII.

But there are others still whose world expanse
Can never measure to their boundless glance,

Because humanity their thought and theme,
And man's great brotherhood their constant dream ;
Obscure it may be, but the bounds of love
The utmost limits of their heaven prove ;
Still Love can have no bounds, since God's great soul
Is infinite and it of love the whole.
Of these imperfect, fragmentary, all
Along the line somewhere their lights may fall ;
We see now gather in the ways around
The promise of a faith whose force profound
Is soon to sweep, like them, the beaten ways
And make new paths for man in coming days.

IX.

O wondrous pageant ! How shall we declare
The growing numbers crowding ev'rywhere ?
The streaming hills pour forth their floods amain,
Like freshened torrents from a sudden rain ;
The crowds descending palms above them bear,
Like moving forests waving ev'rywhere !
While from the city's gates, from tent and field,
From groves their human hives in shade concealed,
From Hinnom's vale and near Jehoshaphat
To where Mount Scopus in the shadow sat,
These meeting in the highways eastward go,
Along the roads which lead to Jericho.
Out from the city pour its gathering streams ;
A thousand hues flash back the morning beams ;
And, as they march, their songs of triumph sing,
And hallelujahs to their coming King.

X.

While to the east the first to meet the gaze
Of Judeth, and to fill her with amaze,
Came on a host who crowd the narrow way,
And o'er the hillsides further widening stray ;
An army marching to the songs of peace,
Whose glad acclaims, as they approach, increase,
While all the air sways with their waving palms,
And songs reëcho through the valley's calms,

While upward float the notes from hill to hill,
And wid'ning echoes cleave the distance still.
The marching columns close from either side
The less'ning distance, and together glide
Like meeting waters of the stream and tide
Where flows the river to the sounding sea,
And halt at last beside Gethsemane.
And who is he who sits the ass's foal,
In raiment white the people now extol,
And leads the host approaching? Strange indeed
Is the approaching host and they who lead!
First run the shouting children on before,
With eyes turned back when pass'd the summit o'er,
Wistful their following might not appear,
Although their shouts and coming feet they hear;
Next come the singers with their palms and song, —
A motley troop, the narrow way they throng;
And next a host no pen can well describe,
Where ev'ry race, condition, clan, and tribe,
And ev'ry land to Eastern nations known
In tribute gave some offering of its own;
Behind them, stretching down the beaten green,
On either slope they crowd the way between
Who follow after, shouting with acclaim
In mighty chorus now their leader's name.
With head uncovered and with brow made bare,
That whitely gleams beneath his yellow hair,
Which falls in clusters o'er his neck and breast,
These on his shoulders in confusion rest,
Where in the light, which burns a golden sheen,
A radiant nimbus crowning him is seen,
Rides he who leads the triumph, sad of brow,
Forgetful of all earthly glory now.
He is the Christ; and crowding thick along,
They fill the way and greet with cheers and song,
While at his feet their boughs of palm they lay,
And carpet with their garments all the way.

XI.

The scene is grand! Not in the tinselled show,
Nor glittering dress, nor jewelled robes that glow

In brilliant dyes or blaze in streaming light,
Of gold and gems resplendent on the sight;
Not in the pageant pomp and power display
In shining arms and trappings rich and gay,
Where kings and warriors lead their shouting hosts
That earthly fame imperial grandeur boasts,
Whose bugle's shrilling strains torment the ear,
And trumpet's blare distracting those who hear,
While in their wake in chains triumphant led
The captives of the conquered with bowed head,
Who grace the triumph, and when it is past
Die on the cross a cruel death at last,
Or if they live, no hope to cheer their path,
Save that to all men left, the hope of death, —
Not such this scene, but, grander far than these,
It hath the power, in charming, yet to please !
This is the people's triumph, not for them,
But by them made, nor sword nor diadem
Shines in the skies, to light with lurid blaze
The hills with flame, or dazzle with fierce rays,
To show how glory must be won, and how
The crown is kept upon the tyrant's brow.
It means to kings destruction, and to thrones
A trembling in the valley of dry bones,
When bone shall cleave to bone, and man shall see
His race stand up alive, forever free.
It means that in those palms those glad hands bear
Waves faintly now the flag of freedom there ;
That in those garments cast before his feet
Lie despots' robes cast off in their retreat :
It means that in those hearts a new desire
Has touched and kindled souls with fervid fire,
Which, as it burns, inspires each separate part,
Then, filling all, shall leap from heart to heart,
Until the world of man shall in it glow, —
Burst into flame and light all earth below !
It means that from these lips the songs that rise
Shall tremble from the earth and mount the skies,
And soar like prophet-birds of song until
Its music shall the whole creation fill ;
And this one song shall ev'rywhere be sung,
In ev'ry land, by ev'ry human tongue.

It means that he who in the conqueror's train
Drags on his bleeding feet the captive's chain
Shall find release, and nevermore will be
Such stains to crimson our humanity;
But in its place enchained and captive crime
Be bound forever to the wheels of Time,
No more to triumph over mortal souls
While through the realms of light his chariot rolls.

XII.

As now approach the meeting hosts, their song,
In challenge made and answered, floats along.
First those advancing from the east proclaim
The matchless glory of Messiah's name;
Those from the city loud the chorus sing,
And hail the triumph of the coming King.

SONG OF THE HOSTS.

THE EAST.

Tell the daughters of Zion, behold their King in triumph is
    now drawing near,
And the chains shall be cleft of her children in twain, and
    deliverance is here.
Tell the daughters of Zion put on their robes of purple, fine
    linen, and gold,
For their king, the Messiah, is coming, and they his beauty
    may now behold.

THE WEST.

Hosanna! hosanna! to David's son blessed, our King, who
    shortly comes
In the name of our Lord and light of his grace, to bless our
    desolate homes!
Crown him with laurels 'mid waving of palms! the King,
    our deliverer, we hail;
Let us sing a new song to the harp and the lyre, for the
    psalms of our fathers fail.

Lo! he comes, bow the knee! spread your palms at his feet,
    our Lord, the Anointed, receive!
The oppressed he will succor, the bond shall go free! O
    daughters of Zion, believe!
Wreathe chaplets of flowers, garlands spread on his way,
    with roses his pathway be strown,
For the son of our King, heir of David, is here, the Lord
    cometh now to his own.

Welcome home, King of kings! welcome home, Prince
    divine! thy children await thee with praise;
In our hands will we bear thee, and chaplets will twine,
    O Victor! in laurel and bays.
The daughters of Zion, with eyes that are bright, await thee
    to cheer and to bless;
Welcome home to thy own, King of kings, Lord of lords!
    let us shout, since our Prince we possess.

XIII.

Just at the garden where the two ways meet,
The mingling throngs anew each other greet,
And crowd together, in their eager haste
Nearer the Christ they follow to be placed,
Which he scarce noting, save that in his breast
A tender pity moves his heart oppressed;
For his weak followers, weak in all beside,
More blindly follow now their unknown guide.
In gazing on the crowds met in the way,
Which for a time his further progress stay,
His wistful eyes beyond the garden wall
On Lazarus and Judeth chance to fall,
When, as if touched by heaven's benignant rays,
A smile seraphic lightens up his face,
And on them benediction sweet bestows,
As with the throng he on the journey goes,
While following after, mingling with the flow
Of those who from the city come and go,
Together toward the gate they onward move,
Joined by the crowds which throng the hills above.

XIV.

Vain were the task attempted here to paint
The moving scene in color strong or faint:
Pen hath not power where brush could not avail,
Nor can weak words succeed where colors fail.
A hundred varying hues distract the eye,
While garbs most picturesque strange shapes supply;
The fisherman fresh from his reeking nets;
The shepherd, crook in hand, his flock forgets;
The ploughman, taken from his team a-field
In headlong haste, is by his goad revealed;
The market-man, who thought his roots to bring,
Finds empty baskets from his panniers swing;
The Jew devout his offering throws away,
While goats and kids along the roadways stray,
Forsaken by their owners, who had thought
Through their shed blood full pardon to have bought;
But caught amid the throng, and from the cry
Believing that deliverance was nigh,
All else forsook to join the hosts, and sing
Their song of praise to Judah's coming King.
From ev'ry side around the tented field,
Their motley crowds sojourning strangers yield:
Jews from all lands, distinctive by their dress,
Upon the moving line excited press;
With these commingling, thick as locusts blown,
Were men of ev'ry clime and country known,
On each, with varying type to mark the race,
Is stamped attesting seal on form and face.
Here Egypt's swarthy son with turbaned head,
The Arab's bonnet there and fez of red,
The Bedouin's mantle and the Greek's capote,
The Roman's toga and the shepherd's coat;
Black, white, and brown, the mingling faces shine
In bold intaglio through the shifting line:
While women, veiled, fair-faced, of haggard mien,
In flowing robes and dainty kirtles seen,
With garments wrought in all the varied dyes,
Veiled heads, bared locks, with sad or laughing eyes;
And children, too, of all conditions born;
The man of wealth, the beggar woe-forlorn, —

Make up the shadow of the moving host,
And all save this must be forever lost!

XV.

With some surprise, a gladsome one maybe,
Our waiting friends Mary and Martha see;
Not of the throng, but following it aside
Along the beaten track, now spreading wide,
Whom friends from Bethany their care accord,
Join in the seeming triumph of the Lord.
Our friends, beholding, join them in the way,
But still along the outward ranks they stray;
For nearer contact would discomfort give,
As each for place would be compelled to strive,
Which gained, at best, would add but to their ill,
And leave them far behind the Master still.
So, with content they followed as they could,
With joyous hearts and mirth-provoking mood:
Filled with the spirit and the soul of song,
They hold sweet converse as they walk along.
Now of their kingdom and their King they speak,
With sight uncertain and with knowledge weak;
For all believe, save it be two or three,
That of this earth his kingdom is to be,
And that the heathen hosts will be o'erthrown
When the Messiah cometh to his own.
In silence Lazarus and Judeth hear
These words of hope now filling ev'ry ear,
Yet hold their peace, uncertain of the course
The Master holds his teaching to enforce.
This scene, so novel to their wondering eyes,
Leaves them uncertain and in sore surprise;
So with the tide they float resistless still,
And wait the guidance of a master will.
If Earth shall see him crowned, they will deserve
His smile approving, as they humbly serve;
If Heaven, through death, begin his princely reign,
They still will serve, through pleasure and through pain;
For well they know how little earthly joy,
Compared with Heaven, can here their hearts employ.

XVI.

The city gained, the sight its streets astound ;
The rulers pale with fear and awe profound,
Since here in triumph rides he as a king
Whom they to death are plotting now to bring ;
While swelling crowds about the Temple raise
Their shouts triumphant in accorded praise.
What shall they do? They dare not seize on him ;
The maddened crowd would rend them limb from limb :
The Roman Legions, if they would defend,
Could scarce preserve them from this fearful end.
This must be stayed! else their devoted blood,
Instead of his, will redden into flood,
And proud Judea's boasted Temple fall,
And utter ruin thus will swallow all!
High offices by them so gravely held
Will cease, or they ignobly be expelled,
While his new reign, with them from it deposed,
Beholds its ancient rites forever closed.
Such thought but maddens! This must never be:
Such is their feeling, such their stern decree ;
And traitor hands at once against him seek
To strengthen theirs, so pitiable and weak.

XVII.

These scenes, so rapid in each changing phase,
As each to each succeeding now gives place,
We cannot follow, nor would it be meet
That in succession we the tale repeat
In our true story ; they but grace the page,
And in its leading thought our time engage.
When the last scenes of this grand triumph close,
And in his several way each joyful goes,
Old Rahab, meeting in the Temple's courts
Our friends, with them unto his home resorts,
To rest a time, and with them break their fast
With generous speech and bountiful repast.
All should be happy, as they cheerful greet
Each other while they sit with him at meat.
Yet over all a shadow of restraint

Represses pleasure, and a trembling, faint,
Uncertain quaver weighs in ev'ry tone,
Like the first whisperings of the tempest's moan,
When in the night is breathed along the sky
The trembling murmur of the sad wind's sigh.

XVIII.

Their speech is fitful, and they one by one
Drop into silence ere the meal is done;
Each following Rahab, who the first to cease
His grudging speech, they with him hold their peace.
The hush is painful; still the fruits and wine
May warm their hearts and cheer them as they dine, —
At least unloose their tongues, whate'er the mood,
And pour in speech a sweet or bitter flood.
Soon Rahab, first to cease, now first renews
The conversation, soon to grow diffuse;
For when one theme engrosses ev'ry mind,
The slow of speech a flow of words will find,
And catching thought, as flint strikes flint, the fire
Will fill each soul, and ev'ry heart inspire.

XIX.

RAHAB.

Pray pardon me, my friends, yet for my age,
If not myself, I would your hearts engage,
And crave attention to my troubling theme
That hath the vagaries of distempered dream, —
Nor half so wild, methinks, such visions cast
As that which met our gaze the hour but past.
We see the pageant of an earthly king,
Amid the thousands that his triumph sing,
With palms and wreaths that strow his onward way
Proclaim him ruler and enthroned to-day,
Whom yesterday, despised, contemned, and sought
By those in place who had his life-blood bought,
Believing that, ere this momentous hour,
He had been safe and helpless in their power:
No monarch on his throne seems more secure
Than he in power, nor stronger to endure.

And yet, to-morrow, he to-day enthroned
May be by these same hearts cast out, disowned,
Because not small nor great he who deserves;
The people's idol is the one who serves:
If it be saint or despot, king or slave,
The hour's diversion is the thing they crave.

LAZARUS.

I am at loss all this to understand,
If it were sudden, or preferred and planned:
I nothing knew until the march began,
And saw the Master riding in the van.

XX.

RAHAB.

And this the more my spirit darkens now,
Since we the truth of prophecy allow;
Which, you remember, strangely this foretells,
And how the seer in triumph on it dwells :
" Rejoice, O Zion's daughter, greatly : shout,
O daughter of Jerusalem, nor doubt;
Behold thy king, he cometh unto thee :
And he is just : thy children shall be free ;
Lowly is he, and rideth on an ass."
How truly hath this word now come to pass !
Will that which follows on his wondrous page,
Too, come to pass in this succeeding age ?
Will battles cease ?   Will War's red-hilted sword
Be sheathed, and all the land to peace restored ?
Will his dominion o'er all nations be,
From farthest river to the utmost sea ?
By God's own covenant he thus doth swear,
And in his book hath he not writ it there ?

JUDETH.

I know, dear father, there are things concealed
That to our eyes through death have been revealed, —
That of this world his kingdom will not be,
But in this world to all eternity.
How this is so, and how it now appears,
Must be made plain in Time's succeeding years ;

Not mine to say, whose eyes are not yet pure,
Of things to come, from vision not yet sure.

XXI.

MARTHA.

We have the Master's word, what more desire?
Should mortal man to things beyond aspire?
I know he is my Saviour, — have him seen,
And through the gates of Death go safe between,
And from the tomb call forth the sleeping dead,
And to its clay restore the spirit fled.
Why ask for more?

RAHAB.

    There is none left to doubt,
But what to do? What should we be about?
Is what we ask.

MARY.

    Leave that alone to him;
Our eyes of faith see darkly and but dim
The things before, and walking in our light
We neither go by faith nor yet by sight;
But stumbling halt, uncertain of the way,
While he can bring us to the perfect day.

XXII.

RAHAB.

That we desire, and, listening to his words,
The truth he speaks sweet comfort still affords,
Yet at the Temple, which again he purged,
And from their seats the money-changers scourged,
The blind and lame to him again appealed,
And all the sick they brought he gladly healed.
The Pharisees and rulers, at the sight,
The people's songs and shouts of great delight,
Now sore displeased, in anger and dismay
Said unto him, "Heard thou what these do say?"
Then answered he, "Know ye the Word so says,
'From babes and sucklings thou hast perfect praise.'

If they should cease their praise, these stones hard by
With many tongues would then take up the cry."
Then to his followers, apart, he said
That soon by these he would to death be led;
That this was meet and right, for thus the way
To life eternal through his suffering lay;
That when he should be lifted up, all men
Would thus to him be drawn : which saying, then
He cried, " Now is my soul exceeding sad.
What shall I say?   My Father, I am glad
To do thy will, yet save me by thy power :
But for this cause came I unto this hour.
Now, Father, glorify thy mighty name."
Then from the skies a startling answer came,
While all the zenith glowed with radiant flame,
In accents deep, and words and speech most plain, —
" I have both glorified and will again."
The people standing in the midst averred
It thundered, some ; others a voice they heard :
But Jesus hearing answered them and said,
" This voice calls not to me, but you instead :
Now is the judgment of this world made known,
The Prince of Earth cast down from his high throne."
And other things, which I cannot recall,
He spake to them, and they were tending all
To show the death which he must soon endure
For man's redemption and for sin the cure.

XXIII.

More they conversed and long in anxious mood,
With faces sober and in tones subdued,
Until the dinner o'er, when they arose
To seek an hour of quiet and repose,
Worn with the toils and scenes exciting past,
Which they a time may thus forget at last.
On Olivet Day's fading torch low burned,
As with his sisters Lazarus home returned,
While Judeth lingered at her father's home,
Expectant with the morrow she might come.
And at their threshold waits with weary feet
The smiling Master, their return to greet ;

For, let his heart be e'er so sore and sad,
His smiles for them are ever sweet and glad.
With them he enters, seeking food and rest,
Nor ever had such home before such guest.

XXIV.

Long would we dwell upon these passing days;
The mind reluctant at each scene delays :
The sacred memories crowd the glowing page,
And all our love and all our soul engage.
How loth we pass them ! how we lingering turn
Where here and there their brighter glories burn,
And gaze transported on the pleasing sight,
As thrills the heart with some new-found delight;
Else, crushed with sadness by increasing woe,
Our tears o'erwhelming in hot torrents flow !
Oh that we could but tell of love so great
As Martha's, as she at the feast doth wait !
Or pure as Mary's, with its care so sweet
Wipes with her hair the Christ's anointed feet !
Could we renew those journeys daily made
Through crowded street, along the wayside shade,
And hear his talks with those who journeyed there;
Write down his sayings as his lips declare ;
Portray the sad Last Supper when he showed
In bleeding wine the emblem of his blood ;
How Treason's plot was there against him laid,
And the black heart by which he was betrayed, —
Then would we go to sad Gethsemane,
To witness there that night of agony,
And watch while he in bleeding sorrow prayed
Against the foe by which he was betrayed,
Tho' others slept, who, stealing through the night,
By Judas led, with swords and shaded light,
In search of him whose love for them there found
A pity deeper than that traitor's wound,
Who comes to meet him with a brother's smile,
With kiss betraying from a heart of guile,
That pierced so deep it robbed his heart of pain,
Which by the kiss and not the cross was slain.

XXV.

Now sit the rulers in their hall of state,
Nor there alone decide the prisoner's fate;
Themselves they judge when justice they deny,
Nor is it Christ, but they, the death shall die!
The sword which they now call from rusted sheath
Gleams red already from their coming death.
Nor heed they now nor friend nor secret foe,
But blindly on to their destruction go.
Tried, judged, condemned, by hate, their only law,
Against the truth, which they most plainly saw,
They gloat in gloomy glory o'er their crime,
Assured their fears are mastered for a time;
Yet they each other with suspicion scan,
Nor dare they trust as judge their fellow-man,
Who sits himself in judgment, lest he may
For greed or gain his fellow-judge betray.

XXVI.

Thus sealed his doom, the day and hour draw near;
Delay waits not upon the haste of fear:
No rest is there for crime while in its sight
Still lives the heart to bring its deeds to light.
Returning reason in the people's breast,
Who now are moving in their deep unrest,
May rise defiant in the passing hour,
And hurl their tyrants from the throne of power.
The night has seen him taken like a thief,
With hand as cruel as the work was brief,
And in the selfsame hour is he arraigned,
Friendless, alone, and of his rights distrained:
E'en Peter, boastful of his zeal and pride,
With cringing soul his suffering Lord denied.
Alone with cruel foes through all that night,
They question him until the morning light;
Then haste to Pilate with the shrieking Jews,
Who Christ of treason now alone accuse,
Themselves, at heart, all traitors to the laws
They now invoke to save their sinking cause.
From him to Herod, in their bloody greed,

Reviling still the Saviour, they proceed.
Where'er they go, the Truth their charge denies,
And Mercy pleads against their bloody cries ;
Since Justice finds no guilt in him, they rage,
And perjured oaths, to speed their cause, engage.
When feared release, their ravings rend the sky
With one shrill note of hatred, " Crucify ! "
The scornful ruler, wearied with their hate,
Despising vengeance so insatiate,
Still moved by pity in him strangely born
For seeming weakness, of his soul's hot scorn,
When they refuse all mercy, choosing first
Barabbas, who with blood their land had cursed,
Insists that in the Christ no guilt is found,
Yet orders that the robber be unbound ;
Then in the bath his guilty soul demands
The sneering Pilate seeks to cleanse his hands :
A thousand years twice told in ceaseless flood
From them has failed to wash that guiltless blood !
The cause is lost, the plea is heard and done,
The world and not the Jew the victory won ;
Christ is condemned, and, guilt by them preferred,
No touch of pity more for him is stirred ;
So from the court, wild with unchecked delight,
They hasten him to Calvary's distant height,
Impatient lest a moment's slow delay
Might snatch from them their now defenceless prey.

XXVII.

So swift their action, and so well concealed,
The morning light, which his arrest revealed,
Showed in the selfsame hour the gathering throng
Which to his death the Christ now bore along.
Old Rahab, feared, somewhat suspected, yet
Knew of the Council and the plottings set,
With plea of age and sickness sent excuse, —
The urgent call he dared not else refuse, —
So went not near, but Haddan sent instead,
To learn how well their secret plotting sped.
From him he learned all that which we relate,
Except the judgment and Christ's further fate :

With this to Rahab he in hot haste speeds,
Who, learning this, his further fate well reads,
And sends his servant on the wings of fear
The tale of sorrow to his friends to bear.
These, hastening back with Haddan, hear the shouts
Of the mad mob ; this ends their hopes and doubts.
As from the heights the first advance they see
Turned tow'rds the slope of distant Calvary,
With urgent haste Mary and Martha speed,
While Lazarus with Haddan foremost lead,
For gathering people on their pathway throng,
And choke the road on which they press along.

XXVIII.

Soon with a rush, like angry torrent's roar,
The crowd will fill the waiting gates before,
As through the city from the tents and town,
And heights surrounding, hastening hosts come down,
Led by the shouts which now their footsteps guide,
Speed through the streets to reach the further side.
So drives the flood where mountain steeps converge,
Pour down their streams through some deep, gloomy gorge,
From sudden rains, or melting of deep snows,
Each swollen rill its separate banks o'erflows.
Choked up by loosened rocks and fallen trees,
Where gathering drift has thickened by degrees,
Until a rising wall from side to side
Behind this dam shuts in a basin wide :
Here strays the wild fowl in the lingering spring,
By huntsman sought, still guided by her wing ;
While on its margin sheltered rushes grow,
And in its shallows water-lilies blow.
The teeming floods, from rains that ceaseless fall,
Rise high and angry up the trembling wall,
And chafe the dam, which in the sudden rise
Half sunk beneath the muddy water lies,
Until the flood the banks no more control ;
Then rushing out, the mighty waters roll,
And roar and surge along in ponderous glee,
In their mad riot, now escaped and free.

XXIX.

Borne on the tide, our friends have passed the gate,
And now at Rahab's door admission wait;
For thither turned their feet, instinctive led
By want of knowledge and uncertain dread.
Hard by his door they Rahab sitting meet;
And him with hurried question kindly greet,
And learn of him the truth now fully known,
That to his death the Christ but now has gone.
E'en as they speak, fair Judeth, bathed in tears,
Shod for the street and closely veiled, appears;
The veil, a silken gauze of spotless white,
Her matchless features half reveal to sight.
" Whither, my child ? " her father shortly said :
" To where my Master to his death is led."
" Thou canst not go alone ; no more can I
Go with thee now, except it be to die :
For at the sight of me upon the street
My doom, without a judge, would be complete."
" Have I no friends ?   Why, who are these that wait
Now just without our home's inviting gate ?
Oh, here are friends !   My sisters, and the one
Who, more than friend, my love now leans upon :
They wait my coming ; let us haste away,
Our faithful Haddan here with you can stay."
" Nay, daughter, if thou goest, I, too, will go !
But sluggish currents through these old veins flow ;
What matters it how soon their streams shall fail !
If thou shouldst suffer, nothing can avail."
" Nay, cousin Rahab," Lazarus replies,
" The soul is strong which destiny defies ;
And grand the heart which dares all things for love,
The brightest crown awaits such soul above !
Let us all go, for love of Christ, and see
If this be ruin, or Christ's victory."

XXX.

No more is said, and soon their flying feet
With urgent haste speed on from street to street,
Through shorter ways to reach the northern gate

Before the throng is there and they too late ;
For they have learned the Council's judgment now,
And that the cross shall crown old Calvary's brow.
By fortune's leading, they outstrip the crowd,
And leave behind the tumult wild and loud,
Soon find themselves in shelter by the way
Along which now the first oncomers stray.
For in their haste, as runs the rabble, stirred
By the first echoes of some rumor heard,
The hosts divide : some on to Calvary haste,
Some to the Temple ; others, heedless, waste
Their time in madly running to and fro,
In all uncertain, back and forward go :
These are the stragglers ever passing still
Between the Temple and the rising hill.

XXXI.

Scarce have they found a place secure and safe,
Where now the crowd against them may not chafe,
When from the city on the waiting ear
The first hoarse murmur of the march they hear,
Which, as the fitful breezes bear along,
Each moment grows in volume fierce and strong ;
While from the deep'ning roar rise, here and there,
Distinctive voices on the perturbed air.
These, as they still draw nearer, deep'ning rise
To words of triumph and derisive cries,
As through the gate a flood of human souls
Its mighty current as a torrent rolls ;
Then, sweeping out, it spreads its swelling tide,
A billowy flood, light-fringed on either side,
Like waves that break upon the stooping shore,
Dash the white spray in spreading foam before.
We may not stop to picture what we see, —
A scene more grand in its diversity
Than was his triumph from Mount Olivet,
And earth had never seen a greater, yet
Earth on this day beholds a greater still
From Herod's court to bare Golgotha's hill !
No funeral march was e'er so grand before ;
No mourners have such gorgeous trappings wore

As these, who, in their maddening zeal, believe
They are the victors, but themselves deceive.
A nation, which in love he came to save,
Here holds its march rejoicing to the grave,
And as the Cross they raise and Christ lift up
They crucify to death a nation's hope.
Yet here they go, with lips just taught to sing
Their songs of triumph o'er their coming King,
Now foul with curses, ribald jest and call,
Which fill with fright the ears on which they fall.

XXXII.

So on they come; the thunder from their cries
Affrights the air, with horror rends the skies;
The sun from golden dun to crimson blushed,
The air affrighted grew to whisper hushed,
As if expectant Nature held its breath
In awe, awaiting the Creator's death.
First march the rabble leading in the van,
From piping child to stooping, gray-haired man;
Next follow soldiers armed with shield and spear,
Then Priest and Levite in the ranks appear,
And following these, a woful sight to see,
With head bowed down, the Man of Galilee!
Now from his bosom burst half-groaning sighs,
While floods of pity drown his weeping eyes:
His garments torn and soiled with ruddy stains
That shed their purple from his weeping veins,
Where clings about his brow the crown of thorns
Which now in mockery his head adorns.
And still from wounds beneath this cruel crown
Some few great drops of blood run slowly down
O'er face and breast, to leave congealing streams,
Between whose tracks the pale flesh whitely gleams;
While through the thorns, escaping from their hold,
In burning shower flow down his locks of gold,
To frame his face, most pitiable the sight!
In the soft radiance of their trembling light.

XXXIII.

His steps are slow; the weakness of the flesh
The soul's great agony now wrings afresh ;
The burning heats, the dust which chokes the air,
The swaying crowd that pushes ev'rywhere,
All sap the failing powers which yet remain
From nature's struggle with consuming pain,
Until his weary feet refuse at last
The further burden now upon them cast,
And prone beside the way he reeling falls
At Judeth's feet. At first the sight appalls :
She cannot stir ; nor has she voice or speech,
Until his pleading eyes upraised beseech
A touch of some kind hand, a look, a word,
To cheer where blows are felt and curses heard.
He does not speak, his parted lips are dumb ;
He bears the sorrows of the years to come
For those who follow him, and feels the fate
Of all whose pity wakes a fierce foe's hate.
An instant thus, then Judeth's trembling hand
Unloosens from her head the silken band
Which bound her veil, and without care or thought
Of where she is, the deed, or public spot,
Removes the filmy folds and bares her face,
In pity careless of the public gaze,
And, stooping down, wipes from his face and brow
The grimy sweat and blood's commingling flow ;
Then snatching from a proffering hand a gourd
Fresh from some spring with cooling water stored,
Gives him to drink that draught which those who drain,
Though soothed a time, shall be athirst again,
While in return she drinks from his sweet eyes
A draught which all her future wants supplies.

XXXIV.

So swift her action, following, as it did,
His sudden fall, so in the pressure hid,
Scarce one beheld it, save the guard and those
Who swiftly round the fallen prisoner close.
Not Lazarus nor Mary sees the deed,

But Martha sees, and aids as is her need,
And from the eyes of the reviving Lord
In gracious thanks receives her full reward,
While from his quivering lips a whisper fell
With a sweet blessing and a hushed farewell!
Refreshed and strengthened, onward now he goes,
His steps supported by his cruel foes :
The crowd behind him forward pressing on,
With them beyond their sight he soon is gone.

XXXV.

Why should we follow to that bloody scene ?
On earth its cruel like has never been ;
And yet we dwell within its shadows dread,
Whose skirts their darkness o'er the whole earth shed ;
And still beneath that gloom, in his own name,
Have those preferring him endured the shame
From followers whose deeds have been the same.
Those hands that crucified were wondrous kind,
Since they to truth and knowledge both were blind,
Compared with those who from this brooding night
Have long come forth into the noonday light :
They by their doubt, despite, and lusts of flesh,
In these their Saviour crucify afresh !

XXXVI.

Our friends, whose souls the ghastly scenes abhor,
Now follow him but in the way afar,
The cruel pain, his suffering, the tears,
The ribald jests, the gross, insulting sneers,
Pierce through their hearts as barbéd darts of steel,
While ev'ry shout as cruel blows they feel.
Still as they pass along they low commune,
With bitter speech these cruel acts impugn ;
Weep as they talk, and weeping onward go
With hearts now bursting with their sighing woe ;
So lost in thought to all external things,
So to its grief each mind tenacious clings,
That they see not, though talking face to face
With Judeth as they walk along apace,

Although remarked her face was worn and pale,
That she no longer wore her silken veil.
Mary the first discovers it is gone,
And says to her, in hushed but eager tone,
" Judeth, my sister, what is this I see ?
Your face unveiled to ev'ry eye is free !
Why is 't withdrawn ? Has it been snatched away ?
Why look you so distressed ?   Oh, answer, pray ! "
" Peace, Mary ! here you see my veil, I hold
Close in my mantle's safe and secret fold.
I have not lost it: money cannot buy " —
" Stay ! Whence those spots of dark and crimson dye ? "
" The blood of Christ ! " Judeth in answer said.
" The blood of Christ ? How on your veil was 't shed ? "
" Peace, Mary ! " Martha cries : " She would not tell,
It is so painful.   When the Master fell —
You saw the fall ? but in the crush about,
From further sight you were a time shut out,
While we were closer thrown, Judeth and I,
And for a time it seemed that he must die
There as he lay, so weak and faint he was,
Beneath the crushing burden of the cross.
Then Judeth, snatching from her brow her veil,
Stoops o'er the suffering Christ, so wan and pale,
With touch of pity in the deed sublime,
Wipes from his face the bloody sweat and grime ;
Then from a proffered cup she gives a draught,
Whose cooling flow is by his parched lips quaffed,
And as he drinks his failing strength revives,
As to his feeble powers new strength it gives."
" O Judeth," Mary cries, " your precious heart
Must claim its richest blessing set apart !
The soul of daring and the heart of love
The grandest riches of your nature prove.
I love you better now a thousand fold
Than e'er before, sweet heart of wealth untold ! "
" Nay, Mary, speak not so ; I only did
What my poor heart, unquestioned of me, bid :
I saw his suffering and his sore distress,
Could I, a woman, seeing it, do less ? "
" You could not, Judeth ! " Lazarus replied,
" For all your heart cleaves fast to mercy's side.

You saw the mansions, Judeth, fair and bright,
Through which as crystal shone the heavenly light;
In them ere long your dwelling-place shall be,
Your soul outshining them in purity."

XXXVII.

" Peace! Speak no more to me of this, I pray;
And let us hasten faster on the way.
Look, Adonai! what is this I see?
My Lord and Master hanged upon a tree!
O bloody Death! O cruel Death! Is Earth
Still to be dumb? Shall not the heav'ns launch forth
Its lightnings from the hand of God to smite
The cruel hearts that do him this despite?
O Adonai! hear, O hear my prayer!
His murderers smite, nor soul of any spare!"
" Hush, Judeth, pray thee! Speak not here so loud;
Your words will draw on us the angry crowd.
We cannot save if he would not: to die
For him here now, — what would it signify?"
" But once! let me speak once, and I am done!
And witness, Heaven, and thou, now bloody sun,
And hear, ye people, Pharisees and Jews,
Who now your Saviour and your King refuse:
The day is coming — in its tread I hear
The thund'rous tramp of armies drawing near —
When from your lofty seats ye shall be hurled,
And nationless be scattered round the world;
Your Temple levelled and its shrine defaced,
Your name in ev'ry tongue on earth disgraced,
And Heaven shut out from you, and God withdrawn;
Then, without hope, you shall through life hope on,
Never to see that hope's fair day arise,
While rocks the earth beneath your feet, the skies
Span with yon arch the boundless depths of space,
And Time is reckoned in the round of days.

XXXVIII.

" Hark! What is that? What mean those mournful cries?
Earth shakes! Night falls, dissolving Nature dies!

Eternal blackness swallows up the gloom,
And Earth itself becomes a mighty tomb !
Let us haste onward to the gloomy hill,
For there some rays of light are lingering still,
A burning halo round his drooping head,
Whose thorns become a golden crown instead,
And in its light behold the wondrous grace
And heavenly beauty of his shining face !
O glorious scene ! O piteous scene ! How long
Wilt thou endure, Eternal God ! this wrong ?
Had I but wings, up to the bending sky,
Cleaving the murky night, I would now fly,
And call the hosts of Heaven, that they descend
And from this cruel world snatch its best friend,
Then, smiting it with Night's eternal gloom,
Bear him in triumph to his heavenly home."
" Judeth, you now forget what was revealed
To us, nor shall it be from man concealed,
That Christ should die the death, and, having died,
We in his death should all be glorified."
" So was the speech, dear Lazarus, I mind :
But why should man to Christ be so unkind ?
What need of brutal death like this ? Shall he
Bear in his wounds all human misery ?
Shall his one death concentrate in its pain
The burdened miseries of the Ages slain ?

XXXIX.

" Ah, hark ! He cries : the list'ning heavens hear !
And his hushed murderers bend in anxious fear.
Feel how the solid Earth beneath our feet
Leaps as to fly his burdened prayer to meet !
The bending heavens stoop down in blacker night,
As if in shame to veil the scene from sight.
Hark ! yet again he cries, then all grows still
As leap the forky lightnings round the hill !
The thunders rage, the vaulted ether burns,
And all the zenith to a furnace turns :
Now in the light which through the darkness plays
Behold his sightless eyes and death-cold face !
The Christ is dead ! and Earth goes back to those
Who all its good and all its hope oppose !

What mean those faces gleaming in the crowd, —
Those gliding forms now clad in burial shroud?
The dead are rising! These are they I see,
And Death is swallowed up in victory!
Well may we shout, and loud hosannas sing!
Where is thy victory, Grave? where, Death, thy sting?
O Christ triumphant! Lord eternal, blest,
In thee the living and the dead find rest!
We have here tasted glory yet to come:
Why wait we longer? let us hasten home."

XL.

The deed is done; triumphant hate appeased,
Doubt from the bonds of grovelling fear released:
Offended Caste, grown out of cruel reign,
Hath set itself upon its throne again.
What matters it if blind no more shall see,
Nor fettered limbs from palsy's touch be free?
What matters it if through the land is seen
The helpless blind? is heard the cry " Unclean "?
What matters it if to the starving poor
The living bread be broken nevermore?
Since altars stand, the rites and service there,
The power of priesthood and its rule declare!
The wrong has conquered in its folly now,
The thorns of Hate are bound on Love's dead brow;
God hangs in death upon the burdened Tree,
And crucified the hope of earth to be!
So read these minds the history of the hour,
And, reading, closer draw their robes of power.
Another reads the portent from the skies;
That reader is of all than man more wise.
It says : " To-day hath to the poor made known
The conquering Christ, who cometh to his own.
Death feels his chains encircling his gaunt hands;
The grave despoiled of power now open stands;
Through it shall pass the Mighty One, and then
Its kingdom ends on Earth and over men!
Eternal Truth stands forth within its light,
And Error sinks defeated into night;
God reigns! his Christ, triumphing from the grave,
A ruined world shall from itself now save!

CANTO TWELVE.

THE VICTORY.

I.

OVER the distant plains of Galilee,
Where flows the Jordan to its tideless sea,
Touching the forests with its purple veil,
Shrouding their niches in its shadows pale
In mountain gorge with misty gloom of night,
Dashing with streaks of gray the crimson light
Which gleams upon the peaks, in distance far,
Of Lebanon, Mount Tabor, and Mount Hor,
While from the eastward, swiftly closing down
O'er verdant plain, on hill and white-walled town,
Reaching the city of Judea's kings,
The Eastern night o'er all its mantle flings.

II.

The hush of Israel's Sabbath day in night
And restful peace succeeds wild Tumult's flight,
Which, on that day of death, unbroken reign
Held in the city and surrounding plain,
When Earth and Heaven and shuddering Nature groaned
With mortal pain, and sighing Silence moaned,
As Christ's white side was pierced by bloody spear,
And Earth in horror shook, convulsed by fear :
While from her wrinkled breast by earthquake rent
The dead to walk the earth once more were sent.
Day from her face shrunk back affrighted ; Night
Came down, but moon and stars withheld their light ;
Shekinah flamed ; the Temple's veil was rent ;
The stooping skies in gathering blackness bent,
And rested on the hills : from caverned gloom
Shot red its lightnings, while the thunder's boom
In hollow bellowings far seaward rolled,
And in its tumult ev'ry heart appalled !

They who had mocked the Saviour's plaintive cry
Wrung out by death's despairing agony,
" Eloi ! Eloi ! Lama Sabachthani ! "
Agape and palsied stood, their blood congealed,
Since they in earth and heaven beheld revealed
The power divine in all stand forth confessed,
That they had slain the Son of God at last.

III.

Now Calvary is desolate and still !
The spectral cross stands on its lonely hill,
Where Christ had hanged, and stretches empty arms
Out to the night, — now hushed its wild alarms, —
A shadow in the shadows, type to be
Of man's grand triumph and his liberty !
Now it with many tongues, yet voiceless, cries
Out to all human-kind beneath the skies,
" Come, ev'ry one, to me ! Ye doubting, come !
Since Christ I bore, for all the world there's room !
He suffered pain for ev'ry heart opprest,
And now in me forever there is rest."
Is there no answer borne upon the night?
Forsaking him, has man fled in affright?

IV.

Ah, hark ! A sound breaks on the stillness now,
A life seems drowned in sighs, it sobs so low !
Then from the shadow to the misty light
A form glides swiftly up the sloping height ;
And with a cry, imploring arms it flings
Up to the cross, then grovelling earthward clings
About its foot, while bitter floods of woe
Upon the blood-stained ground in torrents flow.
Who can it be, forgetting rest and sleep.
Heart-sore with sorrow, cometh here to weep ?
It may be he who dwelt among the tombs,
Some leper cleansed to mourn his healer comes ;
Old Bartimeus, who from unsealed eyes
Pours forth his tears as sorrow's sacrifice ;

Jairus' daughter, born to life anew ;
Or he of Nain, still to his Saviour true.
It might be Judeth, for her love would dare
All things to death, to mourn her Saviour there.
One heart there is which danger cannot fright,
Clings to the cross wet with the dews of night,
In love and hope, with faith in him who died
To save a world which hath him crucified, —
One mourner lingering on that dreary hill,
In night and darkness, unaffrighted still ;
Yet this one, too, ere morning will be gone,
And leave the cross forsaken and alone.

V.

Christ's sepulchre ! Divinely hallowed spot !
Whoever heard its story hath forgot ?
Where sleeps the Master in its awful night,
The outer darkness veiling all the light, —
How broods the spirit of our hope o'er thee,
And waits the morning light of prophecy !
The stone lies sealed against its marble door ;
The guards, unwearied in their march before,
Keep watch beside the Saviour's silent tomb :
The breath of night, rich laden with perfume,
A thousand flowers shed from their bursting hearts,
Blown through the trees, to all its sweets imparts.
The moon sweeps on her course ; the glittering stars
Flame high above, nor aught their brightness mars.
A hush so still oppresses all the air,
And pierces with its pain all waiting there,
That e'en is heard in sighings of the grass,
Caresses murmured as the Zephyrs pass.
Glide on, O silent hours ! your golden sands,
In bleeding hearts poured out by agéd hands,
Drop balm o'er all, since on your noiseless wings
The coming day the gray morn's promise brings,
Which touches now the east with faintest stains,
And tints with purple all the sleeping plains.

VI.

From Calvary's hill, like sweet, ethereal song,
Faint as an echo from some chanting tongue,
Sweeps on a strain than first more constant grown
In near approach and deep increasing tone
Of choral host, which from the cross draws near,
Chanting of Hope secure to mortals here;
While through the air above the tomb is heard
The rush of wings unseen; then voice and word
Swell into song rich, clear, and wondrous sweet,
As in the air the gathering angels meet
To watch the coming morn, and chant the praise
Of the triumphing Lord in heavenly lays;
While the arisen dead join in the strain,
Sending the anthem echoing back again,
They of the earth to question, and reply
They answer back who fill the stooping sky.

VII.

SONG OF ANGEL AND SPIRIT CHOIRS.

SPIRITS.

Lo! the Cross is desolate;
   Those who loved have fled away:
Night and darkness over Earth
   Show no promise of the day.
Is our hope, like Earth, in night?
   Is to man that promise vain
Which has led us to this hour,
   Since the Prince of Peace lies slain?

ANGELS.

Lo! the tomb its precious trust
   Fragrant in its incense keeps;
Still within its sacred rest
   He, the Prince of Heaven, sleeps.
Only wait we for the morn,
   With its promised golden skies;
Only wait we here to see
   From his sleep our Saviour rise!

SPIRITS.

Is the promise still unsped?
Shall the cross our Master bore
Be the world's all-conquering sign,
   Sweeping ev'ry sea and shore?
Are the tidings you now bring,
   Watchers o'er the sleeping Lord,
Promises of joy on Earth,
   Peace to man by him restored?

ANGELS.

Spirits of the risen dead,
   From the Cross behold the Tomb!
Hither through the gates of Death
   Hath the Lord your Saviour come.
Hope, which fled when rose the Cross,
   Stoops above the Sepulchre,
Waiting with her for the dawn,
   Faith, her sister worshipper.

SPIRITS.

Lo! the night is darker grown;
   Hushed the winds: no mortal eye
Watches by the lonely Cross
   Which beheld the Saviour die.
Has his own forsaken him,
   Since his hand no more can bless?
Faithless all his chosen ones,
   Can the stranger now be less?

ANGELS.

Man may turn to earth again,
   Grovelling in its baser things;
Yet behold, from yonder Cross
   Mercy now eternal springs!
While the fountains of its grace
   Shall the drooping heart restore,
Until ev'ry land and clime
   Drink of it to thirst no more.

SPIRITS.

Who shall bear these tidings hence?
Him we trusted there lies slain!

Who shall teach men that the dead
Shall arise and live again?
We by Faith have lived and died, —
Ever with this hope have striven:
When shall Earth behold her lord?
What to man the promise given?

ANGELS.

Lo! Behold your answer there,
Where the opening Heavens shine
With the glory of our God
In his messenger divine!
He who holds the keys of Death
Now descends the blazing skies;
He who slumbers in that tomb
Unto glory now shall rise!

VIII.

As swell the strains of tuneful tongues on high,
Down sweeps an angel from the opening sky,
And in his path the heavens refulgent shine
In the new glory of his light divine.
Awed by the grandeur of this wondrous scene,
The song is hushed; while in the golden sheen
To sight stands forth revealed a countless throng
Of Cherubim and Seraphim along
The glowing hills, with angels ev'rywhere
In shining hosts on earth and in the air;
While thronging Calvary's hill, aflame and bright,
A glorious company, in robes of white,
Of those whose faith had led to see this day:
Their upturned faces watch the shining way,
As downward sweeps the messenger of God,
A blinding glory, shedding light abroad.
As some fierce meteor launched athwart the world,
A blazing terror from the zenith hurl'd,
Rushes in flame across the darkened zone,
In flame and smoke upon the earth is thrown,
So sped the angel from the ether down,
The light of matchless glory now his crown.
But not of woe the messenger he comes,
For joy he bringeth to earth's saddened homes,

And to the hosts that wait him in mute praise
The glorious promise of the vanished days;
And to the ages of all future years,
A solace for their sorrows and their tears.

IX.

The angel, stooping, touches but the stone,
When bursts the seal with low and hollow moan,
As if the parting Death in mortal pain
Within the Tomb of Christ itself was slain;
Untouched the loosened stone now backward rolls,
And on the wakened Christ the glory falls.
Forth from the tomb he comes, upon his brow
A crown of light, his radiant face aglow!
And victor stands he now who captive bled,
Captivity by him is captive led;
The Grave despoiled, and Death robbed of his sting,
And Hope released soars on triumphant wing!
Spirits and angels low obeisance make,
As into song the waiting angels break;
The dead redeemed catch up the glorious strain,
And sing his triumph in a glad refrain.

HYMN.

Angels, spirits, mortals, rise,
    Join the triumph and the song;
Glory! glory! glory! sing,
    Let the Earth the notes prolong!
Catch the song, ye shining hills,
    Where his weary feet have trod;
He has triumphed o'er all foes,
    Leading now the hosts of God.

Day of days forever blest!
    Night and darkness now have flown;
In the fulness of his power
    Cometh he unto his own.
Death is slain, the Grave despoiled,
    Christ, the victor, breaks all chains;
Glory to the Lord our King,
    Christ omnipotent now reigns!

X.

The hills shout back the song; the valleys fair,
Filled with its melody, his praise declare;
And far-off Lebanon with shouts of glee
Catch up the notes; while sleeping Galilee
Gives back in murmurings the grateful strain,
And in his praise lifts up its voice again,
Once hushed by his command, as stern as sweet,
When its mad waves came crawling to his feet.
Then as the morn, which paled before this light,
As fades a taper in abyss of night,
Bursts on the Earth, the singers glorified,
With noiseless wings up through the ether wide
Evanishing before the wondering gaze
While yet they sing, send back their hymns of praise
In echoes sweet down to the waking Earth,
A benison to all of mortal birth,
In whisper soft, yet all the valleys fills,
Then into silence dies along the hills.
Some lingering notes of that glad anthem sung
That morn on earth by rapt, angelic tongue,
Down through the ages ever onward sweep,
In gathering chorus many-voiced and deep,
A gloria to the hope-exultant soul,
Whose gathering praises high the Lord extol,
And yet the Song, in light of Bethlehem,
Is to the sad of heart a holy requiem!

XI.

Now comes the Magdalene with other fair,
In morn's first flush to mourn the Master there,
Grateful for love, bring spices for the dead
And tears to sprinkle their beloved's bed.
Great their surprise to find the Saviour gone,
And at the empty tomb the Shining One!
" Fear not," he says, " I know why you have come;
He is not here; behold the empty tomb!
Come see the place where the Lord lay, and then
Haste quickly back to Galilee again."
With their departure other friends draw near,

Drawn by the love of him to sad hearts dear;
. The empty sepulchre, a sad surprise,
With its white cerements, greets their wondering eyes.
Pale with her weeping, and with sorrow worn,   -
Came Judeth with the first at early morn;
Not hers to fear, not hers surprise to feel;
These but the fulness of her hope reveal,
And as she sees, she clasps her hands and sings,
"All hail! The Christ has risen! Hope now springs
Triumphant from his empty tomb, and lo!
His Kingdom now hath come to man below.
Lend me swift feet, mad Joy, that I may run
And bear the tidings to each mourning one!"

XII.

Old Haddan, who had brought her on the way,
In the sweet freshness of the rising day,
Awaits her near; and now her flying feet
In grave alarm he hastens forth to meet.
"What frights thee, child? Why in such haste to fly?
Is danger lurking here, your pathway nigh?"
"Nay, Haddan; but for joy I hasten here;
The Lord is risen! This the tale I bear
To father and to them at Bethany:
Haste! let us go now quickly; follow me."
"The Lord has risen? Have you seen his face?"
"No; I beheld his empty burial-place,
And one who saw him, Mary Magdalene,
And others who the empty tomb have seen."
"Then let us haste! Thy father waiteth this,
Nor is there faith so true and pure as his."
As Haddan ceased they mount and homeward ride,
And as they go look not to either side,
Where hastening feet crowd thick the outward way,
As on the morning speeds the risen day,
And press the gathering throngs, as rumor flies,
Upon the empty tomb to feast their eyes.

XIII.

Arrived at home, Judeth the scene narrates,
With what she saw and heard in full relates ;
Old Rahab hears her through, and then he cries,
" Praise ye the Lord ! I knew he would arise !
The kingdoms of this world have now become
Our Lord the Christ's.   Here he will make his home !
It is enough ! my day, or short or long,
Shall be an anthem, — a triumphant song.
Haste, Haddan, on to Bethany, and there
To them this wondrous miracle declare,
And bid them come to me, where with one voice
We, through his boundless grace, may all rejoice.
What would you, daughter ? Would you with him go ?
Once such a boon my pride would not allow :
But now, — then thither haste, but quick return ;
My eager arms for their embrace now yearn.
I will in love prepare the waiting feast,
And Joy at such a board shall be chief guest."

XIV.

At Bethany, with love's now mute surprise,
Bathed in their liquid woe their weeping eyes,
The sisters greet their ever-welcome guest,
Who is successive to each bosom press'd,
While kisses warm and true as mother's love
The deep devotion of their pure hearts prove.
No question ask they, so intense their grief,
In the first moments of this respite brief ;
Then Mary, reading in fair Judeth's face
The smile her laughing heart at last betrays,
Cries out reproachfully, " Judeth, how dare
You smile, when in our hearts sits black despair ? "

JUDETH.

Because my heart itself has now grown glad,
And I have come that yours may not be sad.

MARY.

How so ? The Lord, who bringeth joy, is dead ;
And with his death has Joy forever fled."

JUDETH.

The Lord *was* dead : were not his words most plain? —
" I needs must die, but I shall rise again."

MARTHA.

What mean you by these words? we saw him die.

JUDETH.

And so did Lazarus, and so did I.

MARY.

He hath not risen ?

MARTHA.

Can such thing be true?

JUDETH.

You have your witness here in me : will you
My eyes dispute? Then little worth my word,
If I should tell you what I saw and heard.

MARY.

Nay, we believe! What is it, Judeth dear ?
Speak what you will : belief comes as we hear.

JUDETH.

The Christ is risen from the dead.

BOTH.

Risen !

JUDETH.

Yes ; and I saw his cold clay's empty prison,
But he was gone.   His cerements there remain ;
The Christ to life has now returned again.
One of the guards has told that, at the hour
Before the daybreak, with a mighty power
Sleep fell upon him, and as dead he lay
Into the rosy dawning of the day,
And when he woke a form in spotless white
Sat on the tomb ; that, cowering at the sight,
He hid his face, — how long, he could not tell, —
So mighty in his heart had wrought the spell,
But when he woke at last and looked, the stone
Was rolled away, and he within was gone !

XV.

MARY.

Oh, haste, tell Lazarus!   He is so sad :
If aught will please, this tale will make him glad.
Ah! here he comes!   A sight most wondrous strange!
Could I believe there could be such a change !
I never saw a face whose radiant glow
Was so like Christ's ! —   But yet his step is slow
As if some mighty thought beyond his power
Were clogging his light footsteps at this hour.
I will arouse him.

MARTHA.

Nay! do not do so:
The brightest sun must have its evening glow.
But now he hastens on : returning thought
Of life about him, sure this change hath wrought,
And with it what best pleases, since he smiles,
Of all its shadows his fair face beguiles.

JUDETH.

What if I draw aside ?

MARY.

Good!   Do so now —
But Haddan may have seen him, I allow :
No matter ; step aside and hear his tale.
What ails thee, brother, that thou look'st so pale ?

LAZARUS.

I pale ?   I thought my face was deeply flushed,
And had you asked me, sister, why I blushed,
I had not thought it strange.

MARY.

Why should you blush ?
Is it for shame or love ?

LAZARUS.

Neither : but hush
We now this silly talk ; it ill becomes
Hearts that have been so sad.

MARTHA.
Have been ?   Why blooms
The flowers of joy so freshly on your cheeks,
That in their glow the heart expectant speaks ?

LAZARUS.
The Christ has risen.

BOTH.
The Christ !   How know you this ?

LAZARUS.
I have both seen and spoken him.

BOTH.
We miss
The sweetest of the day while here confined :
Eyes when unused would better far be blind.

JUDETH (*coming forward*).
You saw the Christ ?

LAZARUS.
What, you already here ?
I had not thought you risen.

JUDETH.
Ah ! I fear
I suffer in your thoughts.   My question plain
You answer not ; shall I repeat again ?

LAZARUS.
No ; Sorrow hath its modes of speech, and true
Respect forgets them not ; no less its due
Should Joy regard : so I your question passed,
And, now remembering, I answer last.
This morning, as beyond the city's gate,
Where I had gone upon my griefs to wait,
And in my aimless wanderings had come
To that sad spot where once had been my tomb,
There I sat down a little time to rest,
With head bowed low in sorrow sore oppressed,
Wondering the while why I from death should rise
While on that cross the one who saved me dies ;

And there, repeated o'er and oft again,
Came back to me that mocking, harsh refrain
Which filled with terror faithful hearts and brave, —
"Others he saved, himself he cannot save."
I cannot tell my thoughts; I had no tears!
For in that hour were crowded griefs of years,
Stretching across their course, while towering stood
The streaming cross barring their further flood.
Long time I sat, it seemed, in grief engrossed,
To all of life and things around me lost;
Then came a passing foot, with gentle tread
Approaching me. I did not raise my head,
Believing it some neighbor or some friend,
Who, when he saw, his course from me would bend;
And so awaited, scarcely with a thought
That any one for me had thither sought,
Until a hand, with touch as light as down,
Rested in slight caress upon my own.
I then looked up: a stranger's was the face,
But one of manly beauty, wondrous grace!
His eyes were soft as woman's, and his voice
Would move to pity, make the heart rejoice;
While from his brow swept down his golden hair
About his neck, as any woman's fair!

XVI.

" Why grievest thou, my friend? " he softly said.
" For him who now in yonder tomb lies dead,"
I answered. " Weep not," he replied to me;
" He is not dead, but liveth: I am he."
With that upon me broke revealing light,
And my blind eyes anew received their sight,
And knew him as the Christ, — saw each red wound
In hand and foot, and where the thorns had crowned!
Their yet empurpled lips still gaping wide
Where the cursed spear had pierced his snowy side!
With joy I cried, "My Saviour and my God!
No more shall I regret this lost abode:
Mine eyes have seen thy glory in the earth,
Anew in thee I have a second birth:
The grave henceforth to man has lost its gloom,

And souls redeemed shall fly to meet the tomb."
And then I reached my arms out to embrace,
But from my reach he backward drew apace,
And said: "Nay, touch me not! While here below,
It must suffice by sight that you shall know."
I then drew back, by sudden fear dismayed,
At which he said, "'T is I, be not afraid.
To mortal hand to touch it is not given;
I have not yet ascended unto heaven."

XVII.

"My Lord," I cried, "if you my touch refuse,
Have I now found thee but again to lose?
Most desolate on earth all hearts shall be
If they of earth are left alone by thee!"
"It needs that I must go while you abide;
But where I go, a place I shall provide."
With that, before me as a picture spread,
In lights and shadows on a canvas shed,
He drew before my inward-gazing eyes
That scene of earth revealed in Paradise.
You know the scene, my Judeth; and its power
Divinely shown still holds me to this hour.
I may not tell what he to me made known;
The days of darkness and their sorrow shown.
Our cross most heavy seems to human sight:
By him revealed, the burden is most light!
Now, since his work and suffering here are done,
Ours, following it, are now but just begun:
Yet he will be our guide, support, and friend;
If faithful, crown us victors in the end.

JUDETH.

What are the crosses we for him must bear
If in the end we hope the crown to wear?

LAZARUS.

The crosses? Tongue cannot in full relate
The many, but I give some of the great:
The way is not a flow'ry path of ease, —
Some of the bitter fruits you pluck are these:

Fierce persecutions, such as he has borne ;
Of friends and riches for his sake be shorn ;
Father and mother, wife and home, forsake ;
Of earthly power full sacrifice to make ;
Go forth to strangers and to lands unknown,
Bearing his tidings, friendless and alone ;
Place all upon his altar, — ask not why, —
And ever ready be for him to die.

MARTHA.

The cross seems heavy, but for us he bore
A thousand fold more pain.

MARY.

Let us adore ;
Take up the cross which he has just laid down,
And win him souls, though ours the martyr's crown.

JUDETH.

It would seem heavy if to mortal view
Alone were shown the darkened vistas through
Which bleeding feet must walk in constant pain,
The heights of hope immortal thus to gain.
But short indeed the road, and few the thorns,
And these the faithful heart in triumph scorns.
Then, with the journey done, how grand the rest
To us revealed, to faithful spirits blest !
I shall not stay my feet, but where he wills,
That place my hope anticipating fills.

XVIII.

LAZARUS.

Right glad I am, my sisters, and thou friend,
To find you ready for the dark'ning end :
Here have we lived as revellers crowned with flowers,
At life's sweet banquet in its rosy bowers ;
Our homes inviting to their social ease
The friends we love to honor and to please.
Through all our years, for ev'ry thorn of care
Was set by Love a hundred roses there !
E'en in our larger griefs, to our surprise,

We found in them but blessings in disguise.
These homes may soon be desolate, each friend
Forget us, and our dream of friendship end :
Scattered like thistledown before the wind,
No rest for our sore feet shall we then find.
Are we all ready for this time to come,
And for his sake forsake both friends and home ?
Is earthly pleasure now to be contemned ?
Shall bitter seas on boisterous floods be stemmed ?
And are we ready at his call to go
And flowers of life before his altars strow ?
You answer not : the picture is too black !
We must go on, — he 's lost who now turns back.
The world invites us with delusive smile ;
The flow'ry borders of its paths beguile ;
The ways of honor still allure our feet,
While wealth and ease call us with voices sweet.
Thy father's palaces, his lands and gold,
Luxurious offer of their gifts untold, —
And these, fair Judeth, wilt thou cast away, —
All these and more, — to meet that darkened day
Whose dawn is breaking, and its clouds we see,
Dark as the night which hung o'er Calvary ?

XIX.

JUDETH.

All these I would forego if but one friend
Walks with me on the journey to the end.

LAZARUS.

His service in it no condition hath ;
It is in love shown forth by trust and faith.

MARTHA.

I will accept such service ; for his care
Will make the burden such as I can bear.

MARY.

And I the cross will bear and walk alone,
If he so will, since he the way hath shown.

JUDETH.

" Lord, as thou wilt ! " help me in truth to say ;
And when I falter, I can only pray
To him for strength.

LAZARUS.

        Such is the bitter cup
We all may drink when we the cross take up.
While we this sad, sweet joy so tender feel,
Far brighter ways his truth may yet reveal ;
For these we wait, nor let us now forget
The sweeter duties of our friendships yet.
These may be short, for all of joy is fleet,
And yet for that it should be no less sweet.

XX.

Long converse still they held of kindred things,
Until the hours with ever-flitting wings
Brought on the eve, when all, more truth to learn,
With Judeth to the city then return.
Old Rahab greets them with a kiss of peace,
Now doubly sweet in such strange days as these,
And to them, as with age the theme accords,
With circumstance — and many it affords —
Narrates the gathered news which Haddan's care
Had gleaned for him with hand that did not spare.
Then Rahab Lazarus in turn informs
Of his strange meeting.   This his old blood warms
With zeal anew, and with a fervid cry
He shouts amain : " Now let thy servant die,
Since he has seen thy wondrous glory, Lord,
In the fulfilment of prophetic word !
My days are few, and these for thee I spend,
My God, my Counsellor, and faithful Friend :
All glory to thy name, who from the night
Hath brought me into thy most marv'lous light."

XXI.

With them now speed the days in rapid flight,
With rumors rife and themes that all excite.

The Council sits in almost daily court,
To weigh all rumors, hear each new report,
And plot and plan, and try some new-found way
The rising tide of this new faith to stay,
Which seizes on the people as a plague
Endemic grown from sources small and vague,
And which, if they find not heroic cure,
Will in the very soil itself endure.
Work as they will, disease they cannot stay,
Which on the body feeds in its decay.
Their crumbling altars, as their fallen throne,
Now at its touch begin to topple down:
The Christ, the mortal, they to death have slain, —
In the immortal, Christ now lives again;
The venal guards, which they to lies suborned,
As branded perjurers are known and scorned;
While, many-voiced, the people now declare
The Christ still lives, and proof convincing bear.

XXII.

From Bethany to far-off Galilee,
In crowded town, beside the murmuring sea,
In wayside met, in chamber hid and lone,
He to his followers himself hath shown, —
Walked with and talked with them : 't was said
He sat at meat, and bless'd and brake their bread :
And showed his wounds to Thomas, doubting still,
Whose faith grew fixed as his unwavering will.
No farther doubt remains ; the Christ still lives :
Not from the wounds received he yet survives,
But from the death those cruel soldiers gave
Is he restored, escaping through the grave !
Thus Faith, made perfect in the sight, arose
And bade defiance to all earthly foes,
And to the hosts of Hell in power complete
A warfare wages that knows no defeat.

XXIII.

The days speed on.   Once more and for the last
Shall we behold our friends as in the past,

With whom, when now this pleasant journey through,
No longer we their different ways pursue,
As up the steeps of Olivet they mount
To drink the morning from its golden fount.
Slow move their steps, in earnest converse held,
The shadows from their faces scarce dispelled
By the swift light which, shooting from the east,
Glows on the Temple now from cloud released.
They stand transported when in grandeur first
The glories of the scene upon them burst;
It seemed to them the city of the Lord,
The Heavenly one, to Earth had been restored:
'T was but a moment, then with drooping head
Judeth, to Lazarus turning, softly said:

JUDETH.

Is it not beautiful, that templed dome,
Where Adonai long hath made his home?
Can it be true our God, who hath so long
Led this his people, saved from wrath and wrong,
Will now desert them, and that yonder wall,
With city, Temple, palaces, shall fall,
And all this land at last a waste be made,
The prey of vandals and the smiting blade?
Within its walls I almost see the roof
Beneath whose dome was woven warp and woof
Of my young life.   Shall it in ashes lie?
While from its smoke ascending to the sky
Float up as incense memories of the past
With breath of prayer to reach the throne at last.
I would to thee I now might say farewell,
If I no more in thy sweet halls may dwell;
For when my heart goes out to regions far,
As falls through space some fiercely blazing star,
Its place forgotten and its dying light
Sucked down and swallowed in the drowning night,
So thou, fair city, shalt be lost to me
When falls love's star into the engulfing sea,
Not cast away, but in the mighty whole
Is swallowed up of Love's consuming soul.

XXIV.

LAZARUS.

Why are you now so sad ? If duty call,
Should we not to its prayer surrender all ?
You heard the Master in his gentle speech
To us, his followers, that duty teach :
I cannot stand a laggard in the field
While yet the harvest gives but grudging yield.

JUDETH.

Nor do I ask it : I would labor, too, —
Nay, be thy handmaiden his work to do :
Our ways apart need not forever lie,
And where thou lack'st I may the need supply.
'T is said the Evil, when it seeks our fall,
Is like an army storming some strong wall :
When it attacks the strongly guarded heart,
Will ever seek to reach the weaker part.
So is it, too, with woman : long and well
Will she defend her heart's strong citadel ;
But weak and yielding must she ever prove,
When you attack it through the gate of Love !

LAZARUS.

Yet through that gate her heart, unless she will,
Of all the most invulnerable still.
There is no cross for me to bear so hard
As this ; my heart must constant be on guard,
Else it rebel at Love's destroying pain,
Forsaking duty, fly to thee again.

JUDETH.

Fly home, dear heart ! My arms will thee embrace,
And in my bosom give thee dwelling-place.
Oh, this is hard ! I can nor go nor stay
With thee, in work to wear my life away.
A thousand deaths with thee are not as one,
Should I without thee live and die alone !

XXV.

LAZARUS.

O Judeth! do not tempt me: my poor heart
At ev'ry plea is fiercely torn apart!
You know my love for you, — you cannot doubt!
The light within my heart with you goes out,
Save for the torch his love now keeps aflame
In the sweet promises that crown his name.
Remembered well that saying of the Lord, —
Unworthy he who soon forgets his word! —
"That he who loveth aught most dear in life,
Father, mother, brother, or child or wife,
Better than me, unworthy is of me."
How shall I do his will, if this so be?
He gave me back to life! Why should he save
A clod unfallow'd from the wasting grave?
The barren fig-tree withers at his curse;
I, whom he saved, an idler would be worse!
My field awaits me, ready for the grain:
Shall reapers wait the sowing still in vain?
He now hath sent them forth; I, laggard still,
Because through love of you, refuse his will.
No, Judeth! fairest of all earthly fair,
My heart is breaking to refuse thy prayer:
I must be ready when the summons comes,
With heart not doubting, as its task assumes.

JUDETH.

Why may I not go with you?

LAZARUS.

          We must part.
Not well we serve if Love divide the heart.
He who would teach the world must teach in love;
And love of Christ first from our hearts must move.
How can this be if other love invade?
The light withdrawn, how soon the flower will fade!
When love the sunshine to the heart supplies,
It spreads its bloom, and when withdrawn it dies.
I can have but one bride, his cause or thee;
Now in that Saviour's name which shall it be?

Your love for him and me you fully know;
This means eternal life, and that means woe:
Not that our love is wrong, but that it draws
Our hearts away, divided from his cause.
Help me to choose, through love of Christ, I pray:
I trust your hand to guide the rightful way.

XXVI.

JUDETH.

O Lazarus, you make conditions hard!
Without we yield, shall there be no reward?
Can I not follow you? Is there no grace
That will allow I look upon your face?
Beside your home could I not sit me down
And weave some chaplets in your earthly crown?
The fields are many and the world is wide,
Is there not room that I work by your side?
You taught me first to love with heart-love true, —
Would you now teach how I can love undo?
So you, too, taught the wondrous lesson given,
That after death this love should live in Heaven.
Teach me one lesson more, 't is all I ask, —
For you it should be now no irksome task, —
How I can lay that love slain at your feet,
While yet this living heart within shall beat;
Then will I gladly cast it dying down,
And in its blood paint flowers to deck your crown.

LAZARUS.

O Judeth, Judeth! how my heart you wring,
Until its ev'ry nerve leaps quivering
With mortal agony. For you to die
Would be a joy. Within your arms to lie,
With white lips sealed with kisses wet from tears,
The very thought my panting spirit cheers.
But now to part with you and yet to live,
How can I still its cruel pain survive!
But yet how light these pains which o'er me roll
Compared with torments of the sin-lost soul!
Would it be best our hearts should bleed a day,
Or the lost soul forever cast away?

JUDETH.

I yield at last! 'T is woman's cause that 's lost:
Hers ever is the suffering, hers the cost!
There must be then somewhere to her the gain,
Which compensates for her redoubled pain.
Oh, take my heart, dear Lord, myself, my love!
I consecrate them all to God above!
Upon his altar now with humble grace,
The glory of my life, my love, I place,
And pray that from his love the fires may come,
And all its gold as frankincense consume.

LAZARUS.

One last embrace, sweet Love! May all thy power
Fill the full measure of this parting hour!
May all the sweetness of thy precious tide
In quick'ning currents through our bosoms glide,
That ever in our hearts shall cling the taste
Of thy pure joy, and there forever last!
Here we first met to learn thy bliss divine;
Here first we drank thy richly flowing wine;
Here saw thee grow from bud to perfect flower,
Here sip the nectar of thy fruits this hour;
Then with the red cup crushed which faintly bleeds
As crushed pomegranate o'er its scattered seeds,
We fling the rind aside, as through the soul
Thy nectar flows and consecrates the whole.
Farewell, sweet Love! receive our parting sighs;
It is not thee, but grosser nature, dies:
Thou shalt live on forever, and shalt grow
To flower in Heaven from this fair bud below.

XXVII.

JUDETH.

O Lazarus, you wring afresh my heart;
And ev'ry word makes harder still to part.
I drink your breath with kisses as they flow,
And with each draught I still more drunken grow.
My heart leaps up as if it now would flee
And find a dwelling-place for you and me.
I cannot part from thee, O Olivet!

If in thy shadow I cannot forget,
How then shall I, when he from me has gone,
Forget, or, still remembering, live on ?
I cannot say farewell, but I can die !
Here in thy glowing day asleep to lie,
To wake in Paradise, as once before,
And in its rest find all my troubles o'er.
But you, my Lazarus ! Am I so blind
To ask for death and leave you still behind ?
No ! I will live as God shall give me grace,
Until life ends as he shall close my days ;
And if you call for me this side the tomb,
On wings of love with haste to you I come !
So I will say farewell — What makes you start ?
Are you, then, in such haste you would depart
At my first bidding ?

XXVIII.

LAZARUS.

Look ! who hither comes ?
The very air grows rich in rare perfumes
At his approach.

JUDETH.

It is the Christ draws near !
And my poor heart is still from love and fear.
Who are those with him ?

LAZARUS.

They ? Disciples.

JUDETH.

Few

The followers to him remaining true !
Let us draw near, that he perchance may see,
And, if we ask, decide what best will be.

LAZARUS.

Why should we ask ? Has he not so decreed ?
To learn our duty what the further need ?
Still as you wish ; we can but ask once more,
E'en if the answer should be as before.

XXIX.

They now draw near, with steps that hesitate,
To where the Saviour and his followers wait:
The summit reached, lies fair in front of them
The white-walled city of Jerusalem.
Upon the city which beneath him lies
Long looks the Christ with fixed and ardent eyes;
Again within their depths a mist appears,
From the deep fountain of his unshed tears,
A parting look of love and pity shed
From the pure heart that for its crimes had bled,
Yet with no pang of hate, though Justice stern
The scale with heavy hand may downward turn.
This done he turns, and to his followers speaks;
The slumbering echoes his sweet voice awakes;
In rippling murmurs runs its cadence still
Among the groves that crown the sleeping hill;
Then Nature listens, bend the arching skies,
While the soft wind scarce through the grasses sighs.
The God of Nature breathes o'er all a spell,
As Christ from earth now takes his last farewell.
" It is not meet ye know the day and hour:
All these the Father knows, in him the power.
Abide ye here, believe, and him obey,
And wait the coming of his Judgment Day.
When ye receive the Holy Ghost, for me
Throughout Judea and through Galilee
Ye shall be witnesses from now henceforth
Throughout all lands unto the ends of Earth.
Receive my benediction, faithful few;
In it I bid you and the earth adieu! "

XXX.

When he had spoken, all their heads they bowed;
With outstretched hands his blessing is bestowed:
Then in the midst a cloud of golden sheen
Like flame of fire descending sweeps between,
And, rising upward toward the glowing skies,
Bears him away before their startled eyes.
A glorious sight it is to eyes whose power

The triumph witness of this wondrous hour ;
Yet for a time each shields his upturned face,
Like those who on the sun at noonday gaze, —
With sight from his destroying beams secure,
Gaze but an instant, as they can endure.
Our friends, though mortal, with a sight more pure,
Look long and steadfast through the air, and see
A glorious sight ! the heavenly mystery,
As through the opening portals once more shine
The light eternal from the throne divine ;
By them remembered well but to regret,
The Heavenly glories they can ne'er forget.
The scene is ended : Earth's arisen Lord,
Unto his throne resigned, is now restored ;
Salvation's plan secure, man's work begun,
Shall never cease while glows the rolling sun ;
But Hope is his fair harbinger, and Peace
Shall from the chains of sin all men release,
And then in victory his warfare cease !

XXXI.

With songs of joy, toward near Jerusalem
Haste the Disciples, Lazarus following them,
With Judeth by his side ; her silent tongue
To-day forgets its notes of joyful song !
Her heart had hoped when she beheld him near,
As she would say, " with trembling joy and fear : "
As she had thought to tell the Master all,
And at his feet imploring there to fall ;
Then would he not in tenderness reprove
The harsher course, and give to her her love ?
For this she waited trembling at the side
Of Lazarus, whose duty love denied ;
Although in torment he was weak and sore
From the fierce pangs his fainting nature bore.
When Christ had done his speech, her eager feet
Were trembling to fly her Lord to meet :
One forward step she toward him e'en has ta'en,
Their glances meet, she sees his smile again ;
His lips are moving, yet she cannot tell
If it be blessing or a hushed farewell.

Then sweeps the fiery cloud between them there,
And leaves unanswered her unspoken prayer.
O sad undoing of her hope ! How sad
That she must mourn while all beside are glad !

XXXII.

It is not sin to love in human heart ;
His is the sin who keeps such love apart
When pure and true.   Love's altar is the same
If holy incense mingle with the flame.
If souls do penance, they should ever keep
The pain themselves, nor make the guiltless weep.
If for our sin another heart should mourn,
A double guilt upon our soul is borne :
Should we wear sackcloth, let the guiltless wear
Their silken robes with garlands in their hair.
If in the way we walk with unshod feet,
To flow'ry paths let innocence retreat.
Such were the thoughts that troubled Judeth's breast,
Yet these alone in silence are expressed ;
More painful thus to feel but not to hear
When heart responds unquestioned by the ear.
Not more disposed is Lazarus to speech,
And thus in silence Rahab's home they reach.
With smiles he meets them at the outer door,
Which are returned by them with look heart-sore.
His eyes, though aged, this cannot fail to see,
And this arouses keener scrutiny.
To him each face, an open page and clear,
Tells him of sorrow and of trouble near.
" What horror new doth now affright the air,
Or cruel woe do friends for us prepare ?
Your faces read like scrolls from open book,
Where lurks a horror hid in ev'ry look :
What now, my children ? tell me all, I pray,
Nor keep me longer filled with this dismay."
Thus Rahab's piping treble shrilly cries,
To which fair Judeth through her sobs replies ;
Her story told, made by her telling sweet,
We here a second time may not repeat.
At first, with staring eyes and straining ears

The story of her burdened grief he hears ;
Then, as she speeds, to her the saddening tale,
His straining interest begins to fail,
Until the end is reached, when gathering brow
Is smooth and free from ev'ry shadow now :
Although her grief her eyes of tears beguile,
He meets her closing story with a smile.
She, all abashed, looks up into his face,
That type of cunning in the Jewish race,
And almost shrieks, in her betrayed surprise,
" Why, father !   I see not where humor lies !
Is there no pain, no sorrow to the heart,
When we for life must thus be torn apart ? "

XXXIII.

" I grant you, daughter, there is sorrow sore;
But God be praised, since it is nothing more ! "
" Is not this now enough ?   What deeper pang
Can pierce my heart, what shadow darker hang
About my life ? " Her Rahab answering said :
" The blade divides, but leaves unsevered head.
Hark now my speech.   I would not rouse alarm,
Nor hasten on the near foreboding harm.
You know my station, wealth, and high degree:
The Council now suspect and shadow me.
If aught they find, — and much there is to show, —
I to the court and to the Judgment go !
Then my estate — this home, my slaves, and all —
Into old Herod's greedy coffers fall ;
While I go to the cross, — a boon I crave,
Were't not for thee. I hope all these to save.
If thou remain with me, all will be well:
The story of our faith we need not tell ;
It braver is sometimes to silent bear
A hidden cross than strive in open war.
If thou shouldst marry Lazarus, then clear
To them my faith apostate will appear :
This why I smile, and not to mock your grief,
For in this seeming woe lies our relief.
What say you, Lazarus? speak I well or ill?
This plan doth well the wish of both fulfil."

" No better plan than this could I devise ;
It is but just to you, and also wise :
You save your home, your wealth, with it your life,
And keep her safe who cannot be my wife,
As she hath told you, not for lack of love,
But I would do my Master's will above :
And this I can with strong heart if I know
She is with thee secure from ev'ry foe ;
And thou art safe, for in thy weight of years
But little fruit the failing harvest bears.
Let younger hearts and stronger arms perform
The wearing toil and meet the coming storm.
Thy wealth, when thou hast lived thy length of days,
Shall keep her yet in ease and flow'ry ways :
I meet the conflicts braver when I feel
The passing years must kindly with her deal."
" Thou hear'st, my daughter, words that touch my heart ;
And while most loth am I with him to part,
His generous bosom bares he to the blast
To go alone, forgetting all the past,
Save his great love for thee, and reverence
For my old age he blesses going hence.
Oh, had I youth and fire as once were mine
Abreast of him would I march on the line !
Nor Roman Legions could my progress stay
As I to daring conquest led the way !
The rust of time hath wrought me gravest ill,
In limbs now aged, with heart left youthful still !
Here with the women and the crouching slave
Must I, inactive, sighs and tears still brave ;
And with them fret the useless time away,
Lamenting less their wails than my decay.
No matter ; thou art all in all to me :
Martha and Mary will companions be ;
We still can pray while these the conflict wage —
Not fiercest battles where the wildest rage !
Be glad, my daughter, that thou hast the power
To comfort still in this distressful hour."

XXXIV.

With breaking heart Judeth now deeply sighs,
While through her tears she smiles as she replies :
" Father, I feel your words are truth and love ;
And to your own my heart doth strangely move :
As finger touched upon a gaping wound
Makes the hot heart with agony rebound,
So does your speech breathed on my heart of pain
Thrill ev'ry nerve and make it leap again.
And as the wounded bears the surgeon's steel,
Assured the knife which wounds is meant to heal,
So I your cold and tempered words receive :
Although they wound anew, they do not grieve ;
For you, my father, have my tend'rest care —
Your burdens bearing, mine grow light to bear.
So I will fly to you with outstretched arms,
And clasp you to the heart your fear alarms."
With that, about his bended neck she throws
Her snowy arms and to his bosom grows,
While his old frame shakes in her long embrace,
And course the tears adown his wrinkled face.
He is a child again ; his child's the breast
Upon whose downy snow his white locks rest ;
And as that rest, aweary, he now shares,
In his great joy forgets his life of cares !
So woman, be she daughter, wife, or maid,
Frail, trembling, weak, of shadows oft afraid,
In lightest breezes frightened to us cling,
As to the bough the bird with broken wing —
When storms grow black and dangers sore dismay,
She, who upon us leaned, becomes our stay !

XXXV.

Why should we further on such scenes now dwell ?
Upon the Mount was said the last farewell ;
A hundred times could we repeat it o'er,
Each time but makes it sadder than before ;
And then, when at the last its accents die,
To these a sobbing echo makes reply.
When he goes forth, the shadows on the wall

Grow dark and sombre in the misty hall;
The echoing pavements, many-voiced, repeat
The hollow cadence of his hastening feet,
Until the dying sounds from hall and floor
Give back the faintest murmur there no more.
So on the heart the shadows darkly lie;
So in the mem'ry sweetest voices die :
While eyes with watching long and late grow dim,
And scenes they view in lights uncertain swim;
While haunting voices lose familiar sound,
Or in the sea of silence long lie drowned.
Will Judeth's heart forget in love to beat?
Will mem'ry fail Love's accents to repeat?
Will other faces on the pictured wall
Hide this one face, the fairest now of all?
Who answers well these questions only knows
By journeying o'er the way which she now goes.

XXXVI.

Two thousand years their course have nearly run
Since was the story of the Christ begun!
Upon these scenes their suns have rose and set,
And kissed far Lebanon and Olivet
Into a golden glory, bright in glow
On fresh'ning verdure and unfailing snow!
Unchanged in beauty still, this land we see
From distant Syria o'er the Galilee.
The olives grow in old Gethsemane;
The figs still ripen on each terraced hill,
Pomegranates grow in stately gardens still;
The flowers of Judah shed as rich perfume,
And Sharon's roses still as sweetly bloom;
And lilies spread their varied beauties round;
The palms still whisper, and the streams still bound
With joyful laughter on from vale to sea,
With tide as limpid and with course as free
As when upon the glorious advent morn
Angels proclaimed the Son of God was born.
But where are they, in transports of delight,
Who hailed on earth the dawning of that light?
Where are the kings of Judah, throne and crown,

From Herod reigning to the Tetrarchs down?
Where are the Priests and Levites, Pharisees,
And boastful rulers proud of their degrees?
Where the proud Council, Annas and his son,
Under whose word and rule these things were done?
Where the proud soldiers of that hateful reign,
That Empire circling world-wide in domain?
Where now the Cæsars and their boastful lines,
Whose fame uncertain now but dimly shines?
Gone! gone forever! and their crumbling dust
In the wide ruin of their day is lost.
Nor spares the hand of all-consuming Time
The works of beauty and its art sublime;
Since with the ruin of its broken walls
The matchless glory of God's Temple falls,
His house forsaken, and its altar-stone
In the wide ruin of the land, o'erthrown:
Is there so desolate a land, or name
That had such glory or so bright a fame?

XXXVII.

But from the ashes of these funeral pyres,
From the fierce wasting of destroying fires,
Comes forth as gold refined by blood and flame
The wondrous beauty of the Saviour's name!
From torches set by Nero's hate on high
Of living men to light the midnight sky;
From thousand burning stakes and torture-flames
That bear in each earth's unforgotten names;
From flaming cities, sacked by fire and sword
Of those who fought the followers of the Lord;
From homes laid waste and hearths made desolate
By those whose scourge was still the Christian hate, —
The light has shone to lead the triumph on!
From sea to sea and land to land has gone
The Empire of the Christ! His cross the sign
Leads ever forward the advancing line;
The World his Empire and all hearts his throne:
And so Emanuel cometh to his own.

XXXVIII.

We leave this story with a word for those
Who with us journeyed to its darkened close,
Not that our word or what we may relate
Can change their fortune or reverse their fate,
But that the legend of their lives may tell,
And in it bid the waiting guest farewell.
When Lazarus went that morn from Rahab's hall,
The darkened shadows on his pathway fall :
To Bethany he turns his tardy feet,
Ere he from paths familiar makes retreat.
His sisters hear his stern resolve, and fear
The dark'ning sorrows shortly drawing near ;
But when they find him in his purpose stern,
They to his labor and his calling turn.
Through all Judea and through Galilee,
From Lebanon to Siddim's tideless sea,
Their tireless feet together bear the Word
To dying souls of the now risen Lord.
So eager in their work, their home forgot,
Infrequent seen, at last they visit not,
Falls into Ruin's desolating hand,
Else is destroyed by some marauding band.
Thus Mary, tireless, laboring day by day
In work of love wears her frail life away ;
While Martha, longer, with her brother's aid,
In blessing sees her sojourn still delayed.

XXXIX.

Escaped the cruel hand of vengeance, still
Old Rahab, faithful, did his Master's will,
Unflinching in his duty, without show,
To rouse the sleeping minions of the law.
So ran his days until the evening's close,
Which came to him as sweet as night's repose,
When Haddan, feeble grown by weight of years,
Folds his thin hands at last with many tears,
Where still they lie upon his pulseless breast,
Their busy fingers clasped in peaceful rest,
Bathed in the tears and kisses on them shed

By Judeth, mourning now her sainted dead !
Not long it was, it seemed a little day,
When Haddan went himself his master's way ;
While Judeth's hands, with fingers trembling now,
Smooth the white locks that shade his furrowed brow :
The faithful servant with his master gone,
She in her father's hall alone lives on.

XL.

When swept the torrent and the storm of war
Over the city, levelling all before,
This home was desolate, nor was there tongue
A word of light its darkness shed among
The house of Rahab not forgotten, yet
The line of Rahab lost they soon forget ;
Nor would the faintest gleam on it be thrown,
Had not a parchment found within it shown
The story we relate with little change,
That had the seal of truth.   This writing strange,
Whose closing lines foreshadow in their trend
A sweeter sunset when the day shall end,
No better can we close the story done
Than in the words of this heart-saddened one,
With which she ends the record she has made
Of scenes by her so vividly portrayed,
Wrote out to soothe the pain her aching breast
Forever suffered in her love's unrest : —

XLI.

" ' So long ! and now at last, yes, I may come ! '
So writes he to me from his distant home,
Where he hath built a church, and now hath need
Of woman's hand, her sisters there to lead ;
Since Martha — faithful sister, failing saint ! —
In her long labors now grows weak and faint.
And I will go ! Yes, on love's wings will fly,
That I may serve with life until I die.
I may not be to him aught more than now ;
What matters it, since snow-wreaths crown my brow,
And his fair locks in his long labor grown

Like wool whose snow must far outshine my own!
Farewell, Jerusalem! And thou, Judea,
Thy glorious scenes I nevermore shall see!
Yet mem'ry's pictures with me I shall bear,
And where I am ye still shall cheer me there!
A little while I linger, first to close
Dear Martha's eyes in their last sweet repose;
To bear the cup to Lazarus, feeble grown, —
No hand so well can serve him as my own, —
Then will I wait with him the coming shades
While life's sweet twilight into darkness fades,
Our work all done, our crowns with starry gems
Thick set in gold as royal diadems,
Awaiting us; then in that sunset fair
Once more together will we cleave the air
To fields Eternal where we once have gone,
This time to wait and worship by the Throne.
Farewell once more! farewell, farewell to all!
Sweet home of youth and dear-remembered hall!
My heart sinks low with pangs of sad regret,
But Love dies not and neither can forget.
Let all who read this curious writing through
Know Judeth, Rahab's daughter, speaketh true,
As witness Nisan thirtieth day and year,
Since Lazarus beloved went forth from here."

POEMS OF HOME, HEART, AND HEARTH.

MY LAST NIGHT'S DREAM.

I HAD a curious dream last night,
  And thrice ere morning came
I woke, and when I slept again
  I dreamed it o'er the same.

'T was strange! I lay, methought, asleep,
  And yet awake did seem,
And told the tale which now I tell,
  But told it as a dream.

It seemed as actor I was one,
  And yet apart did stand, —
Not on the ship which floated by,
  Nor yet upon the land:
I was and was not, saw and felt,
  And all did understand.

I saw, and yet like one who sees
  A hundred years before,
And as the passing of a dream
  I told my story o'er.

THE DREAM.

The wind blew high; the pitchy sky
  Sank down upon the sea,
Till black waves met the clouds of jet,
  If such a thing might be.
The winds roared loud from sea and cloud,
  And naught was heard or seen
Save thunder's crash and lightning's flash
  That leapt and roared between;
While in the light the sea and night
  Burned instant blue and green!

A blacker wave, a brighter flash,
   What gleams so ghastly white?
It rose up like a masted ship,
   And on its prow a light:
What means a ship with sails all set
   To sail on such a night?

What means the ship? — another flash
   Still brings the prow more near!
I see the light through the gloom of night,
   And the helmsman shoreward steer.

And by my faith I know the ship!
   And by my all held dear,
This morn at dawn, ere the mist was gone,
   It did this harbor clear.

I heard the boatman's whistle call,
   I saw the white sails set:
The helmsman stood beside the wheel, —
   Why do they linger yet?

A boat from the shore with a single rower
   Approached the waiting bark,
Yet two were there, the rower fair,
   The other tall and dark.

Wrapped in his cloak, no word he spoke,
   But watched those white arms bare,
As if he thought it strange to see
   A lad so lithe and fair —
A boy that climbs the tough oak mast —
   With soft and yellow hair.

The boat is moored with crew on board,
   The anchor loosed below;
The sails full set the breeze has met,
   And bravely out they go!

The water leaps from painted prow,
   The waves roll back amain;

A lovely sight this ship to see
Skim o'er the waters light and free,
  As bird o'er waving grain.

" My ship hath got a gallant crew,
  Well used to brave the sea ;
But the lad who rowed thee out this morn,
  I pray thee, who is he ? "
" He shipped last night at set of sun,
  And begged to sail with me."

So spoke the captain of this ship,
  So spoke the mate again ;
The stranger answered not a word,
And it is doubtful if he heard,
  Else answer did not deign :

For all the while with half a smile
  And half a frown sat he,
And gazed upon the passing lad,
  And then out on the sea,
When his blue eyes in glancing round
  Detected scrutiny.

" Now by the cross ! " the stranger said,
  " Now by the cross ! " said he,
" This is a curious tale, forsooth,
  Thou tellest unto me."

He looked again unto the lad,
  Then glanced he to the sky ;
Why follows he still that sailor-boy ?
Why follows he with his eye ?

" A foolish thought ! " he said at last ;
  " Such eyes and hair, I ween,
In such uncultured loveliness
  Never but once I 've seen,
And they — 't is vain to hold such thought —
  Those mountains lie between ! "

This is that ship ; see how she rides
  The waves, now mountain-high,

Down to the ocean's shining depths,
   Then to the pitchy sky.

Before the blast each sail and mast
   Now sighs and creaks and moans,
While in the ship each sailor's lip
   Is muttering prayers and groans.

The helmsman steers with steady hand;
   By winds the sails are split;
The helmsman steers with steady hand, '
   Nor minds the waves a whit,
Though the sailors do all stand and shake
   As in an ague-fit.

Before the wind, as press'd behind,
   Still drives the vessel on ;
The masts now split, the sails are slit,
   The yards and jib are gone !
Still rise the waves as mountains high,
   Still drives the vessel on.

The thunders crash, the lightnings flash
   And blaze along the sea,
Till all around the depths profound
   Is bright as bright can be,
And ship and sky and sea and all
   It showeth unto me !

The thunders crash, the wild waves dash,
   And whelm the ship with spray ;
The clouds are riven with floods from heaven,
   But on she holds her way,
While many a sailor, who swore but now,
   In fervent tone doth pray.

" I 've breasted many a storm at sea,"
   The captain said at last,
" But never before, my long years o'er,
   Doff'd cap to such a blast.

" I 've sailed these waters for many a year,
   And know both sea and shore,

But never have heard nor seen averred
 Such storm as this before."

Up spoke the gray-haired Pilot then,
 And spoke he solemnly :
"Some wicked thing 't is sure must bring
 This storm upon the sea ;
Some wicked thing, and in this ship
 Here hiding sure must be !

" Without a frown the sun went down,
 I watched him to the west ;
Without a cloud to dim or shroud,
 I watched him to his rest.

" The darkness followed o'er his track
 Where down the west went he,
And curtained o'er both sky and shore,
 And muffled up the sea.

" Upon our wake a fire-like flake
 I watched burn blue and white ;
I watched — but what ill-favored thing
 Is that which meets my sight ?

" It rose breast-high above the wave,
 And with its eye of coal,
It looked at me as if 't would look
 Down in my very soul !

" It looked at me, then at the ship,
 And then again at me,
Then shook its crested head, and sank
 Beneath the crested sea.

" Three times, before my watch was o'er,
 I saw it so arise
And glare at me, then at the ship,
 With red and hungry eyes,
And ev'ry time it uttered moans,
 Like woman's wailing cries.

" Three times upon these waves before,
   And in my watch at night,
And also on three different ships,
   I saw the selfsame sight ;
And on each ship a guilty soul
   Was shunning fate by flight.

" One was a Traitor, who for gain
   His country's freedom sold,
And one an agéd man had slain
   To rob him of his gold.

" The last the vilest of the three,
   For he a trusting maid
Had won through love from virtue's path,
   And left her when betrayed,
And sought to flee in other lands
   The misery he made.

" Look to the ship ! "   " But wherefore start ? "
   The captain makes reply ;
" Look ! on yon wave's advancing crest
   There shines that burning eye ! "

The sailors all have been confessed ;
   The lad, — what sins has he ?
There is no crime that he hath done
   That moveth so the sea.

But yet this lad essays to speak :
   " I loved right well," said he ;
With that the blast the maintop-mast
   Hurled crashing in the sea.

None heeded now the sailor lad,
   None heeded now his tale :
'T is sure not he the cause can be
   Which brought so wild a gale.

Then spoke the dark-eyed stranger loud
   Above the sea and wind :
" A blue-eyed lass that loveth me
   I left long leagues behind, —

" A blue-eyed lass with locks of gold,
    And breast as white as swan ;
Oh. she was fair as any there,
    Nor sweeter sun shines on !

" Aye, she is fair and she is good :
    Why turned I from her side ?
I fear me now for grief this night
    Her blue eyes are not dried,
But her pillow is wet as these sails still set
    That drip in the whirling tide.

" She loveth me right well, I trow,
    And my false vows believed,
And, yielding to my tale of love,
    By me was she deceived.

" I loved her, for she was most fair,
    And that she loveth me ;
But then I would not marry one
    Who was of low degree.
And now to seek another bride
    I sail across the sea."

Again the gray-haired pilot spoke :
    " We took the other three,
When we had heard their sins confessed,
    And hurled them in the sea;

" And as they splashed upon the wave,
    All heard that cry of woe,
An instant ere the echo died,
    Then ceased the wind to blow ;
And where they floated on the wave
    We saw that fierce eye glow."

With locks all wet and dark eyes set
    They watch the stranger there,
And if thy sins are not now shrived
    Thou hast great need of prayer ;
For by those looks too much I fear
    There 's little thought to spare !

For he who makes of innocence
  A plaything and a jest,
Should not on earth have pleasant place
  Where his vile foot can rest ;

And he who pleads a love unfelt
  To blast a virtuous name,
Should live in pangs of burning Hell
  And wither in its flame !

Now close they round the stranger dark —
  Whence comes that piercing shriek ?
Why kneels he there with yellow hair,
  Wild-eyed, and blanching cheek ?

Why kneels he there, the sailor-boy,
  And clasps the stranger's knee,
And prayeth them, if one must die,
  To cast him in the sea,
For he hath much of sin to hide,
  And more of misery ?

They seize and drag him from his place :
  Lo ! cap and cape are gone ;
The lightning's flash shows bosom fair
  As ever eye gazed on,
Until in shame to veil from sight
  Her yellow locks drop down !

Back start the sailors at the sight
  To see a thing so fair, —
Back, as if, dropping from the clouds,
  An angel form stood there !

And now confessed a maid distressed,
  She clasps the stranger's knee,
When in his arms he holds her fast
  And gives her kisses three,
And cries, " My Ellen, for thy love,
  Oh, welcome back to me !

" The maid who loves with such a love
  Is worthy of the rest

That she alone can hope to find
    Upon this sheltering breast.

"No other love shall claim my heart,
    Nor shall we part again ;
For, you are mine in love and truth."
    The captain cried, "Amen!"

And ere fair Ellen dried her tears,
    Or found a word to say,
The winds have died and sleeps the tide,
    The clouds have fled away,
And from the portals of the east
    Comes forth the golden day.

I woke, and, lo! the morning sun
    Across my chamber floor
Had thrown his golden banners down,
    And I could dream no more!

THE ROSES HAVE COME AGAIN.

Now the cold, bleak winds of Winter are past,
    The frost and the snow are fled ;
The dry old leaves of the forest are hid
    That Autumn around has shed ;
The waving boughs of the trees are clad,
    The grass grows sweet o'er the plain ;
While wild-flowers spring from their emerald beds,
    And Roses have come again.

The song of the bird and hum of the bee
    Float joyously through the air ;
The shout of the child and the lambkin's cry
    Are mingling together there ;
The whispering breeze through fresh-grown leaves
    Is murmuring its pleasing strain ;
And the earth looks brighter to-day, and why ?
    The Roses have come again !

I love the flowers of my native fields,
    But the wild rose best of all,
For one who was dear to my youthful heart
    Its opening buds recall ;
And now, as the grass in the old graveyard
    Grows green in the warm spring rain,
I think of a form that is mouldering there,
    Now Roses have come again.

I 've gathered the wild-flowers many a day
    And twined of them chaplets fair,
And wove them with trembling fingers oft
    In the folds of that lost one's hair :
But the Rose was the gem in that diadem,
    An emblem of young Love's reign ;
And these words sound sweet though sad to my heart, —
    The Roses have come again.

I gather the Rose from its thorny stem,
    And drink of its sweets with joy,
And with the young leaves of the tender buds
    In wandering thought I toy :
Far away o'er the past my thoughts go back,
    Through scenes of pleasure and pain,
And, thinking of her, awhile I forget
    That Roses have come again.

Yes, a smile I see round her red lips play,
    The bloom on her cheek returns,
And the fire long quenched in that once bright eye
    Again in its beauty burns;
And I snatch fresh Roses to crown her brow :
    But, ah ! my feverish brain
Has called her up from the dead, dead Past ! —
    The Roses have come again.

But the act which broke the magic-like spell
    Has strown o'er the dewy ground
The loveliest bloom of the full-blown Rose,
    To wither and fade around :
E'en thus the flowers that crowned her brow
    Lie thick where my love lies slain,

From the Rose-tree shed which grows by her grave
  Now Roses have come again.

I love the spring, for it brings these flowers,
  But the flowers I love more dear,
For they seem but messengers sent to tell
  Of loved ones no longer here, —
Of the spring-time of life, and youth's bright days,
  When the soul is free from stain ;
And we live those days of childhood o'er
  When Roses have come again.

When I lay my head on the pillow of death,
  I want the flowers in bloom ;
For I shudder to think when I leave this shore
  I leave it in shadowy gloom.
Let me go to those fields of endless bliss,
  With their spring's eternal reign,
From a world in bloom this side of the tomb,
  When the Roses have come again.

THE OATH.

I.

"Swear it !" he said ; "swear on this hand
  Over this heart that is throbbing beneath !
Swear it ! Yes, swear, that the oath may stand,
  Nor perish away in the passing breath.
There ! it is done ! Bound soul and heart, —
Not to the evil, for no black art
The struggling soul shall stain, but good,
Good for thee and for me. Why should
Thy cheek blanch white, as if a fear
Pressed on thy footsteps darkly near ?
Nay ! Thou art saved, not lost ! for now
The gold-woven crown entwines thy brow,
An aureole bright, to shine and burn
  Brighter each day and brighter each hour,

As the days and weeks through the years return,
 Brighter the crown and sweeter the flower
Plucked for thy bosom to wear in love,
Under the skies blue-arched above ! "

II.

Thus did he whisper it in my ear,
 Whisper these words so fond and low ;
Whisper them with a breath so near
 The dew grew wet upon my brow,
As upward it rose from burning cheek,
 Perfumed as breath from flowers, and soft
As the touch of an infant's fingers.   Speak
Not of a love that is vain and weak,
 And changes and faints and fails so oft
It mocks as a shadow Faith : for his
Was not so unworthy a kind as this.
 His was a heart which fed on fire,
And lived as the sacred bird whose life
 Grows in the flame devouring, born
 Living in that where life is shorn, —
Yet pure from the flame where no desire
 Base in its earth-mould is grovelling, rife ;
 Festering with hot, unholy thought,
 Tainting his blood : nor ever wrought
Evil in heart or stain to his soul.
 No !   He was pure, and his love was so, —
Pure as the stars that Godward roll, —
 Pure as the light which paints the bow
Spanning the storm !   And such was his prayer,
To see me ever as he was there ;
Thus in that hour, he bade me swear !

III.

But my idle tale in telling will wear,
 Will weary and wear your patience, I fear ;
But to my heart, like an answered prayer,
 Or even the last slow-falling tear.
It brings a balm, — a soft, sweet balm,
That falls with a gentle, soothing calm,

Peacefully, sweet, and fresh, like rain
Soaking a dry and thirsty plain,
Till odors of life breathe ev'rywhere,
Filling the damp and sweetened air
Full of its life.   That he made me swear
   I bless him now, though I could not see
   Aught in this oath but Love's tyranny!

IV.

Look in my face and read its lines!
   Lines upon lines! the deeper crossed
Gently by those where sweetly shines
   Sunlight of rest for the tempest-tossed!
Just as the sea whose white lips lave
   The storm-ploughed sands of the stooping coast
     Where the tide rolls in, when sunk to rest
The storm which beat to a foam each wave,
     Tracing its track with a white-capped crest
Over the scarred and beaten shore,
Until the sands grow smooth once more!
Such are the lines the tide of years,
Sweeping across the course of tears,
And marks of passion and pain and fears,
Has left with its gentle kiss upon
A face, but for these, with its beauty gone.

V.

But there are years, and tears, and pain,
   Sorrows, and sighs, and hopes, that lie
Buried in doubt, but to rise again, —
   To rise, revive, grow sweet and die,
Giving new birth through death, as she
Who labors in death to infancy;
   Lives in new life, the dead alive,
The living dead, — transposed, transplaced,
Separate, yet both in one embraced!
   Such has my heart's life ever been;
Such is it ever to those who strive:
   Such forever and ever, I ween,
     It passes and changes from scene to scene.

VI.

But from the day he made me swear,
   Yes, from the day upon his breast
I placed my hand — and it trembled there,
   Trembled and shook, and could not rest —
Peace came into my heart, sweet peace,
Such as man dreams of but never sees;
Peace and the holiest calm !   I felt
Like praising some spirit — some presence — knelt
I just where I stood, and raised my eyes,
Silently, wonderingly, up to the skies,
Still breathing no word ! and yet it seemed
(Or else I had fallen asleep and dreamed)
Somewhere above there were faces that shone,
And eyes that looked lovingly into my own,
And voices that spoke; and my heart, as it were,
Gave back a low answer — or was it a prayer ?
I never had prayed before, and knew
But a note and a word of a hymn or two:
Aflame and aglow the heavens above
Shone, and my heart seemed melted with love !

VII.

Oh, it was sweet ! and ever and ever
Down in my heart has it lingered, and never
Faded the light !   It will live there forever
And ever, forever will live and grow lighter,
And sweeter, and richer, and warmer, and brighter !
My soul feels the thrill, even now, as I speak,
And witnesses yet for that love in my cheek.
The gloom there before I did not see ;
My soul had grown blinded.   Sin whispered to me
There was no happiness saving through sin,
Which won all that mortal could hope here to win.
I tasted that fruit ! it palled ; but the bliss
Grows sweeter and richer, — no surfeit in this !

VIII.

My heart grows younger, I know, as the years
Speed on, and my life grows older and nears
That hateful old age, to many a bane —
To all his coming is seen with pain —
Yet I but laugh in his ghastly face,
As he pinches my wrinkles, and lightly lays
The thin, white threads in my hair. My heart
Is young and grows younger : Love's wondrous art
Keeps it as young as the day when first
Love into its chambers as sunshine burst.

IX.

What did I swear ? And did I not tell ?
I thought I had told you all ! Ah, well !
We were parting — you know what that is ?   He
Was all, yet could be as nothing, to me —
At least not then ; yet he loved me, — both
Loved madly, but purely and truly, were loth
To part for an hour ; yet we must sever,
To meet not for years, perhaps not forever !
It may be the last — I look still and wait :
The day, if 't is coming, is now coming late !
My hand on his hand, and that on his breast
Pressing the hand his loving hand press'd,
I swore to be true, and to watch and to trust
Through wearing of years and time's wasting rust,
Loving no other but God and my soul !
While keeping that oath I see the years roll
Faster and faster, and years come and go
O'er those that were younger and fairer than I,
But yet I do not grow older, or why
Should they tell me my youth will not die ?
It may be : for Love, like dew on the flower,
Refreshes my heart with its sweets ev'ry hour,
While hope bids me wait, and faith whispers low,
He is coming, sweetheart ! be true to your vow.

X.

Was I always called Agnes? Why this —
Is there aught in that name found amiss?
Do you know — 't is a fancy — 't is nothing! stay!
You are old, and look worn from the way,
And I 'm sure you want rest and repose for the day.
Did you just speak? Did I hear aright?
Who told you my name? What, you? No, no!
Your form is too bent and your hair too white,
　　And he was an arrow and lithe and fair,
　　While the shadows of night were in his hair —
But then that was years, long years ago!
And my own locks of gold are changing to snow.
But the eye's burning glances the same, just the same!
And the name he now gave was his name, yes, his name!
Open wide, waiting arms, though now feeble grown!
Love flies to his own! yes, flies to his own!
Because my love changed not through sun and through
　　　　storm,
I dreamed of no change in your face or your form.
　　Take me close to your bosom, my sweet; closer, there!
　　My oath is fulfilled! I am true if not fair!

SONG.

　　THE stars are glowing in the skies,
　　　　The clouds have fled away,
　　The mist of night around me lies
　　　　In shadows dull and gray.
　　　　Come stray with me, dearest,
　　　　While stars their watchings keep.
　　Come stray with me, come stray with me,
　　　　Let those that love not sleep.

　　The night grows deeper on the plain,
　　　　Our steps must homeward turn;
　　The dew reflects from earth again
　　　　The heavenly lights that burn.

Come, come with me, dearest,
We can no farther rove.
Come play for me, come play for me
Those melting notes of love.

Ah! sing to me, for in my breast
All tuneless are those strings
That vibrate when the heart is blest,
And rapture inly springs :
Yes, sing to me, dearest,
Thy voice is music sweet;
The echoings, the echoings,
My heart shall still repeat.

And when the last note dies away,
New strings shall catch the strain ;
A viewless hand shall sweetly play
The song of love again.
Then list with me, dearest,
Love tunes the echoing song :
Within my breast, within my breast,
Those notes shall echo long.

MUSIC THAT EVER IS NEW.

I HAVE listened to-night to music so sweet
It charmed all my sadness away,
In the rhythmical sound of merry young feet
Of children in innocent play.

Their laughter, like ripples of water, flows
Enchanting upon the breeze ;
While echo, repeating it, comes and goes,
Refining the notes which please.

I drink of the music as one does wine,
Athirst for the cheer it brings ;
But sweeter to me this draught of mine,
Which comforts but never stings !

The voices come in at the open doors,
  And float through each vacant room,
Like fragrance blown in from the bursting flowers
  Which under my windows bloom.

And yet no feet o'er the threshold come,
  And under my roof-tree rest ;
No nestlings at eve to my gates fly home
  To shelter upon my breast.

Yet a hand once touched the open door,
  A foot at the threshold stayed ;
And a shadow lies there forevermore,
  A sorrow that will not fade !

ON THE ABOLITION OF SLAVERY.

Bring forth that flag, now tempest-torn,
  Fling out its starry shield,
Which long in triumph has been borne
  On Freedom's battle-field :
Its blood-washed folds no longer bear
That living lie to blacken there
  And shroud one half its stars ;
The shackled hand has purged that page,
A stain to Freedom's name and age,
  Attested by our scars.

That barren tree hath borne its fruit;
  In war it bloomed anew :
The driving blast gave deeper root,
  Dispelling poisonous dew ;
A nation's tears dissolved the rock,
First broken in the battle-shock,
  Our blood redeemed the soil !
No blast can snap the laden bough,
While ripened fruit we gather now
  In resting from our toil.

No more the crouching head will bow
   In abject slavery crushed ;
No more we watch the patient brow
   And lips in suffering hushed !
By Freedom's air dissolved in rust,
The broken chain lies in the dust,
   By bloody hands cast down ;
While on the brow of Liberty
These hands she now in turn makes free
   Have placed the victor's crown !

Arise and sing, O land redeemed !
   Let ev'ry tongue unite ;
That sun which through the war-clouds gleamed
   Redoubles now its light ;
And Liberty, baptized anew,
Stands forth the living, strong, and true,
   With skirts blood-purified !
We blush no more with shame to see,
Before the altar of the free,
   Humanity denied !

Praise the Eternal, from whose throne
   Shone forth the promised sign !
And in thy joy, O Man ! make known
   His power prevailed, not thine !
The whirlwind of the battle rose,
Then passed ; the fire consuming glows,
   Then rolls the earthquake by !
A hush comes o'er the scene, — a voice
In whispers soft bids man rejoice,
   For God himself is nigh.

How great, how grand, the work thus done,
   How vast the wondrous plan !
He who directs the blazing sun
   Works through the will of man !
The mortal wills and works in night,
By glimmer of his reason's light,
   Which leads him far astray :
Eternal Justice shapes the course,
And wields at will its feeble force
   In His long chosen way.

The sword and torch, that were designed
    To spread all-grasping power,
In hands they were invoked to bind,
    In turn that land devour;
And chains are cleft, the bond go free, —
In flames the whipping-post we see,
    The block is overthrown:
The hands that bound those fetters there
The chains of slaves have won to wear,
    Most fitting for their own!

The fire of Slavery's sacrifice
    Is quenched by hand divine:
O'erthrown the bloody altar lies
    Upon its broken shrine!
Whelmed in a fearful sea of blood,
The hosts which after them pursued
    Forever lost now lie;
Across its wave the harp is strung, —
Anew the song of Freedom sung
    Beneath our own fair sky.

From battle-clouds our land comes forth,
    From graves the loving come;
Baptized anew in second birth,
    We hail our Free-land home!
The stain is wiped from off our crest;
In war our land has yet been blest,
    Our liberty made pure:
We plant our standard on the heights
Where glow the Truth's eternal lights
    Forever to endure!

A VISION OF LOVE.

THEY told me it was beautiful, the home
    Where Love doth dwell; and in his palace fair
That I should never find night's hateful gloom,
    That Love's own sun gave light forever there,
Nor on its morn of rising noon nor night should come!

I laughed their praise to scorn, and scorned their praise,
   As words that fools delight in, — turned away
And shook my head in mockery. The lays
   They sung I could not understand, — that lay
At least of Love, which hearts with passion madly sways.

I wandered by the gateway, — half looked in;
   The lights were low, and voices softly hushed;
And through the veil — a scarlet veil, so thin
   It showed the flitting forms and faces flushed —
I saw the hidden mysteries of the courts within.

But Love I did not see enthroned and bright
   In the soft radiance of a thousand hues
That mingling fell, — prismatic showers of light,
   A mist of soft and fragrant-scented dews,
In every drop of which there lurked a soft delight.

I would have passed them by, would then have gone
   Out into darkness and the freezing night,
And, not beholding where the veil was drawn,
   The glory hidden to the darkened sight,
Would still as blindly through this life been toiling on, —

But for a voice that called me, — called as low
   As the hushed whisper of the waving grass, —
Called me as softly as the roses blow
   When with red lips they kiss the winds that pass,
And, nodding with sweet blushes, still more crimson grow!

I heard the whisper far away and faint
   As Echo dying on a distant hill!
It trembled with a sad and sobbing plaint
   That sent through all my soul a burning thrill, —
A rapture words, with all their power, can never paint.

I turned and saw! my eyes dropped down, — my heart
   Gave one great, shuddering bound and then stood still!
My lips, with words unuttered, stood apart,
   And all my flesh grew weak, and dead, and chill,
As if my panting breast were pierced by Death's keen
     dart!

I would have fled, but could not, — could not move
    Away from what had charmed, though I had died!
The breath from lips like winds that blow above
    The ice from southern seas, set free the tide
Into the swift, hot torrents of tumultuous love!

Her lithe form, as a reed when winds blow soft,
    Swayed gently, and each motion was a grace;
Her hand and waxen arm, as raised aloft
    In beck, were beautiful — but that sweet face!
The like I never saw, though dreaming of it oft!

I lifted up mine eyes, and looked into
    Those liquid orbs, whose glances took strange hold
Upon my heart, as sweetly they looked through
    Their fringed and waxen casements, where the gold
Drooped down with pendent pearls as grasses wet with dew.

Down in those wells of light I looked, and saw
    A thousand worlds unseen before, and each
Brighter than any dream! My heart in awe
    Rose up and choked the struggling power of speech,
While, fast enchained, my eyes from her could not withdraw.

Her throat was soft and swelling as a dove's
    When the low note of sorrow trembles there;
And white as Spring's fair blossoms in her groves,
    And through the tresses of her floating hair
Courted the rosy kisses of the wingéd Loves.

Her lips the hue incarnadine, the expressed hue
    A thousand roses yield in odorous dye;
And clinging to them in a mist of dew
    The sweets concentrate which within them lie,
A thousand, thousand roses robbed could not supply.

The smile which wreathed them had the joy of years,
    The hope of life, the peace of heaven, complete!
The bow of promise cast upon shed tears,
    To tell of days of sorrow now complete,
And the calm rest which comes when hushed are all our
      fears.

She called me, and I could but come! Her glance
   Drew me like cords of steel, and her white arms,
Stretched out to me, still beckoned my advance,
   While yet the thousand shifting, varied charms
Of face and form divine my senses did entrance.

Close I drew near; yet drawn I know not why,
   Nor could I question with a soul aflame
From the hot passion which her kindling eye
   Had stirred within. My labored breathing came
In short, quick gasps for life, like those who, wounded,
    die.

Just at the portal — at the close-shut door
   Of Love's fair palace — stood she there so sweet
I could have gazed upon her evermore, —
   I could have lain forever at her feet,
Or in the distance meekly watched her to adore!

But her white arms embraced me; as a star
   Hiding each bright eye seemed in dewy mist;
Her breath upon my cheek, perfumes afar
   Faint in their spices as her red lips kiss'd
My own, and with that kiss Love's gates swung soft ajar!

And then she led me in, — in through the gates
   Which I had passed and scorned to look upon —
Into the courts where Love alone creates
   That over which he reigns. No picture drawn
Is this, of which the long beholding palls and sates.

No sight so beautiful! The sun's warm light
   Fell through a thousand sweetly tinted screens
That softened it; and ev'ry color bright
   Played as winged vapors o'er the shifting scenes,
And with each rising image brought a new delight.

Before there are no flowers, but bush and tree,
   Shrub, plant, and creeping thing, and all that bear
The bud for bloom, were pendent, I could see,
   With buds just bursting into blossom there,
But not an open flower beyond to gladden me.

I wondered, and my wonder was increased
 As farther on we trod the paths of green;
There was a noise around that never ceased:
 Beneath my feet, from spreading boughs between,
Were breathed soft sounds like sighs from prisoners re-
  leased.

Where we had trod, those bursting buds in flower
 Bent the high boughs, while shrub and vine, but green
The while, flamed in a thousand hues, each bower
 A gorgeous wilderness of beauty seen,
Like wondrous magic of some great magician's power; —

And such it was, and she, enchantress, trod
 There with bare feet, while in each track sprung up
The flowers which slept beneath the verdant sod,
 And kissed their soft, pink soles, while from each cup
Dripped down the sweets in showers, and down her fair
  locks flow'd.

And even as we walked, the blossoms spread
 Their carpet at our feet; the buds unfurled
Their twisted petals, — from their sweet hearts shed
 The richest odors of a flowery world,
While birds on wing of fairest plumage sung o'erhead.

And there were strains from players in the air
 On strings no mortal fingers could inspire;
And there were songs that murmured ev'rywhere,
 And through each breathed a soul of soft desire,
In love made sacred by the incense of sweet prayer.

But in my ear one name was ever rung;
 A thousand voices whispered it, and light
Wove it in shade; and from sweet flowers among,
 I read that name; and closed my eye's dull sight,
Deep in my soul in song I heard it softly sung.

Voices that syllable her name were sweet;
 The flowers I saw, most beautiful, that bore
On their rich leaves the name I might repeat,
 Softly and slow as all had breathed it o'er,
Each voice in sweeter strain my ravished ears did greet.

But vain my efforts further to portray
  In colors which have tints to charm the eye,
And show to hearts the mystery of Love's way.
  Let each go in, nor pass the portal by,
Afraid to trust a love that never can betray.

A pledge of Love, sweet offering of my breast,
  I bring that heart to her who led me in ;
Out of this wine, in Love's rich goblet pressed,
  There fall to stain no poisoned drops of sin,
A name I breathe not here, since Love has breathed and
    bless'd.

Bright vision !   Love to me hath all things shown !
  He weaves thy name in words for aye to live,
Through these sad years when locks to silver grown,
  Like autumn leaves grown sere, to me now give
Thy kiss of life so sweet that it may check Death's groan !

There now I rest !   And it was not a dream ?
  Not all a dream, since in my hand I hold
Thy fair white hand, and see thine eye's soft beam
  The flame of love flash out, and flowers of gold
For us still bloom along the borders of life's stream.

THE OLD RÉGIME.

SALUTATION.

WE stretch our hands imploring to the Past,
With eager fingers strive to hold it fast, —
Cling to its robes, which, backward flowing, seem
A shadowy vision in a fitful dream,
While speeding onward in its rapid flight,
Pursued by shadows followed fast by night ;
And, as it flies, bears in its potent arms,
Snatched from our own, life's sweetest hopes and charms,
Still glancing back with half-averted face,
Becomes a memory of departed days.

In the dim shadows of its twilight hour
The heart's affections feel its silent power,
When we, long wandering, turn our steps again
Into the paths of youth so dear and plain !
The hills, the vales, the streams that gently flow
Through wood and dale, old friends and dear, we know:
In rapture, we with eager steps draw near,
With smiles for this, perchance for that a tear,
The one dear spot where recollection weaves,
Amid its bloom, her gloomy cypress leaves,
Where pale lips quivering at the parting's pain
We kissed adieu, never to kiss again !
Thus seen, again, from every sheltered nook,
From leafy bower and wayside babbling brook,
From wild-rose vines, from hawthorn's snowy bloom,
From alder-hedge with sweet but faint perfume,
From orchards where the apple-blossoms gleam
With all the richness of a fairy dream ;
From meadows where the lark's first matin lay
Mingles its music with perfume of hay ;
From pastures where the lowing cattle feed
On clover, sweetening all the flowery mead ;
From gardens where in dreamy incense rise
Rich odors breathing of a Paradise ;
From hearth, from home, from every cherished scene
Which once familiar to the heart has been, —
Look forth the faces, now divinely fair,
Of those, lang syne, we loved and cherished there !
Such dreams are life's sweet retrospects, and live
Our hearts anew in the short hours they give.
So turn my thoughts !   So gleam before my sight
These scenes familiar in their settings bright ;
So lift the shadows, and again appear
Faces and forms familiar once and dear,
Dim, shadowy, vague, — or are these mists that rise,
Before my sight, from tears that fill my eyes ?
I may not answer : all I know is, yet,
Though time obscure, my love will not forget !
But turning ever to the past, I find
In memory still a friend most true and kind.
We laugh with it where we before have laughed,
Drink of the cup again we once have quaffed ;

In it again we live a life long done,
With all its flowers and all its smiles and sun.
Enough! So ends for me this hour's sweet dream,
And I now turn, regretful, to my theme.

Sweet are the odors of an honored name
That cling around a bright but fading fame:
As flowers we gather in their fresher bloom,
In fading leave behind a faint perfume
Which clings to all, a memory of the past,
The first to charm us and to cheer the last,
So lives man's honor, so his fame ascends;
A breath declares it, and a breath, too, ends!
His glory withers with his fading bays,
And tongues withhold which late inspired his praise.
And yet how many on a thread so frail
Hang all of hope, and on it rise or fail!
Their deeds, their names immortal hope to see,
Secured by such in Fame's eternity.
As spinners spin, so they these threads entwine
To weave from them a long, immortal line!
These ropes of sand, from Time's frail glass thus spun,
Snap at the touch e'en as the spindles run;
Nor is there known a hand with skill and power
To join the frayed and broken fragments more!
Then, if our fame we strive so hard to win
Hangs on a thread so brittle and so thin,
How shall he stand who lives on others' deeds,
Fame's parasite, which on dead laurels feeds,
And boasts a lineage, if, in him begun,
A bankrupt heritage he leaves his son!
There is a pride which merits our esteem
For those whose boast is of the Old Régime;
A pride of name which still some honor gives
From years long past, and on that honor lives.
We may admire the palace for its art,
While yet the builder we detest at heart;
The one who builds may be in soul a king,
While he who occupies a nameless thing!
We would not hold ancestral lines in scorn,
Not man's the fault if titled he is born;

He who does not go forward must go back ;
The natural color of all sheep is black :
Yet those whose boast is birth, and that alone,
Should not in scorn on nobler men look down.
For such, while yet their folly we detest,
Some sense of pity fills the warmer breast ;
A feeling such as oft will in us spring
When we behold a bird with broken wing,
Which to the empyrean upward might have sprung
Had not the parent bird deformed her young ;
A feeling such as oft will o'er us come
When for the first we enter some fair home,
Where we, expecting faces bright to see,
Are met instead by staring idiocy,
The brain, the mind, a ruin from the first,
A fate inherited in a blood accursed ;
Chained in such clay the soul immortal lies
Wrapped in its cerements nevermore to rise !
To live while dead to honor is scarce worse
Than thus to live beneath dead honor's curse.

Where leaps Niagara from its bastioned walls,
Sheer down the steep the seething torrent falls ;
Forever there o'er roaring rapids play
The pearly mists alike by night and day,
Cold, white, and chill until the sun's warm rays
Burst through the clouds and set them all ablaze,
Then, in the grandeur of their borrowed fires,
What chilled before with ardent joy inspires.
Again, when Winter o'er it rudely blows,
Changing the mists to white and fleecy snows,
Fantastic forms his frosty fingers weave
Where winter gardens bud, and flower, and leave,
In all the cold and icy forms that rise
Created in this Boreal Paradise :
These, touched and thrilled by morning's rhythmic beams,
Glow in each ray that o'er the frost-work streams,
In glory crowned, transcendent, and inspired,
Painted by sunbeams, rainbow-hued attired.
Awed we must stand before such sights revealed,
Our eyes admiring while our lips are sealed !
And yet all this is painted beauty still !
The touch of death beneath is cold and chill.

Such are the garlands, such the glittering crown,
They wear who live upon a past renown.

We walk through gardens where exotic flowers
Surprise and please from unexpected bowers;
We drink their odors, as do gourmands wine,
And scent their beauty as they taste the vine;
Thus, thinking these excel all other bloom,
Nor other flowers distil such rare perfume;
Yet, could we tread the gardens of the East,
Our eyes on their unspoken beauties feast, —
Those gardens whence these selfsame flowers were borne,
Transplanted here and of their sunlight shorn,
Then would we learn that flowers and laurels fade
From native garden torn or rightful head!
As well might we plant roses in the snow,
From Samarkand, and think they still would grow,
As crown a fool from Dante's laurelled brow!

No prodigal is Nature; all her store
She treasures, whether it be life or power.
She clothes the fields in wondrous beauty, yet
The hidden mines of earth does not forget;
The Seasons sends as laborers to their task,
Nor does she Winter's work of Summer ask;
The rose weaves red her flowers, the violet blue;
Where rain should water she withholds the dew.
The blossom fades, then comes the fruit, and then
The leaves grow sere, and rest begins again.
No second fruitage any season knows,
Since labor must be followed by repose;
Save where some hand has plucked the early leaf,
Or summer lingering makes the autumn brief,
Then Nature, forced, from her o'er-quickened womb
From weakling bud brings forth a sickly bloom,
Whose fruit, if autumn ample time endure,
Insipid grows, or drops before mature.
And so throughout the universe we find
The laws that govern matter govern mind.
The points of difference are but in degrees;
Man has his seasons, just the same as these:
Behind them all moves on the great First Cause,
Their pathway hedging by unchanging laws.

As grows the plant, so all its kingdoms will;
As walks the man, so march the nations still:
These facts declared, before we pass them by,
This lesson to our theme we would apply.

Mind marks in man his empire o'er the brute;
Genius its flower and fame its ripened fruit:
Slow in its growth, the flower at last appears,
Like the famed aloe, once a hundred years;
Then, bursting forth in all its wondrous bloom,
The earth grows fragrant in its shed perfume:
The odor lingering when the flower is shed
Breathes but of memories of a beauty fled;
So genius flowering into ripened fame
Drops to the earth and leaves alone its name.
Upon that stock no fruitful branch more grows;
The mind o'erspent sinks back to dull repose;
So those who boast ancestral fame declare
Where genius found their line it left it there!
How clear these truths throughout our lineage run!
The Sulgrave tree bore but one Washington;
And Newstead's branch, luxuriant in its flower,
In Byron bloomed, then failed in name and power.
So Avon's bard, to genius born full blown,
Left fame immortal to a line unknown.
Napoleon fell, and perished Wellington,
Without a heritage from sire to son!
These things have been, and must be to the end:
The laws which shape may break, they will not bend;
As well expect the bloom on Aaron's rod
Without the hand and living touch of God!

It matters not if up or down we go,
The stream will ever to the ocean flow;
He who would cross, the trusty oar must ply:
The laggard waits until the flood runs by.
As well may such dwell in a Capulet's tomb,
The dead alone to chide them for their room!
The living, — what have they this hour to do
With those who perished centuries ago?
There may be heroes in the shadowy line
Whose deeds uncertain on its darkness shine,

Heroes as worthy of the names they bear
As Rome's detested Pontiff-Buccaneer!
Who knows how little honor or how great
Is plucked by merit from invidious fate?
How vain to boast, how worse than vain to build,
On things that blacken what we seek to gild!
It may be meet, in lands where title springs,
Out of the hand or fountain-head of kings,
Where place is sought for power and not for name,
To build our castles on another's fame,
Since rank is place, and place, with such, is power,
Which lasts beyond a little fleeting hour.
But in this land where title is unknown,
Save as a cap, so worn by fool or clown,
How pitiful to see these foolish things
Plume their ambition on such puerile wings!
Knights of the yardstick, heroes of the stye, —
We hold our noses as they pass us by, —
Bearing escutcheons, arms, and monograms,
Heralds to heroes of self-titled shams!
Who in the hall descant on race and blood,
While in the cellar father saws the wood!

They boast of shapely hand and slender foot,
Wear gloves and boots a size too small to suit;
But for the head, I here reverse the charge, —
The hats they wear are found a world too large!
I love a tapering hand as white as milk,
With tint of rose and skin as soft as silk,
If to that hand a shapely arm is pair,
And the proud owner young, and coy, and fair!
So I admire a slim and curving foot,
Well clad and shod in dainty hose and boot,
If just above such witching pedal float
Soft, filmy lace and silken petticoat.
These for the ladies white of hand and heart,
God bless and give them all the better part!
But men! what have they in such things to claim?
Their road lies up the rugged steep of fame,
Where iron hand must second fearless will,
If they would win and hold their vantage still.

Life is too short, while speeding on its track,
To waste its years forever looking back!
No matter what behind us still may lie,
Before us is the mark to fix the eye.
Our life is action : we should not forget
All time is lost we spend in vain regret,
And all regrets are vain, save those which bring
A lesson learned, and healing with the sting.
Not for ourselves we live, then why not we
To others leave our fame and destiny?
As slants the shadow of the feathery pine
When turns the sun the equatorial line,
So will the Now, when it becomes the Past,
Across the future its long shadow cast.
This is the age of manhood, this the day
In the swift race to bear the prize away :
Out of the ashes and the crumbling thrones,
The dust of empires and their mummied bones,
Springs a new manhood, filling every land,
Strong in itself and ready to command.
These are no dreamers, save perchance they dream,
Not of the Old but of the New Régime!
Born of such times and in heroic mould,
Such men love valor, since their hearts are bold.
But theirs a hero-worship which admires
Just as the act they quote itself inspires!
Their theme is action, its success and plan ;
The deeds remembering, they forget the man.
They measure not the sire to judge the son,
But ask alone what he himself has done.
Yet to the great all glory they allow,
As painted halos on a saintly brow!
Still, ever present is this ruling thought,
Not what man is, but what his hand hath wrought.
Thus the dead soul of action, the ideal,
Touched into life, becomes a living real!
Build on such altars fame's sweet incense-fires ;
From rank and name rise Folly's funeral pyres,
Burn up the wrecks now rotting in the past;
Be true to manhood, and on it stand fast!
This marks a man, this evermore declares
Nature's true knighthood on his brow he bears.

Let those who will, sleep on, but thou, awake!
Man of the hour, thy place prepare to take!
Sounds the shrill bugle down the serried line,
Where banners flutter and gay trappings shine,
Cleansed from the smoke, and dark, ensanguined stains
From other fields and slumbering hero's veins:
The blood which bought past victories nought avails;
Your own must flow, or else the battle fails!
These battered swords rest idly in their sheaths,
Its fame alone the past to us bequeaths;
The hands which swayed no more shall rise to wield
Their blades victorious on our battle-field.
As they have ended, so remain their days;
Their laurels wither as their dust decays!
Ours is the conflict, they have fought their last;
Leave them to glory and their fleeting past,
While we press on, to plant our banners high
In the pure sunlight of a brighter sky!
There let them kiss the sun-kissed winds, and stream
Like beacon-fires that from the mountains gleam,
Whilst we look back across the plains to see
Who, after us, the standard-bearers be;
Content if they the higher heights may win,
And where we stop the upward course begin;
Then can we rest, to them leave our renown,
Our country and our cause, and lay our weapons down;
Since not to man in any age is given
The power to reach his bounds this side of Heaven.

THE COMING OF THE RAIN.

THE dusty earth was sere and brown,
   The cloudless sky to bronze was turned;
The sun his blazing flood poured down,
Till hill and valley, field and town,
   As in a seething furnace burned:
Men prayed and watched, but watched in vain, —
There was no sign of coming rain.

The bare hills bowed each sun-brown'd head
  In mute submission to the flame;
The waters from the rivers fled,
The mountains smoked beneath its tread,
  As onward from the south it came,
With hot winds blowing in its train, —
But yet no sign of coming rain!

The winds lay hushed, and scarce a breeze
  Fanned the hot brow of dusky Night;
The leaves are sibilant on the trees,
And silent birds lie hid in these,
  As if they fear the piercing light,
Else with discordant notes complain
Because there comes no sound of rain.

But, see! a speck on yonder sky
  Is rising from the purple west,
Such as the prophet did descry,
When he, upon the mountain high,
  Prayed that his land with rain be blest.
That prayer, once heard, avails again,
Since there is sound of coming rain!

The cloud spreads forth its dark'ning wing
  In grateful shadows o'er the land;
The cool winds from their caverns spring;
The trees their glad arms upward fling,
  And lowing herds beneath them stand,
With sad eyes turned across the plain,
From whence they scent the coming rain.

The ground in fissures gaping wide
  Its parched lips upward turn, as one
Who, long the cooling cup denied,
Beholds the waiting hand supplied,
  And sees the sweet drops sparkling run,
In eager ecstasy of pain;
So waits the earth the coming rain!

Now bursts the cloud, the glad showers fall,
  All nature shouts aloud and sings;

The mountains to the valleys call,
The rivers to the brooks, and all
    Exultant into new life springs;
One glad hosanna leads the strain
In swelling chorus to the rain!

GOLDEN-ROD.

THE winds blow soft as maiden's sighs
    Which answer love's fond dreaming;
The sunlight from the azure skies
    In misty radiance streaming;

The meadows and the orchards lie
    Asleep by wood and river;
To kissing winds the aspens sigh,
    Their white leaves gleam and quiver;

The plover pipes among the reeds,
    The goldfinch from the sedges;
The lark swings on the red-top weeds,
    The sparrow trills from hedges;

The blue haze skirts the distant hills
    In golden sun and shadow;
To silver threads have run the rills,
    That wind through mead and meadow.

Afar I hear the cattle low,
    And faint the fox-dog baying;
The laden harvest wain, now slow,
    Comes from the autumn haying;

Red gleam the berries on the rose, —
    The hawthorn's russet-coated, —
Where sport the jay among the boughs,
    And oriole golden-throated.

The rose, the summer's queen, uncrowned,
    The lily dead and dying

The harebells, while the grass, sun-browned,
  In tangled tufts is lying!

There born of sun in smiling hours,
  Where all beguiles and pleases,
The golden-rod unfolds its flowers,
  Kissed open by soft breezes.

And crowned the reigning autumn comes
  With days of sun and showers,
When golden-rod the sweetest blooms
  In sylvan dales and bowers.

I love it, for it cometh late,
  Unsung in tale and story,
Without the train, the pomp and state,
  Of spring's triumphal glory.

I love it, with its yellow plumes,
  The pride of field and meadow;
The foil of autumn's rank perfumes,
  The sunlight in the shadow.

Sweet memories sleep among its sprays,
  And as they open, waking,
These call me back to other days,
  Of life's young morn just breaking.

The curtained mists fold back amain,
  Past hours swing in their places;
From out the shadow once again
  Look forth forgotten faces!

I touch the veil, — its outer fold
  Seems melting from my vision,
Whilst yet my eager fingers hold
  The gates to life's Elysian!

I dream! They sleep beneath the sod
  Their lowly graves encumbers,
Thy magic wand, sweet golden-rod!
  Has called them from their slumbers.

GRETCHEN.

KATARINA, bring out the old Bible,
  The one we brought over the sea,
Which often your father was reading
  Out under the old linden-tree :
That Bible he gave you when married ;
  It seems it is laid on the shelf,
But nothing we have so reminds me
  Of bright, happy days with yourself.

I would read once again from its pages
  The story of Moses and Hur,
Of Lot in the land of Gomorrah,
  And Abram, that grand man of Ur.
They all left the homes of their fathers,
  To sojourn in lands that were new,
Just like you and I, Katarina,
  With homes for our children in view.

How natural the old wolf-skin cover, —
  Your name in your father's bold hand ;
And the letters, like faces familiar,
  Call back to the old fatherland :
These flowers, pressed between its broad pages,
  You gathered in youth and concealed,
Have the hues of the skies and the meadows,
  The scent of the dyke and the field.

What is here folded up in this paper,
  So yellow with time and with age ?
So long has it lain in the Bible
  It has worn a deep hole in the page !
What makes you look so, Katarina ?
  The mist gathering fast in your eye,
As it used to across the broad waters :
  You surely are not going to cry !

I will open this old, yellow paper —
  Gott in Himmel ! what makes you look so ?
For I see in your face now all over
  The pain of a grief long ago.

What is this in the paper, I wonder,
 Folded up with the tenderest care ? —
Katarina ! good wife ! it is Gretchen's —
 Our Gretchen's — own soft, yellow hair !

And so, with the flowers you have gathered,
 That grew on the banks of the Rhine,
And pressed in these old, yellow pages
 So full of sweet promise divine,
In this Bible your father has given,
 His blessing and mem'ry to bear,
From the land of our fathers, Kat'rina,
 You treasure our lost Gretchen's hair !

I see the old cottage, Kat'rina,
 That welcomed our bright wedding morn ;
Which bloomed, in the beauty of summer,
 The brightest the day she was born.
And I see your sweet face as you kissed her,
 When first she was laid on your breast,
And then, through the shadow of sorrow,
 I see her in death laid to rest.

And she rests by the blue Rhenish waters,
 Our Gretchen, our first and our lost,
Where we left her asleep with the flowers
 When over the ocean we cross'd.
Our heads have grown white, Katarina,
 Her grave we may never behold ;
But her we shall see, says this Bible,
 In that city of jasper and gold.

THEULDA'S VIGIL.

Low sighs the wind ; the darkness deep'ning round
 Falls in thick folds, and earth and air are still ;
The deeper shadows trail along the ground,
You hear a footstep, but no other sound,
 Save low, hushed whispers from the lips of ill.

Just in the shadows of the denser night,
  Where stoops the mountain his majestic crest,
And deepens there the pall of feeble light,
Uncertain as the fire-fly's wavering flight,
  A yellow ray shoots from its rocky breast.

A nearer view betrays a little church,
  Set in the niche of the great mountain's side:
High up the steep, and o'er its stooping porch,
Swing low the branches of a silver birch,
  And with their trembling leaves the entrance hide.

Through these a fitful ray with feeble spark
  Gleams now and then, as sways each bending bough,
But to be swallowed by the hungry dark,
Remorseless, down its caverned jaws. Ah! hark
  The sound of voices rising softly now!

We mount the steps and pass the outer door,
  And lift the curtain, — stand and gaze within,
Where the pale light with dull and feeble power
From the high altar streams along the floor,
  And cleaves the night with trembling shaft and thin.

Like walls of ebon shaded into gray,
  The columned darkness stands on either side:
Between these streams a long and yellow ray, —
Afar and down the mountain-path it lay, —
  Which we had followed with this light our guide.

And in its light before the altar there
  Bursts on the sight a vision glorified!
It is an upturned face, divinely fair,
With eyelids closed and lips apart in prayer,
  And arms outstretched imploring, high and wide.

The prayer is earnest without agony;
  The face is eager without look of pain;
The eyelids quiver o'er each close-shut eye,
And yet the lashes are not wholly dry,
  While on her cheeks there is of tears no stain!

The lips now parted in her prayer are red,
   And ready seem for song or orison;
The ruddy flush, though paling, is not fled
From her warm cheek, but deepens there instead,
   Ere the swift current of her prayer is done.

Her robe is spotless in its filmy white,
   And shines like silver through her golden hair,
As o'er her downward streams the altar light.
What calls her here alone on such a night,
   To spend its hours in vigils and in prayer?

Were she but clad in sable weeds, with tears
   Fast streaming down her hollow cheeks from eyes
Long drowned by weeping in her widowed years,
A fitting time and place, since earthly fears
   Such hearts affect to and may well despise.

But here is beauty, youth, and joyousness
   Made tenfold sweeter in this hour of prayer,
With young life's ev'ry hope waiting to bless
A heart o'erflowing in its happiness,
   And shrouded now with scarce the dusk of care.

Why this long vigil in a spot like this,
   Away from all that can defend and shield?
What in so sweet a life has gone amiss,
Where ev'ry pulsing throb is filled with bliss,
   That must to Holy Mother be revealed?

But hearken to her prayer, now sweet and low:
   " Mother, I come to thee, a trusting child;
My life has been so tranquil in its flow,
I almost feared, at last, to have it so.
   And that my pleasure as a sin beguiled.

" To thee I come, and at thy altar lone
   Reconsecrate my heart and rest on thee!
Wilt thou receive me, Mother, for thy own,
Not from the world, but in it, to atone
   For sins unbidden which encompass me?

" Life is so sweet to me, I almost fear
    I sin in living it unconsecrate ;
And yet my nature cries within me here, —
Life has its duties and the way seems clear :
    Each bird and beast lives sinless with its mate.

" I love my free-born life and love my kind,
    And thee, sweet Mother, love with trusting heart ;
Thy son, the Lord Christ, to my heart would bind,
For he it is who leadeth me when blind,
    And keepeth me from thorny ways apart.

" In faith I come my vigil here to keep
    Alone in prayer to thee ! The gloomy night
Is filled with fear, and in its shadows deep
Lurk dangers, while the eyes that love me sleep,
    And nought can keep me save thy love and might.

" Thou seest my faith which to thine altar clings,
    And trusts thee as a child its mother's love :
Sweet Mother, to my prayer in prayer give wings,
While from thine altar to God's throne it springs,
    That it may draw me answer from above.

"I will await the dawn for answering sign,
    If I forego the world, as thou shalt send ;
Howe'er bestowed, I feel the blessing mine :
The gift through thee sent by a hand divine,
    Although it scourge, is from my dearest friend."

The night is gone ; with pale and sickly gleam
    The taper burns and shadows have grown gray ;
Theulda's Vigil has become a dream,
Since she, asleep beneath the paling beam,
    With smiling face before the altar lay.

A gentle hand but touches her bowed head ;
    She lifts her face, now wreathed in joyous smiles, —
Reflections from her dreams, — and in their stead
A vision sees in them foreshadowed
    So true, she thinks the dream itself beguiles.

It is her lover's face which beams on her,
  Aglow with love and joy and glad surprise !
He came from lands afar, and, first astir,
He seeks this shrine, an early worshipper,
  With zeal as earnest as his course was wise.

He speaks ! Ah, now it is no dream, to cheat !
  The sacred altar, her remembered prayer,
And its swift answer ! At the Mother's feet,
In tears which fall in shower as fast as sweet,
  In thankfulness she kneels adoring there.

Then rising with a face seraphic bright,
  With heart new consecrate to God and love,
She greets her lover, and their troth they plight,
For her long vigil through the lonely night
  With morn hath brought her answer from above.

THE CITY UPON THE HILL.

THERE 's a city with many a mansion,
  In granite and marble laid,
Whose domes without girder or stanchion
  'Gainst winter and storm are stayed ;
There many a shaft and steeple
  Gleams brightly upon the air,
Far above that silent people
  Who make their dwelling-place there.

It stands with its white spires shining,
  Fair valleys on either side,
On a hill with its slopes declining
  To rivers that round it glide :
No door on its hinges turning
  From morn till the day's decline ;
No fires on its hearthstones burning ;
  No lights from its windows shine.

And the days go by unnumbered
  By any one dwelling there.

And never a heart is cumbered
  Within it by Time or Care :
Not a sound of strife or labor,
  No echo of saw or plane ;
And neighbors at peace with neighbors
  Through all that city remain.

No restless hearts are there beating
  Sad marches to other lands ;
No world-weary feet retreating
  From its gates with empty hands.
They enter to dwell forever
  Who pass through the silent gate ;
All ties from without they sever
  Of kindred, of home, and state.

No friend ever enters a dwelling
  Of friend who has gone before ;
No heart finds relief there in telling
  Its hopes and sorrowings o'er.
The gates are all sealed at each portal ;
  No hand from within can unloose ;
All ears have grown deaf to the mortal ;
  All pleadings they coldly refuse.

Man may come, he may go, but never
  A whisper makes glad his ears ;
At their doors he may stand forever,
  But never a welcome hears.
At his home, when he comes, no meeting
  Makes glad his dwelling-place lone ;
Not a hand to him stretched in greeting
  Of the many dear friends he has known.

In the warm, sweet days of October
  I stood in its silent streets,
With its lawns all russet and sober
  And strewn with its faded sweets.
The sky was as clear as a crystal,
  The trees were aglow and aflame ;
From valleys below, the faint whistle
  Of birds through the dreamy air came.

Hands unseen all the hills were dyeing
  A thousand bright hues everywhere ;
Sweet groves through the valleys were vying
  With meadows as beautiful there.
Enraptured I stood at the vision,
  My heart leaped with life born anew !
Was it earth or a dream of Elysian,
  A sunburst of heav'n on my view ?

At my feet lay another fair city,
  As silent as this of the dead,
While noiselessly over it flit the
  Soft shadows from clouds overhead.
Between them, aloft, at each portal
  I stood looking up to the sky ;
Was I mortal to-day, or immortal ?
  Was it gain here to live, or to die ?

I looked on the homes of the living,
  Their beauty I saw was of death ;
Life itself in dying was giving
  The wealth of a world for a breath !
Painted hills, flaming woods, skies of amber,
  To-day were my heritage here :
Blow your blasts bleak and cold, O December !
  And earth lies all withered and sere !

Then I turned to this city of seeming,
  Whose streets are all watered with tears,
Where Death at its portals lay dreaming
  Of empire outlasting the years.
And I cried, " Blow your trump, mighty Angel,
  The Kingdom of Death now divide !
Those who sleep here in Hope's sweet Evangel
  Shall rise and in Eden abide."

THE ITINERANT.

He tried the problem of this life,
　And found it hard and intricate,
Not in its toil and vexing strife,
　The heritage of rich and great ;

Not in its greed for fame and place,
　The world's chief aim, Ambition's goal, —
But in that work, made sweet through grace,
　To win and save a dying soul.

Few were his needs, — an humble fare,
　His Bible with its tear-stained page ;
A book of sacred song and prayer,
　The comfort of his pilgrimage.

He had no home save with his flock,
　Which took him in its fold a time, —
A refuge in that Rifted Rock
　Made perfect through a faith sublime.

A wife gave comfort in those days
　When labors pressed and sorrows pained,
And followed him in lowly ways
　Where duty called and souls were gained.

What need was it her faith to prove ?
　The dullest eye her heart could read ;
A Ruth was she in trust and love,
　His people hers in faith and creed.

A year of sojourn here and there,
　They pitch their tents and call it home ;
The fallow for the seed prepare,
　And sow for reapers yet to come.

They gather sheaves as those who glean
　The harvest field ; the reaping done,
The golden store, though small and lean,
　By thrift despised, they make their own.

His life is one of ceaseless toil,
   With frugal board and humble bed,
And gleanings from a scanty soil
   Repaying grudgingly in bread.

His Master gave the test for all,
   Though clad in rags or purple gown,
By it adjudged we stand or fall :
   " 'T is by your fruits ye shall be known."

So from these lowly fields of grain
   His eager hands their trophies bring,
Well pleased if he at last may gain
   The smile approving from his King.

His Master taught, he followed him
   In faith and patience to the end ;
And when he found his way grown dim
   He counselled with him as a friend.

He faltered not, but went his way,
   Nor questioned where the duty plain ;
Few flowery vales inviting lay
   Amid those steeps of toil and pain.

His seemed a lowly life to those
   Who journeyed not upon his road ;
And yet from height to height it rose,
   And scaled th' Eternal Mount of God !

For him no grand cathedral rung
   With organ-peal and chanting choir ;
No glittering throng ecstatic hung
   On his chaste lips, though touched with fire.

Yet his the broad and echoing halls
   Of Nature, where her leafy shrine
She reared in arches vast, and walls
   Wrought out and decked by hand divine !

There, templed in the fragrant wood,
   Blue-arched and spanned by skies above,

Amid a weeping multitude
  He preached them Christ's redeeming love.

With cause so great, at shrine so grand,
  God's curtained throne, its arch and dome,
Proclaimed his love on every hand,
  Made perfect in a life to come!

Transported by this lofty theme
  Of faith which sees that promised day,
The spirit in a mighty stream
  Swept teacher and the taught away.

A hero great in deed and word
  As ever girded armor on;
By such, and not by fire and sword,
  Are Earth's enduring victories won.

His name a household word becomes
  In all his circuits, far and near;
A benison in all their homes
  His face familiar grown and dear.

The grandsire, father, wife, and maid,
  The babe upon its mother's knee,
On each his hand in blessing laid,
  Baptized them in their infancy.

He labors till life's eventide
  Casts silvery gleams on locks of brown;
And she who journeyed by his side,
  Aweary, lays life's burdens down.

Dark grows the way without her hand
  To clasp in his and guide his feet;
He wistful views the promised land
  Where they across the flood shall meet.

The summons comes, he owns Death's power,
  Yet, victor crowned, he mounts the sky;
He lived each day to meet this hour.
  And, living thus, learned how to die.

THE LAND OF THE HARP AND THE SHAMROCK.

LAND of the Harp and the Shamrock,
  Land of warm hearts and sweet song;
Island of promise and sorrow;
  Island of courage and wrong!
Green are thy hills and thy valleys,
  Fair are thy sky and thy sea;
So is the love of thy children
  True, and devoted to thee.

Never had land fairer daughters,
  Never had land braver sons;
Never at hearthstone and altar
  Tenderer, kindlier ones!
Exiled across the far waters,
  They in strange countries may roam,
Yet, like the down of her thistles,
  Hope wafts their true hearts towards home.

Love such as this for a country,
  Love such as this for a land,
Rises above creed and tenet,
  Rises to heights that are grand!
It is the love of the hearthstone,
  Altar and shrine all enthrone,
Shamrock and harp and sweet heather,
  All here united in one!

Worthy the land of O'Connell,
  Worthy the harp of Tom Moore;
Worthy the green isle of Erin,
  Worthy its sweet emerald shore.
Skies such as these are for freedom;
  Lands such as these for the free!
Homes such as these but for freemen
  Ever forever to be!

Yet lies this land in the shadow
  Darkling from mountain to sea;

Homes still in thrall to the stranger,
  Fetterless, and yet not free!
Names has she written in story,
  Heroes illustrious to fame;
Yet is the nation they honor
  Living now scarce in a name!

Rouse and arise, sons of Erin!
  Stand by the home of your sires!
Grandly the man of the hour
  Strikes for your altars and fires.
Not with the sword is the battle;
  Not with the strong is the fight;
Waving beside Harp and Shamrock,
  Streams now the banner of right.

THE OLD RIVER BRIDGE.

THE old river bridge, with its roof gray and hoary,
  Which spanned in high arches Scioto's broad stream,
Is dear to our hearts in its legend and story
  Of days which grow dim as the mists of a dream.

By the moonlight I stand in the bed of the river,
  While clouds, like black coursers, speed noiselessly by;
As beneath on the waters in dark shadows quiver
  The skeleton bridge dimly hung in the sky.

Dismantled, a ghost of the past, and now fleeting,
  A sword of hot flame hews away the firm wood;
Its death-groans grow loud as the swift blades are eating
  Through strong oaken vitals old Time hath withstood.

As I stand with the night and the shadows above it,
  Weird forms and strange fancies seem gathering there;
And I hear the hushed whispers of spirits that love it,
  In sighs of regret which load the still air.

How many, I ask, are the feet which cross'd over
  Its broad, throbbing bosom, no more to return!

Of statesman and sage, the fair maiden and lover,
  In dust they now sleep in the lone funeral urn.

How bravely with Time it has fought the long battle,
  Triumphantly driving all foes from the field!
The storm's charging squadrons, the thunder's fierce rattle,
  Nor flood's rushing torrents, could force it to yield.

So faithful to friends and defiant to weather,
  A king crowned to rule with a heart made of oak,
Of the millions who journeyed across it together,
  To none was the pledge of safe transit once broke!

Through years of long service, with strength still unshaken,
  No servant more faithful our burdens to bear!
Distrusted, despised, and in old age forsaken,
  How piteous its plea that we trust still and spare!

Ah! where are the hands that set girder and rafter,
  And swung those long arches across the deep wave?
I hear in the echo of Time's mocking laughter
  The hollow responses come up from the grave!

Not one it has sheltered in storm and in danger,
  Not one it has nursed on its broad oaken knee,
Not one, be he born at its feet or a stranger,
  For this friend found in need offers protest or plea!

They have fled from its fall like the flood of the waters
  Which kiss those cold feet, and speed heedlessly on!
They are lost in the march of the sons and the daughters
  Who over the bridge now forgotten have gone.

Of the friends of the past, not a friend longer lingers
  Who once would in pity give heed to its cries;
Across each cold bosom are clasped the still fingers
  That hailed it in triumph with shouts to the skies!

My hot heart cries out in the strength of its sorrow
  Against the decrees of vain man's puny power;
His is of to-day!   God's alone is to-morrow!
  He holdeth the breath in our nostrils each hour!

Ah! see those wild arms reaching up as in prayer,
  As deeper and hotter sinks death's fiercest pain!
The wind's softest kiss fires anew the red slayer,
  And prayer now for help and for mercy is vain!

Farewell, my old friend! The rude hand of the vandal
  Is laid on your timbers now hoary with years;
You, too, are the victim of envy and scandal,
  Which scoff at the past which our memory reveres.

Farewell, dear old Bridge! not a friend of the many
  You carried in safety across the wild flood
Had a word in your favor, and few now, if any,
  Remember how bravely the storms you withstood!

Farewell, dear old Bridge! fare you well and forever!
  The fire's burning fever runs hot through your frame,
And the shafts of the slayer your life tendons sever,
  And you rush to destruction through ruin and flame!

Ah! hear those hoarse groans through the still night now
      ringing!
A shriek of fierce pain from that heart strong and brave,
As upward in terror, its spectral arms flinging,
  The old river Bridge plunges into the wave.

THE SONG WHICH THE ROBIN SUNG.

  HIGH up in the top of a willow-tree
    A Robin sat and swung and sung,
  And sung and swung in a merry glee
    Over a nest that beneath him hung.

  The winds blew soft and the winds blew strong,
    The clouds fled upward from the'sun,
  Still the Robin merrily sang his song
    From purple morn till day was done.

  From morning's dawn till the day was gone,
    On the topmost bough he sat and swung,

As he looked afar o'er field and lawn,
And this is the song the Robin sung: —

" To my heart so gay the breaking day
  Is grand in its lights of gold and green ;
From my perch aloft, as I swing and sway,
  What glorious sights around are seen !

" I see, I see, from my perch in the tree,
  My new-made nest with its mistress brown,
And her eyes are bright as stars at night,
  As she looks up and I look down.

" Just four little eggs in their coats of blue
  Are hidden now in that pretty nest ;
And four little bills just pipping through
  Thrill, as they touch, her warm, red breast.

" And merry the songs we sang the day
  We builded that nest together there :
Sweeter the songs will we sing when away
  We fly with our brood to meadows fair.

" I see, I see, from my perch in the tree,
  A lover fond and a maiden fair,
Through sun and shade in the smiling glade
  Wandering heedless of time and care.

" Over them bending the bright blue skies,
  Under their feet spring flowers full-blown ;
Earth for to-day is their Paradise,
  Blooming and sweet for them alone !

" I see, I see, from my perch in the tree,
  A mother leading a fair-haired child ;
Its eyes of blue from its tears look through,
  As clouds have wept while the skies still smiled.

" O love of that mother, so sweet and pure !
  O love of that child, so pure and sweet !
Earth's flowers will fade, but its love endure,
  For love may be long if Time is fleet."

So the Robin sat, and swayed and sung
   Through the livelong day his merry song;
While the little brown nest beneath him hung
   With its growing brood the whole month long.

But frosts will come and leaves will fall,
   Leaving the meadows all sere and dun:
No more will we hear the Robin's call
   From the willow-tree at set of sun.

An empty nest on a leafless bough
   Will swing and sway in the frosty air,
But lover and maiden that stray below,
   With mother and child, will not be there.

And so we all sing and so we all go,
   If bird or lover, mother or child:
In springtime and flowers, in winter and snow,
   Life is with pleasure or sorrow beguiled.

O heart full of love, sing thy joyous strain,
   Pour'd forth in its flood from silvery tongue,
And sweet in refrain, with no touch of pain,
   As heard in the song the Robin sung.

FUNERAL HYMN.

GRANT sleeps, his battles now are done,
The last his greatest victory won:
Immortal honors crown his name,
Immortal life and deathless fame.

Lift up your hearts, ye lands that mourn,
While to his rest the dead is borne:
Wide as the earth our sorrows go
For him who now in death lies low.

Lift up your hearts, since God who gave
To this fair land, with soul so brave,
That chief of heroes, prince of men,
Has but recalled his own again.

He touched our bleeding land : it rose
Redeemed and saved from mortal foes.
We crowned with bays ; immortal now
Jehovah's crown upon his brow !

O Land redeemed ! let tears and praise
Flow mingling in the hymns we raise ;
God's mercies e'en this hour declares,
The hand which smites in pity spares.

DECORATION HYMN.

GRAND are the deeds of men,
　　Sons of our noble sires,
Who fought to shield and save
　　Home and our altar-fires.

Grand are the hearts that toiled
　　Tireless and sleepless on,
Fainting and faltering not
　　Until the victory won.

Flushed with the mortal strife,
　　Then was it grand to die !
Victory-crowned in death,
　　Under that flag to lie !

Flag of our hope and faith ;
　　Flag that our fathers gave !
Grandly that banner floats
　　Over each hero's grave.

Kiss it, soft winds of May !
　　Kiss it, sweet dews of Heaven !
Kiss it, O Love ! in tears,
　　Blood-stained and battle-riven !

Cover their graves with flowers,
　　Flowers for the loved and known ;

Flowers for the lone and lost ;
Crown them, they 're all our own !

THE DEAD PRIEST.

IN MEMORY OF FATHER A. J. RYAN, THE POET-PRIEST.

WE cannot trace the heart-throbs on this page,
  Nor fill their measure with our tears unshed ;
No words of praise our sorrows can assuage
  In the still chambers where we mourn the dead.

We can but tell the story of our grief
  For the sweet dead, and telling it but show
Through the rift clouds, in glimpses few and brief,
  The soft and golden twilight's after-glow.

It was a little while, — so short, indeed,
  The time we knew him, that, if measured so,
We might be strangers, save for his grand creed,
  Which was for all mankind to love and know !

And so we knew him, and knowing loved,
  And loving weep for him, — not as those weep
In some o'ermastering sorrow, but as moved
  Like mother-hearts for babes that fall asleep.

The priest was poet, and the poet priest ;
  Prayer, sacrifice, and song went hand in hand :
While self with him of all the world the least,
  His work for human souls the theme most grand.

His church was his 'trothed bride, and, wedding her,
  He gave to her his heart in song and praise ;
And, at her holy shrine a worshipper,
  He poured the red wine of his life's best days.

Then on her bosom fell asleep at last
  This knightly prince of men with uncrowned head :
Although her eager arms may hold him fast,
  Her tear-wet kisses cannot wake her dead !

There let him sleep with benedictions crowned!
His songs go singing in the hearts of men,
Where love for him already sits enthroned,
And there will sing until he wake again.

WHO KNOWS?

THE lights flash out along the street,
    And merry feet still come and go,
While distant music soft and sweet
    Floats up, and voices from below
Ring out in laughter; distant call
    And answer back come up to me;
And yet like throbs of pain they fall,
And thrill my heart and soul and all
    With one fierce throe of misery.

I do not know why this to-night;
    I love sweet music, and I love
To hear the merry voice and light
    Which floats to where I sit, above
The crowd which hurries to and fro:
    I close the sash and shut me in,
And press my heart, which flutters so
    I hear the muffled roll within.

It may be that one voice is gone
    Whose tones would harmonize all sound;
One footstep falling on the stone
    Might rhythmic make each step around:
A touch of one fair hand might still
    The tumult of the heart within,
    To joy the saddened thought yet win,
The heart with hope and sunshine fill.
    Who knows? The secret yet unguessed
    Is closed and locked within my breast.

COMPENSATION.

IF it were truly known
To the young bud just bursting into bloom
That such sweet death led to forgotten tomb,
    Yet should it haste to be a rose full-blown,
Although that bloom the richer life destroy,
    Since dying thus gives joy.

    Nor should the lark be dumb;
The skies are his to cleave with joyous wing,
And songs ecstatic soaring there to sing,
    Whose melodies float through the years to come:
Should he, through fear of death, refuse his song,
    He doth the world a wrong!

    The world is full of love:
Some empty heart for want of it is sad;
One breath blown warm will make that faint heart glad!
    O heart love full! wilt thou refuse to move
Because, perchance, false hearts will love betray?
    Give what thou canst alway.

    It is not self alone, —
Nay, less of self and more of all beside
Makes joy so sweet! Our hearts should open wide
    If in them Love, or Song, or Rose unblown:
Of what we have, we should most freely give,
    And thus life twofold live.

REMEMBERED.

THE picture of a summer day,
    A river swiftly flowing,
The breath of flowers upon the breeze,
    The sound of cattle lowing.

The grateful shade of spreading trees;
    A couch of fragrant grasses,

On which I lie, and, listless, note,
  Each moving thing that passes.

Across the meadow smooth and green,
  A fair and dainty creature,
She comes, a flash of joy and light
  Irradiant in each feature.

The lilies bend their golden heads,
  The harebells wake to ringing;
The roses burst their odorous hearts,
  Their fragrance o'er her flinging.

The grasses kiss her unshod feet,
  The ivy clings around them;
And love-entangle's dainty arms
  In sweet embrace has bound them.

The robin on the maple bough
  In merry glee is swinging;
The blackbirds from the distant grove
  Their choral songs are singing.

The breezes whisper to the leaves,
  Which burn with sun-kissed blushes,
For in their shadows hushed and still
  Now sit the silent thrushes.

The winds, that catch and toss her curls,
  With kisses warmly greet her;
Their breath, as blown from clover fields,
  Blown o'er her lips grows sweeter!

She sings a low, sweet song anon,
  With pathos deep and thrilling;
The melody that moves her heart
  My own with rapture filling.

And as she sings there is a sigh,
  That breathes through every measure,
A tender chord that thrills with pain
  Among the notes of pleasure, —

Soft as the faintly breathing strain
  That richer grows in dying;
Sweet as the perfume of rare buds
  In hidden vases lying!

A moment of mad ecstasy,
  A foretaste of Elysian,
A hope which died the moment born,
  Passed with the fleeting vision!

The sunlight ever holds her face,
  That song I hear repeated;
I see those eyes of liquid love,
  That wait to be entreated.

The waters murmur just the same,
  I catch the breath of roses;
Upon the sunshine of this day
  The twilight never closes!

And yet it is far, far away,
  And I may still remember
The glory of that summer day,
  As falls the drear December.

MY GUESTS.

THE bell tolls the midnight; a knock at my door
  Which rattles the hinges and loosens the latch;
Wide open it flies, swinging backward, before
  I had time, if I would, to fasten the catch.

Alone with my books, and the fire burning low,
  Half angered, half startled, I turned to the guest
With reproof on my tongue, a frown on my brow:
  A glance stilled the anger that stirred in my breast.

The darkness without cast its shadows within;
  A part of the shadow, and black as the night,
The robe which she wore, while her face pale and thin
  Looked ghastly, as blazed her eyes fiercely bright.

On the threshold, no farther approaching, she stood,
  As silent as death and chill as the grave;
The sight for the instant seemed freezing my blood,
  And I for the moment forgot to be brave.

Beside her, O wonder of wonders! appeared
  A lovelier vision than mortal can paint,
In robes white as snow, and locks fair and bared,
  With face of an angel and smile of a saint!

Her glance calmed my bosom and lulled every fear;
  I laughed, begged their pardon, and bade them come in,
And waved them to seats at the fire blazing near,
  With the arts of a host both to please and to win.

They sat themselves down on the left and the right,
  With never a token of greeting or cheer,
The brow of one dark, the other glowed bright,
  I waiting between them some message to hear.

"I am pleased," I began, when the dark eyes that burned
  Rose slowly and fastened their gaze on my face,
The blue eyes as quickly as light to me turned,
  And filled my whole soul full of light with her gaze.

Nothing more could I say with their eyes bent upon me;
  Contending emotions left speechless my tongue;
Repelled by the one as the other had drawn me,
  My heart seemed on fire and my nerves all unstrung.

In silence I waited, it seemed, there forever,
  Since moments grow hours with heart on the rack;
I would not, I could not make farther endeavor,
  In the glow of blue eyes and blaze of the black.

At last she in sable, with tones of command,
  Said, " Write! " and instinctive I turned to the theme
I had left but half finished, with pen still in hand,
  But my thoughts had now fled like the mists of a dream.

I paused to recall them; like children at home
  Who shrink from the presence of strangers and fly,

In vain were my pleadings, no more would they come
  At the beck of my hand or the glance of her eye.

" Write ! " she said; "write! write!! " with a rising in-
    flection.
  My pen from my fingers unconsciously slid ;
I sat there aghast, and in utter dejection,
  Unconscious of aught that I suffered or did.

"Write ! " again rang that voice. " I cannot ! " I cried ;
  " Of thought I have none, and no inspiration.
Within me the source of the fountain is dried,
  And my soul is grown blank in my heart's desolation."

A soft sigh I heard, like the sobbing of night
  When out in the darkness its slumber is stirred
By the breath of the winds, or the low, throbbing flight
  Through the arch of the skies of its own dusky bird.

I turned, and the eyes of that beautiful maid,
  Grown liquid with pity and radiant with fire,
Smote my heart, sick with shame at my weakness, and
    stayed
  With glances that burn into thoughts which inspire.

Through my heart, through my soul, as the flood of a
    stream
  Poured into the desert, the tide swept along ;
And the thought of her face was the soul of my theme,
  And the light of her eyes the fire of my song.

Then I wrote with that pen, nor rested nor stayed,
  For thoughts winged with light swept in like a flood ;
The storm of the passion that tossed me and swayed
  Brought zeal to my heart and fire to my blood.

Through the night, through the day, I plied the swift pen,
  My guests sitting silently, watchfully by ;
As I wrote, glancing up to me now and again,
  With smiles on each face and joy in each eye.

What I wrote may be read in my life's closed Evangel,
  For life grew a poem and rhythmic in song ;

At the touch of the hand of its own better angel,
　　The soul that was sinking forever grew strong !

And these guests of the night at my hearthstone are sitting,
　　The strength of my day and the cheer of my night;
Though my life may be long, evanescent, and flitting,
　　Their ministering hands fill its cup with delight.

Ah ! sweet is the night in its stillness and beauty
　　Which sent me my guests from the far skies above, —
The sable-clad, dusky-eyed Goddess of Duty,
　　And the heart's fairest mistress, the Goddess of Love.

THE OLD QUAKER HOMESTEAD.

WHAT ails thee, Jonathan, to-night, thee looks so sad and
　　glum ?
Since sunset I have waited here, still hoping thee would
　　come :
Thee knows we are alone again since Ruth has moved
　　away,
And the old house gets lonesome now with waiting all the
　　day.

Thee knows it was thy father's home, where thou wert born
　　and raised,
And that on many faces gone its cheerful firelight blazed ;
And sitting here alone at night, does thee not know I feel
That to their seats beside the fire those forms departed
　　steal ?

I sometimes fear to look around — it may be weak in me —
Lest in his old arm-chair again thy father's form I see
Just where he in the corner sat, thy mother by his side ;
And yet it is near forty year since he, asleep there, died.

Our children once all gathered here, a bright and happy
　　band, —
There were no better, Jonathan, in all this goodly land ;

And don't thee know that I forget, sometimes when here
    alone,
That all these children we so loved are men and women
    grown ?

I know thee will now laugh at me, yet from the stair and
    hall
I hear their infant voices ring some old and merry call ;
And often from my chair I start, as in the lane near by,
Upon the dusky hush of night, I hear familiar cry.

These make one lonesome, Jonathan, and feel a little queer ;
I cannot say that I am sad, and yet it is not fear, —
Why should I fear those sounds beloved, and why should I
    be sad ?
The very thought of loved ones near should comfort and
    make glad.

But then thee knows we have been taught to view such
    things in dread,
And those we love when full of life, to fear when they are
    dead.
We start when absent voices ring glad peals in mem'ry's
    ear,
And tremble when those silvery notes should fill our hearts
    with cheer.

And does thee know, sometimes I think that it would be the
    best
To sell the old farm, Jonathan, and take a little rest;
Thee is grown old, I 'm not so spry as I was years ago,
And we can live with Solomon, — thee knows he wants
    us to.

This pleases thee, and for the first thee greets me with a
    smile ;
It grieves me sore to see thy mind so burdened with thy
    toil.
I know I will be homesick like to leave the dear old
    home,
But then thee knows, dear Jonathan, that day has got to
    come.

Has got to come, dear Ruth, thee says ; ah ! that I know
    too well :
If we do not, some other one the farm will surely sell.
And this I have been thinking of for now 't is nigh two
    year,
But would not mention it to thee to cause thee pain and
    fear.

But all this day upon my mind a heavy weight it bore,
And in my heart I felt its pain as never felt before ;
I stopped my seeding on the hill, I could not see the flags,
And told the boy a-harrowing he might take home the nags,

As I would seed no more to-day, but go across the field
And fix the fence there broken down ; but when I was
    concealed
Behind the hill, and out of sight of any spying one,
Why, Ruth, if thee believes my word, I broke into a run,

And never stopped my headlong speed, nor turned aside my
    eyes,
Until I fell upon the grave where little Rachel lies ;
And there I lay, not long I know, and yet the time seemed
    years,
And when I lifted up my face her grave was wet with tears.

And father lies beside her there, and mother by his side,
And in two rows, with headstones white, all of us that have
    died ;
And somehow, Ruth, I loved to think that we, too, there
    should lie,
And Jonathan should own the farm when we should come
    to die.

And I had singled out the spot beneath the chestnut-tree,
Between our Rachel and the rest, to keep for thee and me ;
While yet along the other side is room enough for all
For generations yet to come, between us and the wall.

Thee said thee had been waiting me since sunset's gathering
    gloom,
Yet all that time I lingered there beside our Rachel's
    tomb ;

I could not drag myself away to meet thy tender face:
Yet in our weakness and despair God giveth us his grace.

Since thee is pleased to sell the home we can no longer
    hold,
Thy love and smiles, I have them yet, more precious far than
    gold;
And we can keep the burial-ground, it goes not with the
    farm, —
What ails thee, Ruth? thy eyes are wide and staring with
    alarm!

The farm? I bargained it away, it is almost a year,
And he to whom we make the deed to-morrow will be
    here:
Thee knows the debts I had to bear for thy own brother
    John,
Who lost his all to help his friends, — poor fellow! dead
    and gone.

Thee knows how most our crops have failed and I have
    feeble grown,
And that against this adverse fate I have not held my own.
Well, it was sell the farm myself, or have the sheriff come
And over thy now bleaching head sell out the dear old
    home.

And so I bargained it away — but how could I thee tell?
But when thee spoke of selling out, then light upon me
    fell,
And all the gloom which o'er my life had settled in these
    years
Seemed left upon our Rachel's grave, dissolving in my tears.

I did not know — thee startles me — I cannot understand!
Oh, is it true, dear Jonathan, thee has to sell thy land?
Why did thee keep it all from me? I would thy burden
    share;
Thy tender heart is very brave alone this load to bear.

I thought it was our Jonathan who gave thy heart its pain,
And I have prayed with many tears for his return again;

And now it seems I hear his voice and footsteps in the
     gloom —
O God! if thou wouldst whisper him, I know that he would
     come.

What! is this thee, son Jonathan? This is a glad sur-
     prise!
Oh, let me hold thee in my arms, I cannot trust my eyes!
And what a man art thou become, with beard like Esau's
     grown!
No other but a mother's eyes that altered face had known.

What are these papers? Father, here! thy eyes are best
     to read —
Where didst thou get these papers, son? This is my mort-
     gage deed!
Thee paid the debt? God bless thee, son! Thou shalt with
     us abide;
And we will hold the graveyard, Ruth, and he the farm
     beside.

LE CHEMIN DORÉ.

Twinkling bells with music sweet,
    Lightly cadenced, freight the air;
Songs of bird and maiden greet
    Laughing Earth in morning fair.

Down the way with maple trees
    Hedged on either side I go,
Listening to the laughing breeze
    Softly kissing leaf and bough.

Never king such way before
    Trod in purple robe and crown;
Never choir, where saints adore,
    Sang as these in coats of brown!

Prince I am this hour alone,
    Walking in the king's highway;

Never has such glory shone
  Round my path as falls to-day !

Opaline and pearly sky
  Arching hangs above my head ;
Emerald swards and orchids vie
  To adorn the paths I tread.

While the trees on either side
  Flame in purple, gold, and green,
In the sunshine glorified
  Where I proudly walk between !

Prince I am but for to-day,
  Then I lay my sceptre down ;
Yet shall holly branch and bay
  Flower in my triumphal crown,

While I tread these bannered aisles,
  Where the maples flame on high,
Flashing sunshine through their smiles
  From the blue autumnal sky.

ADONIS' INVOCATION TO APHRODITE.

COME up from the sea, come out of the sea,
  My love and my fair one, come up from the sea !
Mine eyes have grown heavy in watching for thee,
  My heart has grown weary in waiting so long:
Thy love is as cold as these waters to me,
  Since thine ear has grown dull to my love-burdened song.

Come up from the sea ! Why tarry below
  In thy bed of green seaweed tossed restlessly there ?
Come out of the sea, my beloved so fair !
  I cannot go to thee and live in the wave.
Thy couch shall be roses my hands shall prepare,
  And I will attend thee, thy lover and slave.

Come up from the sea, come out of the sea!
  Thy bower shall be woven of rainbows of flowers;
The Graces shall deck thee, and rosy-winged Hours
  Shall weave thee fresh garlands of joy through the day:
The night shall bedew thee in love's softest showers
  That fall in sweet kisses to please thee alway!

Come up from the sea, O thou vision divine!
  The waters are moving so softly below, —
They are parting asunder as liquidly flow
  Thy limbs white as marble beneath the clear tide!
I clasp thee! I kiss thee! with love all aglow,
  Sweet Maid of the Sea! my heart's chosen bride.

HER HAND.

THE tapered fingers small and white;
  The rosebud pink of shell-like nail;
The dimpled joints, now deep now light;
  The pearly skin, with pencilling pale
Of tinted blue that hints of vein;
  The hollow palm, like lips of shell
On sun-kissed shore, — a crimson stain, —
  This is the hand I love so well!

And is this all? To you, maybe!
  For what is she or hers to you?
That hand, because 't is hers, to me
  Of all things beautiful to view!
No flower more fair, though rose unblown;
  No shape more perfect in its mould;
Unrivalled since 't is hers alone,
  And mine to touch, to clasp, to hold!

Yet other hands I know there are
  As soft, and white, and fair as hers,
For beauty ever is most fair
  And comely to its worshippers.
And this to me that makes her hand
  The fairest of all hands, and why

I tremble and admiring stand
  And kiss with heart-idolatry.

Why hers, and why its power to charm?
  Once on a morn of May we met;
The bugle-call rang war's alarm,
  The gage was thrown, the standards set:
Sweet flowers she gave with heart love-free,
  Her hand had plucked, — chance made them mine, —
And in them lurked that witchery
  In love's fair phrase is called divine.

Ah! when she snatched the nodding flower,
  And gave the fresh, sweet buds of spring,
Our fingers touched — I felt the power —
  A thrill — a throb of Love's sweet sting
Run to my heart: the blossom grew
  More beautiful! Ah! yet I see
Her hand, as then wet with the dew,
  Still grasp the buds she plucked for me!

And when that hand lay clasped in mine, —
  The flowers had withered long ago, —
Her cheeks were flush as rosy wine,
  And mine were none the less aglow;
It trembled as a frightened dove,
  But clung and clasped my fingers fast;
Ah! then I knew I had her love,
  The shadow of all doubt had past.

The years go on; the touch of Time
  Leaves here and there some mark or stain:
Upon the hair the gathering rime;
  The brow is traced by darker vein;
The shadows turn to day's decline,
  The eastern slopes grow cold and brown;
And still that fair hand lies in mine
  As westward now our steps go down!

Not many years, — they seem so few
  Upon her fingers one might tell
Their number twice since first I knew,
  And owned, and loved that hand so well, —

But, ah! they cheat, these years of joy!
  Their numbers more than touch a score!
Soon Time will touch and then destroy,
  And Earth will see its like no more!

I know that hand will some day fail,
  Will wither as the fairest bloom;
Death-touched, grow limp and waxen pale,
  Within the shadow of the tomb;
But wrinkled, browned be it by years,
  To me the fairest hand shall be!
Youth loved it, love in age reveres
  In twofold love's idolatry!

A SONG.

SHE sat where the sunlight was falling,
  Soft blows the wind o'er the lea!
Gay birds in their love-notes were calling,
  Sweetly from hedge-row and tree.

She sighed as she thought of her lover, —
  Soft sighs the wind o'er the lea, —
For long has he now been a rover
  Tossed on the waves of the sea.

"Oh sing, merry birds!" cried the maiden, —
  Low sings the wind o'er the lea, —
"Ah, sing! since my heart heavy-laden
  Joins not your sweet minstrelsy.

"Each bird seeks its mate in these bowers," —
  Low sobbed the wind o'er the lea, —
"The sunshine and dews kiss the flowers,
  No one has kisses for me."

But hark to a step swiftly nearing, —
  Hushed grew the wind o'er the lea, —
"Sweet Jenny!" came softly, endearing,
  "Love brings sweet kisses to thee!"

She laughs through glad tears softly flowing, —
  Low laughs the wind o'er the lea, —
Her cheeks hot with kisses are glowing,
  Kisses brought over the sea!

THE HAWK'S NEST ON NEW RIVER.

ALONG the pathway's steep ascent,
  Made cool by hidden fountains,
We clambered up the rocky heights
  That crowned the rugged mountains.

The blast of war with fear was heard
  Through valleys where we skirted,
And by our road the mountain homes
  Stood silent and deserted.

The sun shone through the morning's mist
  In streams of golden glory,
Which burned like flame along the crags
  All tempest-torn and hoary.

Above we saw Day's glancing beams,
  Like arrows from his quiver,
Drop noiseless through the pines below,
  That fringe the deep New River.

Above their tops we stood so high
  They seemed like stunted bushes,
Beneath whose boughs the copsewood swayed
  Before the breeze like rushes.

While at our feet, and o'er the stream
  Which round the bleak cliff rages,
Beneath the ledges grooved by time
  The hawks have built for ages!

And far beneath we heard their cries,
  Like voices weirdly ringing,
From out the gray cliff's storm-rent side
  Where tangled vines were clinging.

Upon the Lover's Rock we stood,
   And watched the short waves creeping
About the dark and gloomy stones
   Which in the tide were sleeping.

Upon that Rock I heard the tale
   The white-haired guide related,
Of her, the mountaineer's fair child,
   So beautiful and fated!

Rough set in virgin gold, this pearl
   By Nature formed and fashioned,
Was born of mists soft skyward blown,
   Of Love the most impassioned.

Than opening rosebud far more sweet
   Her parted lips in smiling;
The witchery of dreaming love
   Lurked in her locks beguiling.

Within the halo of her smile
   There fell no shade of sadness:
She caught the sunshine from her hills,
   And flung it back with gladness.

Within the heart like sunshine fell
   Her timid eyes' dark glancing,
While in the ripple of her laugh
   Rose music most entrancing.

Her beauty won a lover's heart,
   Whose love in turn soon won her;
Yet all the wealth he had to give
   Was in his love and honor.

Her father spurned his proffered hand
   That brought no golden treasure;
And love he scorned as idle dreams
   In Folly's vale of pleasure.

Their love denied, their hopes betrayed,
   By hands that sought to sever,

Their spirits looked beyond this vale
  To live and love forever!

One night they stood together here,
  Their arms each intertwining,
While Love undying to their death
  Had borne beyond repining.

Above, the moon sails silently;
  Beneath, where bright beams quiver,
Like silver broken on the waves,
  Flows on the dark New River.

Their hands are clasped, their lips are met;
  Their faces, pale but tender,
Show still the pangs it costs to break
  A cord so frail and slender.

The cold waves kiss each parted lip
  As in their arms they bore them,
And murmur softly as they throw
  Their liquid mantle o'er them.

And gazing now upon the wave
  Where round the white foam chases,
In fancy yet beneath we see
  The gleam of upturned faces!

The low, soft ripple of the waves
  That run along New River,
Above them sing with voices low
  A requiem forever!

THE GATHERING OF THE VETERANS.

Lo! they come, the heroes come!
  Hark! the tread of hosts advancing;
Hear the fife and rolling drum,
  See the banners gayly glancing,

Banners now so grand and glorious,
Rent and torn, but still victorious !
  Let them fly against the sky,
Colors, pennon, flag, and guidon,
That we love to look with pride on,
  Borne triumphantly on high !
Let the battle names now olden
Flash and flame in letters golden ;
  Let the sunshine kiss to glowing !
  Let the breezes still caress,
As their loosened folds outflowing
  Greet the eyes that love and bless !

Hear the bugle ! how its peal
  Sends the echoes wildly flying,
Till their pulsing throbs we feel
  Faintly in the distance dying :
While the trumpet's hoarser braying
Still the moving ranks obeying,
  Sweep along a glorious throng,
Mingling as a rushing river
Grandly on its course forever,
  Ever steady, full and strong !
How they march ! with faces beaming
Underneath those banners streaming,
Banners which now torn and gory
  Still they love as dearest friend ;
Banners that have been their glory
  Once to follow and defend.

Oh, 't is grand ! this once again
  Them to see with glowing faces
As they catch the thrilling strain,
  Marching in their wonted places,
With the step and martial bearing
Born of pride in hearts of daring !
  Now we know how long ago
Lookout's heights were stormed and taken,
Vicksburg's circling lines were shaken,
  Forced and wrested from the foe ;
How Antietam's fame grew crested,
Malvern's Hill the rout arrested ;

How brave Thomas, fate defying,
  Held the rebel hordes at bay,
When our routed hosts were flying
  On Chickamauga's fateful day.

Stream the banners from the walls!
  See them bloom from roof and stanchion,
Where the golden sunlight falls,
  Flower-wreathed, on hall and mansion!
Welcome! welcome! sung and written;
Welcome! still from glad bells smitten;
  Ev'rywhere upon the air
Ring in choruses above them
Glad acclaims from hearts that love them, —
  Tribute praise to hearts that dare!
Love endures if fame is fleeting;
Thus a nation reads the greeting
To its battle-scarred defenders,
  In its fair and peaceful hours;
Such a noble city tenders,
  Banner-decked and wreathed in flowers!

Hail the gallant Sheridan! —
  Patriot hero, how they love him! —
As he leads the Veteran van
  Where the banners stream above him!
Hears he once again the warning
Of that dark October morning,
  As it bore the distant roar
From the field his troops engaging
In that battle fiercely raging
  Twenty miles away or more?
Then, the nearer thunder guiding,
Is he down the Valley riding?
Hears he once again the cheering
  As he stays the wild retreat,
Stops the rebels' mad careering,
  Snatching victory from defeat?

Sherman, lo! he, too, is there,
  Grand old warrior! they revere him;
See them toss their hats in air,
  Hail with shouts and madly cheer him!

They have followed oft his leading;
For him marching, fighting, bleeding,
  On a field they would not yield!
Through Atlanta's gates he thundered,
While the nation watched and wondered
  Whither he would bear his shield.
Sweeping southward sped his legions
Through its yet unconquered regions,
Then before the fair Savannah
  Thundering at its gates is he;
And the land with loud hosannah
  Sings his March down to the Sea!

Who is he approaching now,
  Grand and silent in his bearing?
Eyes that burn and godlike brow
  Speak of iron will and daring.
Hail to Grant!   Send echoes flying,
Dip your standards, crying, crying,
  Gloria Deus! gloria Deus!
He the grand in ev'ry station,
He, the known of ev'ry nation —
  He did lead and he did free us!
Wave the banners worn and tattered,
Crimsoned, tempest-torn, and battered!
Let the cannon boom and thunder
Till the echoes burst asunder;
Set the bells a-ringing, ringing!
  While all hearts in sweet refrain
Beat the time to glad lips singing,
  Welcome! welcome! thrice again!

Hark! there falls upon the ear
  Sounds like distant footsteps throbbing;
Nearer, clearer still I hear
  Voices hushed like low winds sobbing, —
Prayer of priest or mourner sighing
O'er the couch where man lies dying!
  Soft and slow as zephyrs blow,
See the banners lightly playing;
See! the ranks are bending, swaying,
  And the columns wider grow!

See them fill the vacant places,
Phantom forms and shadowy faces!
From the battle-field and prison,
   Lo, they come, an army slain!
From their graves the dead have risen,
   Now to join the march again!

Spirits of the martyred dead,
   Leaders famed on History's pages,
Those who ruled and those who led,
   Valiant knights and hoary sages;
Lincoln, born to fame undying;
Stanton, with the mighty vying;
   Warriors brave whose blood they gave,
Ellsworth, Lyon, Baker, leading;
Mansfield, Sedgwick, later bleeding,
   Kearney, from his warrior grave, —
Crowd so fast I cannot name them,
Yet all hearts will know and claim them;
Gathering wreaths from memory's bowers
   Each its golden legend spells,
Each bids Love, from rarest flowers,
   Wreathe for them its immortelles.

Holds the witchery of the hour
   In this vision soul-entrancing,
As the spirit's mighty power
   Shows the risen hosts advancing;
Warriors dead, whose fame and glory
Live embalmed in song and story,
   Heroes gone whose blood has won
Peace and freedom for the living,
Honored for the gift in giving,
   Be their names and graves unknown!
Sweep they past with banners flying;
Sounds the bugle faint and dying;
Sinks the pennons, fades the column
In the shadows deep and solemn;
Gone the pageant! but the story
   Of their deeds shall never die;
Brighter still shall blaze their glory
   Through the ages circling by.

WHY SILENT?

AND yet thou answer'st not!   Has rank offence
　　His seal with burning fingers on those lips,
Which with their words of trust made recompense
　　For all my ills, now set?   Or rather clips
Thy speech with envious hand cold-hearted Hate?
　　Stung at our innocence, grows fierce to see
That hearts may yet know happiness, though late,
　　As grudgingly at last it came to me?

Has Slander's tongue, dripping with venom hot
　　Like rabid cur's, pursued my honest name
Until thine eye beholds a fancied blot
　　And turns away, while brow and cheek aflame
With shame for me are hid, because thy hand,
　　In more than friendly grasp, once touched and thrilled
In mine?   And cold and careless wilt thou stand
　　And freeze my hope to death, by silence chilled?

No answer?   Then let silence speak and tell,
　　Through Memory's pictures in her misty halls,
The story of our past.   O'er these, how well
　　The painted halos flame!   How softly falls
Each tint upon thy brow!   Love breathed on these
　　And animate they grew, and, voiced by him,
Spoke, and alone of thee!   and yet I freeze,
　　Since turned thy face away the sun grows dim.

Not always thus; ah, no!   There was a time
　　When in the hours of all the circling day
There was not time enough for thee : the rhyme
　　And rhythm of thy low-toned speech a lay —
A song — a melody became, which made
　　For me rest, solace, sleep from night till morn,
From morn till night again, and pleasure stayed,
　　If but an hour by thee was illy borne.

I traced a line upon the shifting sand
　　And bade thee read; thou chid'st me for the thought

In it expressed, since one might understand
   A doubt of constancy expressed; 't was nought:
But with thy foot the sand was smoothed again.
   Above those hidden lines one word was traced!
Those treacherous lines closed slowly, grain by grain.
   Has Time the memory of that word effaced?

A book lay open, and a leaf turned down
   To mark the page: I traced a line beneath,
A cynic truth, to see thy gathering frown
   Meet my raised eyes, — Love's gathering storm of wrath;
And quick thy fingers caught from willing hand
   My pencil but to mark a line which told
In burning words a passion almost banned:
   Hast thou forgot? have those words, too, grown cold?

A leaf fell slowly from its parted stem,
   And fluttered down and rested at my feet;
I caught and kissed it. for it touched the hem,
   In falling, of thy robe. Thou called it "Cheat!"
The why, thou know'st, and kissed it where I kissed,
   As from my hand 't was caught, and to thy cheek
Long pressed the dewy thing. Of this dost wist?
   That leaf is dust, but Love still lives: wilt speak?

I took thy hand, its dainty fingers pressed
   With kisses soft; then saw thy look, which said,
" Why kiss the hand? such kisses are not best! "
   With pouting lips and gently drooping head,
Thine eyes grew humid, and I caught their charm,
   And pressed a hundred kisses on them there,
And yet thou didst not think it then a harm;
   And should I take them back, wouldst thou now care?

No answer? Well, just once to try thy heart,
   I will take all the gifts I gave,
Each separate one, since tired of them thou art;
   I would not force the smallest on a slave,
Much less on thee! With kisses start we, then;
   Now keep the score while I with all my might —
Ha! didst thou speak? It seemed thy voice again:
   And didst thou say it would take half the night?

LUX FUTURO.

Dim, shadowy, vague, they rise,
  Quivering in prismatic light,
Which on the skies
  Flits here and there, now pale, now bright,
    I see these shadows come,
    Born of the spirit from the womb
Of Time, not pregnant with the things
Now shown, but yet to be.   His wings,
Outspread in the deep shadow cast,
Fold back like curtains, and as Past
    I see the Future spring to light.
    From the mystic night
Lifts the dark mantle ; days
Gemmed in the lustrous blaze
    Their crown, the sun, sends forth,
Brilliant with many pictures shine,
    While all the earth
Glows in the light we hail divine.

Creeping they come, like shadows dim ;
  We trace the rugged outlines on the light ;
Yet, as the shivering semblance we would limn,
  It darkens — fades — is lost upon the sight !
Shadow of pale shadows, a memory of those shades,
And even this to paling nothing fades,
And leaves a blank, cold, dead, and chill,
Shading the light as from a form of ill.
Groping among the visions that have fled,
Reading upon the tombstones of the dead,
Thoughts and hopes we trace thus far to find
That at the best, the grandest soul is blind !

Yet we would go beyond, would pass
    The inner veil where mortal eye
        Ne'er gazed,
Where glows the flame more dread to man than was
    The light which fell adown the noonday sky
        And blazed
Around the persecutor Saul.
    Groping among the shadows drear,

Seeking for light where none can fall,
    Blindly we go, and guess our footing here ;
Casting aside the Truth's soft beams
Which on the darkened pathway turn
As beacon-lights which for us burn,
    Shedding their ruddy gleams
O'er the dark clouds as waxen light
Over the shrouding pall
When the dark veil has closed on misty sight !
  Into the mist, into the dim
    Trackless future, we turn,
  Seeking where deeds now grim
    Like priests await their lights to burn
On the razed altar, where
In the soft light wings up a prayer.

Light of the Future ! in whose beams
    Shadows flit by
From the kaleidoscope of life's dreams,
    Startling the eye
With a half-hidden mystery shown,
That we may yet in substance call our own :
But yet we long may chase a joy
    With bleeding feet from cruel, cutting stones ;
Panting in wretchedness, destroy
    In haste the substance sure, while groans,
Bruised limbs, and burning tears
Are all we gain who blight the hope of years.

Upward, beyond this darkened world,
  There is a light which glows
For us when the last breath has curled
  From death-white lips, and throes
Of life are done, — when Time is dead,
And we are dead to Time, and fled
The vision which this nightmare brings
  To bleeding hearts in life's o'erfitful sleep,
Which but awaits the flapping of Death's wings
  To quench the taper which alive we keep
  Till gleams eternal day :
Then we awake but to be borne
  To the Elysian Fields away

Over the waters, where no more to mourn,
But rising in the light, no future dawn
Nor twilight eve can rise or set upon.

ONLY A WOMAN.

SHE is only a woman with unshod feet,
Ragged and sun-browned, walking the street.
Her clothes are all tattered, her throat is bare,
And wildly is flowing her uncoiled hair
Down over her shoulders and bosom lean,
On a faded dress that is not quite clean.
You may taunt, you may scoff at her, nobody cares :
She is only a woman such insult bears!

She is only a woman, — a wrinkled crone,
All sour and sharp in life's conflict grown,
Who sneers at your smiles, as if she well knew
The value of them just as well as of you.
As she hobbles along she is muttering low
Strange words that no one but she may know ;
She is talking to Time, but Time has fled,
And the loves of her life have long been dead
As the heart of the world is dead to her ;
But she 's only a woman, this sufferer.

She is only a woman, who wants a place
Beside strong manhood in life's hard race ;
She has mother and brother, and little feet
And hungry mouths with their needs to meet ;
And while she is asking, beside her stands
A brawny young man with stalwart hands,
Demanding the place, that he may spend
The wages thus earned on a wayward friend ! —
Drink, gamble, and revel in sport and wine,
And dress in the ways of a fashion fine :
But give him the place, he 's a man, you know ;
She, only a woman of so and so !

She is only a woman ; and to her home
With the guile of a serpent some day may come

A man, — or one in the form of a man, —
Who, seeking her ruin, will plot and plan ;
And when she has fallen — if fall she must —
The world will upon her heap filth and dust,
And say she was weak and should have been strong,
And hers was the fault and hers was the wrong ;
While he goes forth in the light of the day,
As the wolf to devour the innocent prey :
And she goes forth to the hell of sin !
But she's only a woman who plunges in !

She is only a woman ! A woman, O man !
Nursed you and kept you when only a span
The length you would measure from head to toe,
And did for you freely what none else would do !
That mother who bore you, stand up for her now :
The crown is her weaving encircling your brow.
Stand up for each woman ! A mother is she
In heart and in soul, and revered thus to be !
She sits at your table, she clings to your arm ;
'T is yours to protect her and shield her from harm :
The man who dishonors, he is not a man ;
His soul has grown shrivelled and shrunk to a span !
Remember your duty ; your manhood still prove.
It is only a woman who knows how to love !

You are only a woman ? Oh, shame on your kind,
Who fault with your sister in suffering will find !
Who will drag your own down, and set in her place
The man who hath brought her and you to disgrace ;
For that which but touches the woman refined
Leaves a stain on the name of all womankind !
Her weakness is yours, her sorrows your own ;
The mercies of God may have spared you alone :
So go to her, fly to her ! tears are her meed ;
Your love and your sympathy sorely her need !
She smiled as you smiled yesterday, but to-morrow
Hath many sad hearts coming in to their sorrow !
Stand up for your own and stand fast ! In the fall
Not one alone suffers, the shock hurts you all !
Oh, then you will triumph, if thus you will stand,
For though but a woman, that woman is grand !

TOUCH THE HARP.

Touch the harp! its chords of gold
Fire anew the heart grown cold,
Waking visions that impart
Pleasure to the fainting heart.

Beauty, breathe thy magic spell,
Weave thy chains of conquest well;
Strong thy yoke, and unto thee
Those who rule must bow the knee.

Yet thy triumph soon is past,
Rule like thine can never last:
Faded roses crushed and dead
Carpet but where beggars tread!

Touch the harp! what vision fair
Hovers dimly in the air;
Turning Hope's delusive glass,
Showing joys that never pass?

Youth, thou morn of joyous life,
With a thousand visions rife,
Dreams as fair as hope can give,
Rise and in thy future live!

Life is what thy wish creates;
Joy is supped till fulness sates;
Shadows pass not o'er thy sun,
Or the fields it shines upon.

Yet the hand of Time destroys
Youthful hopes and youthful joys,
Leaving age with bowed head bare
To the biting breath of care.

Touch the harp! in golden showers
Falls the faint perfume of flowers;
Pictured halls and gildings rare
Charm and thrill while gazing there.

Wealth, thy tinsel charms the eye,
Gilds awhile the roseate sky,
Buys a cup of pleasure still
From the grudging hand of ill.

Yet beneath this gilding lies,
Half revealed to watchful eyes,
Blackened shrines and altars, where
Life's best gifts are offered there.

And the hand which grasps thee clings
Trembling to thy shadowy wings,
Fearful lest some adverse blast
Snatch thee from its hold at last.

Sorrow comes, thy power is vain !
Fairest lips that cup must drain,
Though in golden vessels fall,
One by one, its drops of gall.

Touch the harp ! a sweeter strain
Trembles from its chords again ;
Thrilling hearts that feel, confess,
All its soothing tenderness.

Love, thou anchor of the heart
Drifting from the world apart,
Thou dost draw all things to thee
By thy wondrous witchery.

Beauty fails, and friendship flies
Those who trust, and hope soon dies,
Leaving all, thy tendrils cling
Where all else is withering !

What if beauty's robes grow sere
While thy smile remains to cheer !
What if youth to age has grown
If thy fires undimmed live on !

Count as naught all gifts but this ;
Without love life has no bliss :

Gilded halls are desolate
If in them it does not wait.

Hope in love fruition finds;
Happy brows its chaplet binds:
Victors' crowns, though won in right,
On their brows sit not so light.

Found on earth though born in Heaven,
Love was first to angels given;
Last to man its richest gem, —
Christ, the Babe of Bethlehem.

Harps of angels caught the strain
Rising from Judea's plain;
Through all Heaven its chorus ran,
" Peace on earth, goodwill to man ! "

KITTY M^CDONALD'S RIDE.

A LEGEND OF THE SCIOTO.

A HUNDRED years are passed and gone,
   A hundred days they seem no more !
And as I touch the glass of Time,
   They rise and dimly pass before.

The scene grows wondrous in its change,
   As shadows swallow up the light,
So forests spring from verdant fields,
   And cities melt before the sight.

A hundred years the Past has knelled :
   Turn backward o'er the track of Time,
And pictures that from out them rise
   Seem of another age and clime.

I see spring forth a glorious morn,
   In autumn verdure gold and brown,
Of wild woods skirting vale and stream,
   With neither hamlet, church, nor town !

Oh, rich and rare primeval woods,
  How faintly limned by brush or pen !
God's wondrous pictured page but mocks
  The grandest themes conceived by men.

He walks amid these aisles of green
  In evening shade and golden dawn,
And each and all grow brighter then,
  Which, passing by, he looks upon.

But to my tale : this autumn morn
  Rose sweet and bright as maiden fair
From sleep and dreams of innocence,
  When neither knows nor cloud nor care.

Sweet as that morn, and no less fair,
  Kitty McDonald greets the day,
Her eyes of deeper blue than skies
  Beyond where yet the shadows stray.

Joy flies to greet her with his kiss ;
  With lips thus touched she softly sings,
Amid those aisles of green, a song
  Whose notes would thrill the courts of kings.

Sing on, sing low, sing sweet and long,
  With hope and love in every strain ;
Thy matin song, so rich and pure,
  These scenes may never wake again.

But no ! God walks these woods among,
  And in his steps Peace as a flower
Springs fragrant into perfect bloom,
  And sheds her incense through each bower.

Morn passes, swift pursued by noon ;
  The gates of eve now swing ajar ;
Her yellow sunbeams backward stream
  With gilded radiance from afar.

The lengthened shadows tinged with gold
  Lie slanting eastward up the hill ;

With burnished sunlight glow the heights
   Which catch the sun's hot kisses still.

A robin from the maple's bough
   Sings loud and shrill his evening song,
And sways and rocks him as he sings,
   Tossed by the breeze, the leaves among.

Sweet scene of peace, glad evening time,
   Too sweet, too bright, to end with day ;
And yet, affrighted from her home,
   Peace plumes her wings to fly away.

For gather now beyond these hills
   The savage plumed and painted foe,
Whose tongue beguiles with words of peace
   While yet he arms to strike the blow.

Is there no friend within whose heart
   Stirs yet one throb of faith divine ?
Will all stand silent in this hour
   And turn not, speak not, give no sign ?

Yes, there is one, a dusky maid,
   Who morn and evening ofttimes came
To sit beside the white man's hearth,
   A welcome guest in heart and name.

And as beside her father's door
   Young Kitty lingers in the gloom,
Communing with her heart's sweet thoughts
   That whisper low of joys to come,

A shadow flits among the trees,
   A form glides swiftly through the shade, —
With whispered word of warning given,
   A hand on Kitty's arm is laid !

She turns, but with no sign of fear,
   To meet, it may be, friend or foe,
And sees the Indian maiden there
   With parted lips and troubled brow.

"Speak, maiden, speak!" fair Kitty cries;
   "What means this sign and look of fear?"
"Hark! hear you not that stealthy foot
   Which through the night is drawing near?

"Thy foes are thick as forest leaves;
   And come as silent as their fall,
And, like the winds when frosts have come,
   They soon will rend and scatter all.

"I heard their council speak for war;
   I saw their war-dance in the wood;
The plumed and painted braves go forth
   To revel in the white man's blood.

"My sister, rouse thy father's lodge!
   The wind's swift wings now seize and fly;
There's mercy yet within the night:
   Who lingers till the morn must die!

"Remember who this warning gives;
   Her life hangs on thy lightest breath:
Thy lips while silent bid me live,
   Their lightest word condemns to death.

"I go, farewell!" and with that word,
   The shadows catch and backward bear
Her far within their dusky deeps,
   And hold and hide her safely there.

Swift as the shadow that has fled,
   Her feet winged with compelling fears,
To warn her father Kitty flies:
   With paling cheek her tale he hears.

"O God!" he cried, "our friends are lost!
   For none there is to warn them here,
Since I can scarcely save my own
   From the red foe now drawing near.

"Oh for one true and trusty heart
   To dare the dangers of the night,

And bear the word o'er hill and flood,
    To warn and speed them in their flight!"

"Father, I know the way and dare!"
    "No, no, my child!" "Nay, let me go!
My horse is fleet and sure of foot,
    And can outstrip the swiftest foe.

"Nay! speak no further, I will go.
    Bring out my horse: the night speeds on!"
'T is done! she mounts, and at the door
    He bids Godspeed, and she is gone!

Ride, Kitty, ride! the very air
    Is tremulous with voiceless fear!
The night winds whisper it to the leaves
    That shudder at the danger near.

The wolf's low wail repeated oft,
    The panther's almost human cry,
Strike on her ear like death-notes now,
    As near their lair she rushes by.

Ride, Kitty, ride! the way is long,
    O'er hill, through wood, and valley fair;
The foe is pressing on your track:
    Fear not, be strong to do and dare!

On, on she rides: at every door,
    "Awake! arise! the foe is nigh!
Fly to the fort!" on startled ears
    Rings shrilly out her warning cry.

Her clothes are torn by bush and thorn;
    The red blood drops from hands and face;
She heeds not, feels not, knows no pain,
    But headlong holds her onward pace!

Her horse is gray and flecked with foam;
    With labor heaves his quivering side,
While white plumes stream from trembling lips,
    And pant his nostrils red and wide!

Yet on she rides, till from the hill
  She·turns to look with startled eye ;
And, lo ! behind her from her home
  The red flames paint the western sky !

Ride, Kitty, ride ! the end is near !
  The last poor lodge before you lies ;
Speed, speed the warning, faithful heart,
  The night behind you swiftly flies !

'T is done ! now speed you to the fort,
  God give you strength, your steed still power
To bear you to its sheltering walls,
  Before Time strikes the morning hour.

The morning mists are tinged with red,
  The eastern sky grows roseate,
When slowly up the sloping hill
  A rider nears the fortress gate !

The weary steed toils slowly on,
  Nor heeds he now nor hand nor rein ;
The foam that flecks his quivering lips
  Is deeply tinged with crimson stain !

" 'T is Kitty ! " loud the sentry cries ;
  The gates swing open at his call,
A hundred feet rush out to meet,
  And bear within the sheltering wall.

With shouts of joy they bear her in !
  With tearful kiss and fond caress
Fond mothers greet the noble girl,
  Whilst aged hands now trembling bless.

For she has saved them from a fate
  Too terrible to think or name ;
But they have read it through the night,
  Across the skies portrayed in flame.

But now the foe is at their gates ;
  The woodmen wait assault within ;

When, with a shout that chills the blood,
　The savage conflict they begin.

Not mine is it the tale to tell
　Of bloody conflict fierce and long,
Of wild attack and swift defeat;
　Such is not fitted for my song.

It is enough, since victory
　Remained to crown that sturdy band,
And left its legacy of peace
　To bless in after years the land.

And in those homes that sprung again
　From out the ashes of the old,
The grandsire by the blazing hearth
　At evening oft the tale retold,

With dim eyes that grew wet again,
　And heart that throbbed with generous pride,
The story that his youth renewed,
　Kitty McDonald's midnight ride.

CENTENNIAL.

ROME in her plan made the best out of man,
The physical, ponderous animal man,
And drove him a thunderbolt into the van
　Of armed opposition, in war's deadly thrust,
　And trampled them down and ground into dust,
　　In her all-conquering day,
　　All nations that stood in her way;
Then out of their ruin brought life,
And out of the besom of strife,
　　　If not peace,
　　　Brought ease;
And out of the ignorant night
Brought strength in exchange for light;
　　　Gave muscle and brawn,
　　　Took the light and the dawn

Of the Arts, of Poetry, Painting, and Mind,
Of all the known world in their best, their refined,
From all lands and all human-kind ;
 And gathering the centuries in a span,
 Wrought out and left this, her model of Man.
  Rome's best !
  Stand up, O Man of our West!

Eighteen hundred and eighty-eight !
Turn to the morning that gives this date.
 With the wise men afar,
 Now follow its star,
Seeking the truth as sought by them,
In the low manger of Bethlehem ;
  And there,
  Radiant rare !
 See the Child born to earth,
 Low in its menial birth,
 That should yoke to his car
 Men of heart, men of brain,
 Gathering his mighty train,
Then drive as a victor careering the plain,
Speeding conquests o'er lands, o'er islands and main,
Until the seas bloom white,
 Valleys grow rich with grain,
Out of the darkness of night
Bringing day, bringing sunshine and light,
 And the world grows glad again.
And out of the desert, and out of the flood,
Bringing empire to man without shedding of blood !
Without sword, without chains, without fire,
But with hands filled with blessings to man, —
For the bugle of war, the harp and the lyre ;
 For the spear, — save when dyed
 With blood from his side, —
The plough and the pruning hook. This was His plan
To conquer the world into peace !
  And on to that end
  The years now but tend,
   And never shall cease
The march of the world through its circle of years,
Until upon Time's farthest confines appears

A kingdom most wonderfully blest,
   Believing His creed
   Of Love shall succeed,
Somewhere in the beautiful ongrowing West,
   With Man at his best !

   The Old World had brawn ;
The Old World had men, the best of her best,
Which the East of her East gave the West of her West,
   In her new day's flush dawn.
As the mother would say to the child of her breast,
   She said to her children, Sail over, sail on, —
Sail somewhere !   My people now feel the unrest
   Of birds of the North, where winter is gone.
And they sailed and found land, —
Found seas lapping seas and continents grand ;
   Found hills where the seas
Once swallowed a wide continent,
   Which, risen again, the sun and the breeze
To the virginal bosom of young Earth had sent
   The flowers, the grasses, the reeds, and the trees ;
And then, somehow, came man, not our man,
   But the wild, savage man of the forest and plain ;
The best of his kind, and the best of his plan,
   For God never made mote or mortal in vain !
That man fled before our Man of the Sea, —
Fled fighting and killing the first as he ran ;
   Behind him marched on the hosts of the free,
   For Liberty grew on these shores, as the tree
   Self-implanted, and ever to be
   Fruit bearing, life-bearing, and strong,
Though blooming with death and dripping with blood,
   Embattled against it the hosts of wrong,
To stand where it ever has stood.

     And so
They came over the hills, pressing on the fierce foe
To the rivers that on to the Southland flow,
To the lake whose south shore bends up like a bow,
   And on by the margin of river and stream,
Through the valleys that lie in the shade of their woods,
Into depths of the deepest of lone solitudes,
     To where lay

In the flush of fair day,
Where the noon in the heat of the sun faints away,
  Like a vision of Paradise seen in a dream,
This land, like a maiden half-hidden in flowers,
  Unrobed for a bath in the cool, sleeping lake
Of the outsweeping Northland, embosomed in bowers,
  Asleep on her couch with but hushed winds awake ;
    And the birds in their dream songs
        Singing so low
        As they flit to and fro,
    That we dream they are singing with magical tongues
That ever go on, unceasingly on,
From fall of the night to the rise of the dawn,
From the breaking of day to the drowning of light,
        Day and night
        Night and day,
While asleep she there lay,
This maiden of dreams, this child of the sea,
  Cast up from the depths in the blossom of foam,
  Crowned with flowers as a bride to become, —
The fairest and sweetest of sisters to be,
  Robed in white, queenly crowned, with her feet
Dipping into the beautiful river, her breast
  A garden of spices in all wholly sweet !
Unrolled as a scroll on her lap broadly rest
  The onstretching plain soft aglow,
  Lush with grass, spreading trees, clambering roses ablow,
  And a burden of lakes betwixt her fair hands,
  With a necklace of pearls in their ripple-kissed sands.
O'er the hills set as tent-poles a curtain of clouds,
        So enshrouds
Her beautiful face from the sun glowing warm,
        As they swing to and fro,
        Where the winds gently blow,
  That but glimpses we catch of her beautiful form ;
  Where asleep lies this brightest of all the bright band,
  On the broad, swelling bosom of Liberty's land,
        Lo! OHIO!!

O Muse of sweet song, O Muse of bright waters !
Give me rhythmical tongue to sing the fair daughters
  Born of the morn, of the sun, of the rain ;
  Of hill and of valley, of mountain and plain ;

Born of the river, the lake, and the stream,
Conceived as a hope, brought forth as a dream;
Born unto man, unto progress and brain;
Born to this sister, the fairest of states;
Created of Time, unto Time it creates;
Matchless in beauty, deathless in fame;
Peerless in riches, spotless in name!
Abroad to the breezes thy banner we fling,
   And sing,
   With tongue
To the harp of our heart, touched by love each string,
   Thy Song!

The Burden of Rivers that onrushing flow
Into the broad-bosomed Ohio, —
Miami, biforked, o'er shallows and deeps
Rippling, and purling, and swirling down sweeps,
With its broad-branching elms, hooded alders, tall lyn,
Growing out like the fringe of a ribbon wrought in
A garment of beauty, through valleys it runs,
With smiles that are sweetest to soft-kissing suns.

Scioto, benignant, soft-voiced as a maid's!
The river of whispers, of legends and shades,
Where white-branching sycamores, ghostly to sight,
Cast their phosphorent light on the gloom of the night;
Fill with ghosts their deep shades, and the whispering wind
Breathes a vapor of fears, though with voice not unkind;
Where the valleys run down, blushing red with their bowers;
Where the hills hang above it their festoons of flowers,
As it kisses their feet and laughing speeds by,
With a song to the fields and a smile to the sky.

   Hockhocking,
  With a smile that is mocking,
  Like young maiden's laughter
  In play when her lover runs after,
Shouts out to her hills, sighs sweet to her rills,
And the long rocky glen with sweet laughter fills,
   As it purls,
   As it swirls,
And around the sharp rocks bends in long liquid curls,

Then shoots as an arrow
Down some gorge dark and narrow,
Rushing out with a shout and a sally
Of laughter renewed, watering meadow and valley,
With grasses for robes and flowers for crown,
Then down, rushing down,
From the leap and rebound,
In the Ohio lies lost there and drowned.

Muskingum sweeps out
From the foot of her hills,
Where the dark whispering pine aroma distils,
And the trout
Would dream it a Paradise liquid and cool,
In the swift-flowing channel and tree-shaded pool,
Where it winds through its course,
Deepening, widening alway
With the far-reaching force
Of a giant at play,
Broad-bosomed, wide-shouldered, he bears
With a burden of song a burden of cares,
Out into the plain,
The promise of fruitage and riches of grain.

The Burden of Rivers that flow to the Lake:
Where the wash of the waves on the north borders break,
Lake Erie has carved with her blue-gleaming blade
In her soft liquid hand,
From the uplifted shoulder of land
Of our fair-bosomed Lady, and made
A wide, circling wound,
From whence ceaselessly pours,
From her heart-fountain profound,
Her rivers of life-blood adown its green shores.

Maumee,
Empties into this inland sea
From the gardens, and meadows, and glades,
Sweeping out of the sunshine and into the shades ;
Winding down through the vales, kissing foot-hills that lie
Like emeralds embossing the earth, with the sky
A poem of beauty, while anthems of song
Rise up from each ripple's interpreting tongue.

Like a ribbon of silver through carpets of green,
The winding Sandusky north-flowing is seen,
Where the hills gently rise from the valleys between,
With flags in its shallows and reeds on its shores,
With willows for fringes and maples for bowers;
     And the sky,
     As its waters speed by,
A blue arch bends over the white sands that lie
     In a shimmer of light,
     While the clouds' speeding flight,
Like huge, drifting fleeces, lie mirrored in white.

Cuyahoga, still whispering hushed in its name
Of forests unbroken and man yet untame,
     Flows murmuring on,
     Flows ceaselessly, hurrying on
     The course it for ages has gone:
     And the Grand,
Running northward from out the same land,
Pour their floods from her heart, and yet, as they flow
Still stronger, still richer, more beautiful grow
The charms of her valleys, the pride of her hills,
Until one blooming garden the whole valley fills.

A Burden of Cities! but why should we name?
Of the Rivers and Lakes they have part in their fame;
They sit on their borders, rise up with their tide,
They live in their glory and share in their pride.
A Burden of Valleys! But whispers of these
From Rivers and Cities each outflowing breeze;
Nor city, nor river, in valley and plain,
But blesses, is blest, by their blessings again.
A Burden of Women, fair Women! The flowers
Not sweeter than grow in these valleys of ours!
A Burden of Men! Let the whole land declare
Man has wrought in them all, and his hand is still there.

Come up from these rivers, so beautifully flowing;
Come up from these valleys, resplendent and glowing;
Come up from these hills, in their evergreen growing;
Come up from these plains, lying sweetly between;
Come up from these streams, like gossamers seen;
Come up from the wake of a Century's dream, —

From valley, from hill, from onflowing stream;
From cities that lie in the flash of the sun;
From towns that are dreams of a beauty that none
Ever dreamed when in waking. O Land, now awake!
From city to river, from river to lake,
> Come up with a greeting
> To brother in meeting:
> Come up where with deeds we span
> The oncoming march of man, —
> Learn how the years have told,
> How slow the world grows old;
> Learn how the march of Time
> Makes man and life sublime!
> Come up, O ye people! All
> Answering the call.

Out-reaching, broad arms of iron and steel,
Calling into thy service the piston and wheel,
Sending forth at thy bidding the engine and keel,
> Thy sons and thy daughters,
> By rail and waters,
Now peopling the plains from sun unto sun, —
For their day is a day that never is done, —
Reaching up to the Northland and down to the South,
On the Father of Waters, from source unto mouth,
Where the myrtle is blooming and orange flowers grow,
Or the gleam of their stars light long winters of snow,
> Bring them home, call them home!
> Call them sweetly, again they will come
> To the hands that have blessed them,
> To the arms that caressed them!
Call them home to the feast for them spread;
Call them home to thy natal year's century fled;
Call them home to the graves of thy dead!
Call them home all the living to meet;
Call them home all the smiling to greet;
Call them home to the banquet of Love;
Call them home to the hearth and the grove;
Call them home where the banqueting guest
From the North and the South, the East and the West,
> Comes to meet them,
> Comes to greet them;
> Call them home, soft entreat them,

O thou fairest and best!
    They will come,
    Call them home!

Come, all ye people born
In this land's later morn,
Come, bringing sheaves of corn;
Come, bringing fruits and flowers
From teeming fields and bowers;
Come, bringing loads of grain,
Car-lading or in wain;
From mines and furnaces,
From loom and printing-press;
Come, with the dust of mills,
Come, with the breath of hills,
Come, with the voice of rills,
    Fresh everywhere!
Come, with your flocks and herds,
Come, with your warbling birds,
Come, full of joyous words
    Laden the air:
Maiden and laughing swain,
Up from each swelling plain;
Frost-whitened, stooping head,
Sad-visaged, slow of tread;
Wealth-bearing gilded bloom,
Rough-clad from rustic loom;
Statesman, priest, poet, sage,
Of every rank and age,
    Come!

And thus we will learn, and at the same time
Teach, the lesson of Truth so wondrous, — sublime!
That the years — all the years in their rhythmical rhyme, —
    From the past, with one tongue,
    Shall sing but one song,
    The song the Centuries sing, —
"Crown our king! crown our king!
    The up-leaping, hot-blooded, latest-born!
Of the children of Time, sweeping into the morn
Of the oncoming century NOW!"
    Yes, crown his brow
With laurel, and iron, and silver, and gold!

Weave him robes out of textiles of threads manifold ;
    And with dyes
  That outrival all hues of the skies
  Embalm them in color, — a poem expressed ;
    Then take by the hand
  This unrivalled child of an unrivalled land,
 This daughter of Liberty, born on the breast
Of the grandest of Centuries man has yet known,
Clothed in queenly apparel with gem-studded zone,
And lead to her lord of the Now of all years !
 To whom, in these valleys matriculate-born,
She has borne her fair children in hope and in tears,
  In the glory of Truth, since motherhood's morn !

Why name them ? all know them, these sons
And fair daughters, her own honored ones,
  Ohio hath borne on her breast :
  Crowning acme of time, reigning queen, now our quest,
In thee, in thy homes, in thy daughters, thy sons ;
  In thy lakes and thy rivers, thy valleys, thy plains ;
Thy sky, which the glory of glories still crowns ;
  In thy freedom which is the reign of all reigns,
In thy strength of brawn arms, in the power of broad
     brains ;
  In thy wealth not of gold yet of gold ;
  In thy treasures of learning untold,
In thy youth of fresh hearts that never grow old ;
In thy shot-beaten mail and thy swords rusted red ;
In the tears of thy women and prayers they have sped ;
    From the smoke and the cloud
    Of the red battle's shroud,
Where the faces gleam white of thy brave heroes dead, —
In and out of all these, from thy century fled,
Has come forth of thee born, by thee nursed, by thee given,
The grandest of Earth, blest of Time and of Heaven ;
Stripping laurels from all, snatching crowns from each brow,
Led forth by thy spouse, the all-ruling Now !
 Touching hands with the Christ, in all ages blest.
Ohio, Sweet Mother ! to thee we all bow,
  The Bride of the Century ! Thine is the best
     In heroes and sages
     Perfection of ages,
  Thy Man of the West !

CENTENNIAL SONG.

COME, let us sing a joyful song,
　　Like Miriam's from the sea,
Whence God had brought his children safe,
　　And set his people free, —
A song of praise to him who gave
　　Us victory o'er all foes,
And made through peace the wilderness
　　To blossom as a rose.

His hand our fathers hither led
　　And kept them as his own,
Until within an empire vast
　　An empire we have grown.
Our nation spreads from sea to sea,
　　From snows to fadeless flowers ;
A hundred rivers thread our plains,
　　A thousand cities ours.

And we within this nation grew
　　A part within the whole,
Her cities in our borders stand,
　　Through them her rivers roll.
Ohio, in a hundred years
　　From child to giant grown,
Strides on, resistless in her march,
　　An empire for her own.

Her sons are now the nation's boast,
　　The world declares their fame ;
From fields of battle, halls of state,
　　Are many a glorious name.
Her homes sent armies to the field
　　Which wore the loyal blue,
And armies waited in those homes
　　Of women grand and true.

When peace returned, for sword and gun
　　Exchanged were plane and plough ;

And reapers from those fields of death
  Returned her fields to sow.
Then springing like a steed unreined,
  The eager race to run,
New victories greater than in war
  In peace her sons have won.

Let us rejoice, make glad the land,
  Each heart shout forth its song;
To Him who leads us by his grace
  The notes of praise prolong;
A hundred years his hand hath led
  In his own chosen way,
And in the fulness of his peace
  Brings our Centennial Day.

ABRAHAM LINCOLN.

A MEMORIAL ODE.

WHY write of him with feeble pen
  Who needs no praise from human tongue?
Why sing of him when hearts of men
  Have made his deeds a world-wide song?
Not mine the tuneful harp to string
  For him anew a song to raise;
My trembling lips refuse to sing,
  So great the burden of his praise;
The chords attuned from Freedom's lyre
Alone a fitting strain inspire!

The Nation stood with paling face
  Before the frowning gates of War,
While yet the dying songs of Peace
  Were wafted through those gates ajar:
Her million homes with hearthstones bright
  Were rich in treasure of young life;
There Peace had crowned each sweet delight,
  And hushed from them all sound of strife,
While Love sat on his flowery throne
And ruled the kingdom as his own!

We were so blessed in peace and joy,
    We never dreamed such days could end;
Nor human madness dare destroy
    What every hand must needs defend!
So wild seemed all the threats of men
    Who plotted treason to the land,
We laughed at them, and turned again
    To loom and plough, — forgot the brand
Already kindled for the fire
To light our nation's funeral pyre!

The hammer struck the clanging bell,
    And War's deep thunders from it rolled;
To Peace it was the parting knell,
    For Freedom dead the strokes were tolled;
From heart, from mart, from field and mill,
    Were marshalling armies gathering seen;
A time the merry wheel stood still,
    And Silence sat where Trade had been,
As marched the serried lines of men
From city, plain, and mountain glen!

But men are nothing: theme and plan
    Conceived, applause may win a time;
When for the Cause comes forth the Man,
    Through him the hour becomes sublime!
Without its Cromwell, Marston Moor
    Were but a sterile battle won;
While Yorktown would be tame and poor
    Without the name of Washington:
And Liberty shall lose its power
When men shall speak those names no more!

When on the dial-plate of Time
    Turned to the hour its hands we see,
Upon the stroke, as peals the chime,
    Stands forth the man of Destiny!
Disunion, ripe for war and blood,
    Struck on the brazen shield, when, lo!
Before it clad in armor stood
    The Nation to avenge the blow!
And, towering at the front, the Man
Seen ever after in the van!

Miltiades to Greece gave fame
   When victor crowned at Marathon;
St. Denis gave her Oriflamme,
   Beneath which France grand victories won;
A Cromwell cleaves the Briton's chains,
   And Washington our land sets free;
O'Connell pours through Irish veins
   The seething fires of Liberty:
But Lincoln with one stroke of pen
Sets free four million fettered men!

Unskilled in arts of those who rule,
   He governed as one born to reign;
His lessons learned in life's rough school
   Were not to him thus taught in vain!
He knew the worth of Liberty
   To poor and lowly, when denied;
None felt their weakness more than he,
   Since he with them their lot had tried:
A kinship broad as all the land
Was his, and he touched every hand!

To every heart, to every home,
   Where warmed the hearth with Union fire,
Was his in simple faith to come,
   And all to noble deeds inspire!
The camp, the field, in battle's rime,
   The hospital and prison grim,
In hearts heroic grew sublime,
   Because all felt akin to him,
And knew his tender, watchful care,
And his great heart was with them there!

Each soldier knew his brother's hand
   Was reached to him to shield or stay;
Each mother's heart could understand
   The friend she found in him alway!
Firm as a granite rock he stood
   When he was battling for the right;
Unmoved he saw the red sea's flood
   Flow back from fields where surged the fight,
And yet the bird from storm-tossed nest
Found pitying shelter in his breast!

He hated War and cried for Peace,
  As mother-heart cries for its child ;
He longed to hear its thunders cease,
  And see its grizzly hosts despoiled :
But well he knew this could not be
  While Slavery ruled with whip and chain, —
That Peace which brought not liberty
  To every man was made in vain :
Far better War's redoubled woes
Than compromise with Freedom's foes !

And that great heart which felt each stroke
  Of bloody hand on bleeding breast,
Which shrunk and thrilled and almost broke
  By the great burden which oppressed,
Was smitten by the hand of Hate
  When all of hope was past and vain,
And in blind mockery of fate
  That one which would have spared is slain !
While Treason's last, most cruel crime
Has made the Patriot's death sublime !

We move with measured step and slow,
  A Nation in his funeral train ;
The land lies shrouded deep in woe,
  Though smiling Peace has come again !
The World with hushed lips stands aghast,
  While Freedom mourns her martyred son ;
The thunders of the battle past,
  We know how dear the victory won :
But yet know not how great the price
Was paid in this last sacrifice !

As towers some beetling crag on high,
  Scarred, seamed, and rent, with many a stain,
Menacing with its head the sky,
  And frowning darkly on the plain,
So looked he in his roughness wrought,
  A monarch rude, as we drew nigh ;
Severe in Truth and strong in Thought,
  With nought to charm the startled eye.
We scarce had dreamed there could be grace
Or beauty in such mind or face.

As evening falls with golden glow,
  Across the level plain we gaze
Upon that towering crag, and, lo !
  A scene that fills us with amaze :
That rugged peak, all scarred and riven,
  Transformed, a golden glory gleams,
As, falling from the purple heaven,
  A crowning radiance o'er it streams !
So Lincoln towers, with brightening name,
Upon the gilded heights of Fame !

THE ROSES WERE BLOOMING ON CONEMAUGH.[1]

THE roses were blooming on Conemaugh,
　　Gardens were fragrant and meadows sweet;
And hills in their green were smiling upon
　　The river which flowed a song at their feet.

The roses were blooming in Conemaugh,
　　And life was a joy in the homes of men;
Love wove his bowers where children played,
　　Carol and bird-song filled garden and glen.

Sunshine and shower had clothed the fields
　　In the bright dress of blooming spring;
And never a whisper foretold the flight
　　Of bird of ill omen on dusky wing.

Lover and maiden their tales retold,
　　Weaving fair visions of hope between;
Fragrant with spices from gardens blown
　　Softly through night from bowers unseen!

So sped the days in the Conemaugh,
　　Rich in their hope and sweet in their joy;
Never a dream casting shadows before
　　Over the track where Death would destroy.

Swifter in flight than an arrow sped,
　　Sure as the lightning from God's right hand,
Leaped from the shadowy mountain heights
　　The deluge of waters which smote the land.

Leading his squadrons of foaming waves,
　　Death rode aloft on the waters, and high
Over the roar of the seething flood
　　Shrieked his mad glee to the weeping sky.

Down through the valley his squadrons charged,
　　Ruthless as warriors, o'er fields of grain;

---

[1] This was suggested from seeing among the ruins of Johnstown roses in full bloom when all about them was a waste and ruin.

Trampling a city beneath their feet,
   And strewing its streets with children slain.

Homes which had been but a moment before
   Edens of beauty and bowers of love,
Were tossed on the bosom of mountain waves,
   Or sank where the waters rose high above!

Moaning of women and shouts of men
   Mingled with wailings of children there;
Horrors which darkened the frown of Night
   Out o'er the waters stalked ev'rywhere.

Then from the waters the living came
   Out from the ruins, like ghosts from graves,
Whispering the names of their loved ones lost,
   Lying asleep there beneath the waves.

Fatherless, motherless, widowed, were there,
   Saved from the waters but left to weep;
Hearthstones were robbed of their jewels, or lay
   Buried with them far under the deep.

Breasts throbbed for lips that should press them no more,
   Babes cried for bosoms now pulseless and cold;
Under the waters lay white limbs half bare,
   On its dark currents streamed tresses of gold!

Oh, it was pitiful! Night, alone kind,
   Drew its black curtains around the scene;
Save for the wailing of desolate hearts,
   Love could have fancied it had not been!

All that night long, yes, all that night long,
   Out of the flood rose voices in prayer,
And He who had walked the blue Galilee
   Was walking with them the dark waters there.

What tongue hath the speech, what pencil the power,
   To picture this night's unspeakable woe?
Unwritten the tale forever must be,
   A story that man shall nevermore know!

Yet there is no valley so dark on this earth
  But what on its gloom some light breaks through ;
No desert so parched by a cloudless sun
  But what is refreshed by some drops of dew !

As out from that night the morning came,
  So out of the waters of death arose
A beautiful flower of blood-red bloom,
  That only from gardens of weeping grows.

Its sweetness and richness, like spices blown,
  Fill the whole land from sea to sea ;
'T is the blossom of Love from the Crown of Thorns
  First found in the valley of Galilee !

And so in this valley of desolate homes,
  That blood-red blossom full blown I saw,
In this garden of weeping, where, fresh and sweet,
  The roses still bloom in the Conemaugh.